DETERMINER D	PREPO-SITION Prep	VERB-MARKER v	CLAUSE-MARKER Cl-M	CON-JUNCTION
CHANGES IN WORD-FORMS				
a, an this, these that, those		be, am, are, is was, were, being, been have, has, had, having	who whose whom	

OTHER WORD-GROUPS				
NOUN-GROUP	NOUN-CLUSTER	VERB-GROUP	VERB-CLUSTER	VERBAL GROUP

THE BASIC STATEMENT-PATTERNS		

FOUR A: **N LV N**
     B: **N LV A**
     C: **N LV A,**
	FIVE A: **N VG**
	      B: **N VG Prep N**
		SIX: **N VG N Prep N**

SELECTION

In **Prep N** and in **V N** the **Prep** and the **V** select me, us, you, him, her, it, them; mine, ours, yours, his, hers, its, theirs. Also in **V N N** the **V** selects as the first **N** these forms.

Cultivated usage varies in **LV N**; the **LV** may take I or me, you, he or him, she or her, it; mine, ours, yours, his, hers, its, theirs.

THE FOUR SIGNALING-SYSTEMS			
WORD ORDER	WORD-GROUPS	STRUCTURE-WORDS	CHANGES IN WORD-FORMS

INTERNAL PUNCTUATION					
COMMA	SEMICOLON	COLON	DASH	PARENTHESES	BRACKETS

FORMAL PUNCTUATION			
QUOTATION MARKS	ELLIPSIS	BRACKETS	APOSTROPHE

*

AMERICAN ENGLISH

IN ITS

CULTURAL

SETTING

*

Donald J. Lloyd

WAYNE UNIVERSITY

AND

Harry R. Warfel

UNIVERSITY OF FLORIDA

19 56

NEW YORK: ALFRED A. KNOPF

*

AMERICAN

ENGLISH

IN ITS

CULTURAL

SETTING

*

For permission to reprint copyrighted material, the following acknowledgments are gratefully made:

BRANDT & BRANDT. "Portrait VIII" by E. E. Cummings. From *Poems 1923–1954,* published by Harcourt, Brace and Company. Copyright 1923, 1951 by E. E. Cummings.

THE DETROIT NEWS. The column by Jane Lee of November 17, 1952; copyright, 1952, by the Evening News Association.

HENRY HOLT AND COMPANY, INC. The last stanza of "Stopping by Woods on a Snowy Evening." From *New Hampshire* by Robert Frost. Copyright, 1923, by Henry Holt and Company, Inc. Copyright, 1951, by Robert Frost. Reprinted by permission of the publishers.

THE JOHN DAY COMPANY, INC. "Fife Tune" from *Selected Verse* by John Manifold. Copyright, 1946, by The John Day Company, Inc., publishers.

ALFRED A. KNOPF, INC. Five lines from "Winter Remembered" from *Selected Poems* by John Crowe Ransom. Copyright, 1945, by Alfred A. Knopf, Inc.

LITTLE, BROWN, & COMPANY. Five lines from "I Like to See It Lap the Miles" from *The Complete Poems of Emily Dickinson,* 1947. Edited by Martha Dickinson Bianchi and Alfred Leete Hampton.

PRAIRIE SCHOONER and UNIVERSITY OF NEBRASKA PRESS. "Bridal Couch" by Donald J. Lloyd. From *Prairie Schooner* (Winter, 1947), published by the University of Nebraska Press.

KENNETH FEARING for five lines from "Dirge." From *Poems* by Kenneth Fearing. Copyright, 1935, by Kenneth Fearing.

THE UNIVERSITY OF CHICAGO PRESS. A base map from Goode's series of base maps, Henry M. Leppard, editor; published by The University of Chicago Press; copyright, 1939, by the University of Chicago.

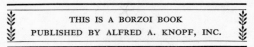

THIS IS A BORZOI BOOK
PUBLISHED BY ALFRED A. KNOPF, INC.

✳ *PREFACE* ✳

agencies, and the Department of State.

THIS IS A BOOK for all those who have tangled with the English
language in school or out and have come away bruised. It is a book
for anyone who needs to understand English and how it works in
American society. It is a book for the slow, halting reader or for
the good reader who wants to be better. It is a book for the unwill-
ing, inarticulate writer or for the competent writer who wants to be a
stylist. It is a comprehensive treatment of English speech and writing in terms of modern studies of language, a display of our language in terms of the various uses we make of it, and a practical,
orderly procedure for moving to a command of English in speech
or in writing to serve any need of expression. It is, in short, the
intelligent person's guide to his native tongue.

The twentieth century has brought us much knowledge about
language in general and about English in particular that has shat-
tered centuries-long traditions and turned a brilliant new light on all
the processes of language and language-learning. Research findings
have tumbled over one another as individual scholars and teams of
scholars have refined their methods into analytical tools of un-
imagined precision, and turned a cold scientific scrutiny on that
mystery of the ages—the means by which men and women in human societies communicate with each other. We could not list here
in any reasonable space the colleges and universities—let alone the
individual scholars—engaged in bringing this new knowledge into
being. At Michigan, Indiana, and Cornell, teams of investigators
work together, and in the city of Washington alone the Institute of
Languages and Linguistics of Georgetown University, the American
Language Center of American University, and the School of Language and Linguistics of the Foreign Service Institute of the Department of State have made massive advances in our understanding of language and of English. The support of this work has been

among the finer accomplishments of the great foundations through grants to both individuals and institutions; and the American Council of Learned Societies must be honored for seeing, in the days before our entry into World War II, the coming need for language experts and for drawing them together in projects which developed into the great language and area programs of the Army Specialized Training Programs. Today, though badly starved for funds, the ACLS continues to press the study of language and of language teaching in cooperation with colleges and universities, individual scholars, and the Department of State.

Linguistic knowledge has developed so rapidly that it remains almost unknown outside the company of the experts; though it has begun to affect second-language teaching to some extent, it has scarcely touched the teaching of English. Yet it has its meaning for us, too, who use English as natives and wish to move to an easy and effective command of our native tongue in speech and writing as efficiently as possible. The authors of this book are not linguistic scientists and do not pretend to be; our object has been to master the findings of the specialists and apply them to the problems of reading and writing English. We feel that it is the right of every American citizen to know in detail what his language is and how it works; we feel that it is his right to handle the language for all his purposes cleanly and efficiently in the expression of what he has to say.

In this book we have drawn together all the knowledge about English which seems to us to bear on the learner's problems; we have shaken the mass of research results through the teacher's grid and excluded everything, no matter how interesting, that does not seem to us to bear on those problems. The result is a comprehensive display of English in relation to the society that uses it, in relation to language learning, and in relation to the individual whose force in society and whose very sense of well-being is tied to his understanding of English and the effectiveness of his reading and writing. We have tried to bring the commonplaces of advanced study of language within the range of any person with the equivalent of a high-school education, and offer a step-by-step procedure by which he can move from where he is to the limit of his native ability.

This book may be used by any reader working by himself. It may be used in the freshman composition class, where its materials have been worked out and tested in actual teaching over a number of years. It may be used in advanced classes for teacher-training candidates, and by working teachers who wish to bring their approach to the language into line with the best modern knowledge, since the display of the language is thorough enough to serve any normal needs. It may also be used by any person who has to deal with language as part of his work—the doctor, the lawyer, the psychologist, the business writer, and even the creative writer who needs to be briefed on the shape and functioning of this instrument. It is a translation from the jargon of the specialists into standard written English—a humane introduction to that most human of all activities, human language: American English in its cultural setting. We have tried to make sure that the reader will reach the end of the book with a concept of language acceptable to the best modern students of language, and be able to proceed by orderly, rewarding steps to a control of reading and writing and to a personal distinctive style of his own.

DONALD J. LLOYD
Wayne University
HARRY R. WARFEL
University of Florida

✳ *ACKNOWLEDGMENTS* ✳

AMONG THE AGENCIES which have directly aided in the preparation of this work, we must jointly and separately acknowledge our special debt to several:

Under its Executive Director, Dr. Maxwell H. Goldberg, the College English Association has since 1952 sponsored a series of "Institutes for Liberal Education and Industry," an ongoing inquiry into the meaning of humane education to the business and industrial community. Both authors are officers of the Association and have been active in the Institutes; at these conferences we have sat with academic, business, and labor leaders in penetrating discussions on all matters where the interests of education and commerce come into contact. For this book we have drawn freely on these consultations for the picture presented here of the place of English in our modern technological society.

A Faculty Study Fellowship in Linguistics at Yale awarded to Donald J. Lloyd in 1951–52 by the American Council of Learned Societies made possible systematic study of linguistic findings and their meaning to the study and use of English. A Grant for the Summer Study of Linguistics by the Council in 1952 permitted further study of the structure of English and of dialect geography at the University of Michigan. In 1954–55, when the first draft of this work was substantially complete, a Faculty Fellowship in English awarded by the Fund for the Advancement of Education permitted consultations with scholars throughout the country on current linguistic studies. In 1953–54, during the composition of the work, a Fulbright Lectureship awarded to Harry R. Warfel at Philipps-Universität, Marburg/Lahn, Germany, put him in touch with European scholars and with the agencies of the United States Government concerned with overseas education. We are indebted to these generous awards for much of the substance of this work.

In addition, it is a pleasure to make special acknowledgment:

To Professor Maxwell H. Goldberg, Executive Director of the College English Association, University of Massachusetts, for guidance in the teaching of English language and literature, and in the place of language in the industrial world;

To Professor George Borglum, Chairman, Department of French, Wayne University, for wise counsel on language teaching and encouragement throughout the composition of the work;

To Professor Paul McHenry Roberts, San Jose State College, San Jose, California, for careful criticism of the text and many valuable suggestions;

To Professor Robert A. Stockwell, Jr., School of Language, Foreign Service Institute of the United States Department of State, for critical reading of the phonemic treatment and provision of the phonemic text of a poem by E. E. Cummings;

To James P. Gillespie, Douglas Aircraft, for valuable technical advice;

To Professor David W. Reed, Director of the Linguistic Atlas of the Pacific, University of California at Berkeley, for the map showing the main channels of migration;

To Freda Kimel, Walled Lake, Michigan, for the figures and illustrations;

To Vida K. Malik, Wayne University, for critical observation of classroom procedures over several semesters, and for her analysis of student writing in terms of psychiatric insights;

To Robert G. Donaldson, Denby High School, Detroit, Michigan, for aid in the critical appraisal of current dictionaries;

To Joseph Blumenthal, Mackenzie High School, Detroit, Michigan; Professor MacCurdy Burnet and Mrs. Burnet, Salisbury State Teachers College, Salisbury, Maryland; Professor Alva Davis, American Language Center, American University, Washington, D.C.; Professor W. Nelson Francis, Franklin and Marshall College; Professor Archibald Hill, University of Texas, Secretary of the Linguistic Society of America; Professor Charlton G. Laird, University of Nevada; Professor George McCue and Mrs. McCue (Lillian de la Torre), Colorado College; Professor James Sledd, University of Chicago; and Dr. Robert Suczek, Clinical Psychologist, Lafayette, California, for illuminating discussions of structural and pedagogical problems which enriched the texture of the book.

✳ CONTENTS ✳

Part Four: How We Form Our Sounds

Part Five: How We Write

Part Six: The Arts of Reading and Writing

Part Six: The Art of Reading and Writing

*

AMERICAN ENGLISH

IN ITS

CULTURAL

SETTING

*

First Words

LANGUAGE IS THE MEANS by which men and women reach searching fingers toward one another, understand one another, ward one another off. It is the prime vehicle of our conduct as members of a human society; it is the basis of our writing and the instrument of our literature. Each person who hopes to apply his full powers to his relations with other people in business or professional life must look to his language and to his reading and writing. These are the means by which he takes in the knowledge on which he builds his career and makes that knowledge effective in his work.

Effective command of the English language is the use of speaking and writing with conscious control of their effect on the people we address, and the use of our ears and eyes to bring into our minds the full intention of people who address us. In these processes language should be a channel through which messages flow with the least friction and the most significance. The processes are easy and within the capacity of any normal person; reading and writing are not mysteries revealed only to the bookworm and the genius. Anybody can learn to read and write well, once he understands the working of his native speech.

In the pages to follow we offer the story of our language, a story every American is entitled to as part of his birthright. In Part I we tell how and when the English language came to America and spread to every corner of the continent, where it came from, and what it was like when it came. We describe its part in the boom that has gripped Western European civilization since the discovery of America. We relate English to the persons and communities which use it. We distinguish speaking as a creative act from speech, its product, and the process of writing from what is written. Most books about language are books about words, but this is a book about the patterns and structures that give words their meanings. Part II is an orderly display of the language system, a step-by-step exposure of the way it works in use. This display lifts the habit-patterns by which we speak and write to the level of consciousness so that we can examine them, and it provides exercises by which the reader can drill them and make them available for conscious control. Part III displays our vocabulary in terms of the sets and classes we sort words into. Part IV dissects the sound-signaling mechanisms of our speech; Part V describes the means by which we translate the speech sounds that die on the empty air into the writing that lives on paper. Parts II and IV are the core of the book on which all the rest depends; Parts III and V spell out their meaning in detail.

In the final section of the book, Part VI, the arts of reading and writing which constitute literacy are developed step by step for practical use. The pattern approach to the display of the language is here extended to the use of the eye in reading and of the hand in writing, to vocabulary building, to the problems of usage. We describe the nature and use of the dictionary—the reader's guide and the writer's friend. We treat the use of language in business where efficiency and accomplishment hinge on effective communication. We treat the use of language in the literary world as the base for a form of art, and sketch an approach to literature grounded in the structure of our language. In the final chapter, building on all that has gone before, we offer a guide to a personal writing style, distinctive, individual, and effectual.

This book is meant to be read for delight and understanding. We recommend taking it lightly. The reader should aim at a general comprehension of the entire matter which he can apply to his own reading and writing. The fruit of his grasp of this story of the language will be a new vision of the language and a new orientation of thought. The reader who wishes to accompany the book with practice should hold off until he is well launched into Part II, the display of the language. He should then skip ahead and read Chapter 25, "The Way to Read by Structures," and Chapter 26, "The Way to Write by Structures," and follow the suggestions there. In his practice he should always read and write for ideas, and go for the ideas without much regard for anything else. We become literate by putting ourselves into the company of the literate and moving in this "peer group" of thinking minds with urbanity and light-hearted self-possession. Too prim or too grim concentration on the manner of writing muddies up the matter and defeats the end we seek—the clear, clean, adequate conveyance of meaning.

*

PART ONE

*

Language, Man, and Society

✳ CHAPTER 1 ✳

Our Land and Our People

Our Land

A SPACE SHIP approaching the western hemisphere of our whirling globe would see the continent of North America as a great, sprawling, raggedy-edged triangle which floats in the seas around us almost without contact with any other land. Its very southern tip reaches a long finger down the Isthmus of Panama to South America. At its northwest apex Alaska falls short of touching Siberia by some twenty miles, and at the far northeastern angle Newfoundland is separated from northern Europe by the wild waters of the North Atlantic.

The whole northern side of North America facing the Arctic Ocean is a vast, deeply scalloped, treeless plain not much lifted above the icebound sea. The long western side from Alaska to Guatemala is a chain of tumultuous mountains, at some places crowding almost into the sea, at others separated from the shore by beaches, deserts, and fertile valleys. These mountains are the highlands, the backbone of the continent. Water which falls on their western slopes runs off into the Pacific; on their eastern slopes into the Atlantic by way of Hudson Bay, the Great Lakes, and the Mississippi basin. At some places 1500 miles from the Pacific, the eastern edge of this vast chain of mountains is a wall or escarpment lifting stark out of an arid mile-high plateau.

Along the shorter eastern side of the continent runs another, lower chain of mountains, the Appalachians, which begins just southeast of the Bay of Fundy and flattens out in central Alabama. These mountains wall off the jumbled hills of New England and the rich coastal plains of the eastern seaboard from the central heartland of the continent. Few passes cross the Rockies and the Appalachians, and those have channeled the movement of settlers across the nation. But the Appalachians can be passed at both ends; to the north the wide St. Lawrence River leads to the Great Lakes, a string of freshwater inland seas. Above the St. Lawrence lie the brutal granitic barrens of the Laurentian Shield, a rocky outcropping so old that it is thought to be the primal material of which mountains are made. To the south of the Appalachians, in Georgia and Alabama, the Atlantic coastal plain merges with the lower Mississippi Valley in a fertile, well watered upland of clays that are sometimes almost blood-red. The heart of the continent is drained to the south by the Mississippi River and its tributaries, the Missouri, the Arkansas, the Platte, the Ohio, and the Tennessee; drained to the east by the Great Lakes and the St. Lawrence; and drained to the north by the chain of lakes and rivers that empty into Hudson Bay. In the heart of the continent the land slopes from the Mississippi Valley east in a jumble of hills to the feet of the western Appalachians, and west in a high, dry, sometimes almost desert plateau to the eastern wall of the Rockies.

Whatever your taste in physical nature, you have only to look for it: towering mountains, shudderingly deep and beautiful canyons, endless prairies. There are deserts drier than the Sahara, which yet spring to life with delicate tiny flowers whenever it does rain. In New York there are two-hundred-foot pine trees, their tips lost to sight from the ground, and in California ancient redwoods which were old when civilization was young. There are the thick rain-forests of the Pacific, the floating swamps of the southern Mississippi Valley, and the dank retreats of the alligator in southern Florida. There are springs gushing millions of gallons of cold water, and geysers shooting millions of gallons of hot water. There is a measureless untapped wealth of petroleum, coal, and minerals underground, and a measureless cultivated wealth of plant and animal food aboveground.

Wherever we have settled down to live on this continent, the land as it is where we settled has put its mark on us. The husbanding New Englander grubs the rocks from his hills, and turns the rushing streams into power and his hands into tools; the midwestern farmer keeps one eye on the sky and the other on the river, either of which may make him or ruin him; the laconic cattleman, browned and hardened by the sun, watches his herds; the miner gambles with dynamite and coal gas a half mile underground; the factory hand has his day rounded at either end by the time clock; the salesman and the textile worker north or south—each has his character, his appearance, his speech, his way of looking at the world molded by the land he stands on.

And each in his way has put his stamp on the land. For over its multitude of forms, the length and breadth of the continent, run the wires, the rails, and the roads; in the skies above, following the trackless lanes of the airways, the silver airliners drone. Looking down from these, more clearly than from any other point of vantage, we can see the straight lines of section and quarter section, the furrowed imprint of plow and harrow, the twin ribbon of the superhighways curving through valleys and plunging through mountains, the line of channel buoys in river, lake, and harbor, and the sprawling network of streets and buildings of our cities. Wherever we have built our fires and done our work we have left our mark—the integrated order of our civilization.

Our People

WHEN the first European waded ashore in the Caribbean and announced, "I have arrived!" not the least of the wonders the New World had to offer was its inhabitants. The European was in no state of mind to appreciate them. He had not arrived in India, where he thought he was; nothing in his experience had prepared him to understand the ways of a myriad of peoples so different from himself.

The Indians, too, had come to the New World, but in the very childhood of mankind. As far as is known, they had crossed into North America from Siberia, and during thousands of years of migrations had occupied the Americas. Their technology was of a kind that let them live mainly off the surface of the continents. Where there were forests, they were hunters and fishers; where agriculture was possible, they cultivated and grew their own food.

The mountain tribes knew how to wring a living from the mountains; the desert dwellers submitted to the harsh regimen of the arid land and made the desert feed them. Some tribes followed the migrations of animals; some stood their ground and holed in throughout the winters.

The Indians spoke intricate languages of great age whose complexity we are just beginning to penetrate; in these they had expressed their dignified, often mystic literatures, their codes of laws, and their religious sense of dwelling not so much beneath the hand of God as in His heart and mind. They often felt a kinship with the animals about them, free dwellers with themselves upon the land. Their orientation was toward the community; the idea that one man could own a plot of land (the earth's bounty granted to the tribe) was beyond them. In Mexico they had reared a respectable culture of cities living under the reign of law; elsewhere their communities were sized to what the earth and their labors could support. At war occasionally among themselves, they were not uniformly warlike, and they often welcomed the Europeans. If today in our myths they always seem hostile to the whites, probably their hostility is the implacable anger of those who find themselves being dispossessed.

At any rate they are still with us in myth and name and body, the only Americans who look back to no other home: the Nausets, the Mohawks, the Seminoles, the Caribs, the Sioux, the fierce Dakotas and the Apaches, the Hopi, the Pueblos, and the Kwakiutl of the Pacific Northwest. Some, like the Navaho, remain aloof and detached on their reservations; some, like the Cherokee, have mingled with the nation. Some have been soldiers; one tribe specializes in walking the high steel on bridge and building-construction jobs; Charles Curtis has been Vice-President, Maria Tallchief a prima ballerina, and Jim Thorpe one of our greatest athletes.

The English were not the first Europeans to come to North America; when they came they did not get hold of much of the continent. The Spanish, looking for gold and El Dorado as all men were, had taken the empire of the Caribbean to themselves; their holdings stretched almost in a line from northern Florida around the Gulf of Mexico, across Texas, and west to the Pacific. They had possession of the wealth of the Aztecs; they had pulled down the pagan temples of Mexico City, and they were mining the gold of Montezuma. St. Augustine in Florida was forty-two years old when the English landed at Jamestown in 1607; while the British were establishing their beachheads along the middle Atlantic coast, the Spanish were setting up missions in southern California and pushing on to San Francisco.

As the Spanish were passing the Appalachians at the southern end, the French were passing them to the north. By way of the St. Lawrence, French missionaries, soldiers, and hunters got in behind the mountains and set up outposts in the western foothills— Fort Duquesne and Fort Le Boeuf. They drifted down the Ohio and the Mississippi and met the Spaniards at its mouth. The names they gave to the landmarks, to the Indian tribes, and to their settlements still remain in common use. Along the St. Lawrence and the Great Lakes they made permanent towns—Quebec, Montreal, Detroit, Marquette, and Joliet—settled by soldiers, workmen, and mariners whose provincial dialects formed the base of the French language still spoken by millions of their descendants in eastern Canada and northeastern United States.

Meanwhile the British took over the narrow seaboard from Massachusetts to Georgia and dug in. There was a Swedish settlement on the Delaware that the Swedes could not hold on to, and a Dutch settlement at New York that the Dutch lost; otherwise the points of entry on the coast—Boston, New Haven, Philadelphia, Baltimore, and Charleston—were all English. The settlers were mostly people from the middle and lower classes; each man had his reasons for giving up what he had at home and staking himself and often his family against the unknown in America. Some left poverty behind, some political or religious oppression, some prison for debt or theft, some merely the tangle that men's lives fall into. Records do not clearly tell us what part of England they came from, but many were from the west and south. The records tell us fairly well what became of them.

It is important for the shape of modern American culture that the English settlements were small and feebly peopled, relatively unfriendly to each other, widely separated. A hundred years passed before any real break through the mountains was possible and before any continuous communication between the settlements was established; each colony meanwhile developed its own way of life, raised up its own leaders, and formed its own common speech from the dialects brought in from home. In these matters it is who comes in and gets a grip on the country first that counts. Later

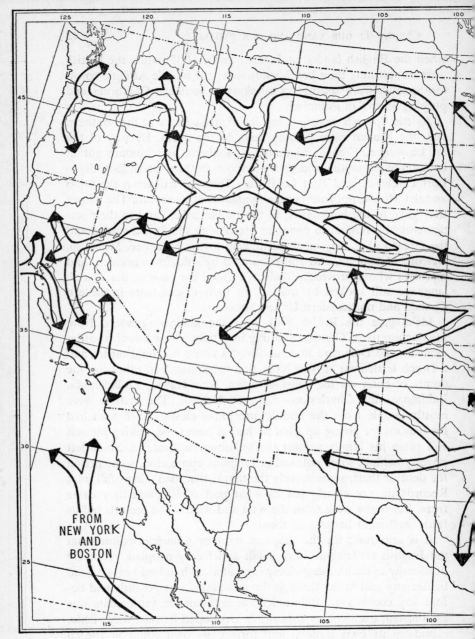

The Filling of

THE MAIN CHANNELS OF MIGRATION. The map shows only the western movemen
of the eighteenth and nineteenth centuries, and only its central tendencies. It doe
not show the Canadian story, which is similar; not enough detailed evidence i

FROM
NEW YORK
AND
BOSTON

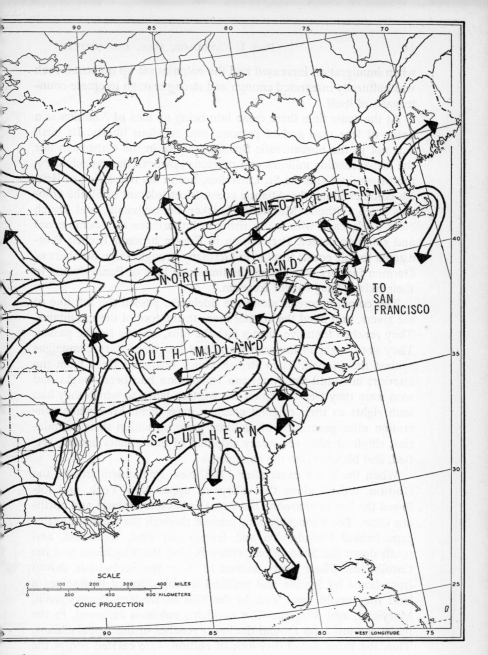

the Continent

available. It does not show the population movements of our own times, e.g., the
Oklahoma-Arkansas-Texas migration to California, the South Midland move on
northern industrial cities, or the exodus of southern Negroes to the north.

when immigration increased and the colonies set up outposts, each was culturally integrated enough and strong enough to create counterparts of itself.

At the same time there came into being an idea of America as a home of free men and of personal and religious liberty. Its birth was not in the bureaucratic Spanish empire in the Caribbean nor the fast-spreading military and religious power of the French along the Mississippi and the St. Lawrence, but in the thin string of British colonies along the Atlantic coast. Most tolerant of all the colonies were Catholic Maryland, Quaker Pennsylvania, and Dutch New York, each with a city rising in importance as a commercial and shipping center. Persecution in France brought French Protestants to this coast; trouble in Germany brought large numbers of German farmers who found the limestone hills of Pennsylvania to their liking. They sought freedom.

The colonies spread along the tidelands, passed the fall line of the rivers, and filled the coastal areas to the foot of the mountains. They reached tentative fingers into the hills, looking for the passes. They got caught in imperial wars, and fought military campaigns against the French. Then British policy restricted them from the interior; not until the American Revolution had been fought and won were they free to exploit the western lands to which they had such rights as their original charters gave them. Meanwhile generation after generation of children grew up within their boundaries; shipload after sea-weary shipload of immigrants landed, settled, and blended into the amalgam.

When the break came after 1783, New Englanders crossed the Hudson, moved along the valleys of upper New York, and followed the low land around the Great Lakes into Ontario and northern Ohio. The Pennsylvanians pressed through the wind and water gaps behind Philadelphia and fanned out west, southwest, and south down the Shenandoah valley behind the Virginians and the Carolinians. Ulster Scots, known to us as the Scots-Irish, driven from home by famine and political troubles, found themselves a land they could cope with in the hills of western Pennsylvania, Maryland, and Virginia. The Southern colonists followed, in the main, the low land around the lower reaches of the Appalachians. Thus the three broad divisions of culture were carried across the land by those who settled it and cleared it: the Northern, across northern New York and the great lakes; the Midland, through the passes behind the coastal regions and down the Ohio River; and the Southern, along the coast and below the mountains.

Besides the frequent removal of Indian tribes and nations to reservations, at least three forced migrations of peoples had a great deal to do with the present shape of our society. The best known was the importation of Negroes as slaves. Human servitude, often attended by incredible brutalities, was commonplace in Africa and Asia, but in Europe the Christian doctrine of the brotherhood of men before God had pretty well eliminated it except for criminals and those who had fallen into debt. Slavery had an uneasy acceptance among the Indian nations of America, usually as the aftermath of war. The European, breaking out of the confines of the narrow world he had known and meeting a multitude of peoples like—but not quite like—himself, was not sure whether they were men or animals. To work the rice, tobacco, and cotton plantations of the southern lowlands, he brought in the black African used to the hot sun and the tropical damps to do what white men could not do and live.

At first slavery was a rather benign paternal system of servitude not too unlike indenture—the binding of a servant to a master for a specific term to work off a debt. Slavery could be terminated, and freed Negroes were not uncommon in both northern and southern cities. As cotton growing spread, as the invention in 1793 of a mechanical gin to separate seed and fiber made large impersonal commercial operations possible, the system stabilized, found apologists, and clamped a tight grip on the economy of the South. It spawned a profitable and inhuman shipping and marketing industry that brought thousands of new victims from Africa to be bought and sold like horses or swine. The system followed the spread of cotton growing into the opening lands to the west of the southern colonies. Further movement west of the Mississippi tended to weaken the slave system. Escape among the Indians became possible. To the north, as public opinion hardened against slavery, a few aggressive fugitives made their way to freedom; the least tolerance of the whole idea of human servitude was found in Canada; many slaves reached there to become free men in Canadian society.

The presence and the problem of the Negro became an integral part of North American culture. The method of capture and transportation of the Negroes splintered tribal customs and replaced them with a depressed and limited form of white culture. Except in the coastal portion of the Carolinas and Georgia, the African languages were erased as languages; even in this area a kind of pidgin English developed, an amalgam of eighteenth-century English and the native tongues, called Gullah. Otherwise the Negro learned the dialect of his masters, introducing only occasional words from his own cultural heritage. Negro speech in America is not a distinct entity; generally it is the speech of whatever group of whites of whatever economic and social level the Negro has spent his life with. Fifteen million Negroes are now distributed throughout the nation. They share our economic life; they contribute significantly to our music, art, and literature; they serve with our Armed Forces in the common defense.

Another forced migration—the theme of Longfellow's *Evangeline*—took place during the French and Indian War in 1755. The French inhabitants of Acadia, now Nova Scotia, were transported by the British to Louisiana, then a French possession. They reinforced there a thriving colony of immigrants, French, Spanish, and Negro—some slave, some half free, and some free—and became as Cajuns part of a society still French in language, law, and customs within American culture. Again the principle emerges: if you wish to understand the local peculiarities in language and customs of an American community, look to the history of its settlement.

The third of the great forced migrations, little remembered in the United States, was the transfer of some fifty thousand United Empire Loyalists to Canada. As a part of the conclusion of the American Revolution these Loyalists, mainly solid citizens of the eastern seaboard, were transported in British ships and distributed in British territory from Nova Scotia to Ontario. The penalty for their active or covert support of the British crown was the loss of their property in the colonies where they had their stake, the hardships of the voyage, and a pioneer existence in uncleared land. The hostile and unreconstructed appraisal of American life and policy of these Loyalists still lives in the coolness of Canadian reaction to the friendly family-feeling of visitors from the United States.

In order to understand why slight differences separate Canadian from northern English in the United States, we must look to the early resettlement of these proud, educated, honest, and industrious citizens of the American colonies. Without them, no doubt the Canadian speech would be much closer to the Scottish and English accents spoken on arrival by generations of later immigrants.

In some forty years after the Revolution, the territory east of the Mississippi had been occupied; settlers were beginning to push beyond it. Immigration continued at a steady rate. We must not think of this occupation as that of an army. It was a filling of the land. Forests were cleared, fields planted, communities started, stores opened. Factories went to work, villages became towns, towns expanded into cities, and the cities grew. As Franklin pointed out, it was a family matter. Americans married, settled down, and had children, lots of children. The children grew up, married, and chose whether to stay where they were or move on. Their staying as much as their moving gave permanence to the way of life that had come into being along the seaboard. The stable community of children growing up in their father's homes decides which features of a welter of differing speeches are to survive. A person's life is a matter of seconds and minutes, hours and days lived one after another; and though a period of forty years seems short to the historian, it is two-thirds of the span of a human life. Each movement into the wilderness was a spurt after a long gathering of forces; the children of those who had earlier come from back east leaned on the fences and watched the plodding teams and the banging, rattling, dusty wagons moving on west.

East of the Mississippi River the three main currents of American culture absorbed the immigrants from Europe and filled the available land. Between the Great Lakes and the southern lowlands the vaster migration from Pennsylvania, centering mainly on the Ohio River, mingled with northerners in Ohio, Indiana, and Illinois, and with southerners pressing up into the Tennessee and Kentucky highlands. From pure northern Michigan to pure southern Mississippi speech was a slow gradation, with no sharp boundaries between. There were political and commercial differences, as the land fed the settlers in different ways.

West of the Mississippi River lay a vast land lightly explored by the Spanish and the French, highly imagined but little known. An early map shows it as an ill-defined blank white space, occupied by "various Indian nations." In the far Southwest the Spanish Mexican empire, with its administrative center at Santa Fe, New Mexico, sent explorers and prospectors as far north as Colorado and laid claim to the land. Spanish missions and military posts were established throughout Texas, Arizona, and New Mexico, where numerous deposits of gold and silver were mined for the king of Spain. Along the Pacific coastline Spanish galleons were nosing by 1750; fifty years later there were missions as far north as San Francisco, and a thriving cattle industry shipped beef and hides from coastal ports. Meanwhile the Russians, following the path of the earliest human entry into the continent, were discovering Alaska and claiming it for the czar. They edged their ships down the rocky coast of the Pacific Northwest. Southwest from Hudson Bay, British fur traders followed the trails first laid out by earlier French traders, crossed the Canadian Rockies, and came into conflict with American fur hunters working for the Astor interests.

In the hundred years from 1800 to 1900 the stream of American settlers occupied this great empty area without much regard to anybody's claim to sovereignty but their own. Slaveholders from the South contended against slavery haters from the Midlands for Missouri, Arkansas, and Kansas. Settlers from the American border moved into the Mexican territory north of the Rio Grande, peacefully at first; then they fought a sharp war with the Mexicans and set up the Republic of Texas. Other settlers followed Lewis and Clark into the Oregon country; others found the passes and crossed the deserts into California. Texas joined the United States; this and other frictions embroiled the nation in war with Mexico in 1846. When the war was over, all California and the lands of Spanish-speaking peoples north of the Rio Grande as far as the state of Washington were in American hands. New Mexico today is the only state with two official languages—English and Spanish.

The discovery of fabulous deposits of gold in California set off a rush for claims, with people traveling overland, around South America, and across the Isthmus of Panama. A whole religious sect, the Mormons, in 1846–1847 crossed the plains from Illinois and colonized Utah. The nation fought a savage civil war and settled the slavery question. Railroads inched their way west. Cattle gave way to corn and wheat; the wheat territory pressed its way north. Canada and the United States drew the border between them; settlers came from eastern Canada and from the United States to farm the rich northern land. The dialects of the eastern seaboard gave way to western dialects with only such local differences as local settlement, local history, and local ways of life put upon them.

In French Canada and Louisiana, in the Spanish lands of the Southwest, and in all the areas where the Indian tribes and nations have kept their cultural entities, English is used in interchange with other languages that have even older and deeper roots in the local culture; English has invaded the society and in effect comprises a cultural overlay. Most speakers of the other tongues are bilingual: they also speak and read and write English.

Besides these primal bilingual areas in America, there are many of a different sort, second-language areas consisting of knots of people who came together to America or drifted together, and who found in the company of others speaking the language of their homeland the profound security of something familiar in a strange land. Every immigrant in America is an exile far from the home his fathers have known and loved for generations; he is a wanderer among people who speak in a different way and live in a different way. He finds comfort in having close beside him others who remember the villages, the customs, the literature, the religious faith, and the day-to-day manifestations of earth and sky in the homeland half a world away. Migrations were often group enterprises of a whole religious sect, a whole band of political dissidents, or a community of famine or persecution-driven persons who, suffering privations beyond endurance, pooled their resources. In America countless communities have another language, not English, as the common speech at home, in the church, and even in the daily intercourse of business life.

One of the earliest and best-known of these second-language areas lies in Pennsylvania in the triangle bounded by lines run from Philadelphia to Easton and Harrisburg. This land was occupied after 1685 by members of several Protestant religious sects in Germany, invited to settle there by the Quakers. These Germans formed a sober, close-knit community, avoided all worldly vanities in dress and behavior, and continued the use of their native German dialects among themselves. As their contacts with English-speaking people enlarged, these Germans added English words to their vocabulary, so that the dialect today has a German grammar and pronunciation. The English of some of these people retains some German pronunciations and idiomatic twists, as in "Don't fall the steps down" and "I have the butter gebought." They are commonly known as Pennsylvania Dutch, a term which derives from German *Deutsch*. Because of the integrated, devotional nature of their society, they have kept their entity through three centuries and fostered other colonies farther west.

Early German immigration came largely through the ports of Philadelphia and Baltimore and spread throughout the Midland area, into upland Virginia, Kentucky, and Tennessee, into Ohio, Indiana, and Illinois. Later migrations like the one in 1848 brought more German settlers into these areas and into Iowa and Missouri. There are large German-speaking areas still in Iowa, Wisconsin, Texas, and in most of the larger cities. Scandinavians and Finns clung to the cold, wooded North—in Maine, along the northern Great Lakes in the upper peninsula of Michigan, in Wisconsin, and in Minnesota.

The Irish came. After the potato blight of the 1840's, about a million and a half persons migrated during the seven years preceding 1854. They settled in the cities of the eastern seaboard, contributing their lilting, colorful speech tones to the English spoken in Halifax, Boston, New York, Philadelphia, and other cities.

The peoples migrating to the United States down to the latter quarter of the nineteenth century came largely from northern and western Europe. In 1842 the number coming each year passed a hundred thousand. With some lags, the annual flood increased until in 1881 over six hundred thousand came. Then overpopulation and political and religious troubles began to drive eastern and southern Europeans to our shores. In 1905 more than a million immigrants entered, and from then until 1914 the flow averaged over a million persons a year. In spite of wars and restrictive laws the number coming each year did not fall below a hundred thousand until 1931. In 1946 it passed a hundred thousand again.

Italians, Poles, Greeks, Hungarians, and Russians stayed near the points of entry or moved on into the larger cities of the Middle West. Central and eastern Europeans—Poles, Hungarians, and Russians—settled in mining and industrial areas—West Virginia, Pittsburgh, Chicago, and Detroit. Jews had been in the country since 1654, but a new tide brought into existence the large and characteristic Jewish sections of the cities, with their Yiddish-language newspapers, libraries, and theaters. By 1900 some hundred thousand Chinese had entered the western states, mainly as laborers, and had established Chinatowns in the major cities. In Canada the Doukhobors, a strange Russian religious cult, still maintain themselves aloof in the western provinces.

We never know in what corner of the land or in what section of a city we will come suddenly upon an integrated community in which the only things that look familiar are the automobiles and the chain stores with brand-name articles. There may be an onion-domed Orthodox church, a street of kosher butcher shops and delicatessens, a vast expanse of tulip beds, a row of Persian restaurants, and a people speaking to each other in a language we do not know. Many other communities show no particular outward difference, but are just the friendly fraternizing of fellow immigrants come to some favorite gathering place. All these represent a part of our cultural heritage.

Some figures may give us an idea of the enormous number of foreign-born within our shores, and where they have come from. As late as 1930 almost fourteen million persons alive in the United States had been born elsewhere. Even with immigration sharply curtailed there were in 1940 about eleven and a half million, and in 1950 ten million. Of these ten percent were from Germany, about eighteen percent from Poland and Russia, fourteen percent from Italy, and about ten percent from the lands once included in the old Austrian Empire. Looked at in another way: by 1947 more than four million people had come from Austria and Hungary, almost five million from Italy, over a half million from Greece, and over six million from Germany. The original colonies were mainly Protestant in faith. Along with some fifty-six million Protestants there are in the United States over thirty-two million Catholics and five million Jews—besides all those millions who belong to other faiths or to no faith at all.

Except for a few minor dialect areas, most of the characteristics of American speech can be traced back to the differences in speech that arose in the British colonies during the first hundred years of their existence.

In Canada the lines of immigration followed the broad St. Lawrence and the Great Lakes, settling a narrow strip of habitable land between the stony mass of the Laurentian Shield on the north and the cultural mass of the United States on the south. The harsh winters bred a durable, self-reliant people, and the mingling of nations made a string of cosmopolitan cities: Halifax, Quebec, Toronto, Winnipeg, Vancouver. Of the present inhabitants, over four million continue the French Catholic culture of the earliest settlement; almost seven million look back to Britain and more than six hundred thousand to Germany. There are four hundred thousand Ukrainians, three hundred thousand Scandinavians, two hundred and sixty-five thousand Dutch, two hundred and twenty thousand Poles, a hundred and eighty-two thousand Jewish from whatever origins, a hundred and fifty thousand Italians, and almost a hundred thousand from Russia. Among these, some on reservations and some assimilated into Canadian citizenship, live over a hundred and fifty thousand native Indians and Eskimos. Immigration has lagged and spurted in this century; in 1951 it almost touched two hundred thousand, and it has run over a hundred and sixty thousand each year since. The exchange of citizens with the United States has balanced almost exactly in numbers, in some years exceeding the immigration from Britain; the migrants from the States remaining in Canada form a larger proportion of the total than Canadians south of the border and have had more influence on the society.

The migrations of Americans were by no means ended when in 1912 Arizona, the last territory within the borders of the United States, was admitted to the Union as a State. Beginning with World War I with its demand for an army and navy and floods of expendable war materials, our people set out on a new kind of shifting about, this time internal to the nation. That war caused a redistribution of the population which brought many Americans out of the places where they were born and into other, often far different, places and ways of life. There was the gathering of the largest army we had seen since the Civil War, and its training in camps variously located, often for political as well as military convenience. The war forced the cultivation of lightly settled marginal lands to provide stores of grain and other farm products. Booming war industries drew a large proportion of rural and small-town dwellers into the eastern, midland, and northern cities. Though the end of the war in 1918 saw a great return, much of the shift was permanent. The migration of many Negroes out of the South into northern cities got under way; at the same time the agriculturally depressed areas of the South began slowly to industrialize.

Between the first World War and the second, the mobility of Americans increased. Mechanization bred mechanization; tractors, harvesters, and other machinery industrialized the farms, while farm laborers drifted to the factory cities to make the machines. A vast road-building industry came into being; the automobile and the truck began to take much of the long-distance carrying from the railroads. The manufacture of motor vehicles became the largest single industry in the nation; with the motor car more Americans began to see more of the nation. Economic prosperity and recession brought tides of people into the city and back to their homes again, but more always came than went back. Industry swallowed up the last great flow of foreign immigrants. Then the economic depression which gripped the entire world during the late 1920's and early 1930's laid its cold hand on this country. Americans who had always known cycles of boom and bust endured the biggest bust of all.

As the depression began to ease in the 1930's, the threat of a second great war began to speed up the growth of industry, which concentrated larger numbers of people in the factory cities than ever before. Development of natural power brought industries (and people) into parts of the country which had never seen them. The presence of a large labor supply in such areas as the South drew factories there. The manufacture of munitions started again, and an aircraft-building industry came into being, notably in the Far West. With American entry into World War II in 1941, a greater industrial demand than ever before multiplied all these effects; a vaster mobilization than anyone could have imagined drew off some twelve million men from the productive labor force. Many were sent into the parts of the world from which their ancestors had come, and many more into parts of the world they had never even heard of. As the airplane came into use as a common means of transport, the mobility of Americans increased again.

Since 1945 the chronic belligerence of our times has kept up our war production; the need for supplying ourselves, our allies, our garrisons, and our fighting armies strains our industries. Urbanization has continued, but now in a new form; the growth of our cities has changed to the development of satellite areas with their own industries, the whole vast semiurban complex linked by the motor car and truck. Suburban shopping centers with broad parking lots supply these areas, but apparently without cutting much into the business of the older centers. Radio, television, air conditioning, and home appliances of one kind and another seem to create a new standard of living for Americans and a new way of living available wherever the power lines of the nation carry electricity on an ever expanding network of wires. By train, car, and plane, Americans move about more freely than ever. We are living now through the biggest boom of all.

This highly organized, dynamic society—which puts its mark on every North American and takes its shape partly from him— depends at every turn upon language. It depends mainly upon the English brought by the earliest settlers to the eastern seacoast and to a lesser extent upon the second languages which are as much "American" as our English is. Any language spoken here by our people is an American language, no matter where it originated; it is part of our heritage. But it is English by which we communicate, face-to-face across a table, by telephone or radio across a city or the continent, by telegraph or teletype, by letter, newspaper, pamphlet, periodical, or book, to carry on most of our daily business and weave the texture of our literature. To use it most effectively we must understand it as it works in our society, as a learned pattern of habits in each individual, and as a system in itself—the code by which we transmit our messages. Let us consider, point by point, what English is and how it works.

CHAPTER 2

Our Language

ENGLISH-SPEAKING PEOPLE who were born and brought up in North America speak one or another of several characteristic American dialects. They can be identified as North Americans as soon as they begin to speak, but often they cannot be identified by Asians or Europeans as coming from any particular part of the continent. To the outsider the differences between the varieties of American speech are so slight that it is hard for him to think of these varieties as dialects. A European, accustomed to British English with its clean-cut social-class differences, does not hear comparable differences in American speech; he has to look for other evidence in conduct or knowledge to judge whether a person has little or much education. A few quirks in some American dialects would remind the European of Scottish, North-of-England, or Irish speech, but they are in the sounds we make; our grammar and our vocabulary are dead giveaways of our origin.

American English is a colonial speech. It has been carried to this continent by settlers; it was not used here before the settlers came. In this respect it is like Pennsylvania German, Australian English, South African Dutch (Afrikaans), American French, Spanish, and Portuguese, and a host of other transported languages. It differs from Afrikaans in that this African form of the Dutch language was spread from a single point of entry; it is like Afrikaans in that the shape of the language was established by immigrants who lived for several generations in close community life. Immigrants smooth out original differences in favor of the speech of the families who rise quickly to eminence in the new land and hold that eminence through fifty to a hundred years. There were several points of entry into North America—Charleston, Baltimore, Philadelphia, New York, Boston, and Halifax. Settlers came from various parts of England to these colonies; in each they entered into a way of life characteristic of that colony and of none of the others.

Aristocratic or upper-class English was not much represented in the colonies; few lords and ladies found reason to emigrate, and most of those that came did not stay long. The people who came and stayed were from the middle and lower classes; even in the southern colonies, where an aristocratic way of life developed, the language of the new aristocracy was the speech of the middle class. Since a good proportion of the settlers could read and write, a press and publishing industry soon came into being. Though the people looked back wistfully to England and tried to write according to British standards, they could not keep their local speech from creeping into what they wrote. Visitors from England were not slow to sneer at Americanisms in American writing; it was quite a while before Americans stopped apologizing. Some never have.

As the American settlements expanded, more immigrants came from the different parts of Britain in a succession of mass movements, so that American English was continually reseeded with British dialects of different times and places. Thus the chances of immigration brought diverse influences to bear on the developing American dialects. On the eastern seaboard and in eastern Canada the educated and ruling group was much more sensitive to British attitudes and influences than in the West, and much more imitative of current British usage. Their attitude did not save them from British criticism; but it led to a continuing contact with British literature, history, government, and philosophy.

On the basis of recent studies we can now make a fairly accurate division of the dialects of American English. First, there is a string of dialects along the eastern seaboard showing marked local variation. We divide them broadly into South Atlantic; Middle Atlantic; Eastern Pennsylvania, New York, and New Jersey; and New England (from the Connecticut River east). Around the mouth of the

St. Lawrence and to its east and south there are the distinct
speeches of the Gaspé, Newfoundland, New Brunswick, and Nova
Scotia, shading off into northern Maine. There are probably more
speakers of Gaelic in eastern Canada than in Scotland.

Back of these coastal dialects but east of the Mississippi, three
broad language divisions parallel the cultural entities we have mentioned: Southern, Midland, and Northern. Midland is basically
Pennsylvanian. Midland speech south of U.S. 40, which is mixed
with southernisms, is called South Midland. North of U.S. 40 in
Ohio, Indiana, and Illinois, Midland speech is mixed with northern
characteristics, and is called North Midland. Northern speech north
of the Great Lakes is Canadian, being influenced by cultural ties
to Great Britain that the United States does not share.

West of the Mississippi, dialect studies are unfinished, but it is
clear that the strong current of Midland speech has carried through
most of the West, especially across Iowa to California and over the
Oregon Trail. It mingles in the Southwest with southern influence,
and in the North and Northwest with northern. Regional differences in the West are tied in with local economic, political, and
religious life or with the underlay of original Spanish or (in Canada) of the original British settlement.

It is too easy to emphasize the distinctiveness of the English
language in America, since most of its peculiarities are obvious to
any discriminating ear. Certainly the Scottish, the Irish, and the
English do not talk the way we do. Nor do they live the way we
do. There are cultural differences within the American continent
quite as deep and far-reaching as those that separate us from the
British; these differences rise out of the manifold origins of our
people; yet we share with the British a set of social institutions and
social ideals that mark us both off from the rest of the world. The
linguistic differences tend to be systematic—they run through our
whole speech. That is, if we pronounce a different t from the British t, one only has to hear a few words in each dialect to make the
substitution with fair accuracy wherever t occurs.

Since the distinctive features of American dialects go back to
differences within the British dialects, one American dialect will be
close to British usage in exactly the respects in which another will
differ. British English has always displayed far greater differences
between dialects than American English has, especially between
London English and local rural dialects. American English, origi-

nally based on middle-class British usage and influenced for at least a couple of centuries by the developing forms of educated British, has more in common with the speech of the cultivated Briton than rural or lower-class British speech has in common with either. All differences are greatest in the everyday speech of the two peoples, and it is precisely in everyday speech that they do not have to get along together. All differences are minimized in our common traditional system of writing, the main means of intercourse between the two peoples.

In the United States and Canada today there are about one hundred and seventy million people. For most of these, English is the primary speech; often it is the only language they know. For the rest, English is a familiar second language. In the British Isles there are fifty million people, for most of whom English is the native tongue. Those who speak Welsh, Gaelic, or Erse usually speak English quite well. In Australia there are twelve million native speakers of English; in South Africa there are thirteen million. With the other smaller groups of English-speaking peoples, there is a total of about two hundred and fifty million native speakers of English. An unknown number scattered throughout the world speak English with varying degrees of fluency. English is one of the official languages of India. English, French, Spanish, Chinese, and Russian are the official languages of the United Nations; they are world languages. English is taught as a second language throughout the Scandinavian countries; it is part of the curriculum in almost every country that has schools and colleges.

Yet in 1545, about the time the explorers were nosing along the coast of North America looking for the Northwest Passage (that was to lead them to the Pacific Ocean and the untold wealth of China, India, and the East), there were three million three hundred thousand people in England. If these all spoke English, they were almost all the English-speaking people in the world. Back in 1087, when William of Normandy surveyed the wealth of England in his famous Domesday Book, there were about one million seven hundred thousand people in England. If they all spoke English, they were all there were who did. In about four and a half centuries, between 1087 and 1545, the number of native speakers of English just about doubled. In the next four centuries, from 1545 to the present, it jumped from three and a half million to two hundred and fifty million, and the total is still climbing. The English

language got caught in a four-hundred-year boom. A large multipli-
cation of the number of speakers was not all that happened to it.
Let us review the history of this language, of which the American
story is only a part.

The Continental Period

WE have no means of discovering the origin of the English language: its beginnings are shrouded in the past. The earliest historical records carry us back only to the fifth century, when English
was brought to Britain by several German tribes who lived along
the shore of the North Sea just east of the Rhine River. It was
originally a Low German dialect related to Dutch and to the German dialects still spoken in the Frisian Islands. Thus it belongs to
the same group of languages as modern German, Yiddish, Danish,
Swedish, and Norwegian.

From internal evidence we know that all these languages belong
to the great Indo-European family of languages. Most of the lan-
guages of Europe belong to this family, notably the Romance group
(Latin, French, Spanish, Portuguese, Italian, and Romanian), the
Slavic group (Polish, Russian, and Czech), Greek, Albanian, Ar-
menian, and some of the languages of India (Sanskrit, Hindi, and
Hindustani). As far as we know, English is not related to Estonian,
Basque, Finnish, or Hungarian.

These German tribes were not uncivilized. From internal evidence we know that they had some contact with the Roman Empire
in Gaul—that is, France—at a time when many young German
tribesmen were happy to join the Roman army and defend the empire. Such common words, borrowed from Latin, as **copper, dish,**
and **church** come down to us from these early days. How numerous
the people were or precisely where they lived in Germany, we do
not know. According to ancient British records, they called themselves the Angles, Saxons, and Jutes. Their leaders in the invasion
of Britain are reported as Hengist and Horsa—which to us is about
as good as calling them A and B.

At the end of the Continental Period in the history of the English language, Old English was already a highly developed, even
sophisticated tongue with the following characteristics:

1) Old English shared with the other, older Indo-European

languages a method of indicating the relations of words in sentences by changing the forms of their endings. German, Lithuanian, Sanskrit, the Slavic languages, Greek, and Latin work this way. A word had a root syllable; to this root any one of a group of endings could be attached to show how the word was to be taken in a particular sentence. There were several sets of endings for nouns, several for verbs, several for adjectives. The speaker chose an interlocking set of endings to show which noun performed the action in the verb, and whether the action of the verb occurred in the present or in the past. The system is called inflection. As inflectional languages go, continental Old English showed a pretty rickety set of endings. The original eight or nine cases found in the older Indo-European tongues had been worn down to four, and these were not very well distinguished from each other. Old English was in the process of giving up this way of working.

2) Old English shared with the other Indo-European languages a "lineal" actor-action-goal sentence which it still favors. In this kind of sentence a "performer" does something to something:

The dog eats a bone.
My brother drove my car.

When the "performer" is not a person or animal but an inanimate thing or group of things, it is still treated the same way:

The waves are eating the shore.
New York stands on an island.

When the "performer" is not a person, animal, or thing, but a concept or idea, it is still treated this way:

Reading maketh a full man.
Peace threatens the stock market.

Many languages outside the Indo-European group do not have this sentence pattern, which emphasizes action or causation; they use static or situational patterns which might be translated this way:

Time now; there is an eating and a dog and a bone.
Time past; there is a brother to me, a driving, and a car.
Island place, New York City.

3) Old English had special verb-forms to distinguish the speaker from the person spoken to and the person or thing spoken of.

Old English had special verb-forms to distinguish an action that happened (in the past) from one that happens (in the present or in the future).

Old English had special verb-forms to distinguish an action that might have happened (in the past) from one that might happen (in the present or future).

Old English had special verb-forms to indicate that a sentence is a statement or a command.

4) Old English had a system of word-formation that worked by combining word-roots, prefixes, and suffixes so that forms could be created at will to meet any need for new forms that might arise; as a result it was peculiarly resistant to borrowing from other languages.

The Island Period

IN early times (to 400 A.D.) the Roman Empire had included Celtic England, and the Romans had defended their territory with fortifications and Imperial troops. As the Roman Empire was invaded again and again by Germans, the troops had been withdrawn. The Island Period of the English language began in the fifth century when the Angles, Saxons, and Jutes left the lowlands of Germany and invaded Britain. The record is confused; the historical notices of the event were all written some time after it, so that we do not know just what brought it about. There seems to have been during this age an enormous pressure of peoples coming out of .eastern Europe. The Romans and the Celts in France and Spain were squeezed by the Germans, who ultimately swamped the Roman Empire. The Germans were being pushed in their turn by the Slavs, and the Slavs by the Magyars and the Mongols. Possibly the Anglo-Saxon invaders of Britain were caught as if in a vise between the tribes east of them and the Roman fortifications to their west; possibly they sought to escape the pressure by taking ship for Britain. In any event they occupied the Celtic territory in Britain which the Romans had held; what happened to the resident Celts we are not told. Some, no doubt, retreated into Wales; some took ship across the channel and settled Brittany.

From the fifth century to the ninth the Anglo-Saxons held their land, which they called England—land of the Angles. Clearly they were of different nations; they occupied the island in tribal groups speaking at least three different dialects. The Angles took the northern and middle portions of the island, the Saxons the south and southwest, and the Jutes occupied Kent in the southeast. As time passed, the Anglian dialects split into two: the Northumbrian north of the Humber River, and the Mercian south of the Humber. The English received Christianity both from the Irish and the Roman church; they were thus drawn into the orbit of Western European culture.

In the ninth century the English were harried by the Danes, searovers having their period of expansion. The Danes were invading France, where they cut a bite out of the land and held it; they were raiding and trading throughout the Baltic and the North Sea. In France they became known as the Normans and their territory as Normandy. In England they cut off the northeast section known as the Danelaw. In both countries, once they had secured their holdings, they became assimilated into the native culture and language and gave up their own. In England the assimilation was easy enough; their customs and language were not much different from those of the English. It is difficult today to estimate the Danish element in English; so many of the forms that might be Danish might also be native.

After about the year 1000 contact with the French across the channel became frequent; some borrowed words from French entered the English vocabulary. In terms of medieval life, the stretch of time from 500 A.D. to 1066 was a "normal" period in the life of the English language. A Germanic people living on the very fringes of Western European civilization had removed itself to an island off the coast, where it maintained an integrated and relatively isolated pagan society. It used one language for all the business of society: the day-to-day talk of all the people about all their affairs, the conduct of commercial and social life at all levels; the intellectual and literary life, and the poetry and prose of thought and emotion. The Old English language of this early period is a true "culture language."

The Anglo-Saxons began to trade and intermarry with the Christian people of France, and were drawn into the orbit of the Christian church. Christianized rather quickly, they absorbed with

Christianity a good part of the philosophical ordering of thought that accompanies Christianity. Their intellectual life became Latinized, or rather bilingual, since their own native tongue was capable of expressing just about what Latin expressed. They translated rather freely from Latin into Old English. Then in the ninth century they were subjected to a new pagan invasion; the parts of the country that were invaded and sacked by the Vikings were the northern kingdoms where learning had most flourished. Absorbing and converting the invaders, the English turned more and more to Latin learning, and borrowed what is for them a fair number of Latin words. Old English remained throughout this period a "culture language," fit for all the expressive needs of a thriving civilization. The remains from this period in architecture, handicrafts, manuscript illumination, and literature show a diversified, mature society.

In 1066 England was invaded again, this time for keeps. William of Normandy defeated the military forces of the English king, Harold, at Hastings, where Harold was killed in the battle. William moved quickly to clean out all opposition. He put his own men in all sensitive posts in the government and in the Church, reaching as far down into both organizations as necessary. For several centuries afterward England was part of a domain that included at times half of France. By this invasion England was encompassed within the community of Western Europe. Religious and intellectual matters were discussed only in Latin, and translations into English came to a stop. Social and commercial life, where it involved the sort of people who count for something, drifted naturally into the Norman dialect of French. The court was French.

The English language was by no means erased. It remained the speech of the farmers and laborers, but its use was limited to the matters farmers and laborers have to talk about. Thus a good part of its vocabulary fell into disuse. The period of French domination happened to coincide with a structural change which had been going on in the English language, the abandonment of many interlocking inflections as a primary means of conveying meaning. These were being replaced by patterns of meaningful order that had been evolving for some time. The net effect was that a large part of the vocabulary and a substantial number of grammatical structures disappeared permanently from the language at about the same time.

Probably even in 1250, when French was the official language of the law courts and of Parliament, when French was used in poems, epics, and long tales of fancy, and familiarly spoken by the landed aristocracy, no large proportion of the people of England spoke French. There are always many more of the common people than of any other element in society, and the common people spoke English. Many of all social classes were bilingual, using at will both languages—probably with a dreadfully bad accent in one or the other. Among the clergy and the scholars at universities, who did their heavy thinking in Latin, no doubt everybody used French or English also, depending on the people they ministered to. Some must have switched from French to English with considerable ease. Yet almost all the writing of the time was in French or Latin. English had reverted to what it had been through thousands of years of prehistory, a language that lived in the mouths of its speakers. As such it left little record, but it never had been or never will be more instinct with vitality.

Very gradually after 1250 the great weight of common use began to make itself felt. Certain cultural changes helped it along. The English kings, who had been riding high in France as the Dukes of Normandy, began to lose out to the French king. Prestige swung to the King of France; military successes came his way, and in the end the French dynasty broke the French power of the Dukes and took over their possessions in France. It became fashionable and perhaps even wise to use the dialect of the King of France. Norman French began to sound a little rustic and Anglo-Norman worse even than rustic. The brilliant interchange of courtiers between Norman France and Norman England dwindled to a formal exchange of ambassadors between the French king and English king. The English aristocracy began to send its sons to France to learn "correct" French. That delicate network of social and political advantage which had sustained the French language in England began to fray a little. In England it no longer seemed quite worth the effort to speak French, because right at home was familiar, homely, generally understood, and easy-to-use English. The habit of writing French continued beyond any utility, until at last legal and parliamentary records became crude word-by-word translations, English sentences with French words.

Only after 1250 did any large number of French words begin to appear in English. In the early days, smarting from their defeat and hostile to the invaders, the conquered people were in no mood to intrude the language of the foreigner into their own. Furthermore, William the Conqueror seems not to have cared much about language; he was concerned about administration, and he published his orders to the English in English. The intrusion of French was an intrusion of French people: its superior social status reflected their superior social status. They brought in Western European feudalism with its specialized terminology, and carried on the social life of a French ducal court—a court into which few Englishmen of the old aristocracy survived to enter. Thus the languages existed side by side for different social uses; extensive borrowing either way was unnecessary. The borrowing occurred when English returned to the social uses from which it had been excluded, and when the French terms in law, clothing, food, and religion were so familiar that they came naturally to the tongue.

The return of English to public life in England may have been part of another great change in medieval life, the rise of a sense of being Englishmen, Frenchmen, Italians, and so on. The feeling was growing all over Europe that a people should use its own language for all purposes, even for the kind of heavy thinking that had always been done in the great international medium, Latin. And so in the latter part of the Island Period, from 1250 to 1550 and beyond, English moved into the sphere of Latin as well. Just as it had added to its vocabulary by adopting words from the French, it ate up the scholarly and learned vocabulary of Latin. Again the reason was the same. All educated men concerned with learning used Latin familiarly; when they began to write in English, the Latin words offered a technical precision not lightly to be given up.

By 1550 English was again a "culture language," used for all the business of a civilized society, but it was a far different language from English in 1066. It had undergone a dramatic-seeming but very gradual erosion of its system of grammatical endings, and developed in place of it a system of meaningful order of utterance. After it had given up a grammar like that of Latin, it took on about a quarter of the whole Latin vocabulary known to us. From being a language with a system of building new words out of old ones, English became a language almost more ready to borrow words than to create them. It kept its original Indo-European actor-action sentence pattern, but it related the actor to the action in a new way. It kept the old past-present distinction in its verbs, building around them a whole troop of verb phrases, often employing several verb-forms in a row to pinpoint a verb idea, as, for instance, "He **would have been hired.**" English had assumed substantially its modern structure.

The Global Period

ABOUT the middle of the sixteenth century the Global Period of English began. The fourteenth century was the beginning of such a period for Spanish and Portuguese, and the fifteenth century for French. In those times the various European nations broke out of the world they had known, roamed over the encircling seas, and moved into far and fabulous lands. In the eighteenth century the Russians crossed the Ural mountains and began an eastward march across Siberia much like our conquest of the West.

The whole history of American English falls within this Global Period, and it is only one facet of the outward movement of the English language. The era was "a four-hundred-year boom" in the sense that hungry and gold-hungry Europe found land—fertile, mineral-rich land—beyond all its greedy dreams. For four centuries the frontier has been permanently with us; there has been an edge of settlement and of exploitation—beyond that the unknown, the unmapped, the unmined, and the untilled, the virgin country where no white man's foot ever made a track. Here a little capital offered large rewards; here a few men's hands could carve an empire. The new world offered riches for the mind, too: strange philosophies, fantastic religions, plants and animals and men hitherto unseen, unnamed, and uncatalogued. When we think of English in the New World, we ought to think not merely of a language transported where it has not been spoken before, but of a language enriched, as Europe was enriched physically, by being permitted to behold the wonders of all creation.

In the sixteenth century, too, thought in the Western World began to take on new dimensions. The most startling development was in science. Medieval thought, before the global expansion of Western European culture, was a strict and ordered system of thinking about the conduct of man in the presence of his God. The world of physical nature was not left out of this body of thought, but it was not systematically observed or examined. The important questions were such as these: given a certain idea, such as an idea of God, or of his angels, or of good and evil, what *must* you think about it, with emphasis on *must*? Modern science began to pose a different kind of question: given a set of facts—that is, given certain primary observed evidence—what must you think about it? Or, better, what must you *do* with it in order to produce more strictly controlled and carefully observed facts? Then, how can you rethink your whole system in order to make room for new sets of facts as you go out and get them?

The basis for this new science lay in the structure of European languages, among them English, because their structures separate *things* (which have *qualities* and *properties*) from *actions,* and fit the things and the actions together in actor-action sentence patterns. The idea of *cause* is embedded in the structure, in the very heart of the favorite sentence. The idea of *time* is also embedded in the action, in the varying forms of the verb. Thus when a language lets you think of one thing coming before another in time and causing another, you have the starting point of modern science.

What we call the scientific view of the world originated only in Western European culture and has developed nowhere else. It has been carried with English, French, Spanish, German, Russian, and the other European languages to all the other societies in the world. Western European society thinks of time as a series of things, like days, hours, and minutes. It counts and measures these things; thus the American or European is forever being exasperated by other peoples who do not have this idea of time, and he is forever annoying to them in return.

The western nations have done a good deal with their science. The habit of investigating the properties of things in nature has given rise to the techniques of using these properties that we call technology. In the Middle Ages most people felt that old things and old ways were best; they were indifferent or even downright hostile to new things and new ways. In the modern world people are inclined to feel that new things and new ways are better, and a large part of our effort is put into finding new things and new ways to use them; we actively go out and try to develop new ideas and new methods of technology. We enjoy a cultivated dissatisfaction: we want easier ways of doing housework, of running factories, of building roads, and of mowing lawns. We want faster cars, bigger and faster airplanes, bigger and more destructive atom bombs.

Other intellectual disciplines, such as philosophy, theology, metaphysics, and logic, have developed almost as exuberantly as physical science and technology. As knowledge of the physical world—of the physical universe, in fact—has advanced, we have come to want to know more about human beings in that world. The techniques of investigation first worked out in the physical sciences have been applied to the study of man himself, as a kind of organism and as a builder of societies. Biological and social sciences—biology, zoology, psychology, sociology, political science (the theory of government), and anthropology—have been amassing knowledge and developing concepts, haltingly at first but ever more rapidly. Economics and theories of business, whole sets of doctrine such as Capitalism, Socialism, Fascism, and Communism, concerned with the production of goods and their movement to the consumer, theories of money and exchange—all are being elaborately thought through and set up against each other, not only as ideas but as actual practicing social systems.

The arts and the technique and theory of art have been developing. Not only do we have painting, sculpture, architecture, and literature being created by the artists, but new forms of art are coming into existence, such as the movies, radio, and television. These forms would be impossible without all the other advances in science and technology. There is a vast amount of thinking and theorizing about the arts, and an enormous publication of critical writing about specific works and about the nature of the experience that art gives us.

An accelerating dynamism marks the present Global Period of the English language. The whole history of American English has taken place within this Global Period. The new ways of thinking that have been multiplying so fast are more than new ways of talking; the dynamism of society is matched by a comparable dynamism in its language. A people talks about what it cares about; and, in our times more than earlier times, such talk leads to writing.

The speakers of English react to new things and new ideas demanding new terms in several ways: 1) They extend the meanings of old and familiar words. 2) They build new words out of older roots, prefixes, and suffixes in the old Germanic way. 3) When the things or ideas come to us from a society using another language, the speakers of English borrow or adapt words from the other language. 4) They continue to use "prestige languages," such as ancient Latin and Greek, as mines of new words. 5) They condense long explanatory names or titles into shorter terms by making words out of initial sounds or letters, or by making words out of syllables picked from the original descriptive titles. It is extremely rare for words to be invented from scratch, without having elements of other words used in them. At the same time the slow development of the sentence structure goes on, as speakers of the language try to achieve the main purpose for which they use language—an easy and complete transmission of what they mean to those they are talking to.

It is hard for us to get the feel of the present dynamism of our society, because we have come to take change for granted in our world. We can guess only with difficulty how different the lives and attitudes were of the generations before us. We can feel the difference between ourselves and Asiatics or Europeans more easily than the difference between ourselves and our ancestors. It is hard for us to feel the dynamism of our language, since we do not know the origin of the terms we use or the sentence forms we use them in. Unless we have studied our language with an eye especially to the first use of words or constructions, we cannot tell which is new and which is old; they all come to use with equal authority from our community. We ourselves without knowing may be the first and only users of a term or an expression; our present need for communication brings us to the borderline of what has been said before us, and beyond it.

The language we speak is a system in equilibrium which has attained its present point of balance by encompassing what has been said up to the moment at which we begin to speak; our next words may tip the balance and bring about a new equilibrium as delicately poised as the last. Our life with this language is a kind of adventure and an exploration as we use it to express what we have to say in a society that is forever presenting us with new things to say. It need not be a blind adventure, a lifelong struggle of trial and error; the language need not be a barrier between speaker and hearer, reader and writer. The English language can be understood by any intelligent person, in its own nature and in its cultural setting. Such understanding leads directly and efficiently to that conscious control of the instrument of communication that makes us more effective in all we have to do. We begin, therefore, with a glance at the community within which language habits are formed.

✳ CHAPTER 3 ✳

The Speech-Community

A SPEECH-COMMUNITY is a group of people who commonly and habitually talk to one another. The basic speech-community is of course the family: father, mother, and children, and often grandparents and great-grandparents living together in a close-knit relationship. Families make up villages, towns, and cities. Linked in our times by the telephone, radio, television, and newspapers, by railroads and highways, the cities group into dialect areas whose limits are the result of history. Larger than these areas are nations such as the United States, Canada, and Great Britain; including all these is the speech-community of the English-speaking world.

Ease of communication is the main thing that determines the tightness or looseness of a speech-community; the easier the communication the more closely knit and distinctive the speech of the community is. The easiest communication of all is constant face-to-face talk; in casual everyday conversation the language habits of most people are shaped. They are shaped rather early; a six-year-old child is pretty well integrated into the language used by his family and friends. He has fair control over their sounds, their structures, and a remarkably large part of their vocabulary before he starts to school. Conversation continues throughout his life to modify his speech. The facts of nature, human life, and human society which act so as to channel, restrict, or encourage conversation are the primary shapers of speech. A large, diverse, and stratified community has more features in it that cut off easy conversation than a small tight one, and has within it many smaller groups distinct within themselves.

When a speech-community is a geographical part of the earth's surface like a town, city, state, or nation, we learn a good deal about its language by examining the history of its settlement. In most instances the speech of the first settlers lives on when they come in substantial numbers and people the land with their descendants. The rural dialects of England often can be traced for a thousand years to the particular dialects of Old English brought in by the Angles, the Saxons, and the Jutes. Most American dialects go back to the English speech of the thirteen colonies. Settlements too weak to survive on their own or resist their neighbors are sometimes absorbed into another dialect area. Danish place names in northern England and the North Sea coast of Scotland survive all local tradition and history to mark the Viking invasions of the ninth and tenth centuries; and in the local speech many words of Danish origin are still used. Settlements may disappear without leaving a mark like the Swedish colony on the Delaware Bay, or they may live on in place names and in local dialects like the Dutch colony of New Amsterdam, taken over by the British and renamed New York.

A geographical speech-community may remain static; it may stay within the same area. It may expand, swallowing up surrounding areas; or it may contract, exchanging its forms for those of its neighbors until all its peculiarities have disappeared. In New England, Boston is an expanding area and its close neighbors contracting; year by year peculiar features of Boston speech, like **tonic** for **soda pop** and **spa** for **soda fountain,** are found farther and farther inland along the roads and highways of the communication network of which Boston is the center. In our present age of swift economic development, changes in business methods may swing a community from stagnation to prosperity, and from contraction to expansion of its influence on local speech. The boom and bust of American life is quickly reflected in the boom and bust of language.

America has absorbed millions of immigrants speaking other languages without absorbing much from their languages. Even such a polyglot area as New York City with its welter of local dialects turns out to be not as foreign in speech as one would expect. New York City is in some respects a contracting area, since many features of its speech were formerly common in the coastal areas to the east and south of the city. The English spoken today in America is not much different from what it would have been if the great wave of immigrants had come from English-speaking lands. The many newcomers filtered into a culture strong enough to absorb them, and they were so eager to become Americans that they gave up traditions which no oppression could have forced them to abandon.

A speech-community may, on the other hand, be swamped by immigration. There seems to be a critical point in the capacity to absorb a flow of immigrants. Thus northeastern Ohio, which was originally the Western Reserve of Connecticut and settled by New Englanders, has lost almost all marks of New England speech in favor of general Northern and North Midland features; the change reflects also a shift from farming to industry, for the growth of factories and commerce in this area drew the immigrants.

Neighboring communities borrow from each other, even when they don't like each other. When it is easy to get back and forth and a good deal of trading, courting, and intermarriage goes on, there may be so much mutual borrowing that no distinct border can be found. A person moving from the center of one speech-community toward the other will begin to notice features of sound, structure, and vocabulary that he associates with the other dialect. As he advances, he notices more and more. At the border he may find a kind of interdialect in which features of both are indiscriminately used; then as he goes on, familiar features drop out one by one until at last he hears no more. It does not take much of a boom at the border to swallow up both dialects in a new blended one, if the area involved is not too large.

Political boundaries of long standing and such geographical features as mountains, deep canyons, deserts, and broad and turbulent seas are excellent obstacles to the flow of conversation and serve to give boundaries to speech-communities. In countries like Germany where in 1870 many small states were combined into one, political boundaries between petty dukedoms and kingdoms, erased fifty or a hundred years ago, still form dialect boundaries. The border between the United States and Canada is a dialect boundary because of the different histories of the two countries and because a continuing British influence in politics and trade, very strong in Canada, stops at the border. Yet it is a minor boundary because of the give and take between the two American nations, the history of their settlement, and their tireless border-crossing.

Small bodies of water, valleys, and rivers are no good as dialect boundaries; the speech-community tends to settle on them and around them. Thus the Ohio River does not separate South Midland from Southern speech; the borders of South Midland are well up into Ohio, Indiana, and Illinois and well down into Alabama. A river, like a railroad or a highway, is a means of communication, not an obstacle to it.

Since the flow of everyday conversation makes speech-communities, anything that affects that flow affects the communities. Time is such a factor. We would not expect the English we use today to be like the English spoken a hundred years or even fifty years ago, since nothing stops the mouths and ears of men like the grave. It does not matter much to us that Shakespeare or Emerson or George Washington used a certain expression; many others that they employed have dropped out of use. The speech of each generation is an integrated system, and that of a later generation is another. We have only the writing of earlier speakers of English to go by; out of their writing we have been able to reconstruct some aspects of their speech but not the system, even of someone as close to us in time as Emerson, Calhoun, Lincoln, or Jefferson Davis. Future students of language will be better off than we are; our age will leave them some first-rate descriptions of our speech and a mass of high-fidelity recordings of our present speakers speaking. In this respect the past is closed to us. We know that our forefathers' speech was different from ours, but precisely what the differences were or how they fitted into a system we do not know.

We do not know whether language changes faster in one period than another, but it is a fair guess that the rate of change through the centuries is pretty constant. The generations follow each other in order: human beings have to pass through childhood and adolescence before they get married and start having children. They commonly live to see their children's children; sometimes they see their great-grandchildren, but not for long. Taken the other way, children grow to adulthood in the homes of their parents; they may know their grandparents; rarely are they born while their great-grandparents are alive. The age of marriage and first childbirth varies in different societies, but the span during which men can beget children and women can bear them has been, until modern times, fairly constant. Whatever modifications modern medicine may be bringing about in the rate of language change are beyond our present measuring.

We can use the idea of the speech-community as applied to the family to understand something about the inexorable nature of linguistic change. The infant is born into a going community; humans of all ages surround him. In America he is a "house child" until he is about three, tolerated and largely ignored by older children unless they have to look after him. His speech-contacts are largely with his parents, and by three he may well be doing a fair imitation of their speech. About three he becomes a "yard child" permitted to range within certain limits. His speech-contacts with his mother and the adult world diminish as his contacts with children about his own age increase.

At five or six the child starts to school. School opens up wider though limited contacts with adults outside his family; his speech-contacts with his parents diminish again in proportion; though, in the time they have with him, his mother and father may actually have more to say to him. The school also opens up wider contacts of a limited kind with other children—wider in that they involve thirty to forty children, limited in that most of the children are about his own age. Older children do not bother much with him except to tease him. Year by year he progresses through school, always with children of his own age group, often with almost exactly the same children. He forms with his contemporaries what the sociologists call an in-group, one of the tightest in-groups he will ever belong to. The out-groups include almost everybody else, certainly all adults who have authority over him. He learns to read and write.

In our society the age for leaving school varies from fourteen to eighteen. It is usually marked by the school grades the youngster has completed. For some it is the sixth grade, for more the eighth, for still more the tenth. Most children leave school at the end of the twelfth, the completion of high school. A small proportion go on to college, and the drop-outs continue each year. At the end of four years of college very few of the age group that began together in the first grade elect to go on to further study. Most have already left the school community where the adults live in one world and the children in another.

Leaving school means, for most young people, entry into a new relation with adults and a breaking of many ties with their families and their school friends. Each begins to move in a world of grownups on even terms with the others. At first he favors people of his own age. As he goes on through his twenties, age differences of five or ten years that formed uncrossable barriers during adolescence and youth diminish in importance, and he moves easily among adults of all ages from twenty to sixty. He breaks his close day-to-day contact with his family, marries, and establishes a home of his own. Contacts with his parents and his brothers and sisters become casual and occasional, often even formal.

During the years from three to sixteen or eighteen his closest association has been with youngsters of his own age or near it; his relations with grownups have been tinged with the hostility that people feel toward authority. Youth is the period of his greatest exuberance, an exuberance that is reflected in his growing awareness of language and his manipulation of it. He plays with language-patterns and with words; he makes great puns; he and his companions construct a password language different from that of the children older than he is and deliberately obscure to adults. His language provokes criticism and even punishment that give him satisfaction and nourish his grievances against a community that will neither let him alone nor let him in. The standardized English the school tries to impose on him is for him not standard English; his standard is what the community of young people of his own age permit and enforce. Only when he breaks these ties, leaves school, and stands nervous and full of bravado on the brink of adulthood does he move into the wider speech-community of the workaday world. It is a speech-community that has its own kinds of stratification and its own ways—sometimes subtle, sometimes brazen, and often cruel—of enforcing them.

Surely in these years of relative isolation, of growth and mastery, the imprecise transmission of speech-forms from generation to generation comes about. There may be societies and speech-communities in the world that do not stand off from their offspring and mold them as a group into the ways of adulthood; but for most youngsters throughout the world, childhood and adolescence are long hours and days of preparation and waiting, marked at the end by some formal ceremony, such as a high school or college graduation, to signify their coming of age. Whatever the cause, it must be cultural, for the organs of speech of any normal child anywhere are equal to all the peculiarities of any language.

Change is an aspect of human language as regular and as relentless as the birth and death of men. It asks no man's permission and waits on no man's approval. No will of man can speed it up or slow it down; it marches like the changing seasons. All known languages of which we have records covering a span of decades show differences between the earlier and the later forms. Where the records span centuries, the changes are great enough to make the earlier speech partly or even wholly unintelligible. As far as we know, the sheep bleats and the cow lows with exactly the same sound as in Homer's day. In contrast, every human language has changed its sounds, its forms, and the meanings of its forms. Possibly the faculty of change marks language as human; certainly the fact of change allows each language to cleave close to the needs of the people speaking it. A language at each point in time is adequate only to what has been said; it is capable of the utterances that have been made. It is a set of completed actions. The next need may be old and familiar, or it may be new; and the next action may be an old familiar complex of acts or some new one. Speech is one of the vehicles by which human beings meet their needs. The test of speech is not its familiarity or its repetition of the past but its adequacy to human need.

A speech-community is a group of people who commonly and habitually talk to each other. Each member of the group is such a person as you and me, an individual human being who comes into life, who matures, and who ages and dies, unless accident or disease cuts him off before his time. In the United States he is one of about ten thousand infants born the same day. The society into which he is born presents a different face to him than to his parents or to his older brothers and sisters; it forms, in terms of his experiences, a different cultural complex.

A child born within the past four or five years will never know a world without television and jet bombers in it; his youth will be colored by the tortured self-questioning and testing of responsibility our people have gone through in regard to the Korean war; he will expect to celebrate the end of his adolescence with a term of military service. He will grow up to handle unalarmed a multitude of machines of frightening speed, power, and intricacy.

The young adults who are his parents see television as a new instrument they have gingerly become accustomed to, the jet bomber as a frightful marvel of their adulthood. They take automobiles, airplanes, and radio in their stride; they have never known a world without them. They have grown up amidst threats of war and thunderings of international hate; they have taken part in one of the catastrophic wars of all time, and they bear its scars. For them the Korean problem was a new issue to which they have had to react in new ways; military service has been an on-again off-again threat and hindrance to their married life. Their idea of speed is what an automobile can do on a level road or how fast an outboard motor hung on the back of a rowboat will pull a water-skier.

The grandparents of the child born recently can remember the first radio and the Model T Ford, Lindbergh fluttering across the Atlantic in 1927, the long pacifist years between the first and second World Wars, and the iron grip of the Great Depression. The modern age seems to them like a world gone mad—war mad, speed mad, money mad. They resent its claims upon their pocketbooks and their security; they resent and fear its threats to their children. What are for their grandchild the basic conditions of being alive, unquestioned as gravity and the falling rain, are for them monstrous innovations and diabolic assaults on their peace of mind.

The speech-community thus has age differences within it, differences that channel the flow of conversation, for each age group finds its most satisfying company in its own members. Each aggregate of people of roughly the same age forms a kind of speech-community within a geographical speech-community.

Another primary division of the geographical speech-community is based on sex. Girls and unmarried women are fenced off from boys and unmarried men in dress, in housing, and in many subtler ways. Girls and women form a language community quite apart from that of the boys and men with a special vocabulary used only among themselves about their own concerns and with many specific taboos against "rougher language" current among the males. Similar special language and taboos set the boys and men apart. "Masculine" and "mannish" applied to a woman and "feminine" and "girlish" or "womanish" applied to a man are terms of social reproach. The division is most marked during the years of growth in childhood and adolescence; it is weakened somewhat among adults, but not very much.

Another division of the geographical speech-community with far-reaching effects is that of religion, since each religious group is attentive to its children and tries to bring them up in its own ways. Through the centuries Roman Catholics, Greek Orthodox, Protestants, Jews, Moslems, and other communions among us have maintained distinct languages of church organization and worship which are passed on to the children. Adult converts have to go through a special training to orient them not merely in the way of life of the church but in its manner of discussing all matters which it considers religiously or morally important. The training is necessary for an outsider; if he has not lived through the patterns of worship from childhood, he may not be conscious of them, either in their open and obvious or their subtler and unspoken meanings.

The speech-community also has money differences within it, for most people find it embarrassing or annoying to run with a crowd that has noticeably more or less money to spend. Wealth and income act to channel the flow of conversation by penning people in the company of others who can afford the same level of expenditure. Wealth buys many things—possessions, travel, spacious living, privacy—that give its possessors a sense of community with each other and common bases for conversation. Poverty restricts possessions, travel, living space, and privacy, bounding and localizing the common interests of the poor. Between these extremes a multitude of variations stratifies our society, though not so much as in other countries and not so much as in former times here. Often wealth combines with occupational and educational differences to isolate groups within the larger speech-community more narrowly.

Studies of the prestige of various occupations have been made, but the differences are apparent to the casual eye. Business and professional men, such as doctors, lawyers, and college professors, enjoy high prestige in our society and think highly of themselves. Scientists, engineers, officers of the Armed Forces, and high government officials are well thought of. Ranking below these in order are minor executives, teachers, "white-collar workers," skilled labor, semiskilled and unskilled labor. Lowest of all are the criminal element and the practitioners of many enterprises that are on the borderline of crime. There is a loose relation between these prestige levels and wealth, one that does not always hold. The prestige levels have a closer relation to educational levels, though again one that is not absolute.

Our population is usually divided into four educational groups, although boys and girls may leave school in almost any grade. The first group leave school at the eighth grade or below and go directly to work, usually as unskilled or semiskilled laborers. The second group drop out at the twelfth grade, the end of high school. Often, after an apprenticeship or a spell in a training school or business college, these people enter the ranks of the semiskilled and skilled labor groups or the "white-collar class." The third, the college graduates, fill the multitude of managerial jobs as engineers, psychologists, government officials, businessmen, and so on. The last group go on to graduate and professional study to become teachers, chemists, physicists, physicians, surgeons, and research men and scholars in many subjects.

Finally there are a multitude of special-interest groups in the speech-community, the members of which are informed about some specific subject matter and use its vocabulary among themselves. Hunters, fishermen, camera users; soldiers, sailors, coastguardmen; baseball, football, basketball, and hockey fans; stamp collectors, members of business and social clubs, of unions, political parties—the list of such groups is very long. Being a member of a group involves some kind of special knowledge and familiarity with its special vocabulary; often the language, as for instance that of sailors, is as traditional as the terminology of religion and as piously maintained among those who care. Unfamiliarity with the language is the mark of an outsider.

People being what they are, it is not possible to splinter a man into various classifications as he moves among his speech-communities and predict what kinds of things he will say before he says them—what system of sounds he will use, what features of language structure, or what vocabulary. Thus we may know that a man of about fifty years of age is a businessman from Chicago, a Methodist, a former army officer, a hunter and fisherman, of the college-educated, high-income group—but we still cannot predict his language before we hear it. Nor can we deduce his group memberships from his speech, for men and their lives are complex with much hidden from the public eye. They react differently to the influences that play upon them, embracing some things, accepting some, and actively rejecting others.

We cannot listen to any indiscriminately chosen person's speech and use it as a base for fitting him into the speech-communities in which he moves. There are too many gaps in our knowledge both of men and of their speech, and there is too much passage between groups. Americans feel quite free to move about their vast country; each generation goes to school somewhat longer than its parents did. They are not likely to carry on a tradition of entering the same kind of work as their fathers have done; for one thing, in our highly mechanized culture many new trades and professions have come into existence; and, for another, the new power of the United States in the world has added a wide frontier of international opportunities. In this situation of increasing flow and change, membership of individuals in most speech-communities seems to be tentative at best except in one respect—men are men and women are still women.

We are not what we like to picture ourselves, a simple undivided people with our roots in a quiet Vermont village or an Indiana farmstead. We are a composite people of many origins and fiercely divided loyalties. Some ten million of us were born in other lands around the globe. All the children of these ten million have grown up in households whose language, religious faith, and ideals were formed and matured within other societies. Ideas differ about the relations between children and parents, the family and outsiders, the husband and wife, and the citizen and the state. Many of us show the marks of the struggle between parents and school, home and community for our submission and our loyalty.

Far more of us look back to childhoods of kicking broken bottles along gutters than remember kicking pebbles along country roads. Some of us have seen our first cow in a zoo, our first robin perched sassily on the tree that grows in Brooklyn, itself an immigrant from China. Some of us have never seen snow, a mountain, a mile-wide river, a desert, a prairie, or white-capped waves along a churning beach. Some have never seen an orange on the tree, an automobile factory, an alligator in a swamp, a real live cowboy, or an Indian. Some have never known a hand raised in anger; some have taken and given slaps and kicks and blows since our feet could toddle. Some of us believe that we have never lost a war; some of us live within gunshot of battlefields where our grandfathers lifted up their faith and their flag and had them both shot down. Some of us have never seen a strike, have only grumbled when the coal or oil or milk supply was cut off; some go to work daily through the gates where picket lines were drawn and the confused bloody turbulence of labor war swirled briefly and was put down. Some of us have never baited a fish, loaded a gun, or set foot on a boat; some of us have been living bait for other men and have chosen men or ships or planes or cities for targets.

It is possible to describe the characteristic usage of any speech-community. If it is oil-well workers or carnival showmen, ski-jumpers, deep-sea divers, oceanographers, or house-trailer dwellers, we can join the group frankly as recorders and set down any expression that has the faintest hint of strangeness about it. Often persons who have married into such a group become interested in its speechways and record the oddities they observe; or a new worker, noticing what insiders seldom are aware of, tries his hand as a recorder. Some valuable records of prison talk have been made by people jailed for one reason or another. We owe much of our knowledge of army talk to the reluctant draftee whiling away the "hurry up and wait" of military service. We owe many records of Colonial speech in America to outraged people from Britain who considered us, even then, worth watching.

Such records, usually labors of love by people with no particular training for the work, vary greatly in the accuracy of the observations. These amateurs often miss the system involved, because each observer puts down only what strikes his ear as different. Scholars need to get at the shape and scope of the total speech-habits of the community, not merely the curiosities. Nowadays scholars like to brief themselves thoroughly with everything known about the group, including such studies as those we have mentioned. They try to get personal and family histories and, if it is a geographical speech-community, the history of its settlement. Then these skilled and highly trained investigators choose representative members of the group and make exhaustive studies of their habits. Or they sample the practices of a large number of people in regard to a selected list of items. Both these methods are time-consuming and expensive. They have been used in the surveys of American speech-communities which have given us our present limited knowledge of the geographical dialect areas on this continent. The studies have to be repeated at intervals to catch the changes that time brings about, and at best much escapes being written down. The description amounts merely to a statement of fact that certain communities do use or have used certain sounds or expressions; it offers no guarantee that the people will continue to speak the same way.

The differences between speech-communities result from interruptions in the flow of conversation, interruptions due to time, space, or lack of common interests. People share speech-habits in regard to matters about which they communicate with each other. Each one is thus a member of all the groups he customarily moves in, and an outsider in all the groups in which he does not. His language is a coherent system; it is all of a piece. He may not find it easy to tell which of his familiar expressions is generally known and used, and which is current only in one place or among a few people. That is no great problem as long as he is content to stick close to home where he is automatically accepted and where he knows all the signals. The group detects an outsider and fences him out. Its response to the outsider's ignorance of its signals need not be open or even noticeable to him; it may be a simple avoidance of everything peculiar to the group. Several men joined by a woman or several women joined by a man slip easily without any clashing of gears or embarrassed silences into a conversation all can share. But they don't let the outsider in.

Our happy security in belonging to our own speech-communities is ruptured when we try to enter a speech-community that is new to us. What the community is—geographical, occupational, or social—does not matter. We have to go through some kind of apprenticeship; we are tested and measured. We feel ourselves tantalizingly held off by some kind of organization of speech that is unspoken and that seems over and beyond the specific terms applied within the group to the things and concepts it handles. We may be content to remain on the outside or to establish a pattern of being in but not of the group, keeping some kind of detachment. Or we may desire very much to be accepted and included. In any case it helps to recognize that we are not facing anything perverse and mysterious in human nature, but a patterned organization of conduct evolved by a community of people over a long period of time.

The American continent has produced a civilization that looks for opportunity in movement and change. To a greater extent than most other peoples, Americans are ready to leave their homes and the occupations of their parents, ready to educate themselves beyond their parents' education for professions beyond their parents' reach. We are continually upgrading ourselves in work and way of life. More commonly than other peoples we move into new speech-communities that we have learned from childhood to hold in respect: the mechanic's son becomes an engineer; the pharmacist's son becomes a doctor; the farmer's daughter becomes a teacher, dietician, or nurse; the minister's son becomes a college professor; the factory hand's son becomes a manager, and the hill farmer's son a lawyer, a diplomat, a soldier, a politician. Entering a new way of life, he wishes to be integrated into it and become a respected member of the group.

The way into a new speech-community is to learn its signals by humbly, honestly, and alertly observing them, then to imitate them and fix them by practice so that they become automatic. It is not a matter of giving up the practices we know and use, any more than we give up our English when we learn French or German. We learn a new set of sounds for familiar words, a new integrated vocabulary, a different set of sentence-patterns. In this effort we do not have to give up what we know unless to break the ties we have with our family and our childhood friends. We simply add new practices which let us move unnoticed in the new group, saying what we have to say without calling attention to our language as such. We enrich our expression and we increase our range in order to make ourselves more effective human beings in all the circles we move in. The person who begins with the speech of the uneducated and masters the language of the educated is in an enviable position to make himself felt in both worlds; when the effort to be sophisticated and cultivated tires him, he can drop back easily into the security of the familiar, homely, easy utterance of his family and his old friends. And he can move forward at will into larger and more satisfying worlds of professional activity.

Learning to read and write is almost like moving from one speech-community into another. We begin with a secure feeling of being at home in our native speech because it is our native speech. What dialect it is, where it is used or by people of what education or occupation does not matter. Nor does it matter whether it is the talk of our ancestors or the broken French-English, German-English, Russian-English, Polish-English, Greek-English or any slightly skewed, heavily accented English that exists for a while among the foreign peoples who have learned this language in addition to their own. For each of us it is ours; it provides the grooves of habit according to which we say what we have to say. We are secure in it. It is the base of operations from which we adventure into the world-wide community of those who read and write in English.

CHAPTER 4

Speech into Writing

SPEECH IS A KIND of human action—the act of making sounds with the mouth to be heard by the ear. Like any other constantly repeated action, speaking has to be learned, but once it is learned it becomes largely unconscious and apparently automatic. As far as we can tell, human beings do not need to be forced to speak; the drive to utter sounds seems to come by itself to most babies. How to speak and what to say are learned from the society the baby is born into. Like all conduct which is learned from a society—that is, from the people around us—speech is a patterned activity. The meandering babble and chatter of a child is channeled by imitation into the few orderly grooves accepted by the people around it as meaningful, just as its indiscriminate putting of things into its mouth becomes limited to putting food into its mouth in a certain way. The sounds that a child can make are much more varied and numerous than the sounds any language makes use of; born into a language, he is encouraged to make a small selection of sounds and make them over and over until it is second nature to him to make those sounds and no others.

An act of speaking is a continued activity which begins in silence and ends in silence. Between the silence at the beginning and the silence at the end, the speaker gives out a patterned arrangement of sounds that takes up a certain amount of time. The created sounds are given qualities of resonance and pitch by the delicate muscles of the head and throat; electronic measuring instruments tell us that the sounds of speech are never repeated exactly the same, even by the same person. We do not need measuring instruments to tell us that some people speak slowly and some fast, that women's and children's voices are generally high-pitched and men's voices pitched low, that some women like Talullah Bankhead and Marlene Dietrich have lower voices than most men, or that some men have voices pitched higher than most women. Our ears tell us those things, and our ears tell us more—they listen to all the different voices that sound so different to the machine, and they pick out, as no machine can, the system of signals that really count for meaning. As a speaker issues a stream of sounds, some of which count and some of which are just there, the ear of the hearer picks out the ones that count and ignores the rest. The rest of the sounds are just noise.

Our mouths make the sounds of our language; our ears hear just those sounds and no others, just as our feet and legs go through the right motions for walking or our hands do any thoroughly learned process like feeding ourselves or typewriting without the conscious interference of our minds. It is possible to put our minds on speaking or walking, but when we first do it we grow confused and begin to stumble; we cannot distinguish what motions are essential from those that are not. It takes an outsider—a person not involved in the action—to study what we do and describe it for us, so that we can come to a conscious awareness of our speech. Once we understand speech, we can move more easily and more economically toward knowing how to use our speech as a basis for our writing, and for reading what is written. Reading and writing are activities based on speech and derived from speech; the better we understand speech, the better we understand reading and writing.

The study of speech-sounds just as we utter them is called *phonetics*. Phonetics is a way of describing all the sounds we make when we speak. A good phonetic description will show all the differences between identical utterances by the same person—a remarkably large number of differences. An experienced and well-trained phonetician can hear one hundred and thirty separate vowel sounds in English. We only have to mention that number—one hundred and thirty—to know that ordinary men, women, and chil-

dren are not capable of managing a system that has that many
vowels in it besides all the consonants and other sounds that can be
distinguished. In those sounds there has to be some simple system
of order, a way of making some differences count for more than
others. There is such a system: the hundred and thirty separate
vowel sounds are simply variants of nine vowels that count. Nine
vowels is a group that any man, woman, or child can control.

If we study English speech not so as to hear everything but so
as to find the important signals, we find a beautifully regular simplicity running through it all. Three sets of sound-signals—vowels,
consonants, and semivowels—with a few units in each are used
in such a way as to set each other off. There are nine vowels—
sounds made with the mouth and throat open and the larynx or
voice box in the throat vibrating. There are twenty-one consonants,
sounds like /b, p, t, d, m, n, k, g/ that are made by closing the mouth
or throat; /p, b/ by putting the lips together; /t, d/ by putting the
tongue up against the front teeth; /f, v/ by shoving the back of the
tongue up against the roof of the mouth and pressing the lower lip
up against the bottom of the front teeth; the others are made in
some similar way. There are three semivowels /w, y, h/ that are
made with the mouth open like vowels, but are used like the consonants before and after vowels, as in **hah, wow,** and **boy.** Thirty-
three units in all, repeated in different arrangements, make up the
words in every sentence that we utter. We will not look at these in
detail until Chapter 18; the main thing at the moment is to get a
general idea of them and of the way they work by repetition and
combination. We call these sounds *phonemes;* we apply this word
to no other thing in the world but the basic sound-signaling units
of a language.

When we speak English, we do not speak at a level monotone;
our voices go higher and lower in *pitch.* Here, again, the phonetician with his electronic measuring instruments can distinguish dozens of different pitches in our speech. Most of them are just noise.
Women and children generally use a group of high pitches; men
generally use a group of low ones. That is the way their mouths and
throats are built. But everybody who speaks English uses four levels of pitch to which he gives just enough distinction to keep them
apart from one another. We can call these levels low, normal, high,
and very high; when we are writing speech down phonemically,
we number them, starting at the lowest /1, 2, 3, 4/. We make all

our utterances using combinations of these four pitches, relating them to each other; we hear English speech in terms of these four pitches.

When we speak English we also signal with *stress*—that is, we say some words and some parts of words more loudly than others. A good deal of the loudness and softness in our speech is noise—it doesn't count. Otherwise, we use loudness as we do pitch, distinguishing four degrees of loudness, not four particular degrees of loudness, but four just kept apart from each other. We call the loudest stress primary and others secondary, third, and weak. In phonemic writing we indicate them /´/, /^/, /`/, and /˘/; mostly we just leave weak syllables unmarked.

Finally, we signal in English with *junctures*. It is hard to describe a juncture, even though we use junctures all the time. It is best to give examples in which we can hear them. When we say "one, two, three . . . ," there is a pause and a rising pitch after each word that tells the hearer we are not done; we are going to go on. It is a kind of "crescendo effect," a rising pitch-pause. We mark it in phonemic writing this way /‖/. We say "one, two, three, and four." The **four** ends on a falling pitch-pause that tells the hearer we are through; the utterance is done. We mark this juncture /#/. We say, "I don't know; I haven't studied it." The pause at **know** is not accompanied by a rising pitch or by a falling pitch; the pitch stays level. It is a level pitch-pause that we use between groups of words that are not in series but are closely related to each other. We mark it in phonemic writing this way /|/. All other junctures between word units we leave unmarked or mark this way /+/. These are the four juncture phonemes we use.

The basic sound-signaling system of English consists of forty-five units called phonemes: nine vowels, three semivowels, twenty-one consonants, four degrees of pitch, four degrees of loudness, and four kinds of juncture. That is all there are, as far as we know now. In themselves these basic units have no meaning, any more than the bricks and lumber in a builder's supply yard "mean" a house. The house is a matter of pattern and design, and so is a sentence. In the sentence the pattern consists entirely of arrangements of these forty-five meaningless units in combinations that do have meaning—but the meaning exists only in relation to the sentence as a whole. Compare **He is dead, sure** (Certainly he is dead) with **He is dead sure** (He is absolutely certain). Or **What are you**

looking for? (Why are you looking?) with **What are you looking for?** (What object are you trying to find?)

We can think of the phonemes by themselves for the sake of analysis, but it is next to impossible to say a phoneme by itself. It occurs in our speech only as a member of two larger organizations. The one next larger than the phonemes, a unit that may have one or many phonemes in it, is called a *morpheme*. **A hat** is two morphemes, **a** and **hat. Re-** in **reduce** is a morpheme; **-duce** is another. We can see that morphemes are sometimes words and sometimes not. Written sentences break up into words, but spoken sentences break up into morphemes. Or, put the other way, phonemes pattern into morphemes; and the morphemes pattern together into utterances. The patterning of morphemes is called *syntax*.

One thing about speech makes it hard to analyze: the speaker offers us all the levels of organization at once, very fast, and as a unit. Furthermore, he accompanies his utterance with two other patterned systems that reinforce his meaning. One of these is *gesture*. The members of each speech-community have a system of gestures to go along with speech. The scientific analysis of gesture is only beginning; no one has worked out a good system of notation for gestures; we cannot yet write them down. We do know enough about gestures now to know that the shrugs, head movements, and hand and arm movements of Americans are differently organized from the movements of the French, British, Chinese, and Eskimos. Persons familiar with them recognize different meanings.

The other patterned system that accompanies normal speech is the *vocalizations,* including a set of "vocal qualifiers" that convey not meaning but the attitude of the speaker. So far fourteen of these qualifiers have been identified, analyzed, and described. None of the fourteen seems to have any meaning in itself; but they work in combination with what we are saying to show how we feel toward what we are saying, or toward the person we are speaking to. They are

1. Overloudness or shouting (raising of the voice).
2. Oversoftness or muting (lowering of the voice).
3. Overhigh pitch.
4. Overlow pitch.
5. Overfast tempo.
6. Overslow tempo.
7. Rasping (an added vibration through the whole utterance).

8. Rasplessness or openness (a "hollow" voice).
9. Drawling (dragging the utterance out slowly).
10. Clipping (biting the words off sharply).
11. Singing (Come here, dear; I have something for you-u-u!).
12. Tonelessness.
13. Whispering.
14. Overvoicing.

Thus in any normal utterance of one person to another, the speaker uses three distinct systems at once to convey his meaning. He uses a *linguistic system* of consonant, vowel, semivowel, pitch, stress, and juncture *phonemes* combined into *morphemes,* and the morphemes combined into the patterns of *syntax.* He moves his eyes, head, body, and arms in a system of movements called *gestures.* He colors his utterance with a selection of *vocal qualifiers.* His whole performance is meaningless to a person from another language community, and parts of it are sure to seem odd, vulgar, affected, rude, or in some other way strange to a person from a different speech-community which uses the same language. It will not be noticed or call attention to itself among members of his own speech-community. In many cases, if it is called to their attention, they deny that they do what they do or retreat to that old excuse for everything, human nature. It is not human nature—it is simply the patterned conduct of a specific human society.

A complete record of a human utterance, written down in the various systems of notations that have been devised or are being devised for each aspect of it, would be very cumbersome to write. It would occupy several lines, and provide the following information arranged somewhat in this way:

The pitch and stress phonemes.
The consonant, vowel, semivowel, and juncture phonemes.
The vocal qualifiers.
The eye, head, body, and arm gestures.

Such a systematic presentation would be just as cumbersome to read, but it would have its uses. Like a musical score, a complete notation would tell a reader how to read aloud a poem or a prose work written to be recited before an audience. The author, like the composer, could maintain rather strict control over the interpretations to be put upon his work by directing the whole procedure of the reader. A playwright or a director could use such a complete notation to control the staging of a play. Any actor familiar with the system could translate the symbols and follow their direction to make the character on the stage a living embodiment of the writer's intentions.

The standard written form of English is not such a close and complete record of speech as a phonetic or a phonemic alphabet; it is only a rather loose parallel to speech. Speech is making sounds with the mouth primarily for the human ear to hear; writing is making marks with the hand for the human eye to see. Speech is the basic human invention, much more extensive and highly developed than writing. Many languages have never had writing fitted to them; all systems of writing are relatively modern and relatively crude; and some of them are in their childhood. In comparison, speech is sophisticated and mature; no single language in the world lacks the polish of centuries of human use. The first invention of speech produced something as simple as the wheel or the lever; all existing languages are complex, like fine chronograph watches.

We begin to speak so early that we have no memory of learning to talk; speaking is a system of acts or of potentialities for action that grows in each of us as his needs grow. It is always exactly equal to the sum of things we have finished saying; we do not know whether our next utterance will be a ritualistic retracing of old sayings or a saying in which some aspect of vocabulary or structure occurs for the first time. Our lives up to the point of our next utterance have been our preparation for speaking; thousands of years of human experience have given us the instrument we are to use. We are like truck drivers threading our way over a road full of surprises for us; our eyes and our minds are intent on the road and what it offers us. Long experience at the wheel has reduced the physical movements by which we control the vehicle to automatic responses. As we shift the gears or come up to a stop sign, we do not attend to the movements of our hands and feet; they seem a part of the mechanism of the machine. And so we speak without attending to our speech; our minds are intent upon the purpose of all human speech, the clear and complete conveyance of what we mean. We do what we have to do to bring that about.

Writing is a system parallel to speech but different from it. It is a means of achieving the same end, the effective transmission of what we mean. The persons whom we address are not in our presence; they do not meet our eyes with theirs; they do not lean into the communication and help coax it into being. At another time and at another place they will pick up what we write and turn indifferent eyes upon it, eyes that challenge the writing to make them keep on looking, eyes always ready to drift to the window or the dancers on the TV set. Writing lacks the face-to-face immediacy of conversation; it lacks the support of our actual presence, the reinforcement by our vocal qualifiers and our gestures, and the help of our hearers.

Writing is a system that is relatively new in time. Early attempts to devise writing systems were based on theories that ran them into a multitude of separate forms that quickly went out of control. One theory was the notion that language is made up of symbols, for which writing substitutes pictures; another theory was the notion that language is made up of syllables, each one of which has its own written sign. The Greek alphabet, from which ours is descended, seems to have been developed about 1200 B.C. from a Semitic alphabet worked out about five hundred years earlier. Alphabetic writing was based upon a crude perception of the phonemic principle—that language consists of a flow of sound-signaling units, relatively few in number, repeated over and over in various combinations. If you attached a separate mark to each one of these signals and used that mark whenever the signal recurred, you could get by with from fifteen to thirty separate written signs. The Greek alphabet used with the Greek language seems to have been reasonably phonemic at the beginning, but the Greek language went on changing; and the alphabet stayed, as most alphabets do, somewhere near the original sound-values. Nevertheless it was a great invention.

The Greek alphabet was adapted to Latin, but with a little less neat adjustment to the phonemes of Latin; from Latin it was adapted to English, again with a little less clear perception of the actual sounds involved. The earliest English writing had been in the runic alphabet, a script (used throughout the Teutonic world) apparently adapted from an Etruscan development of the original Greek letters. The Latin alphabet lacked any letters that could be used for the sounds of **th** and **w.** To fill it out, two symbols were borrowed from the runes. After the Norman conquest, French scribes unfamiliar with these letters substituted the combinations of letters that we now use. As the sounds of English changed through the centuries, the relation of letters to the speech-sounds became constantly more casual and occasional. The actual sound values of English phonemes drifted, and the phonemic system changed; the letters tended to cling to the original sound values. At the introduction of printing in 1476, for the most part they simply froze. English spelling remains a not very good representation of fifteenth-century English speech used to record the talk of our own times.

From one point of view, then, writing is new and crude in relation to the old, complex, and polished systems of spoken signals; instead of getting better, it has been getting continually worse. And from this point of view, the written form of English is bad and getting worse; for we don't pronounce the way we spell, and we don't spell the way we pronounce. People who know other languages like Romanian, whose writing systems represent the sounds of their speech more closely, almost universally agree that English spelling is difficult, cumbersome, and very hard to learn.

It may well be. But if we consider the multitude of speech-communities within the English-speaking world and the host of minute differences between them, we might ask whether a writing system that adequately represents any one of them—no matter which one—could very well represent the others. The historical chances that brought our standard system of writing into being have created a system that does not have to cling closely to any particular speech, but can represent and suggest all varieties of English equally well. English writing is a vehicle in which any man can set down his thoughts in his own native dialect as he writes; and all other men can read what he writes and hear, in the mind's ear as it were, their own native speeches. This is a virtue not to be despised, for the writing system serves as a medium to persons of all occupations, all levels of education, and all the towns and counties of the English-speaking world. Furthermore, it offers itself to all those native speakers of other languages who know a form of spoken English heavily affected and distorted by the phonemes of their mother tongues, so that what they write, too, reminds each reader not of their heavily accented speech but of his own.

The standardization of English spelling does rather more than let us read out in our own dialect what people alive in our times write down in their dialects; it lets us read in our speech what people long dead wrote in theirs. It makes available to us with very little extra study most of the literature in English produced in the last four hundred years. The sounds that Shakespeare spoke have drifted down the wind, and earth has closed his mouth for good; what he wrote we can read with pleasure and profit: his writings come to life in our sounds, not in his. What we write today will offer puzzles to our descendants some four hundred years from now, but if there will be in the future such minds as the past has left to us, our writings will be read, not in our speech but in sounds far different from ours. Our standard writing by being universal and conservative gives each of us a reach of space and time that merely being alive does not, one that otherwise would be granted only to the scholar who makes it his business to crack the puzzles of language.

Our system of writing has adapted itself through the centuries to the needs of the eye. This system is indeed somewhat hard to learn, but once learned it shows itself very economical in operation, permitting a large and comprehensive grasp of meaning with little effort and considerable speed. A skilled reader can grasp some 800 to 1200 written words a minute, many times as fast as most people can talk. We shall take up the ways in which our writing makes such speeds possible in Chapter 25; we can consider here the development of writing away from a mere notation of the sounds of the language to an efficient medium for the eye.

The first alphabetic writing used capitals in a line without breaks, the same uninterrupted sequence of letters as of the sounds in an utterance. A typical sentence would look like this:

ATYPICALSENTENCEWOULDLOOKLIKETHIS

Since this line of letters in space represents a series of sounds in time, early writers had to decide which way to carry the line. Some settled on one way, some another. Hebrew and Yiddish read from right to left, and Chinese reads from top to bottom. Some runic inscriptions read from bottom to top. Greek, Latin, and the languages that borrowed their alphabets read from left to right. The problem recurs with each little child making his letters; he puts down the letters in the proper order but everywhere on the page. He has to learn to put each succeeding letter to the right of the last and then come back to the left to begin another line.

A next step is to break the line into what we call "words." We noticed earlier that words as we usually think of them are not separated in speech; the phonemes combine into recurring groups which we labeled morphemes. The word is a writing unit—a group of letters set off by a space before and after. Whether you write **never the less, never-the-less,** or **nevertheless,** the sound in speech is the same; the difference is one for the eye alone. A word may be one morpheme like **for,** two like **forget,** or three like **forgetting.** Word divisions depend upon tradition or occasionally on the practices of a particular publishing house. Trying to find consistency in them is one of the headaches of dictionary writers.

Our example divided into words would look like this; there is a considerable improvement in readability:

A TYPICAL SENTENCE WOULD LOOK LIKE THIS

During the Middle Ages, notably around 800 A.D., various manuscript-writing establishments (called scriptoria) played very artistically with the shapes of letters and worked out new alphabets easier to write and easier to read. One of the more beautiful of these was called the Carolingian minuscule (small letter), developed at the court of Charlemagne. Gradually the capital letters (majuscule) came to be used for titles and for the beginnings of pages, paragraphs, sentences, and important words. The small letters were reserved for the general run of the text.

Since the eighteenth century the use of capital letters has been considerably restricted in ordinary prose. For a while during the 1920's there was a revolt against all capitals; leaving them off became a sign of devilish mad modernity. Some of the modernists of those days seem to have ended up in advertising agencies, for advertising displays, besides making use of all kinds of alphabets— block, italic, script, and so on—often try to give an effect of frightfully fashionable up-to-dateness by sticking to the lower-case alphabet. Possibly they succeed. Most writing uses capitals to begin sentences and for some other purposes, all of which are sketchy remains of the early use of capitals.

Punctuation, the last set of signs to be introduced into the writing system, arose during the fifteenth and sixteenth centuries as a way of marking pauses for a person reading aloud; the reader might himself go over a text and indicate where to pause and for how long. The marks were primarily aids to orators and preachers. The names we now give to punctuation marks were once terms applied to kinds of sentence constructions. The colon, the comma, and the period were rhetorical units; we still can say, "He spoke in long, rolling periods." The semicolon was half a colon. The units were ways to make up sentences and phrases so as to produce certain guaranteed effects on audiences. As time passed, these devices went out of fashion and are now long forgotten. Their names linger on, applied to the marks which once warned the orator when to take in wind and when and how to let it out. Once detached from their original use, the marks kept the names and went their own way. The eighteenth century was the big time for punctuation marks as for capitals; practically every small group of words got some sort of mark.

Nowadays we take close pointing of a sentence to be overdoing it; it is actually an impediment for a skilled reader rather than an aid to understanding. We have switched from the principle, "If in doubt, put it in," to its opposite, "If in doubt, leave it out." Punctuation is one aspect of writing that is always in a gradual slow process of change; it differs greatly not only between British and American usage but between publishing houses and individual writers. Originally pretty much determinative of the way to read a sentence, punctuation seems to have become sketchily suggestive; writers assume that readers have a generalized understanding of the marks and certain mental sets or expectations; with these expectations in mind, authors play artistically around, now against the reader's anticipation, now with it. Printers and typists, on the other hand, prefer regularity, economy, and attractiveness, so that many "rules of punctuation" are simply the preferences of the printer codified into law.

The practices of modern writing relate to the linguistic notation of speech about this way:

SPEECH	WRITING
1. Stress and pitch phonemes	Sketchily indicated by punctuation and some capitals
2. Vowel, consonant, and semivowel phonemes	Paralleled loosely by spelling
3. Juncture phonemes	Sketchily indicated by word divisions and by punctuation
4. Gestures	Omitted
5. Vocal Qualifiers	Sketchily indicated by quotation marks and italics.

Obviously, writing indicates considerably less than the total performance of a speaker; obviously, too, it contains signals for which
there are no counterparts in speech. A remarkably large part of the
vocabulary of written English is eyewords; a person reading or
writing them has no occasion to use them in speech. The persons
who write pronunciations for them in dictionaries have to guess
how they would be pronounced if they ever were spoken. **Quintuplets** was such an eyeword until a woman in Canada gave birth
to a set which lived to become famous. Editors reasoning logically
from **quadruplets** put the accent on the first syllable, but the public
did not consult the dictionaries; it accented the second syllable of
quintuplets and later dictionaries record the decision. **Hegemony**
is a word useful to social scientists in their writings; when they say
it aloud in public they give it many pronunciations. All renderings
of dialect in novels are suggestive to the eye alone. Unless you
speak the dialect, you cannot really translate the writing into
speech. Some publications frankly give up all pretense of representing speech; *Time* notably is organized for the hasty eye. Captions
of photographs in *Life* and *Look* often cannot be spoken; one wonders sometimes if they can be read by anyone but the writers of
them.

These two systems—speech and writing—are only loosely parallel to each other. Writing is mnemonic, merely a swift shorthand
reminder of speech. The person who writes has the same purpose
in mind as the person who speaks—the clean, clear, efficient transmission of what he means. He writes for people who have the language on their tongues and in their ears. To receive his message
they must also have the writing in their eyes and in their fingers;
they must themselves also be both readers and writers. They must
have learned the written signals and practiced them; the more they
have practiced them in reading and writing, the more sensitive they
are to the delicacies of an author's manipulation of them. It is not
true that you cannot be a good reader unless you have written
enough to be a good writer, but to expect to read well without writing much or expect to write well without reading much is certainly
taking the hard way.

Writing is an action, like speaking. Instead of being performed
with the face, body, and arms in the presence of the listener (and
observer), it is done with the hands and fingers to be read later on.

It suggests to the reader what would be said if the speaker were present; that is, it is a kind of sketch of talk. We have seen that it has grown into rather more than this; by a gradual accommodation to the needs of the eye, it has become a system loosely parallel to speech that exists in its own right. Because the material on which writing is done is not the thin and empty air but stone, metal, or paper, the written word has a permanence that speech does not share with it. It survives the persons who set it down; for many of those persons it is today the only visible reminder that they ever walked the earth.

This permanence of what is written fools us and diverts our attention from the act. Just because written matter lasts we make a full-scale production out of each act of writing, as if what we do is going to echo down the halls of time. If we were to approach speech in the same mood, we would never say much; and we would not become very good speakers. But the human child with a drive to speak is encouraged to practice enough to become an accomplished performer before he is old enough to take an attitude toward what he is saying. If he went on with the same encouragement to write with disappearing ink on self-consuming paper about his interests of the moment, he would develop a comparably wholesome unself-consciousness about the act of writing, and he would write more in the end that is worth saving.

Not all speech is intended for a listener; people often talk for no audience but themselves. Nor is all speaking done out loud; when we sit silently brooding over what we should have said or what we are going to say, we think words that we do not put into sound. The various muscles that would work if we were speaking start into action and then subside, so that we feel faint motions of the vocal organs and have the distinct impression that we "hear" our thoughts. Often as we sit with pen or typewriter composing something that we are about to write, we "talk" our sentences through before we set them down; no ear hears them but our own inner ear, though we may catch our mouths silently moving in complete but soundless acts of speech.

It is only a little further step to develop the habit of writing for no eye but our own, knowing that our thoughts are likely to vanish from our minds like actual speech if we do not make a record of them. They may be worth saving; most certainly they benefit from being traced on paper, and we benefit from the practice. At some times we think better than we do at others; we are in a sense hot, and our thoughts tumble into words; at other times we are cold, and nothing comes into our heads. Good moments are moments to catch, not for the purpose of impressing anyone else but for developing with practice the skillful translation of speech into writing. In the same spirit the golfer practices his strokes on the rug at home; the photographer sets, points, and snaps an empty camera; the sculptor carries in his pocket a piece of soft stone and a knife to carve it; or the surgeon thrusts two fingers through a slit and practices tying knots. It is to be ready, familiar with the instrument and practiced in its use, when there is no more time for practice, when you either do it right or do it wrong, and that is that. To every educated man the time comes, again and again, when he has something to express and needs to express it well; if he has developed the habit of expressing everything he has to say as well as he can, he meets each occasion master of his subject and himself.

The question naturally occurs: at the moment of writing how much attention should you pay to language as such? At that moment you should pay no attention to language at all. When you have something to say in writing and the occasion for saying it, your concern should be to trace the outline of your idea and hold as closely to your idea as you can. That is not the time to fret about your language. If you have not been concerned about it before, the moment of writing is too late. You don't concern yourself with the techniques of basketball while you are in a game; if you haven't thought about them and practiced them day by day during the week, you are a dead duck on Friday night. A swimmer does not wait until he hears the starting gun to practice his strokes.

The moment of writing is no time to try out new words that you have not used before, no time to fret about spelling, no time to worry about punctuation—where to put commas, how to use quotation marks. It is a time to accept your present competence and work within its limits, a time to do what you know how to do. At that moment the words that come easily and naturally are the right words, no matter how common and familiar they seem; the more common and the more familiar the better. At that moment the spelling that occurs to you for a word that you know is the right spelling if it reminds you of the word you mean—you can check it up in the dictionary later. At that moment the sentence-patterns that occur to you are the right ones, and the punctuation marks that drop automatically into place are the right marks. You keep putting one word after another until you finish.

If you have learned to care about your expression, you will be of two minds as you write. The writing part of you wrestles with your subject and puts it down on paper. The critical part of you notes every difficulty you get into and files it away for your attention. While you are writing you are like a pianist at a recital; you have to rest on your competence. You are aware of every discordant note that you make, but you must go on to the end and take your bows, if there are any. Or face the boos.

Each time we write is a test, but not merely of our skill at writing. The test is more comprehensive; it is a measure of our experience, our perception, our education, our reading, our cultural level, our command of our native speech, and our understanding of ourselves. Good writing is not a trick to be turned by some magic of the moment; it is the result of all the training we have done up to then about how to bring all our powers to bear on our expression of ourselves. The manipulation of language is a small part of writing.

After the first draft is finished, the critical half of our minds takes over. Unlike the pianist we can correct and improve our performance before it reaches an audience. We can test what we have written against the ear, to see whether it sounds right and feels right. We can test it against the eye, to see whether it looks right. When we have done what we can, we run off a clean copy and call the job done. Our writing may not be perfect, but perfection does not come often to us in this life. It is good enough if it honestly represents the best that we can do then. It will teach us what we have to learn before we write again.

✳ CHAPTER 5 ✳

Writing into Print

I N SPITE OF all the books, magazines, newspapers, pamphlets, leaflets, and other printed matter that come our way, very little of the writing that is done in this world ever gets into print. It is probably a good thing that it doesn't. Most of what we write is practice, the use of the instrument of writing to develop our skill with it. What we write is the residue of an action, like the wake of a boat in the water; and much of it should be permitted to disappear in the same way. Everybody who gets excited enough about some issue to set down his thoughts sends them off in a letter to the newspaper. Everybody who writes a poem wants to get it into a magazine, and every short-story writer finishes his story and starts hunting for a publisher. This kind of hasty try at publication is something like a sandlot ballplayer wandering into the Yankee Stadium to look for a place on the team. He may have some stuff, and it may look good under the lights out at the edge of his home town, but it will take him a while to get ready for the big leagues.

On the other hand, no ball club applies the standards to a beginning player, no matter how good he looks, that it automatically expects a big-leaguer to conform to. No boxing manager worth anything matches his young fighters against the champ or against any boxers he doesn't think the youngsters have a fair chance of licking.

He doesn't want to let beginners get the feel of being beaten. He measures them against what can reasonably be expected of them, considering their age, their skill, and their experience. Those of us who are learning to write generally don't have managers, but we ought to take a leaf from the manager's book and measure our accomplishment against what can reasonably be expected of us, considering our age, our skill, and our experience.

Tracing the progress of an article from manuscript to publication will give us some idea of the difference between writing and printing.

Let us say that a college student has special knowledge of a subject which he turns to account in writing a term paper. In arriving at the finished paper he has had to plan the visual impression given by his text. After his first draft he has gone over what he has said, making minor changes that give his work more impact. Then he has prepared a final clean typewritten copy. Since this student is a smart one and he knows what he is doing, he has found time during his high-school or college life to learn how to operate a typewriter by the touch system; he has his own machine and he is used to it. He has reduced to routine such matters as keeping a left margin of an inch and a half, a right margin of an inch, and top and bottom margins of two inches. Automatically he puts the page numbers in the center of the top margin, he centers his title on the first page, and he starts his text about a third of the way down the first page. He doesn't have to decide whether to make a carbon copy of his work; he knows that a second copy protects him against the loss or damage of the first one. All these matters he has routinized to get them off his mind.

He shows his term paper to a friend, who reads it with some excitement. "Say, this is good," the friend exclaims. "You ought to see if you can get it into print." That is the first faint note of a siren song.

From this point on in our tracing of the progress of the article from writing into print, we are going to falsify the story somewhat: we will pretend that the student does exactly the right thing, and that everything goes right. Neither is very often the case.

The student looks over a number of magazines in the library and makes a list of those which might print his article. He lists about twenty periodicals, because his article has not been given a fair chance unless he has peddled it in twenty different markets. He provides himself with manila envelopes in two sizes, so that he can send the smaller envelope out in the big one for the return of his paper.

"By the way," his friend remarks as he hands the article back, "I marked a few typos." Typos are typographical errors, mistakes in spelling or punctuation or some such thing. The friend has found these errors in the already carefully revised and finished paper. The student reads the paper over again, finding more typos. He makes some changes in the wording. He gives the paper to a professional typist. She does it over in the manner of a professional, noting more typos and letting her fingers correct them as she goes along. The fact that her fingers do correct them makes her a professional.

The student begins the long process of mailing and remailing, enclosing return postage each time. If he runs through his whole list, he spends from six to ten dollars in stamps; a book would run him sixty to a hundred. One day, instead of a printed rejection slip or a noncommittal note, he gets a letter from an editor. The editor likes the article and wishes to print it if—a big if—the author will consent to certain changes specified in a memorandum enclosed.

Let us assume that the writer does not get up on his high horse and insist that his text is sacred. He takes a sane attitude: if his paper has one more word in it than the editor wants, that is one word too many. He sits down with the memorandum and revises his text point by point according to the suggestions. In one or two cases he stands by his original; but the points are minor and do not really matter. Possibly he has to cut out a thousand words or so; to cut, he reads the article over and over, looking for dead wood and for sentences that can be shortened or recast. He has another clean copy run off, and drops it into the mail.

In time he receives another letter from the editor, accepting the article and naming a price for it, but stipulating that the magazine will have the right to make whatever changes it finds necessary. Possibly a check is enclosed; possibly he will have to write back before he gets the check; possibly he will not be paid until the date of publication. But he's in; his work is accepted.

In the editorial office the article is the subject of a conference. It turns out to fit the plan of a forthcoming issue exactly. Various questions are raised: whether to illustrate it, and how; what kind of place to give it in the magazine, and so on. Then one of the staff goes through it, restyling it according to the practice of the magazine and marking it with instructions to the printer. Restyling involves spelling and punctuation; it also means toning down the treatment of issues that the magazine does not want to get into controversy about. Restyling may mean a kind of rearrangement and rewording that the writer does well to compare with his original; he can find that what he intended to say is given a clarity and emphasis that he could not have given it. He may also find changes that make him writhe. In the process of editing, some typos that have escaped all readers up to this point are corrected.

The manuscript now goes to the printer to be set in type. The type is clamped into frames called galleys. Several printed impressions are taken by hand; those are gone over by proofreaders looking for inverted and broken type and for the inevitable errors of the composing room. A set may be sent to the author for his corrections. The frames are unlocked; the corrections are inserted; the type is clamped together again. Then the pages of the magazine are made up, and a set of page proofs is taken. These new proofs are read by several people; more errors are found and fixed. Finally the magazine goes to press. A couple of copies go to the writer; his article is in print. It is a great day for the student; he has entered the big time.

The thing for us to observe about this process is that it is a group enterprise. Modern printing has reached a high technical perfection out of the reach of the individual writer. What happens to the manuscript after it leaves the writer's hand is of slight interest to him; he is at work on something else. For the author, the preparation of his work for printing is like the washing of a car in a nine-minute car wash where swarms of specialists work over it as a conveyer belt drags it along. It is his, but it is out of his hands. He could not do as good a job himself; he wouldn't want to. Without his original act of putting his ideas into words, none of the specialists could turn a hand. His original composition with all its imperfections—the result of his struggle to find out what he thinks by tracing it on paper—is the fertile germ about which the whole printing plant grows.

Absolute precision in writing is limited to professionals; it is possible to the professionals only when their work is combed over and over by other people whose specialty is finding and correcting errors in the text. We need to set ourselves in our own writing only such standards as we can reasonably expect to meet. Conscious that there will always be some imperfections in our work, we can accept that fact with good humor. We can concentrate on our primary business, developing the habit of phrasing as precisely as we can whatever we have to say. If we work honestly and consistently on that, our work, too, will take on the external gloss that speaks of a careful workman. It is constant use, not polishing by hand, that keeps the tool of the craftsman shining.

The development of the printed work might seem to have little interest for most of us, since we do not write or plan to write for publication. Yet any person who is educating himself is taking the road that leads to publication whether he recognizes it or not. The inescapable burden that our society lays on the educated man is to use his knowledge for the public good. Wherever he lives and wherever he works, he walks with the people whose taxes or contributions to a church or other fund for education have provided the buildings, bought the equipment, and underwritten more of the cost of his education than he has paid out of his own pocket. They expect to use him and his knowledge. Their respect for him throughout his life will be based on the extent to which he can make his knowledge available where it is needed. Teaching is not the private domain of the teacher; it is demanded of most of us when sooner or later somebody says, "This is your field—tell us what we should do."

Further than this, we need to maintain some kind of balance in regard to the standards of writing. We are surrounded by publications of all kinds; the books, magazines, and newspapers we read show an amazingly high level of technical perfection. The sentences run without a hitch; the spelling is precise; the punctuation is exact. It doesn't matter that there are errors and imperfections we don't see. We do not know of the libel actions newspapers, magazines, and book publishers face because of garbled reporting or garbled editing; we do not know of the bitter castigations managing editors deliver to the men on the copy desk. We see the glossy surface, the chrome plate of the printing industry. It helps to know that no one man could achieve it.

*

PART TWO

*

How Our
Language Works

*

CHAPTER 6

The Patterns of English Speech

BEFORE YOU can settle on what you want to know about such a matter as language, you have to be sure what you need the knowledge for. If you are concerned about a few hundred acres of the earth's surface, for example, you are in the middle of a situation. The rains fall, plants grow, and animals, birds, and insects lurk among the plants. All this life has its feet in the soil—the crumbly, grainy overmantle that covers the rocks. Beneath this mantle lie the heaved, twisted, and extruded strata of rock, some formed by fire and pressure, some by the sediment of vanished ancient seas. Among the rocks rest the minerals: gold, iron, silver, tin, and the transformed remains of primeval forests—coal, oil, and natural gas. The ground waters seep and surge or flow in underground streams. There is a good deal to be learned about this plot of land. What the farmer needs to know about it is not what the miner does, or the oil prospector, or the builder of cities needs to know. Each examines it in terms of his own needs; what is vital to the one may well be completely irrelevant to the others.

Our language presents the same kind of complex situation.

There is a world of knowledge embedded in it, not all equally important to all men. Therefore we deliberately turn our backs on a good deal of very important information about the language that does not particularly contribute to our ability to read and write. We assume here that we need to know about our language what will help us to read it and write it well.

The use of language is the performance of certain actions with the mouth for the purpose of making ourselves clear to other men. Our language consists of habit-patterns according to which we act on impulse when we have something to say to other people. These patterns are provided for us by the community in which we live and move; they are basically patterns of speech determined by our contacts in conversation. The give and take of face-to-face talk from the cradle on has disciplined us to express ourselves according to well-worn grooves of nerve paths and muscle responses. The constant chatter and play of talk has disciplined us not to wander into other grooves and other patterns that are used in other communities. To become as good readers and writers as we are speakers and listeners, we need to know which of these patterns of speech are used in writing and what they are like in writing.

Our analysis must lead us to observe, imitate, and practice complicated patterns of habitual action and make them a part of us as our speech-habits. It must expose the likenesses and differences between the speech we start with and the writing we are trying to learn. It must give us the means of observing for ourselves what we have to do, so that we can practice until we have a new and trustworthy set of habits. We must find a clean line through the sentence. We must start at the beginning of a sentence and go through to the end, picking up the sense and a grasp of the structures that make the sense at the same time. We must detach the structures, hold them up for inspection, and manipulate them apart from any sentences we find them in. We must shake the structures free from any particular words so that we can see the kinds of words that work in them.

The patterns important to know are those most commonly used in speech and writing. The two systems do not completely overlap; some patterns common in speech rarely appear in writing, and some used in writing are almost never spoken. Many speech-patterns are excluded from writing by taboos of various kinds, just as many words commonly spoken are kept out of writing. Writing is not only a crude and loose parallel in space to the stream of speech-sounds emitted in time; it is a limited and restricted system in comparison to the plenitude of speech. Writing is a formal garden in which what doesn't want to grow is nursed and forced, and what wants to grow is weeded out.

Our analysis will be characterized by four things:

1) The speech-patterns will be presented in the forms they take in standard writing.

2) The patterns will be those most widely used in most varieties of English speech and writing; they will be representative.

3) They will be basic patterns, the ones that form the core of the system, the ones on which other patterns model themselves.

4) They will be sentence-patterns. We treat the sentence as the equivalent in writing of the spoken utterance; we begin with the sentence as the one overall structure which is capable of revealing the twists and turns our language takes.

We begin with the form of the sentence called the statement, which is at its least in such a sentence as **Jesus wept** or **Men work** and at its largest when the element **Men** and the element **work** is each qualified and subqualified to the limit. We will arrive at a series of six basic statement-patterns capable of infinite variety; the means of bringing all six from simplicity to complexity will be about the same. We will begin with simple patterns and move to the complex, but constantly reduce the most complicated entities to simple elements again, showing the unity which exists in variety, the simplicity underlying complexity. Comparable simplicity will appear in the display of question and command sentence-patterns.

The English language is a system, not a random outpouring of sounds and gaps between sounds. A system is of course an organization of units into general classes of similar items and general classes of similar relationships. It is comparatively easy to show the organization of things we can handle, like hats, buttons, or pencils, just by setting like things together and unlike things apart, and by tracing the lines between them. It is harder to display a language-system because you can't take its elements into your hands and shift them around. Therefore you have to devise an analogy, some kind of tangible items which you can handle and shift into position, things that are not language but can be used to stand for language, things that can be seen, that stay put until you want to move them, labels that represent classes of words, and spaces that represent intervals of time.

For the model which we use in this book to display the working system of our language, we have turned to the "exploded diagram" used extensively in industry to show the parts of a machine in relation to each other. In the exploded diagram of an automobile speedometer, for instance, each part of the mechanism is shown in line with the part it fits, but drawn back and separate from it. The part is pictured "in the round" so that you can see exactly what it looks like, and in position so that you can see exactly where it fits. Each larger bit of machinery is shown as a whole in relation to the pieces with which it joins, so that you have a quick picture of each item in its closer relationships and in relation to the whole. To achieve a similar effective display of the sentence and its parts, we tag each class of words with a label, and we distribute the labels in boxes on the page. We use space to stand for time in the same way standard English writing does: we put the first things said on the left of the page and everything that follows in order to the right. We "explode" our diagram for clarity, spreading the display wide on the page, but we never disturb the order in which one element naturally follows another in speech and standard writing.

Useful as the exploded diagram of a speedometer is for displaying the internal workings of a speedometer, it is most useful to the person who is most familiar with speedometers and not particularly illuminating or interesting to someone who has had no experience with them. And so with our display of the language: it is of most use to the native speaker who brings to his reading a thorough command of English speech in at least one of its many dialects; it arranges, describes, and illuminates a kind of conduct with which he is already adept. He finds in the display the knowledge that he brings to the display; each abstract pattern is illustrated by words that fit it; he must agree that the words in the sample do fit it and he must be able to produce others that fall comfortably in the slots also. The value in the display lies in this production of real utterances to fit the patterns, one sample utterance after another, each one a little easier to think of than the last. He is like an assembler provided with kits of speedometer parts that he must put together for a living: he painfully assembles the first few according to the diagram, refers less and less to the book as he goes along, and finally does not need it at all. By that time he is an expert. These diagrams produce experts at sentence-assembly; the kit of parts is the language of our birth.

The whole aim of the display of the language is to help the reader bridge the gap between the speech that he knows so well and the writing system he must master to join the company of the educated; its object is to put him in conscious control of the word-classes and the patterns they fit, so that he makes deliberate choices among possibilities in order to achieve any effect he wants. In the view expressed in this book, there are four major classes of words into which almost all the English vocabulary may be sorted, with some words falling into one class only, others falling into two, three, and even four. We have one word of each class in such a standard English sentence as **Small children tire easily;** we tag these words (in order) with the labels **adjective, noun, verb,** and **adverb** because these are familiar names which let us devise an easy symbolism for the display: **A N V A.**. All the other machinery of the language relates these four classes of words to each other. Any meaningful occurrence of any of these classes of words is within a structure of some sort, a pattern that somehow relates the word or its class to other words, or to the language as a whole.

What then is a **noun,** a **verb,** an **adjective,** or an **adverb;** how is each term defined? It is never defined, really, except by a kind of sorting: experience tells us that a word which distributes itself, in a large body of utterances, in about the same structures as does **children** belongs to the same class and should have the same name. And so we call it a **noun** because we call **children** a **noun;** calling it a **noun** distinguishes it from **small,** which has a different distribution and a different class-name: **adjective.**

Simply shuffling the four words of our sample sentence gives us a notion of structures or patterns, since these four words cannot be used indiscriminately to produce a meaningful utterance. **Small children** makes sense; **children small** does not. **Children tire** makes sense; **children easily** does not. Some patterns are immediately and sharply meaningful; some are not. Those that are meaningful with these words are meaningful with others of the same class: we can say **small children, young children, busy children, small boxes, young animals, busy work.** Therefore we can drop actual words and make up patterns of symbols; the symbols evoke words of the same class, and the patterns are meaningful. **Small children** gives us the pattern **A N**; into this pattern we can fit a multitude of words from the two classes **adjective** and **noun;** usually they make sense. When they don't, some factor requiring further analysis has intruded to alter the relationship. We have named the patterns necessary to our display: for example, **noun-group, noun-cluster, verb-group, verb-cluster;** sometimes we do not. We avoid a soggy multitude of badly digested names, heavy on the mind; we try to keep our terminology within strict and useful limits.

Watching the operation of word-classes in sentence-patterns gives us the concept of *function:* the function of a noun or adjective is simply a name for its occurrence in patterns: that is, its distribution. We thus can call a certain occurrence the function of a noun or a noun function because it is the occurrence of nouns. When some other word-class or word-group occurs where we have learned to expect a noun, we can say that it is substituting in the function of a noun. Thus we have the pattern **N V Children tire, Men work.** When we find a word like **poor** which we have sorted as an adjective replacing **men** in a sentence like **The poor work,** or a group of words like **Whatever men we can get** replacing **men** in a sentence like **Whatever men we can get work,** we can say that the adjective or the word-group is substituting in the function of a noun. The notion of function gives us a base of operation that lets us deal with a multitude of substitutions. Thus we have noun functions, adjective functions, verb functions, and adverb functions, and we have other elements substituting in these functions. *Substitution* is a fact of language; the notion of function gives us a way to deal with it in the display.

Any use of language is a matter of making choices. Language is not the random occurrence of isolated items in any order at all, but a controlled organization of word-classes in patterns. We make choices at every step in the utterance, but the further we go, the more our later choices are controlled by the ones we have already made. Choice is always between alternatives; and at certain chinks in the utterance more possibilities of choice present themselves than at others. What we call "style" in human expression is a way of summarizing the kinds of choices that a person habitually makes wherever choice is possible. After any noun, for instance, there is a multitude of alternative ways of going on with the sentence; but the next word we say cuts out the other possible ways and may determine quite a stretch of what follows. Practice with the display will reveal the range of possible choices and enrich the store of alternatives which we actually do employ at each of the major *points of choice* in utterances; it will permit each reader to give conscious thought to the total implication of the kinds of choices he makes. It will help him build toward his own most personal and effective style.

There is one specific kind of choice in language to which we give the name *selection*. A person who just uses English innocently as he has learned it from the people around him makes this kind of choice unconsciously; but dialects differ in regard to selection. A person who wishes to learn a dialect that differs from the speech of his childhood, or a person who wants to follow the practices of standard written English in his writing must become conscious of selection and make his choices consciously.

Selection occurs in English when the first word spoken demands a particular form of a following word and forbids others. Thus when we follow the word **he** with the verb **go** we have to say **He goes** and not **He go.** We have to say **I am** and not **I is** or **I are;** we have to say **The boy is** or **The boy was, The boys are** or **The boys were.** Selection proceeds in the order of utterance; the first word spoken selects the next. We say **The bell goes bang** and **The bells go bang: bell** selects **goes** and **bells** selects **go.** If we say **Bang goes the bell,** then **goes** selects **bell;** in **Bang go the bells, go** selects **bells.** In **A man comes, a** selects **man** instead of **men,** and **man** selects **comes** instead of **come.** For selection to occur, there must be alternatives; thus there is no selection in **The man came** and **The men came;** there is no alternative form for **came.** Selection is spotty in Modern English, and it differs between dialects; it also differs between familiar and formal English and between most English speech and standard English writing. The selections made within our own local dialect are enforced by long experience and are performed outside our awareness that the selection is there and is possible; any other selections must be consciously studied and drilled into habits.

The whole use of the display is to expose the machinery of the language for our attention and to permit conscious exercise with it. The pattern-practice permits us to work over the materials by which we communicate. These materials are already in our minds and muscle-sets but largely below the level of awareness. The pattern-practice draws them up into the center of attention, where they can be manipulated as if for their own sake without regard to communicating meaning. The pattern-practice works over the materials of expression in the same way anyone improves his skill by going through motions to be put to serious use at another time. The pattern-displays have been invented to permit what has never been possible to the student of language except in translation between languages: the planned and controlled manipulation of the units of language-structure in the arrangements in which they occur.

It should not trouble you to be able to think of expressions not touched on here. You have a knowledge of your own speech-habits that no one else can have; and if you know that you use a form or pattern, that is sufficient evidence for its place in the language. If you find patterns here that you did not know of, that is a sign of the boundaries of your speech-habits, and you should drill the new ones until you have made them your own and can produce them when you want to. That way you can expand your range and move by observation, imitation, and practice toward assuming the usage of the literate—the usage of readers and writers.

We have not tried to be exhaustive. First, not all patterns have been identified. Researchers who use English as natives frequently miss patterns because they are familiar; outside researchers not concerned with what our utterances mean attend to the signals simply as signals. Contrasting our system with other systems and reporting what they observe, they still have not filled out the picture. People who know most about English often speak of it as the "great unknown," a bitter name coming from those who know it best. We could not treat everything in the language even if we wanted to.

Second, since we do know English as natives and are only seeking to deepen and enrich our control of it, we don't have to touch on every peculiarity it shows. We can content ourselves with the common, the typical, the ordinary, trusting that what we do not mention will be like what we do mention. Sure that the items that come to mind outside our analysis will fall in with those touched on, we sketch in broad outline the main units in their most important arrangements.

✳ CHAPTER 7 ✳

The Four Signaling-Systems

WE BEGIN with the aspects of speech that do get fairly regular and orderly handling in writing—the words and their arrangements in sentences. English is able to encompass any human need that requires expression, from a blunt demand for food to the most subtle and discriminating perceptions of an artist. This power arises from its great richness of vocabulary and its simplicity in uniting words into patterns. As one looks at written sentences, they seem to be endlessly varied. Yet a basic unity underlies all sentences. Our first step is to learn how the sentences reveal their structure through signals. The four systems of signals are:

1. The order of the utterance of words—word order;
2. The grouping of words into units which substitute for single words and do the same work;
3. The use of structure-words that serve as pattern-signals to relate other words to each other; and
4. Changes in the form of words—such as the addition of an **-s** to **cat** to make **cats.**

We shall examine these four signal-systems one at a time.

1. The Order of Utterance

THE order of utterance in language rises naturally from our inability to emit all the words in a sentence at once. Something has to come first, and other things must follow in sequence. In writing, some words have to be put down at the left of the page and the other words one after the other toward the right. Certain languages use this order very little as a way of conveying meaning. In Latin, for instance, the order of words is not an important system of signals; what little it contributes to the meaning of a sentence is the kind of emphasis we get in English by raising our voices or speaking some words more loudly than others. The Latin sentence **Puer puellam amat** could just as well be written **Amat puellam puer** or **Puellam puer amat** or any other possible combination. Any order you give these words means 'Boy loves girl.'

But if we take the same idea in English, it can have only one order: **Boy loves girl.** If we write **Boy girl loves** or **Girl boy loves,** we have no meaning—we just have words. If we write **Girl loves boy,** we have a different though perhaps equally desirable situation. If we write **The boy gives the girl a present,** we have another rigid pattern of order; if you start moving the words around, it is hard to get the meaning or it just goes right out the window. If you change the sequence, you change the meaning.

The principle of meaningful order runs through the whole language; it has been developing for centuries and it has been refined to a very delicate instrument. It is perhaps the dominating principle: whenever any of the other principles collide with it, they have to give way to it. Thus in **Me and him slugged the guy** the forms of the pronouns may seem to collide with the order, but we have no doubt who did the slugging, and the sentence is a perfectly familiar one in speech:

> **George washed the car.**
> **I am going to do the work.**

The principle of meaningful order controls the shape of every working unit in the language. Thus we have **the principle** and not **principle the.** We have **of meaningful order** and not **meaningful order of** or **meaningful of order** or **order of meaningful.** We have **controls the shape** and not **the controls shape.** If you change the order, you either change or destroy the meaning in the smallest as well as the largest units. It is as if the value of a card in a deck of cards is not dependent entirely on the marking on the face of the card, but on the order in which the card is dealt. Some would have one value in one sequence and another value in another.

We have to remember that the order of utterance is the order of the whole utterance, not merely a part. Not only the specific meanings of words but actually their whole function in the sentence is held undecided until a final, usually falling, juncture /#/ indicates that the utterance is done. Compare the changing function and meaning of **pretty** and **fat** in these utterances: **That girl is pretty. That girl is pretty fat. That girl is pretty fat in the head.** If playing cards worked this way, we might let the ace represent the last word. Then the value of every card dealt would be held uncertain until an ace came up, and the whole sequence of all the cards before the ace would settle the value of each of the cards. It would make a complicated game.

2. The Grouping of Words

THE order of utterance in English is not merely a raw sequence of words coming out one, two, three, four, not a steady flow but an emission of words in groups. Within each group there is an internal relationship. To the ear of a Frenchman, whose sentence seems to come out in a perfectly rhythmical sequence like the tick of a metronome, the English sentence seems a very irregular and broken flow. Several words will be said quickly in the same time given to a single word; the utterance seems to rush and then stall, rush and stall until the end. The sentence is a succession of waves of varying lengths. Many a Frenchman has unconsciously tried to improve our sentences by saying the syllables in a regular rhythmical way, but even when he has all the individual sounds perfectly right, he leaves his American hearers wondering what he means. The jerky flow of our utterance is not a bit of trimming but an essential element of meaning. We have to have it.

In English speech the grouping of words, their union into working units, is brought about by a combination of several sets of signals. One of these is the set of pitch and stress phonemes. We recall that there are four levels of pitch and four degrees of loudness that we give to syllables, and we are capable of changing the pitch of a syllable before we let it go for the next. Thus we say, **the book on the desk.** The word **desk** gets the strongest stress. But if we say, **The book on the desk is mine,** then the word **mine** gets the strongest stress, and both **book** and **desk** get a second-level stress. **Desk** also gets a lower pitch in the second utterance than it does in the first, and **mine** gets the pitch in the second that **desk** got in the first. The effect is to clot the words that work together in the sentence in this manner:

> **The book   on the desk   is mine.**
> **The English book   on the desk   is mine.**
> **The English book   on the teacher's desk   is mine.**
> **The new green English book   on the desk   is mine.**

Besides the pitch and stress signals, we use time to help clot these words. We take about the same time to say **the book** as we do to say **on the desk.** Moreover, when we have a longer unit like **the English book** or **the new green English book,** we seem to be trying to squeeze the whole unit, no matter how long it is, into the same time we give to the words **the book.** This rushing through the group, then lagging a little as we go into the next group, is what gives our utterances their peculiar wavelike progression, with the higher pitches and the louder stresses forming the crests of the waves. The time it takes to let out an utterance is determined by the four juncture phonemes in our phonemic system.

The four junctures control the flow of words in a sentence the way traffic lights control the flow of cars on a highway. The common, ordinary juncture is like an unmarked cross street; the flow of traffic just goes on by. The flow of vowel, semivowel, and consonant phonemes comes on out without hindrance, within words and between words. (We recall that the spaces between words in writing have little to do with the separations in the flow of speech.) The "level" juncture / | /, as in **I don't have your book; I left it at school,** marked here by the semicolon (;), is like an amber flasher which warns of cross traffic and slows down the cars on the main road. The "rising" juncture / || /, often marked by a comma as in this sentence after the word *juncture,* is like a red flasher or a stop sign that brings each car to a halt but then lets it go right on. And the final or "falling" juncture /#/ which comes at the end of utterance is like a red traffic light that stops all the cars and holds them until it turns to green. The junctures thus determine the time given to each separate working group of words in the sentence, and, in fact, the time given to each word within each group.

3. Structure-Words as Pattern-Signals

THE MARKERS

WE remarked before that stress, pitch, and juncture are very loosely paralleled in writing by punctuation; there is really no orderly representation of them. To find word-groups in reading, we have to read these signals in from our knowledge of speech; it takes practice to do so. Certain words are clear indicators of groups; these words are starters of groups, and their presence in a line of writing is a good sign of the intonation contours. These words mark and define the nature of the groups that follow them so clearly that their presence in all writing is all the signal we need of the stress, pitch, and juncture system of speech. We call these words *markers;* when we need to indicate them, we do so with the letter **M.**

Whatever else a marker does in a sentence, it begins a set of words that work as a unit; our experience with our language provides us with the proper pitch, stress, and juncture overlay that characterizes such a group. The marker suggests a certain span of words; each succeeding word following the marker gives us another hint about the length of the span. Each kind of marker is a warning of a particular kind of span. Another analogy from driving may be useful: the marker is like a road sign set up some 500 feet before we run into the actual road condition it warns us of: "CURVE AHEAD"; "STOP, THRU HIGHWAY"; "SLOW, SHARP TURN"; "BUMP AHEAD," and so on.

Markers of Nouns

Some words are markers of nouns. **The, a, an, this, these, that,** and **those** warn of the imminence of a noun.

> **the television**
> **the television set**
> **a new mahogany radio**
> **a not very good-looking young man**

this new and completely revised edition
those spoiled vegetables

The last word in each of these groups is its *headword*. The group
is the span between marker and headword. The whole group does
the same job in the sentence that the headword would do if it were
there alone; the headword determines the function of the group.
These headwords are *nouns*.

Certain forms of the personal pronouns serve as markers of
nouns. These are **my, your, his, her, its, our,** and **their:**

> **my hat**
> **your new car**
> **his wholesale and retail business**
> **her engaging smile**
> **its rather rough surface**
> **our final offer**
> **their reply**

Markers of Verbs

Another kind of word serves as marker of an oncoming verb-
headword; this set of markers consists of the so-called helping
verbs or auxiliary verbs. Many of these words can stand alone;
but their function that concerns us here is to warn that they are
part of a span of words that will end with a verb. Typical markers
of verbs are the following: **is, are, was, were; has, have; can, could;
may, might; must; do, does.**

is going	**may go**
are coming	**might have gone**
has gone	**must have been able to go**
have been going	**do sing**
can easily read	**does write**
is going to be reading	

The whole group performs the same function in the sentence as
the verb alone would, though the verb working alone might not
have the exact form as the last word in the group. But when
marker and headword are both present, they fence the beginning
and end of the group and tell us to treat the words within the span
as a single working unit in the sentence.

Markers of Phrases

The other sets of markers are quite different. Instead of warning that a group is performing the function in the sentence of one word —the headword—they warn that the group will work in a different way. The most common markers with this capacity of conversion of functions are the *prepositions*. These little words, it may be said, signify whatever a squirrel can do in a tree: **over, under, through, between, across, by, beside, in, out.** Of course not all eighty prepositions are as simple-minded as this characterization of them might seem to suggest: **of, about, concerning,** and others are beyond the gymnastics of a squirrel. With its trick of letting groups take over the function of single words, English uses group prepositions also: **out of, with reference to, in regard to,** and so on. The prepositions precede nouns and noun groups. This is the way prepositional phrases look:

> **on the street**
> **by the television set**
> **for a new mahogany radio**
> **with a not very good-looking young man**
> **in this new and completely revised edition**
> **with regard to those spoiled vegetables**

Markers of Clauses

The one other important set of markers introduces a clause. A clause is a word-group which contains all the machinery of the sentence; its function as a unit within a sentence is the same that a single word might carry. These markers include **who, which, that, where, when, after, before, because, although, since, if, so,** and numerous others.

> **who knew my father**
> **that came in the mail**
> **when we finish this job**
> **whenever you meet her**
> **if you can stop at our house**
> **since you have already seen him**
> **after we sent the message**

These four sets of markers are not all we have; they merely illustrate the kinds of words that warn us of coming groups and

advise us to suspend our interpretation of individual words until
we have reached the end of the whole unit. When we read aloud,
the markers guide us to the stress, pitch, and juncture overlay that
we commonly give to such groups in speech. The intonation warns
the hearer not to take any part of the group at its face value until
the whole sequence is in.

OTHER STRUCTURE-WORDS

BESIDES the several kinds of markers which slice the utterance
into related groups of words, there are many similar forms that
do not seem to have reference to the world outside language; they
make words work together in meaningful patterns. In Chapter 16
will be discussed *conjunctions, intensifiers, pattern-fillers, starters,*
and *proposers.* They are pattern-signals. There is a counterpart in
the world for **house, green,** or **run,** but it is hard to find such
counterparts for **the, this, a, an,** for **can, will, ought to,** or for **and,
but, very, many, too, please,** and many others treated in Chapter
16. They are "structure-words," because they build sentence-structures; they build sentence-structures as much as the order of utterance does or as changes in form do, like **cat, cats; go, goes, went,
going, gone;** or **quick, quicker, quickest.** The structure-words recur
constantly in utterances; if we count every word every time it appears, we find that structure-words make up eighty or ninety percent of the running line of speech or writing. We also find that the
structure-words are a relatively closed group and a small one; as
we count along, noting each word, we build up a full list of structure-words rather quickly; and no matter how many millions of
words we count, we never find more than two or three hundred in
all. Structure-words are mostly learned when we are very young;
later we blunder into new ones only when we read something written long ago or far away by a person whose signaling-system is
slightly different from ours: **Hast thou the fire a-burning, old man?
Lackaday, the cold hath eat my bones!**

4. Changes in the Form of Words

THE fourth system of signals that we use is a set of slight and
orderly changes in the sounds of words. Normally the change

leaves a recognizable core of the word intact, but not always; fortunately when the change is drastic enough to give us a word of totally different sound, the words involved are familiar and give us no bother. Typical of these changes are the following:

Changes in the sounds of nouns:

cat, cats	**dog, dogs**	**leaf, leaves**	**mouse, mice**
tooth, teeth	**man, men**	**woman, women**	**ox, oxen**

Changes in the sounds of pronouns:

I, my, mine, me   **we, our, ours, us**
you, your, yours
he, his, him
she, her, hers   **they, their, theirs**
it, its
who, whose, whom

Changes in the sounds of adjectives:

quick, quicker, quickest   **good, better, best**
bad, worse, worst   **much, more, most**

Changes in the sounds of adverbs:

well, better, best   **ill, worse, worst**
little, less, least   **far, farther, farthest**
fast, faster, fastest   **far, further, furthest**

Changes in the sounds of verbs:

be, am, is, are, was, were, been, being
have, has, had, having
talk, talks, talked, talking
go, goes, went, gone, going
buy, buys, bought, buying
drive, drives, drove, driving, driven

These are typical of the changes we play with in speech. Compared to languages that rely on this sort of change to bear the main burden of structural meaning, English has relatively few such changes remaining. The ones we have are the last relics of a complete and elaborate set that English once had, but during the Island Period in its history (Chapter 2)—and largely before the language was carried to this country—that intricate and interlocking set was eroded away, and various of its structural meanings shifted to the order of utterance, the unit groups, and the structure-words. The pressures of language change still lean against the set but with different force against different aspects of it, so that probably most differences in usage exist right here—differences between dialects and between educational and occupational groups. As usual, writing, being conservative, preserves many forms seldom heard in speech—any speech.

That is not to say that this is a negligible aspect of modern English; we rely on these changes in sound and form to express those structural meanings they do express. A large part of the intricate interlocking that they once displayed among themselves (as in German and Latin) they now display in relation to the order of utterance, the unit groups, and the structure-words. They have less to do, but what is still left to them to do is their part of the burden of expression.

Lewis Carroll's poem "Jabberwocky" can be used to show the way these signaling-systems work with each other to compose the structure of a sentence. It is a good example, because this poem is a kind of double talk—it seems almost to make sense, but not quite.

> 'Twas brillig, and the slithy toves
> Did gyre and gimbol in the wabe:
> All mimsy were the borogroves,
> And the mome raths outgrabe.

The order of words here is the English order of utterance—the stanza goes like an English sentence. The groups are all defined. The structure-words are all there. The choice of sounds that have structural meanings is perfectly ordinary. But what the author Lewis Carroll did was introduce nonsense words as nouns, verbs, and adjectives. If you leave these out, you have a sentence into which you could put your own words.

> 'Twas _____, and the _____y _____s
> Did _____ and _____ in the _____:
> All _____y were the _____s,
> And the _____e _____s _____.

This skeleton is a nice example of structural meanings detached from all other meaning. Looking at it makes us sharply aware of the framework into which we fit the expression of our thoughts. Yet this awareness is not enough; it is only a partial step toward conscious control of English in speech and writing. Each native speaker has systematic habit-linkages between mouth muscles and ear; each writer has set up some habit-linkages between hand and eye and some relation of the two sets of habit-linkages with each other.

As we expose the patterns by which we speak and write, real grasp of them for writing will come only through practice. Exercising the patterns can fix them in mind. Throughout this display of the language, we suggest exercises at appropriate places, to be done not with pencil and paper but by looking at the pattern, thinking up words to fit it, and saying those words in the normal manner of speech. We recommend oral practice because it is quick and trouble-free.

ORAL EXERCISE: Put words that make sense into the framework of "Jabberwocky" as outlined above.

✳ CHAPTER 8 ✳

Meaning—Structural
and Otherwise

An aspect of language that is very hard to grasp and harder even to accept is the evasiveness of meaning. We hear a person speak and we understand him; his utterance has meaning. He says, "Coke?" We say, "Sure." He says, "Snack Bar?" We say, "No time." And we walk off together, both knowing that we are going to the machine in the basement, which is closer and faster. But if a man from Mars, wrapped in his invisibility suit, were to overhear us and try to find the meaning in the expressions we have used, he would be baffled. The meaning isn't in the expressions alone, of course; it is in the situation. A large part of the situation is the fact that two members of the same speech-community are standing on familiar ground and talking about familiar things.

The meaning here is in the system of signals only as the signaling-system is part of a larger complex of common and repeated actions. The making of the signals is a set of actions related to other actions that we perform and propose to perform with our bodies; they sound cryptic to an outsider because they are economical. In speech we tend to say what we have to say to make ourselves clear, and no more. A person who says more than he needs to say is a bore, and we don't like to be bores. In the act of communication, writing has less than speech of this situational support to which we can apply the general term *context*.

Context in the broadest sense is all of the human acts that bear on a specific act of communication; in its narrowest sense it is the words that come immediately before and after any single word in the communication. The richest contexts are shared by members of one speech-community in constant face-to-face contact with each other; therefore, their actual speech can be a sketchy kind of oral shorthand. The skimpiest contexts exist between a writer and reader who are strangers to each other when the writer is trying to explain something that is new and outside the reader's experience. In a relationship where the contexts are many and rich, the actual burden of expression that falls on the communication itself is very light; but in a relationship where the contexts are skimpy and remote the communication has to contain within itself all that is necessary to its understanding.

One of the problems always facing a speaker or writer is the problem of guessing how much context—how much mutual understanding—exists between himself and his audience before he launches on the actual communication. Much depends on what the audience knows about the subject to begin with. Much depends on the overlap there is between the signals habitually used by the person trying to express his meaning and the person trying to grasp the meaning. The speaker or writer must guess: he has to feel his way; but the speaker is better off than the writer because his audience is in a position to let him know as soon as they cannot understand. The writer's audience may never get a chance or may never bother to tell him. Any act of writing is in this respect a blind flight into the unknown, but there is one precaution that the writer can take—he can risk getting too much in rather than too little.

Even within the utterance or sentence—assuming that it is complete in all that is necessary to understanding—meaning is still evasive. It seems to reside everywhere—and nowhere. We can break the utterance down into the signals that compose it, right down to the phonemes; but we find that specific phonemes taken alone mean nothing in particular, the morphemes mean nothing in particular, the words mean nothing in particular, and the structural patterns mean nothing in particular. Take the utterance as a whole, and it has meaning; take it part by part, and you do not arrive at parts of the meaning in little capsules. The meaning of an utterance is held in solution until the speaker indicates that the utterance is done. The meaning of a sentence is held in solution until the writer indicates that the sentence is done.

> **He made a little bow—a short, sharp thing—to the ladies.**
> **He made a little bow—a short, sharp thing—for his boat.**

Nothing is the same in those two sentences, but you don't know it until you reach the final word-group. **He** in the one is a person out in society; **he** in the other is a person building a boat. **Made** in the one sentence is the performance of an act; in the other it is the construction of a thing. **Bow** in the one is a movement of the body; in the other, **bow** is a part of a boat. The important thing is that you don't know any of this until all the evidence is in, and if you try to jump the evidence you go wrong.

It is really hard to believe that a word has no meaning except in context, but if we once get the idea we have a key that unlocks language. A word has meaning only in a complete utterance as a part of the total meaning of the whole utterance. A word is not a thing, but a complicated set of acts, a fast and integrated set of motions of the organs of speech. Before it is spoken, a word is merely a set of potential, well-worn grooves of nerve impulse and muscle action, more like a swimming stroke or a golf swing that comes into existence only when we are in the water or addressing a golf ball. Writing a word is a set of finger motions, pushing a pencil or hitting a key. The sound or the written letters are only the product of the act, comparable to the swimmer's progress through the water or the golfer's drive down the fairway. We should not be confused that we write a "word" with spaces before and after or that we can say or write the word alone without any other words. That is not communication.

We can understand the way a clock works by taking it apart, but we cannot find time in it. Time does not reside in the clock; it can't be divided among the gears. Lay the works out on a table —the spring, the gears, the hands, the balance wheel—and you don't have little bits of time—seconds in this gear, minutes in that, hours in the spring. You have intricately formed bits of metal; they could be put to work doing many kinds of things. Such a spring is used to scoot a toy across the floor, arm a mine to sink a ship, or drive the mechanism of a movie camera. Assembled and adjusted to each other, the parts of the clock tell time; spread out on a cloth, they mean nothing. So it is with the parts of an utterance: individually they mean nothing; engaged with each other in the total utterance, they mean what the utterance means.

This conclusion is a hard one to accept; it runs counter to what we feel to be our experience, and it contradicts ordinary notions about language. We have a habit of depending on dictionaries to tell us the "real" meanings of words. But the dictionary, useful as it is, can only tell us what seems to be the part of the total meaning of a sentence associated with the word in question; the dictionary record is constructed out of an examination of whole sentences written in the past and, therefore, finished as acts. It is a kind of history; and history, as we well know, is a record of what has been done, not a promise of what we are about to do. It is not an essay in prediction. *The Oxford English Dictionary* records over 14,500 "meanings" for the two hundred most common "words." What kind of a jungle is that for us to hunt in for "real meanings"?

Let us consider the word **man**—surely a common word. Almost anyone feels that he can define it: 'an adult male human being.' Try it in a few sentences:

> **Man the boats.**
> **Man has lived on this earth for fifty thousand years.**
> **Man has never been able to get along with woman.**
> **She wore a man-tailored suit.**
> **He tipped the chess-board, dumping the men to the floor.**
> **The visitor sent his man for the luggage.**
> **When the factory closed, the men went home, but the staff stayed to take inventory.**

We have not repeated a single meaning of the word **man** in these sentences, nor have we run the range of the meanings recorded for it. What, then, is its meaning: 'take your places in,' 'mankind,' 'the male half of the human race,' 'according to the tailoring standards of men's clothing,' 'a counter used in chess,' 'a servant,' 'an employee'? Is it really a verb as in the first sentence; really an adverb as in the fourth; or really a noun as in the others? In each sentence it really means what it means in that sentence, and nothing else. Its meaning is the product of its interaction with all the other structural signals in the sentence.

Let us examine the meaning of a couple of structure-words, **the** and **a.** These are noun-markers; they commonly begin noun phrases: **the book; a book; the morning; the bright morning; a clear, bright morning.** They are among the most often repeated words in our language, so often repeated that they seldom bear any stress in utterances. Any native speaker uses them unconsciously and negligently; if he feels that he has any problem with his language, you can be sure that it does not involve these. Yet their use has never been adequately described. A foreigner is likely to make all sorts of mistakes with these words, but a native cannot tell him what is wrong. The native can set him right but cannot explain the difference between acceptable and unacceptable usage. If the foreigner has a sharp ear and a flair for imitation, he soon smooths out his trouble; but when he begins to use these words our way, he is no more prepared than we are to describe what changes he has made in his employment of them. Here is a little exercise in variations:

At the time of the day when the bell rings, we go home.
At a time of the day when a bell rings, we go home.
At a time of a day when the bell rings, we go home.

There are differences between the meanings of these sentences, but what are they? Each answers the question, "When do we go home?" We can cut the problem by saying, **When a bell rings, we go home** or **When the bell rings, we go home.** Both leave out something. Whether **the** or **a** means 'a certain instance' of the noun or 'any instance' of the noun must be decided more broadly than by examining these words: we have to look at the whole utterance. Their meaning is the product of their interaction with all the other structural signals in the sentence.

Or we can consider one of the sound changes—one of the morphemes—added to nouns, the one written **-s,** as in **cat, cats.** This is a very common signal: **book, books; dog, dogs; board, boards.** We might try to say that the noun without the **-s** signifies one instance of the noun, and with it more than one.

The paper is on the table.
The papers are on the table.

But try this:

The wheat is in the bin.
The wheats are in the bin.

The oat is in the bin.
The oats are in the bin.

Or this:

The worm crawled into the wood.
The worm crawled into the woods.

He made good time on the way to the party, and good
times for everybody after he got there.

The meaning of this signal is the product of its interaction with all the other structural signals in the sentence.

Words, stresses, junctures, pitches, inflectional changes—all taken by themselves—are empty. Each, taken by itself, means no more than a slot punched in an IBM card. We have all seen the checks, registration cards, employee records, file cards, and so on, punched with a pattern of little oblong slots. The slots mean nothing in themselves. They mean what the person who uses the machine wants them to mean. As part of a situation outside the machine, they have meaning. In themselves they merely trigger the mechanism. And so with all the separate elements of language. Each in itself means nothing; it merely triggers the mechanism of the utterance.

We have seen that such a word as **man,** taken by itself outside all sentences, has so many possibilities of meaning that it has no meaning. It has two kinds of possibilities, old and new. **Man** can fit again into such utterances as it has been found in through history, and it can fit into new utterances of a kind in which it has never appeared before. The first is more likely, but we can make no greater error about language than to rule out the second, for language is constantly alive with first utterances—combinations of signals that have never been made before. The user of language does not know from moment to moment when he will blunder into a new experience, make or find a new thing, think a new thought. Yet the continuity of language rests in its repetition of old combinations, in its saying again what has been said before.

In such a word as **man** there is a range of potential meanings, and each word that might be combined with **man** has its own range.

A word, then, is a generalization; and a sentence is a fitting together of generalizations. Let us take a list of words arranged in alphabetical order: **at, beats, corner, his, man, mild, seems, the, very, who, wife, young. Beats** is 'repeated striking' or 'winning'; **corner** is 'any coming together of two sides'; **mild** could be 'soft, gentle, not sharp to the tongue'; **wife** is 'any woman linked in marriage to a man'; and **young** refers to 'that stage in life between birth and maturity, as of a flower, a man, or a planet.' Taken as a list these words mean nothing. They are only capable of meaning.

Let us make a sentence of them:

> **The young man at the corner who seems very mild beats his wife.**

Here we have a statement, something specific, something as definite as the list of words taken separately is indefinite. What turns the trick? We can see what relates the words to each other by removing the nouns, verb, and adjective from the sentence, leaving this:

> **The** _____ _____ **at the** _____ **who seems very** _____ _____s **his** _____.

And we can fill this framework with other words:

> **The old soldier at the front who seems very frightened risks his life.**
> **The shrewd salesman at the market who seems very gullible cheats his customers.**
> **The tired boy at the counter who seems very hungry eats his lunch.**

The other words give a different total meaning. It is clear that the pattern sets up relationships that allow the meaning to become specific. We have to come at the problem of meaning in a different way.

Let us choose one word, **man,** as our key word. We can strip the sentence to its very core and come out with this: **Man beats wife.** We are in a sort of intermediate stage between the very general potentialities of the alphabetical list—**at, beats, corner, his, man, mild, seems, the, very, who, wife, young**—and the specific sentence: **The young man at the corner who seems very mild beats his wife.**

Beginning with **man,** let us use a circle to indicate all the possible meanings of **man** in all potential utterances:

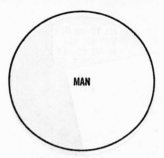

We will take **the** as pointing out one instance of **man**—whatever **man** means. We put a dot in the circle to stand for this one instance.

The word **young**—whatever it means—has the force of cutting out of consideration all meanings of **man** that cannot accept the description **young:**

The group **at the corner** cuts out of consideration all meanings of **man** that cannot be located in that bit of space:

The group **who seems very mild** cuts out all **young men** who do not **seem mild**:

The word **beats** cuts out all such men who **do not beat**—whatever **beat** means.

The group **his wife** limits **beats** and by doing so puts a further limitation on **man.** It excludes all other objects of beating, such as **dogs, opponents,** or **rugs.**

The force of the pattern is to cut away meanings not intended, and the pattern works on **soldier** or **salesman** or **boy** the same way. Each word or word-group removes from consideration all instances of the key word that do not accept the qualification expressed in the word or in the group. The utterance reveals a successive removal from attention of the instances of the key word that are not affirmed by the successive elements in the sentence. It cuts a large and unmanageable area of meaning down to size. The whole sentence becomes the equivalent of what has traditionally been called a proper noun: a noun "used to designate a specific individual, place, etc." It is a marvelous operation.

✳ CHAPTER 9 ✳

Patterns of the Statement

The Noun-Group

WE HAVE dealt so far with the overall ordering of English in terms of the four main signaling-systems: the order of utterance, the word-groups that work as units, the structure-words as pattern-signals, and the changes in sound and form in words. These signals interlock with each other. Now we have to work our way through the most common arrangements that sentences fall into. Taking up the patterns specifically one after the other, we shake them free as much as possible from the individual words we normally fill them with. For convenience we start where the speaker starts, with the first important word in the utterance.

N = NOUN; V = VERB

WE go back to a sentence we touched on before, one with the main elements of the sentence in it: **Boy loves girl. Boy loves girl** is the basic English sentence; it represents the pattern noun verb noun. Using the letter **N** to signify a noun and **V** to signify a verb, we make the pattern **N V N** and fit some other words into it:

N	V	N
Boy	loves	girl.
Children	drink	milk.
Kindness	makes	friends.
Meat	makes	the meal.
The man	supports	his wife.

D = DETERMINER

WE will deal here with the first noun and the words that work as
a unit with it in the sentence. One of these words is **the.** As we
have seen in Chapter 7, **the** is a marker of nouns; it precedes its
noun and starts a noun-group: **the boy. The** is one of a set of
noun-markers called *determiners* that occur in the same position
and put the same general kind of limitation on the noun. In our
display of the patterns we will mark the determiner with the letter
D. D stands for any of the words in the set: **the, this, these, that,
those, a, an, any, some, no, many, each, every,** and **all.** There are
certainly more, and some of these words may occur in other positions and serve other functions. We include the numbers from **one**
to **ninety-nine** in this set when they occur in this position and perform this function.

D	N	D	N
the	boy	some	people
a	girl	any	money
an	orange	each	time
one	day	six	stamps

ORAL EXERCISE: Fit determiners and nouns together until you
have this pattern clearly in mind. It is one of the most common
noun-group patterns.

In the noun-group the determiner is the *marker,* and the noun is
the *headword;* such noun-groups as **the boy, an orange, some people, any money** consist only of marker and headword, like a railroad train made up only of locomotive and caboose. In the noun-

group the marker fences the beginning of the group, and the headword fences the end; between these two the group is expansible. It stretches to accommodate whatever we want to put in; generally we put in a word or words that in some way limit the vague and undetermined bundle of meanings lurking in the noun.

D	— — → — — →				N
a					boy
an				American	boy
a			young	American	boy
a		noisy	young	American	boy
a	rather	noisy	young	American	boy
one					stamp
one			rare		stamp
one			rare	postage	stamp
one	expensive		rare	postage	stamp

Often a word spoken after the marker and before the noun could well end the noun-group—as it ends other noun-groups—and serve as the noun: **an American.** The pitch, stress, and juncture overlay tell us not to stop, to go on until we have said **an American boy** or **a rather noisy young American boy.**

Some selection—that is, some choice of forms—goes on between marker and headword. **A, an, each, every, this,** and **that** select a "singular" or base-form of the noun: **boy, man, stamp, kindness, idea. These, those,** and **many** select a "plural" form (the base with and added **-s** or a similar ending or sound-change): **boys, men, stamps, kindnesses, ideas. The, some,** and **all** may select either singular or plural: **the boy, the boys; some cheese, some cheeses,** etc. When it is necessary to represent a plural noun, we use the symbol **N-s.**

A = ADJECTIVE; D ⟶ N

As we shall see in Chapter 10, much substitution goes on within all the elements of the sentence and between them; but each of the main functions of the sentence is primarily performed by a certain class of words or word-groups. The headword of a noun-group is most commonly a noun. Following the marker and preceding the noun-headword is primarily the function of an adjective, though again other kinds of words may serve. **A/an** warns us of the coming of a noun: **a boy.** When we intrude **American** between the marker and the headword, as in **an American boy, American** cuts out of consideration all boys who are not American. In **a young boy, young** eliminates all boys who are not young; in **a rare stamp, rare** eliminates all stamps that are not rare. Adjectives occur in this order and put this kind of limitation on the noun; we mark an adjective in this position **-A**. The basic pattern is **D -A N**.

D	-A-	N
the	green	tree
a	long	road
this	new	car
five	pretty	maidens
some	ripe	fruit

ORAL EXERCISE: Put determiners, adjectives, and nouns into this pattern until you are sure you have it fixed in mind.

N IN ADJECTIVE POSITION; D -N- N

WE don't want to muddle the basic patterns of the noun-group by taking up variations, but certain words that are clearly not adjectives must have occurred to you as you were working out this exercise. You should not let that fret you; any word that naturally comes to you in this position belongs there. Nouns occur so frequently here qualifying the headword of a noun-group that we have a second basic pattern of the noun-group: **D -N- N**.

D	-N-	N
a	stone	wall
the	garage	mechanic
some	beef	stew
no	college	student

A fairly reliable test whether you have a noun or an adjective is to try an intensifier **very** before it or **-er** after it. You can say **a very green tree** or **a greener tree; a very long road** or **a longer road; five very pretty maidens** or **five prettier maidens;** and so on. You would not normally say **a very stone wall** or **a stoner wall; the very garage mechanic** or **the garager mechanic; some very beef stew** or **some beefer stew; no very college student** or **no colleger student.**

We shall leave other variations on this pattern to be treated in Chapter 12.

ORAL EXERCISE: Put determiners, nouns, and nouns into the pattern **D -N̶- N** until you are sure you have it fixed in mind and distinguished from **D -A̶ N.**

Going back to our original sentence **Boy loves girl,** we can now play some tricks with it:

D	-A̶		N	V		
			Boy	loves		girl.
The			boy	loves	the	girl.
The		**American**	boy	loves	the	girl.
The	**young**	**American**	boy	loves	the	girl.

D	-N̶-		N	V		
The	**Detroit**		boy	loves	the	girl.
The	**Detroit**	**college**	boy	loves	the	girl.

					D	-A̶	N
The			girl	loves	the	young	boy.

					D	-N̶-	N
The			girl	loves	the	college	boy.

Since the patterns **D N, D -A̶ N,** or **D -N̶- N** can perform any job in the sentence of the headword **N** alone, we can feel quite free to let **N** stand for the noun; for the determiner and the noun; for the determiner, adjective, and noun; or for the determiner, noun, and noun. As a unit in the sentence **N = N; N = D N; N = D -A̶ N;**

N = D -N- N. Thus in the sentence-pattern **N V N,** the headword **N** can stand alone or with any of its premodifiers, either before the verb or after it.

You may well wonder why we say in our oral exercises, "Take this empty pattern **D -A- N** and fill it with words of your own," rather than "Take this piece of prose and find the patterns in it." We know that you can learn a good deal about writing by looking at the written work of other people. In the same way, a swimmer can learn about swimming by watching other swimmers. But unless he gets into the water and does the strokes, he will not learn to swim. His own efforts help to teach him what to watch for, and they set his muscles. At first he produces a big splash but goes nowhere; at first the strokes fill his mind, and he is an awkward, unco-ordinated windmill in the water. Analysis, observation, imitation, practice, correction, and more practice set the motions of his limbs in grooves and take them out of the direct concern of his conscious mind, which can go back to his main purpose in swimming—getting across the pool. There is scarcely a motion of the body or limbs in swimming that the swimmer does not use sometime for some other purpose. The motions are not new to him; using them in the water to get through the water is new.

Writing is a co-ordinated unity like swimming—separate motions combined to achieve a specific result in certain limited circumstances. The writer has an edge on the swimmer; he already performs as speaker a co-ordinated unity of separate actions combined to express meaning. By filling empty patterns with familiar words, we lift these motions to the level of consciousness, keep them before the mind until we know them, and by practice pound them down out of the focus of attention. We can then get our conscious minds back on the purpose of writing: the clear, clean, painless communication of what we mean. Seeing the patterns is important, but drilling them until they work at your will is more important.

The Noun-cluster

WHEN we start a sentence, **The young man** . . . , we find ourselves at a kind of crossroads in the sentence after **man,** a parting of the ways. We can say, **The young man at the corner** . . . or **The young man who seems very mild** . . . or **The young man beats**

his wife. Following the word **man** is a "point of choice," a spot where any of several different kinds of units may begin. We can follow **The young man** with the phrase **at the corner** and the clause **who seems very mild,** but we have to do it in that order. Both these word groups put the same general kind of limitation on the noun **man** as the adjective **young** does; for easy handling in our display of the language, we call them "word-group adjectives." Most single-word adjectives that limit a noun come before it; most word-group adjectives follow it. We are going to call the word-groups which follow a noun and limit it *adjective phrases* and *adjective clauses*. The noun-group **D ⊹ N** and its following phrases and clauses make up a larger unit which we will call the *noun-cluster*. Let us look at these pattern-parts and the overall cluster one at a time.

⊹AP = ADJECTIVE PHRASE

A MOST common marker of the adjective phrase is one of the prepositions. A prepositional phrase following a noun usually refers to the noun and limits it, especially when the noun precedes the verb as in **Boy loves** . . . . The pattern within the phrase is **Prep N.**

Prep	D	N
for		men
in	the	room
at	the	house
through	a	window

We mark the whole adjective phrase **⊹AP**. Adding the adjective phrase to the noun-group, we have this basic total pattern:

D	⊹	N	⊹AP		
			Prep	D	N
the	young	man	at	the	corner
a	bright	light	in	the	room
this	new	act	on	the	program

The adjective phrase occurs in several different forms, but we will not take up its variations now. We are concerned with the position of the adjective phrase in the order of utterance: we say it immediately after the noun.

ORAL EXERCISE: Call to mind some prepositions you know and make a series of noun-clusters using the prepositions in this pattern. If you can't think of prepositions at will, there is a summary list of prepositions in Chapter 16.

~AC = ADJECTIVE CLAUSE

THE adjective clause follows the adjective phrase in the order of utterance if there is a phrase. If not, the clause follows the noun directly. The adjective clause is a word-group beginning commonly with **who, whom, which,** or **that** as marker. Other words are often used here as markers, but these four give us the type of the set. We mark the adjective clause ~AC, and fit it into the pattern this way:

D	A	N	~AP	~AC
the	young	man	at the corner	who seems very mild
a	bright	light	in the room	that hurts my eyes
this	new	act	on the program	that we now come to

ORAL EXERCISE: Playing with different prepositions and clause-markers, make a series of noun-clusters consisting of noun-groups, adjective phrases, and adjective clauses. There is a summary list of clause-markers in Chapter 16.

The noun-cluster is the whole aggregate of single-word adjectives before the noun, the noun-headword itself, and all the word-group adjectives that follow. Only the headword must be present; it can occur alone or with any or all of its modifiers; in the utterance, the headword has elbowroom before and after for the words and word-groups that limit or modify it. Fitting this expansible unit into the place of **boy** in the basic sentence **Boy loves girl,** we get the following effects:

N					V	N
D	~~A~~	**N**	~~AP~~	~~AC~~		
The	bright	boy	in the office	who does our typing	loves	the girl.
The		boy			loves	the girl.
The	bright	boy			loves	the girl.
The		boy	in the office	who does our typing	loves	the girl.
The		boy		who does our typing	loves	the girl.
The	bright	boy		who does our typing	loves	the girl.

ORAL EXERCISE: Run through these changes, making all possible substitutions of individual words.

Whatever the noun alone can do in the sentence, it can do with all its cluster. We have touched briefly on three of the functions of the noun:

1. The noun or noun-cluster can join with the verb in the pattern **N V:**

N	V
Men	**work.**
The men from the gas company	**work.**
The men from the gas company who are on commission	**work.**
The service men from the gas company who are on commission	**work.**
The service men who are on commission	**work.**

2. The noun or noun-cluster can follow the verb in the pattern **V N:**

	V	N
We	watched	the service men from the gas company who are on commission.
Mother	made	a new dress for Margaret which she fitted this afternoon.
They	sold	the old house in Boston that was almost falling down.

3. The noun or noun-cluster can follow a preposition in the pattern **Prep N:**

Prep	N
with	the service men from the gas company who are on commission
for	a new dress for Margaret which she fitted this afternoon
from	the old house in Boston that was almost falling down

And so, in our original sentence **Boy loves girl,** we can weave variations:

> **The young boy at the university who is studying for the ministry loves the pretty girl at Oberlin who wants to be a singer on the concert stage.**

ORAL EXERCISE: Within the limits of the noun-cluster in the sentence-pattern **N V N**, substitute words and word-groups until you can produce any chosen arrangement at will.

The noun-cluster is important because of its order; the sequence of units in this cluster is constant no matter where the cluster occurs in the sentence. The cluster can be intruded on, but the intruding element must fit a pattern-part in the cluster; if it is not within one of the pattern-parts, then it helps to compose a different total pattern. There are no negligible differences between the order of utterance of one sentence and the order of utterance of another; any difference in the order of units is important to the total meaning:

The lurid sun in the morning which caught our eye was a pretty sight.

The sun which caught our eye in the morning was a pretty lurid sight.

The lurid sun in the morning was a pretty sight which caught our eye.

In the morning the lurid sun which caught our eye was a pretty sight.

The four sentences all use the same words combined into the same groups; each sentence conveys a different total message from each of the others, because the units have a different order. In writing or reading we have to control more than the raw sequence of words as they come along; using all the signals of speech— pitch, stress, and juncture—we have to slice off the word-groups, the phrases, the clauses, and the clusters. These operate as functioning units. The units most consistently related to each other by the order of utterance are those that arrange themselves around a noun-headword in the typical noun-cluster.

The Verb-group

WE may now advance along the sentence **Boy loves girl** to the second word, **loves.** The sentence forms the pattern noun verb noun, **N V N.** We know that the order of this pattern is not a matter of chance, because the sentence has a meaning it does not have if we change the order; we understand it in a certain way. We can make more sentences just as understandable on the same pattern:

N	V	N
Boy	loves	girl.
Girl	loves	boy.
Men	catch	fish.

We have seen how expansible the unit marked **N** is; it can consist of one word, as above, or the whole cluster **D -A- N -AP- -AC-**.

The unit marked **V** is expansible in the same way into a verb-group and ultimately into a verb-cluster. Like the noun-group, the verb-group begins with a word from a set of familiar markers and ends with a verb-headword; like the noun-cluster, the verb-cluster begins with a marker and goes on to include elements that follow the headword and relate to it.

Most verbs standing alone in the function **V** in a sentence can assume one of three familiar forms, as **make, makes,** and **made. Make** is the *base-form* of the verb, the one that is used as the entry word in dictionaries. It is uninflected; that is, it has no final **-s, -ed,** or **-ing. Go, make, sing, manufacture, read,** and **write** are all uninflected base-forms. The base-form is selected by nouns which have the ending **-s** or its equivalent forms: **Trees stand, Men go, Cars run, Children play.** When the **N** function in the pattern **N V** is carried by one of the "personal pronouns," **I, you, we,** and **they,** it selects the base-form of the verb: **I go, You make, We stand, They play.** The base-form of the noun selects a verb with the ending **-s: The man goes, The tree stands, The car runs, The child plays.** The pronouns **he, she,** and **it** select a verb with the ending **-s: He goes, She makes, It stands.**

All nouns and all personal pronouns select the form of the verb with the ending **-ed** or a form equivalent to it: **went, made, drove, cooked, used, manufactured.** The language offers no alternative form, and so there is no selection: **I made, You made, He made; The boy went, The boys went, She went; They cooked, The woman cooked, He cooked.**

The base-form **go, make, write** and the form with the **-s** ending **goes, makes, writes** are called "present tense" forms, and the form with the **-ed** ending (or its equivalent) is called the "past tense" form. It would be good to have better names for them, for they do not consistently represent any particular time. All are used to refer to events that exist only in memory (the past), to events we are actually going through (the present), and to events that have not happened but that we anticipate in our thoughts (the future). In our display of the forms in patterns, we shall simply indicate the forms: **V, V-s, V-ed.**

The verb **go** does not have a form **goed;** the place of this form is taken by **went.** Somewhere in the history of the verb **go** a gap developed in the system, and the word **went** drifted from another verb to fill in. **Goed** exists in some varieties of spoken English, as **I goed, He goed,** but not in the varieties from which most written English is derived. We normally write it only to indicate that someone is speaking in a local dialect. Many common verbs have these irregular forms like **went;** you know them so well that you think of them automatically when you need to use the **V-ed** form of these verbs. We do not make special indication of them in the patterns.

Selection of the verb-form in the sentence-pattern **N V** may be summed up as follows:

N	V
N-s, I, you, we, they	select **V.**
N, he, she, it	select **V-s.**
N, N-s, I, you, he, she, it, we, they	do not select. **V-ed**

N	V
The boys	**talk.**
The boys	**cook.**
The boy	**talks.**
The boy	**cooks.**
The boy	**talked.**
The boys	**cooked.**

ORAL EXERCISE: Choose ten or twelve familiar verbs and make sets demonstrating selection or absence of selection: **N V-s; N-s V; N** or **N-s V-ed.**

VG = VERB-GROUP

A VERB-GROUP consists of two or more words performing as a unit the function **V** in a sentence:

N	V
The girl	**sings.**
The girl	**is singing.**
The girl	**was singing.**
The girl	**has sung.**
The girl	**will sing.**

N	V
The clock	**stops.**
The clock	**is stopping.**
The clock	**was stopping.**
The clock	**has stopped.**
The clock	**will stop.**

The verb-group like the noun-group begins with a marker and ends with a headword. The markers are verbs often capable of performing the function **V** in the sentence: **The boy is here; He has the ball; The team willed our victory.** Beginning a verb-group and marking it is only one of the functions of these verbs. In the verb-group they are usually known as *helping* or *auxiliary* verbs. We indicate the verb-markers in the pattern with a small **v;** we indicate the verb-group with the symbol **VG**. Verb-marker and verb-headword together look like this in our display of the patterns of the sentence; often one, two, or three of these "helping verbs" or helpers precede the headword:

N	VG	
	v	V
The bus	is	coming.
Our car	has	stalled.
My brother	can	go.
	v	v	V
We	have	been	looking.
The cars	must	be	sold.

Selection works within the verb-group between the verb-marker and the verb-headword as it does between noun and verb in the pattern **N V**. The selection often begins with the noun. We have seen that when the **V** is a single word, the **N** often chooses among its forms: **The boy talks, The boys talk; The car stops, The cars stop.** When **V** is not a single word but a verb-group, the **N** may select the form of the marker, and the marker may select the form of the headword: **I am talking; The boy is talking; We, you, they, or the boys are talking.** Selection does not occur with such verb-markers as **can, could, may, might, would,** and **should.** When a second helper follows the marker, the marker may select the form of the helper and the helper may select the form of the headword: **He is being heard; He has been hearing; He has been heard; He could have been hearing.**

N	V			
I he the boy	say says said			

	VG			
	v	V		
I it they the boy the men they	am is are is can have	saying said saying saying go gone		

	v	v	V	
the woman the boy the money the books	is will has were	being be been to be	called called sent sent	

	v	v	v	V
the train the bills	may will	have have	been been	coming sent

We can approach the verb-group by taking the four forms of the headword—**V, to-V, V-ing,** and **V-ed/en**—in terms of the markers which choose them. Or we can take the various sets of markers and see how they combine with helpers and headwords. We begin with the markers instead of the headwords, partly because the markers lead us more easily into the verb-group, and partly because we want to keep moving through the sentence along with the order of utterance by taking first things first.

The structures of the language interlock and distribute the burden of meaning, each carrying a part. The order of utterance does not work alone even in the noun-cluster where it is dominant; it meshes with the clotting of words into units, with the structure-words, and with the changes in form. Some sentences favor one or two of these ways of signaling; any sentence that contains a verb-group displays them all, because they all work together within the group. The verb-group is at once old-fashioned and up-to-date, like a 1932 Ford with this year's Mercury engine in it. Long ago every verb in an English sentence may have been a single word. This original mechanism is preserved in the single-word verbs still in use. The verbs have fewer endings than they used to have, but they still have endings: **I talk, he talks, the boys talk; I talked, he talked, the boys talked.**

A more flexible verb-system developed when the verb-group combined forms of the verb **be (am, is, are, was, were, be, been, being)** with the verb-headword (**V, to-V, V-ing, V-ed/en**) in the pattern **v V: is to go, is going, is gone.** **Be** makes up a common verb so familiar that we scarcely notice how different its forms are from each other in sound and sight. The modern verb **be** is an old patchwork of three separate verbs, each lacking exactly the forms provided by the two others. **Am, is, are** come from one verb; **was, were** from another; **be, been, being** from a third. Frequency of use through thousands of years has preserved in the verb **be** more separate forms than in any other verb. Those who know the history of language often see in this set of verb-forms a remnant of the real bedrock of language, the oldest words spoken in the Western European world.

Frequent as a single-word verb, **be** is even more frequent as marker and helper in the verb-group. We might wish that a simpler verb like **set, sets, setting** had been the one to pop up again and again in utterances. Probably the same frequency of use kept the verb **be** complicated and made it available as marker and helper in the verb-group. That is the way it is in life: the busy man is constantly burdened with more jobs to do.

Here is the setup of this important and useful verb:

Base		V-s	V-ed	V-ing	V-ed/en
be	I	am		being	been
	he she it N	is	was		

	V-s	V-ed	V-ing	V-ed/en
you we they N-s	are	were		

Other verbs use the base-form **go, talk, run** and the form with the -s ending in the **N V** pattern: **I, you, we, they, N-s go, talk, run; he, she, it, N goes, talks, runs. Be** uses three forms **am, is, are.** If you had to learn these forms, they would give you trouble, but every native speaker uses or hears them used from infancy. In some dialects we hear **I is, you is,** and **they is; I was, you was,** and **they was;** but in most writing these very sensible simplifications of the verb are used only to give an impression of the speech of the illiterates. **You was** in reference to one person is especially wide-spread, even in the speech of the educated, but the persons who say **you was** usually write **you were.**

The invention of the word-group by combining **be** with a head-word opens large possibilities of combinations; the idea is so good that it does not stop. We see a continual march of other verbs, usu-ally the most common and familiar verbs of our speech like **get, make, start,** and **keep,** into the position of marker at the beginning of the verb-group. Once the span between marker and headword lets two or more verbs combine to say what one alone cannot, one verb can step down a peg and introduce another, like an actor who is a star in his own right taking a job in a supporting cast during slack seasons.

A marker is a structure-word which serves more to relate other words to each other than to refer to the world outside language; hence a verb seems to undergo as marker some "freezing" or cut-ting down of its potentialities as an independent verb. We see this freezing best in the second-most-common verb and marker **have.** As an independent verb, **have** has the general sense of 'control,' 'own,' 'possess,' and other senses that gather loosely about these: **He has money; I have a book; A week has seven days; Have a good time; He has measles,** and so on. We do not find these mean-ings or anything much like them in a verb-group with **have** as its marker: **They have gone; We have been talking; He has to go;**

George had bound his book; Jean had her book bound. In these last five examples **have** is part of the verb-group with a bit of the unit-meaning assigned to the group by the whole utterance. No signal in **have,** as it is written, tells us of its reduction from full verb to marker; the signals are sentence-signals of interrelation among all the elements in the utterance.

Here is the setup of this other important and useful verb:

Base	V		V-s	V-ed	V-ing	V-ed/en
have	I you we they N-s } have	he she it N } has		had	having	had

In the common verb-group all the forms of **be** and all the forms of **have** combine fluidly with each other and with other verbs. **Have** combines in verb-groups with **be** as headword to give **be** much more range than it would have alone:

	V	V-s	V-ed	VG		VG	
				v	**V-ing**	**v**	**V-ed/en**
I	am	he she it N } is	was	am is was	being being being	have has had	been been been
	we you they N-s } are		were	are were	being being	have had	been been

Be combines in verb-groups with **have** as headword to give **have** more range than it would have alone:

V	V-s	V-ed	VG		VG	
			v	V-ing	v	V-ed/en
I have	he she it N } has	had	am is was	having having having	have has had	had had had
we you they N-s } have		had	are were	having having	have had	had had

The order of utterance and the structure-words provide the pattern of the verb-group with its span between marker and headword. The patterns vary little between American dialects; but in the selection of the forms of marker and headword there is variation, and each speech-community insists on its own way. Those of us who move between speech-communities have to be alert in order to convey our meaning and control the impression we make as we speak. "I has putted the box on the floor" and "I is putting the box on the floor" are clear; out of the speech-community where they are used they sound very odd.

Be AND Have WITH OTHER VERBS

WE have seen how **be** and **have** combine with each other as marker and headword to produce a number of verb-group units. So far the system is simple compared to the multitude of verb-groups developed when **be** and **have** combine with each other as marker and helper in verb-groups where another verb is the headword. English verbs sort into three groups, depending on the number of separate forms each verb has. Most verbs have four: **V, V-s, V-ed,** and **V-ing.** A few have five forms: **V, V-s, V-ed, V-ing,** and **V-ed/en.** A few have only three: **V, V-s,** and **V-ing.**

In our display we set all verbs up as if they had five forms, marking such forms as **talked, drove, went, set** and **sang V-ed** when they serve as single-word verbs; and **talked, driven, gone, set,** and **sung V-ed/en** when they serve as headwords in a verb-group.

We will take first the common four-part verb with a base-form to which three endings are added: **talk, talks, talked,** and **talking.** Most English verbs work this way; if we make any new verbs we usually make them on this model. The four-part verb represents a very live formula.

Base	V	V-s	V-ed	V-ing	V-ed/en
talk	talk	talks	talked	talking	talked
move	move	moves	moved	moving	moved
repair	repair	repairs	repaired	repairing	repaired

Fewer in number than the four-part verbs, but very frequent in use, is a set of five-part verbs like **drive, drives, drove, driving, driven.** This set of familiar old verbs has been declining in number for centuries. In old English there were about three hundred of them; today there are about sixty-five. They disappear one by one, mainly by assimilation to the regular four-part system. New verbs according to this formula are rare; it is an unproductive or dead formula.

Base	V	V-s	V-ed	V-ing	V-ed/en
drive	drive	drives	drove	driving	driven
choose	choose	chooses	chose	choosing	chosen
sing	sing	sings	sang	singing	sung
break	break	breaks	broke	breaking	broken
eat	eat	eats	ate	eating	eaten
draw	draw	draws	drew	drawing	drawn
fall	fall	falls	fell	falling	fallen

Fewer even in number than the five-part verbs is a set of three-part verbs like **put, puts, putting.** New verbs according to this formula are rare; it, too, is an unproductive or dead formula.

Base	V	V-s	V-ed	V-ing	V-ed/en
put	put	puts	put	putting	put
set	set	sets	set	setting	set

The combination of **be** and **have** with each other as headword gives us the mechanism for the verb-group using some other verb as headword. The verb-group can run to some length with a marker and several helpers. No matter how long it is, the verb-group works in the sentence as a unit, performing the sentence-function **V** in the basic pattern **N V**. **Be** and **have** in combination with other verbs use **to-V**, **V-ing**, and **V-ed/en** as headwords. Here we combine these forms of **be** and **have** with the verb **talk:**

VG		VG			VG		
v	**to-V**	**v**		**V-ing**	**v**	**V-ed/en**	
am	**to talk**	**am**		**talking**	**am**	**talked**	
is	**to talk**	**is**		**talking**	**is**	**talked**	
are	**to talk**	**are**		**talking**	**are**	**talked**	
was	**to talk**	**was**		**talking**	**was**	**talked**	
were	**to talk**	**were**		**talking**	**were**	**talked**	
have	**to talk**	**have**	**been**	**talking**	**have**	**talked**	
has	**to talk**	**has**	**been**	**talking**	**has**	**talked**	
had	**to talk**	**had**	**been**	**talking**	**had**	**talked**	
have had	**to talk**	**have**	**to be**	**talking**	**have been**	**talked**	
has had	**to talk**	**has**	**to be**	**talking**	**has been**	**talked**	
had had	**to talk**	**had**	**to be**	**talking**	**had been**	**talked**	
am having	**to talk**	**have had to be talking**			**am being**	**talked**	
is having	**to talk**	**has had to be talking**			**is being**	**talked**	
are having	**to talk**				**are being**	**talked**	
was having	**to talk**	**had had to be talking**			**was being**	**talked**	
were having	**to talk**				**were being**	**talked**	
					have been		
					being	**talked**	
					has been		
					being	**talked**	
					had been		
					being	**talked**	

These are not all the possibilities we can dredge up, using only **be** and **have** with a headword. We say these as groups and we hear them as groups; they are set into our muscles as units defined by contours of pitch, stress, and juncture. Yet we do not feel them as units unless their unity is called to our attention; hence some seem strange to us laid out like this out of context. A sharp ear will pick them up out of running speech and a sharp eye will see them in writing, though the speaker or writer, intent upon his meaning, will not be conscious of what he has produced. You may find yourself adding new specimens to this display as a heightened interest brings them to your attention.

ORAL EXERCISE: Try some other verbs in this display, using each one as headword and running it through all the verb-groups.

Let's not lose sight of the whole utterance and its needs as the controller of all the choices made within it. We do not have somewhere in the back of the brain a little box full of **is, have, am, has, having, are,** and so on, that we choose from. It is rare for us to think of these words as belonging to any kind of set. Our life with language is a kind of conduct, a way of acting according to certain grooves of habit. When we say **I have moved,** it is not with a sense of not saying **I have been moved** or **I am moving;** it is simply a march through a pattern that we know whether we are aware of any of the other patterns or not. If we live within a speech-community that uses only a few of these patterns, we use the resources that the community provides for us, meager or rich as they may be. The limit of those resources is always being tested by somebody in some utterances; when something beyond the limit seems workable and useful, it spreads from speaker to speaker, and English has a new word or a new structural device.

Thus we have a slow movement of other verbs into the position and function of marker. The verb-group is relatively new in the utterance and has not been exploited to the limit. It is flexible and expansible; it may never see its limit until the language undergoes another of its grand shifts and develops some new mode of patterning only being hinted at today. Some verbs become markers in sets, all pretty much at once; some one by one with no particular association with others.

THE MODAL AUXILIARIES

Now that we have seen the intricate mutual aid rendered by **be** and **have** as markers and helpers, we can glance at a set of words quite similar to one another in their way of working and in their forms. These are the *modal auxiliaries*—verbs that combine with a headword and often with **be** and **have** as helpers to produce verb-groups of rather special significance. Verbs of this interesting set have only one or two parts, instead of three, four, or five. They make a short list. In the verb-group they now serve only as markers, though they were once full verbs (though lacking a full set of forms) and are always under some slight pressure from the regular four-part verbs to conform. Every now and then we hear a verb-group like **hadn't ought, could might,** or **used to could** that points to a fracturing of their regular use. The modal auxiliaries may be briefly listed:

V	V-ed		V	V-ed
can could	could		shall should	should
may might	might		will would	would
must			ought to	

We pair them this way because they once were related as present and past tenses and because the meanings of the paired forms center in the same basic idea for each pair. All these auxiliaries introduce verb-groups that skirt direct statement in favor of the possible, the permissible, the doubtful, the obligatory, or the future; they express what is wished, desired, hoped, or expected, rather than what is happening or has happened. They overlap in significance; in many instances we make a free choice among them. In the **N V** pattern, the **N** exerts no selection; each auxiliary has one form.

The modal auxiliaries combine into verb-groups on the following model:

VG		VG		VG	
v	V	v	V-ing	v	V-ed/en
can	move	can	be moving	can	be moved
will	move	will	be moving	will	be moved
ought to move		ought to	be moving	ought to	be moved
		can have been	moving	can have been	moved
		will have been	moving	will have been	moved
		must have been moving		must have been moved	

ORAL EXERCISE: Try each of the modal auxiliaries in this pattern with different headwords. Test the verb-groups you make in sentences to be sure that they fall naturally on the ear.

OTHER VERBS IN THE VERB-GROUP

OTHER common verbs used as markers and helpers in the verb-group are **keep: He kept going; get: He got going; do: He does go, He did go; go: He is going to go, He was going to go; used: He used to go; dare: He doesn't dare do it, He daren't do it; need: He need not go; He doesn't need to go;** and many that may not occur to you when you try to think of them but will turn up in any account of what people say and write. The position and function of marker and helper in verb-groups is open to any verb; many a verb that would seem at first glance too important to be subordinated to another as marker turns up in actual use doing the work and making its own special contribution to meaning.

OTHER ELEMENTS IN THE VERB-GROUP

THE negative form **not** follows the marker in the verb-group. Its effect is to deny the action or statement in the headword, whatever it is: **He can not go; He is not going; He is not going to go; He has not gone. He does not study; He has not been studying.**

Never, usually, often, always, and similar words are often found immediately after the marker: **He has never worked; He is never seen; He is usually singing; He has often called; He has always lived.**

When a form of **be** is the marker, such words as **about to, ready to, able to,** and **soon to** follow it: **He is about to go; He is ready to stop; He is able to rise; He is soon to finish.**

VERB-ADVERB COMBINATIONS AS VERB-HEADWORDS

IN most verb-groups the headword is the last word in the group, but in many the headword is followed by an adverb that must be taken with it. This is an old and honorable way of making two common words do the work of one; for each of these combinations there is usually a single-word substitute with the same significance but a slightly different tone: **come in** (enter); **come on** (advance), **give up** (surrender). **He will get in, get out, get over, get around, get through; He will give in, give out, give over, give up; He will break down, spin out, get ahead, buy up,** and so on. The trailing word is tied in speech by pitch, stress, and juncture to the headword, and is part of the group. We mark this combination **V- A$_v$, V-ing- A$_v$,** or **V-ed/en- A$_v$.**

ORAL EXERCISE: Using such verbs as **keep, get, do, go, come,** and **give,** make as many such combinations as you can think of, and match each to a single-word synonym: **get over** (cross; convey).

The verb or verb-group is the second main unit in the sentence. The verb or verb-group follows the noun in the pattern **N V.** Selection occurs before it and within it, the noun selecting the form of the marker, the marker selecting the form of the helper, and the helper selecting the form of the headword. We do not always select forms in this way, but selection is a factor, and it is one of the factors on which various speech-communities differ. The verb-group works as a unit in the sentence; it is spoken as a unit, heard as a unit, and understood as a unit. It should be read as a unit. As a whole the verb-group performs the function in the sentence that can be carried by a single-word verb; in analyzing whole sentences we treat the verb-group as if it were a single word.

The Verb-cluster

WE come now to the last of the fixed elements in the basic sentence, the noun that follows the verb in the typical pattern **N V N:**

Boy loves girl. In the Old English sentence of King Alfred in 900 A.D., the main machinery of the sentence consisted of a rather rickety set of interlocking endings that told which adjectives went with which nouns, what noun was the performer of the "action" of the verb, and what noun was the receiver of the "action." At first the order of utterance was a mere prop to this system; it threw in corroborating information. What the endings left muddled, the order cleared up. Order is simpler to control than endings when the system of endings is so shot full of holes that it is not up to its work. The order of utterance gradually muscled the endings into a corner and left them with little to express. The process was progressive; having to begin somewhere it began with a constant **N V** relationship in which the **N** before the **V** took over the functions of the so-called nominative case to point out the "actor" or "performer of the action" in the verb. The pattern **Boy loves** was the first to become stabilized as a trustworthy signal. But boy loves what? The word that answered this question floated without any regular mooring for a while; then it stabilized after the verb. The regular pattern became **N V N: Boy loves girl.**

It doesn't take a dictionary writer to think of verbs in English that do not express action; whatever the verb **be** expresses in the sentence **George is a doctor,** it is not an action. In **The picture hangs on the wall, hangs** is not an action; in **The pencil lies on the table, lies** is not an action. The relationship **N V** in Old or Modern English is more complicated than a mere actor-action relationship, and it cannot be summed up in a word. For our purpose it is best left undefined; whatever this noun is to its verb is sufficiently indicated by saying it first and then saying the verb in the sequence established as a pattern by the multitude of sentences in which the noun is really an actor and the verb an action. With **Mother bakes pies** we have **George likes pies** and **George sees the pies.** We know enough about the eye to know that in **George sees the pies** the action if any is a reflection of light waves from the pie to George's eye. **George** is, if anything, receiver of the action. Still, **George sees the pies** is an intelligible utterance.

The **N V N** pattern has developed from its simple beginnings so that it now expresses a variety of relationships. The pattern is constant, though the particular words that fill it are not; we can take the empty pattern **N V N,** put into it any suitable words, and come up with an utterance-meaning that satisfies those words.

When the whole complex of individual words and structures is in any way defective, confusion results; we don't know what you mean by what you say. The pattern must be sufficient; in Modern English the most nearly sufficient patterns are in the order of utterance, because this order is king of the sentence.

The typical noun-group is the span between marker and headword, as in **the particular words;** the typical verb-group is the span between marker and headword, as in **can be understood.** The noun-group is part of a larger complex that runs beyond the headword; this more comprehensive unit is the noun-cluster. An example would be **a larger element of the sentence which reaches beyond the headword.** In a similar way, a verb-cluster is a larger sentence-element which begins with the verb-marker and reaches beyond the verb-headword. The verb-cluster typically includes the following noun. In simple sentences that fulfill the pattern of the utterance **N V N—Boy loves girl; George is a doctor; Mother bakes pies;** and **George likes pies**—the verb-cluster consists of **V N: loves girl; is a doctor; bakes pies;** and **likes pies.** The verb-cluster has many forms, but we start as usual with the simple ones and work up to the hard ones.

We split the verb-cluster out of the sentence and look at it separately as we did the noun-cluster. We can take clusters without sentences because the cluster does several different jobs in sentences depending on its place in the total pattern. The verb-cluster limits the verb or verb-group which begins it. Its elements are not all confined to the position following the verb in the way that adjective phrases and clauses have to follow the noun if they are going to be in its cluster. But we can see the elements in verb-clusters more clearly in the position after the verb; once we can identify them, we can pick them out wherever they stray.

We refer again to **Boy loves girl:**

N	V	N
That boy	**loves**	**the Armenian girl down the street.**

In the verb-cluster, the verb or verb-group is the first element. All that follows the verb is the *complement.* In **Boy loves girl** the verb-cluster is **loves girl,** and the complement is **girl.** In **That boy**

loves the Armenian girl down the street the verb-cluster is **loves the Armenian girl down the street,** and the complement is **the Armenian girl down the street.** We indicate the complement with the symbol **Comp** in our display of the patterns.

Basic Statement-Patterns

So far we have stuck to the one pattern **N V N,** taking up its elements one at a time. This is only one of the six basic statement-patterns according to which we build our utterances. On these a number of variations occur. The six statement-patterns are a manageable minimum, a bedrock on which we build.

ONE: **This affects that.** The **N V N** pattern, which may be generalized into the statement **This affects that,** is known as *transitive* because the "action" of the verb can be thought of as going from the first noun through the verb to the following noun. The complement is the "receiver" of the action.

		Comp
N	**V**	**N**
Father	wrecked	our new car.
The puppy	bit	Aunt Emma.
Death	rides	the highways.

ORAL EXERCISE: Make a few sentences to fit this pattern as a warm-up for the patterns which follow, playing with the elements in the noun-cluster which comprises the complement.

TWO: A. **This calls that that.**
      B. **This gives that that.**

In the second pattern the complement has two nouns. The formula is **N V N N;** within the formula may occur two different statements, depending on whether the verb may be loosely translated 'call' or 'give.'

   A. **This calls that that.**

		Comp	
N	V	N	N
The boy	will call	the girl	his wife.
She	has chosen	her school friends	maids of honor.
We	nominated	her	secretary.
I	consider	that man	a fool.

In place of the second noun of the complement in this pattern, we often have an adjective: **The boy will make the girl happy; I consider that man foolish.**

The following verbs occur in this pattern: **call, appoint, choose, consider, elect, name, nominate, think,** etc.

B. **This gives that that.** The basic statement of the "gives" pattern is remarkably different, considering that the formula is so nearly the same. The two nouns in the complement refer to different persons or things, but the key signal is in the verb.

		Comp	
N	V	N	N
His mother	will give	the girl	some dishes.
The girl	will bring	each bridesmaid	a gown.
We	sent	the fellow	a letter.
Hawaii	ships	us	pineapples.

The following verbs occur in this pattern: **give, afford, ask, allot, assign, bring, buy, cause, deny, do, envy, fetch, grant, guarantee, hand, lease, leave, lend, let, offer, owe, pass, pay, rent, sell, send, show, spare, teach, tell, throw, write,** etc.

Some verbs occur in both patterns: **make, leave.**

ORAL EXERCISE: Make up sentences to fit these two formulas until they occur to you at will.

THREE: A. **This acts.**
         B. **This acts thus, there, or then.**
         C. **This acts so.**

The third pattern is the *intransitive* sentence; the "action" begins in the noun and ends in the verb.

   A. **This acts.**

N	V
She	sings.
We	are done.
The car	has stopped.
Company	has come.
Bees	sting.

This is a common sentence with nothing necessarily special about the verb, though there may be. Add **N** as complement, and you have pattern ONE: **She is singing a song. The car has stopped its rattling. Bees sting people.** Drop the complement from pattern ONE, and you often get pattern THREE: A. **The boy drives a car. The boy drives.**

   B. **This acts thus, there, or then.** We have not so far discussed the adverb, but we have to mention it here because it forms the complement in this cluster. Basically the adverb makes a statement of manner, place, time, and the like about a verb. These classic functions of the adverb are demonstrated in this verb-cluster where it follows the verb as complement. We mark the adverb **A,** in our display. This sentence pattern is **N V A,**:

		Comp
N	V	A,
She	is singing	well.
We	are done	now.
Bees	sting	hard.
The help	works	here.

C. **This acts so or such.** In this formula the complement is an adjective which indicates the effective result of the "action" of the verb. The pattern is **N V A**:

		Comp
N	**V**	**A**
The door	slammed	shut.
Our boat	broke	loose.
The weather	has stayed	mild.
Our well	ran	dry.

ORAL EXERCISE: Make up sentences to fit these three formulas until they occur to you at will.

FOUR: A. **This is that.**
      B. **This is so or such.**
      C. **This is thus, there, or then.**

The fourth pattern comes in three formulas, all containing a verb that may be loosely translated 'be,' 'seem,' or 'become.' The complement refers back to the first **N**, describing or identifying it.

The following verbs occur in these formulas: **be, seem, become, appear, taste, feel, grow, continue, remain,** etc. We mark these *"linking verbs"* **LV**.

A. **This is that.** The first of the three formulas takes a noun as complement. The pattern is **N LV N**:

		Comp
N	**LV**	**N**
My brother	is	an engineer.
That car	is	a Ford.
He	seems to be	a bum.
The new play	is	a hit.
I	have become	a new man.

B. **This is so or such.** The second formula takes an adjective as complement of about the same set of verbs as the first formula. The adjective, like the nouns above, refers back to the noun. The pattern is **N** ʟ**V A**:

		Comp
N	ʟ**V**	**A**
He	seems	busy.
Those flowers	are	pretty.
My hands	are	dirty.
This school	is	terrible.
That new boy	looks	rather stuffy.
We all	grow	old.

C. **This is thus, there, or then.** The third formula takes an adverb as complement and about the same set of verbs as the others. The pattern is **N** ʟ**V A**ᵥ:

		Comp
N	ʟ**V**	**A**ᵥ
The books	are	here.
He	feels	badly.
The store	is	not far.

ORAL EXERCISE: Make up sentences to fit these three formulas. You will find C to be the trickiest of the three, less common than the others.

FIVE: A. **This is affected.**
      B. **This is affected by that.**

Pattern FIVE differs from those we have been looking at in that the sentence-function **V** is always carried by a verb-group with the headword **V-ed/en**. The pattern is **N VG**.

A. This is affected. The pattern is **N VG**:

N	VG
The walls	were washed.
These books	were donated.
That young fellow	has been hurt.
The painting	is finished.

B. This is affected by that. The complement in this formula is always **Prep N**, bearing the sense in the formula of 'means' or 'agent.' The pattern is **N VG Prep N**:

N	VG	Comp	
		Prep	N
The walls	were washed	by the men.	
The walls	were washed	with muriatic acid.	
The books	were donated	by a rich alumnus.	
That fellow	has been hurt	by your nonsense.	
No work	will be done	by non-union labor.	

ORAL EXERCISE: Make up one sentence to fit each of these two formulas. Surely no one has to practice this one.

SIX: A. **He is given that by that.**
      B. **That is given him by that.**

The two formulas in this pattern have complements consisting of **N Prep N**. As in pattern FIVE, the prepositional phrase bears the sense of 'means' or 'agent.' The verb may be loosely translated 'give'; the sentence-function **V** is carried by a verb-group with the headword **V-ed/en**.

A. He is given that by that. The pattern is **N VG N Prep N**:

		Comp		
N	VG	N	Prep	N
We	were given	a prize	by the committee.	
She	was sent	flowers	by her family.	

B. **That is given him by that.** This formula is a reversal of the preceding. The first **N**, instead of naming the receiver, names what is given. The pattern is **N VG N Prep N**:

		Comp		
N	VG	N	Prep	N
A prize	was given	us	by the committee.	
Flowers	were sent	her	by her family.	

ORAL EXERCISE: Make up some sentences to fit formula A; then reverse them to fit formula B. Note that the alternatives permit you to throw the element you wish to emphasize to the beginning of the sentence.

These are not all the possibilities of the verb-cluster, as anyone can tell by examining a book, magazine, or newspaper. They are typical or more than typical; they are basic. Each is a tool fit for one of the kinds of communication; like the tools of a good workman, they are ready to his hand when he needs them. If the workman is intent on his task, his hand will reach and find the tool he needs. He does not say to himself, "Now I will use a three-quarter-inch socket on a torsion wrench with a three-inch extension and a half-inch drive." He reaches absently for the wrenches; his mind comes off what he is doing only when someone has borrowed one and failed to bring it back. In the same way these patterns are available to us for our communication; we think about them only when for some reason the right one does not pop into the mind.

Now let us look at these statement-patterns all together.

	N	V	Comp	
	N	**V**	**N**	
ONE:	This	affects	that.	
TWO: A.	**N** This	**V** calls	**N** that	**N** that.
B.	**N** This	**V** gives	**N** that	**N** that.
THREE: A.	**N** This	**V** acts.		
B.	**N** This	**V** acts	**A** thus, there, or then.	
C.	**N** This	**V** acts	**A** so.	
FOUR: A.	**N** This	**LV** is	**N** that.	
B.	**N** This	**LV** is	**A** so or such.	
C.	**N** This	**LV** is	**A** thus, there, or then.	
FIVE: A.	**N** This	**VG** is affected.		
B.	**N** This	**VG** is affected	**Prep** by	**N** that.
SIX: A.	**N** He	**VG** is given	**N** that	**Prep** **N** by that.
B.	**N** That	**VG** is given	**N** him	**Prep** **N** by that.

ORAL EXERCISE: Make up sentences to fit each pattern. Once you are sure of yourself, vary the elements serving as **N** and **V** in the patterns; play with the range of the noun-cluster in each position: **D** ~~A~~ **N** ~~AP~~ ~~AC~~. Substitute verb-groups for verbs wherever you can: **v V; v v V;** and **v v v V.** See if you can write one continuous paragraph, using each sentence-pattern just once. And we mean play; don't underrate frivolity as a tool for learning.

The Free-wheeling Adverb

No doubt many of the examples made up to fit the patterns have lacked something, like ice-cream cones without ice cream. They are possible utterances; we say them; they ring right on the ear; but they are a little flat. They have no fizz. They plod from word to word like the army of unalterable law. What is wrong? They have no adverbs in them.

Earlier we compared the junctures in our speech to traffic lights that stop, slow, and otherwise regulate the flow of traffic. In the flow of the utterance the nouns, verbs, and adjectives are like cars and trucks maintaining a relatively constant relation to each other. The adverbs are like a fleet of motorcycle cops who keep that flow moving, clear up clots and stoppages, and shift cars from one lane to another. Adverbs are not tied as rigidly as adjectives to fixed positions in the flow of the utterance; they bring their force to bear where it counts most. The adverb is the free-wheeling element in the sentence.

A_v = ADVERB

LET us go back to our basic sentence, **Boy loves girl**—the basic **N V N** pattern with which we began—and introduce some adverbs.

A_v	N	A_v	V	N	A_v
Nevertheless	the boy	still	loved	the girl	dearly.
Still	the boy		loved	the girl	dearly, never- theless.
Still	the boy,	nevertheless,	loved	the girl	dearly.
Nevertheless	the boy	still dearly	loved	the girl.	
Nevertheless	the boy	dearly	loved	the girl	still.

These examples show the two main functions of the adverb. The adverb steers and directs the whole sentence, or it limits the meaning of the verb. **Nevertheless** lays down a condition for the whole following sentence. **Still** and **dearly** cut down the potential meaning of the verb by denying all meanings of **love** which are incompatible with themselves. Adverbs are movable elements in the sentence, though still not completely free. They have favorite positions: **still** and **dearly** can come before the verb-headword or in the complement. **Nevertheless** can begin the sentence, fit in the middle, or bring up the end. We mark the adverb **A** in our patterns.

| | | | | | Comp | |
A	N	A	V	A	N	A
Then	**he**	**suddenly**	**pounded**	**down**	**the nail**	**hard.**
Later	**she**	**still**	**ran**	**up**	**bills**	**freely.**

Since the adverb limits the meaning of a verb-headword, it can occur within the verb-group, between marker and headword as well as immediately after the headword.

| | VG | | | Comp |
N	v	A	V	A
He			**talks**	**quietly.**
He		**quietly**	**talks.**	
He	**is**	**quietly**	**talking.**	
He	**is**		**talking**	**quietly.**

Any sentence and any verb is thus subject to limitation by adverbs. Scarcely a point of choice in the sentence offers no opening to the adverb. Not all positions, however, are open to a particular adverb or even to a particular set of adverbs. The position immediately following a verb-headword in the verb-cluster **V N**, for instance, admits some adverbs and excludes others. We can say **He broke the door violently down** or **He broke down the door violently** but not **He broke violently the door down.** The position is open to some adverbs but not to all.

The functions of the adverb are as diverse as the elements it modifies. It limits as the situation demands, sometimes broadly affecting a whole utterance, sometimes quite narrowly restricting a single word. In its classic and primal function, the adverb restricts the verb as the adjective restricts the noun, coalescing with the verb in a fusion of meaning that is the product of that combination in the utterance. The adverb is free of the limitation that binds the adjective to the close vicinity of the noun; it can combine so closely with the verb that we have to treat the two as one unit, as in **break down, give out, add up;** or it can stand off at a distance and peck at the verb. Its effect depends on the kind of verb, the kind of verb-cluster, and the kind of adverb.

The beginning of a sentence before the **N** in the **N V** pattern is a usual place for sentence-connectors that place the whole utterance in some relation to what has gone before. Adverbs of time frequently occur in this position:

A͜	N	V
Moreover,	**we**	**consented.**
Still,	**the man**	**has to pay.**
Nevertheless,	**he**	**refused.**
Afterwards	**the business**	**closed.**
Earlier,	**we**	**had phoned.**

ORAL EXERCISE: Make up sentences to fit the pattern above.

In one of the sentence-patterns on page 139 the verb-cluster permits us to see how adverbs fall into sets. This is pattern THREE B: **N V A͜,** This acts thus, there, or then. We can say **We go in; We go quietly; We go now.** We can say **We go quietly in now** or **We go in quietly now.** For **in** we can substitute **where?** and answer it **there.** For **quietly** we can ask **how?** and answer **thus.** And for **now** we can ask **when?** and answer **then. There, thus,** and **then** can stand for three large sets of adverbs that limit in place, manner, and time the verb-headword that precedes them.

The adverbs that answer the question **where?** in regard to the action of the verb by any variation of **there** have a favorite position in the verb-cluster immediately after the verb. Many of them are the same as prepositions in form: **in, out, over, around, through, between, along, under,** and so on. Furthermore, they have been used so much with common verbs like **get, give, come, go, keep** that we often have to think of them as a part of the verb-group:

get over, give out, come on, go over, keep out, and so on. Like these are such words as **away: go away; ahead: get ahead; across: come across; abroad: range abroad.**

N	V	Aᵥ
George	came	in.
Some people	got	on.
The money	came	through.

Words like **homeward, backward, outward,** and **inward** and various words ending in **-where** like **everywhere, somewhere, nowhere** often follow the verb directly: **He went somewhere.**

Adverbs that answer the question **how?** in regard to the action of the verb by any variation of **thus** come either before or after **there** adverbs in a series of adverbs. The list of these is unlimited; the dictionaries have not recorded them all, nor can they ever, for old words are constantly dropping out of use and new ones coming in. It is an open-ended class. These are the adverbs we usually think of as having the ending **-ly: quickly, quietly, slowly, brutally, positively.**

N	V	Aᵥ	Aᵥ
He	went	homeward	quietly.
He	went	quietly	homeward.

Adverbs that answer the question **when?** in regard to the action of the verb by any variation of **then** almost always come at the end of a series of adverbs, if they are not used to start the sentence or tucked into the verb-group. They close the verb-cluster.

N	V	Aᵥ	Aᵥ	Aᵥ
The money	came	through	regularly	afterward.

Besides these a whole host of adverbs do not shake down easily into **thus, there, then** sets: **certainly, reasonably, probably, exactly,** etc. It is not too much to say that you can expect anything from the adverb; it is versatile.

ORAL EXERCISE: Fit adverbs into the patterns above until you are fairly sure you know what an adverb is and what it does.

A_vP = ADVERB PHRASE

ONCE we see what the adverb does in the sentence, we are aware of an adverb function that may be carried not only by single words but by phrases and clauses. We recall that the adjective function was carried by phrases and clauses but not in the same positions; we built up the noun-cluster by recognizing that single-word adjectives commonly precede their nouns: **fresh milk,** and adjective phrases commonly follow their nouns: **fresh milk in clean bottles.** The adverb is different. Adverb phrases sit where the single-word adverbs do when they are doing the same modification, as in **He went hurriedly** and **He went in a hurry.** The same prepositional phrase **Prep N** that works as adjective also works as adverb with no internal difference. We mark the adverb phrase A_vP.

N	AP	V	A_v	A_vP
The train	into this station	comes	regularly	on time.

N	V	A_vP	A_v	A_vP
The train	comes	into this station	regularly	on time.

A_vP	N	V	A_v	A_vP
In spite of the rain	we	drove	on	into the city.

ORAL EXERCISE: Substitute adverb phrases for adverbs in these patterns, and substitute other words in all these phrases and sentences.

A͜C = ADVERB CLAUSE

THE adverb clause differs from the adjective clause in the same way. The adjective clause usually follows its noun, or if there is an adjective phrase, the clause follows the phrase: **the book that I have to read; the book on the desk that I have to read.** Not so with the adverb clause. It substitutes for the single-word adverbs in most of their positions. It occurs most freely at the beginning of the utterance and as a verb-modifier in the verb-cluster after the verb and usually at the end. When an adverb phrase and an adverb clause both limit the same verb in its complement, the clause follows the phrase. We mark the adverb clause **A͜C** in the patterns.

N	V	A͜P	A͜C
He	fell	into the lake	when the boat tipped.

A͜C	N	V	A͜P
When the boat tipped,	he	fell	into the lake.

The adverb clause begins with a clause-marker, one of a set which includes **after, before, once, since, when, whenever, until; where, wherever; as if, as though, like; that, so, so that, in order that, because, since, as; if, unless; though, although, while, even though.**

A͜C	N	V	N
When we get our pay,	we	spend	it.
Where we get our pay,	we	spend	it.
If we get our pay,	we	spend	it.
Though we get our pay,	we	have	no money.
Because we get our pay,	we	have	money.

Markers of adverb clauses steer their clauses in terms of several broad areas of significance:

TIME:	**When the clock strikes**
	As the train stopped
PLACE:	**Where the road turns**
	Wherever the cat got to
MANNER:	**As if he could tell**
	As they think best
	As though he were a stumbler
CAUSE:	**Because the fuse blew**
	Since there is no soda
	In that he would not speak
COMPARISON:	**As if his foot were in his mouth**
	As much as I love you
CONCESSION:	**Though the car stopped**
	While they never had seen a yak
	Even though the trees gave some shelter

CONDITION (on condition that . . .):

> **If the department store closes**
> **If the store closes**
> **If the store should (could, may, might, etc.) close**
> **If the store had closed**
> **If the store would have closed**

ORAL EXERCISE: Make sentences to fit the pattern A͜C, N V . . . . Convert your sentences to the pattern N V . . . , A͜C. (Take the signs of ellipsis— . . . and . . . . —to mean any or no complement following the verb, and any noun-cluster within the complement.)

The adverb steers and guides the sentence and cuts down the potential of meaning in the verb. It can affect the utterance largely and grandly or pinpoint narrowly a specific segment of it. It is not bound to the fixed order of the noun-cluster and verb-cluster; at any point where these show a chink, the adverb can do its work. It is the movable, the wandering, the free-wheeling unit in the utterance.

CHAPTER 10

Substitution within the Patterns

W E HEAR a good deal about "primitive" languages, but the people who study language, though they have searched the world over, have yet to discover one truly "primitive." A primitive language would be crude in its machinery and clumsy in grappling with human needs and experiences. Every known language is a subtle and sophisticated mode of talking, far more minute in its discriminations of meaning and far more copious in its resources than any known form of writing. If we cannot find a primitive language in living societies, where then would we look for it? We would look right in our own language in the basic mechanisms we have examined so far.

We have been dealing with the outlines of a primitive system of communicating that we would cheerfully trade off for Eskimo, Bantu, Hopi, or Swahili if it were all we had. At the heart of this lies an even cruder system, though still one that would have taken human beings thousands of years to develop—a system in which nouns are nouns, adjectives are adjectives, verbs are verbs, adverbs are adverbs, and each is a single word. The utterances we could make with single words invariably performing one function would be pretty crude; yet we have to sense this crude central machinery in order to grasp the complexity of utterances we actually make.

Almost every language has certain words for the closest and most immediate human experiences: **hand, head, strong, hit, hard.** They make a primitive utterance:

A͞	N	V	N	A͜
Strong	**hand**	**hits**	**head**	**hard**

The nouns are things, the adjective is a quality of things, the verb is an action, and the adverb is a quality of actions. Here is real primitive language; we might imagine our ancestors talking to each other like this as they lounged around their cold caves on bearskins or hunted the saber-toothed tiger. It is an advance over the dog's bark and the coyote's nightly song. No living tribe is so brutish as to be content with such brute expression; even a child of three or four in any known society has expressive needs that outrun such language as this.

To increase the range of such utterances, small knots of words may carry these functions, each with a marker that forewarns of a composite unit acting as a single word:

NG	A͞P		VG
D N	Prep	N	v V-ing
The hand	**of the strong man**		**is hitting**

NG	A͞P		A͜P	
D N	Prep	N	Prep	N
the head	**of the weak man**		**with full strength.**	

These are relatively primitive word-groupings. In all but the verb-group the key word is a noun; the markers **of** and **with** serve to convert the noun to another function; in a sense they suppress the noun to the function of adjective and adverb. The markers introduce a kind of conversion into the system and start us toward the mechanisms that make our language apt to our needs. But they start us only.

The next step is to fit a marker to an utterance to signal that we are dealing with this group of words as a unit, not as a separate utterance. We let this marked unit serve within another utterance as if it were a single word. This is the clause. The clause as a unit has all the internal complexity and all the discriminated meaning of any sentence, and yet the clause can substitute within utterances for single-word nouns, verbs, adjectives, and adverbs. It is something like an automatic washer-dryer in the home laundry; outwardly simple, inwardly complex, it substitutes for soaking tub, washing machine, wringer, or clothesline—or for all of these, as the user desires.

A noun clause is a clause serving as **N** in the **N V** pattern:

N	V	
What I want	is	a good time.

A noun clause is a clause serving as **N** in the **V N** pattern:

N	V	N
A good time	is	what I want.

A noun clause is a clause serving as **N** in the **Prep N** pattern:

		A͜P	
N	V	Prep	N
I	can pay	for	what I want.

An adjective clause is a clause modifying **N** in any pattern:

N	A̶C̶	V	N	A̶C̶
The noise	that you make	bothers	people	who are trying to rest.

An adverb clause is a clause modifying a **V** in any pattern:

A͜C	N	V	Prep N
When you quiet down,	your mother	will talk	to you.

N	V	Prep N	A͜C
Your mother	will talk	to you	when you quiet down.

Can we then use a clause as a verb? If not, there would be a hole in the system (as there often is, like the lack of **V-ed/en** in the modal auxiliaries) and there would be occasional attempts to fill it (like the expressions **could might** and **used to could**). Verb clauses are not frequent in English, but they do occur:

VG		
N	V V-ing	N
Your mother	is always "I told you so"-ing	me.

ORAL EXERCISE: Make up sentences to fit these patterns.

The Four Functions

UP to this point in our breakdown of the language, we have discovered four word-classes: the noun, the verb, the adjective, and the adverb. We have seen these classes of words work in patterns, and from the patterns have picked four functions: the noun, the verb, the adjective, and the adverb, each mainly served by the corresponding word-class. The four functions may be performed by any one of four units: the word, the word-group, the phrase, and the clause. In general these units are interchangeable in the performance of the four functions, though, as we have noted, they differ somewhat in their workings. Single-word adjectives precede the noun; adjective phrases and adjective clauses follow the noun. The noun clause replaces the noun in the same relative position in the order of utterance. Adverb phrases and adverb clauses replace single-word adverbs in the same positions in the utterance, though with some limitations. Nevertheless, the four units—the isolated word, the word-group, the phrase, and the clause—are capable of serving in utterances as nouns, verbs, adjectives, and adverbs.

At first glance one can miss the immensity of the increase in range when we have four kinds of units to work with instead of the single word alone. The noun, for instance, normally precedes the verb, follows the verb as complement, or follows a preposition. In each of these functions the whole noun-cluster **D A N AP AC** can occur; it can occur in any noun-function in any unit—in the adjective phrase, for one, or in the adjective clause. Thus we can have cluster on cluster on cluster. The whole noun-cluster can fulfill any noun-function in the noun clause or in the adverb clause, too; so that the sentence is almost infinitely expansible in its noun-functions alone, to say nothing of the verb, adjective, and adverb.

EXERCISE: Copy the sentences given below on a separate sheet of paper and analyze them according to our diagrams. First put a symbol over each determiner, adjective, and noun; then mark the verb-markers and headwords and the prepositions. When you have gone this far, set off noun-groups and verb-groups, prepositional phrases, and clauses, and determine the function of each.

The efficient reader leaves to his eyes all the work they will do. He lets them carry to the brain the widest span of related words that they can handle at each pause they make along the line.

These four units would seem to give the utterance sufficient range, except for the subtlety and delicacy of human expressive needs. If we created an artificial language having just this measure of substitution and no more, we would soon find that our needs outran it. Such a language would be adequate to simple emotions, simple ideas, and simple technologies that no community on earth now tries to get along with; we have to push the principle of substitution even further. Four players in four acts are not enough; we need either more players or more acts.

Still staying within the materials we have treated, we might ask questions that have been answered in the ceaseless flow of the English language toward meeting the needs of human expression. Does a noun *have* to be a noun? Can a noun substitute for a verb, an adjective, or an adverb on occasion? Can an adjective substitute for a noun, adverb, or verb? Can a verb substitute for a noun, adjective, or adverb, if there were a way for it to work in the other function? We have a hint of the answer in the pattern **D -N- N**, which is at least as common as **D -A- N**; we say **a ticker tape** as freely as we say **a sticky tape.** We have another hint in the prepositional phrase **Prep N**, which certainly converts a noun to part of an adjective or adverb phrase. What about pushing conversion further?

In English one word-class such as the verb can readily perform the functions of other word-classes, holding to its essential quality of verbness in the function of noun, adjective, or adverb. We shall now see how we accomplish this change of function with the verb and pass from the verb to treat each of the others.

The Verbals

A VERBAL is a verb-headword detached from its marker and substituted for a noun, an adjective, or an adverb in any pattern where these other word-classes normally occur. The typical verb consists of four parts or five: **talk, talks, talked, talking; drive, drives, drove, driving, driven.** Of these the first three are used as single-word verbs in utterances. The parts **talk, talked, talking** and **drive, driving, driven** are used as headwords in verb-groups:

v	V	v	to-V	v	V-ing	v	V-ed/en
can	talk	is	to talk	is	talking	has	talked
can	drive	is	to drive	is	driving	has	driven

The forms **talk, drive,** and **drove** are not considered verbals, because they lose their verb characteristics when they substitute for other form-classes. The verbals are **to-V: to talk, to drive; V-ing: talking, driving; V-ed/en: talked, driven.** As verb-headwords these forms can be limited by a complement in the verb-cluster:

1) With a noun as complement:

v	to-V	N	v	V-ing	N
is	to talk	sense	is	talking	sense
is	to drive	the car	is	driving	the car

v	V-ed/en	N
has	talked	sense
has	driven	the car

2) With an adverb as complement:

v	to-V	A͜	v	V-ing	A͜	v	V-ed/en	A͜
is	to talk	later	is	talking	now	has	talked	earlier
is	to drive	fast	is	driving	fast	has	driven	fast

3) With such units as the noun-cluster and adverb phrase as complement:

v	V-ed/en	N	A͞C	A͜P
has	talked	sense	that has not often been heard	to the American people

4) With a pre-modifying adverb, noun, and adverb phrase as complement:

v	Aᵥ	V-ed/en	N	AᵥP
has	quietly	talked	sense	to the American people

When these verb-headwords, **to-V, V-ing,** and **V-ed/en** are set free from the marker and detached from the verb-group, they become available for other uses, for service in the sentence not as verbs but as substitutes for nouns, adjectives, and adverbs. As such they retain their quality as verbs and keep all their verb-qualifiers and complements. They straddle two word-classes, being noun and verb, adjective and verb, or adverb and verb at once.

THE VERBALS AS NOUNS

ALL three verbals, **to-V, V-ing,** and **V-ed/en,** can serve as nouns in the sentence; they substitute for **N** where it occurs in the sentence patterns. When a verbal serves as **N** in the **N V** pattern, it selects the **V-s** form of verb-marker or single-word verb: **To err is human; Complaining has been futile.** When **V-ing** is equivalent to **N-s (V-ing-s),** it selects the **V** form of verb-marker or single-word verb: **The chimings of the various bells mingle in the air and their echoings interpenetrate.**

1) The verbal **to-V** as noun substitute:

To-V as **N** in the pattern **N V:**

N	V	
to-V		
To work	is	the burden of man.
to-V N	V	
To work the radio	is	all he enjoys.

To-V as **N** in the pattern **V N:**

N	V	N
		to-V
He	has never liked	to work.
She	made	a big to-do about it.

To-V as **N** in the pattern **Prep N:**

Prep N	Prep N	V	N	Prep N
to-V N	to-V N			
From to say yes	to not to say yes	is	a matter	of time.

2) The verbal **V-ing** as noun substitute:

V-ing as **N** in the pattern **N V:**

N	V
V-ing N	
Working the radio	is all he enjoys.
That quarreling	must stop.

V-ing as **N** in the pattern **V N:**

N	V	N
		V-ing N
Father	never stopped	shouting.
Oscar	tried	selling cars.

3) The verbal **V-ed/en** as noun substitute:

V-ed/en as **N** in the pattern **N V:**

N	V	N
V-ed/en		
Beaten down	**is not**	**knocked out.**

V-ed/en as **N** in the pattern **V N:**

N	V	N
		V-ed/en
He	**has never helped**	**the fallen.**

V-ed/en as **N** in the pattern **Prep N:**

N	V	N	Prep	N
				V-ed/en
The winners	**got**	**no cheers**	**from**	**the defeated.**
The doctor	**has**	**some hope**	**for**	**the wounded.**

V-ing as **N** in the pattern **Prep N:**

N	V	N	Prep	N	
				V-ing	**N**
Farmers	**get**	**that stoop**	**from**	**hoeing.**	
The prisoner	**spent**	**his time**	**in**	**writing**	**letters.**
Elwood	**withdrew**		**from the**	**dancing.**	
The children	**annoyed**	**her**	**with their**	**shouting.**	

4) The verbals **to-V, V-ing,** and **V-ed/en** as headword in the second **N** in **VNN:**

N	V	NG	
		N	**N**
She	didn't like	Father	to work.
She	didn't like	him	to work.
She	didn't like	Father	working.
She	didn't like	Father's	working.
She	didn't like	him	working.
She	didn't like	his	working.
They	were to see	the team	beaten.
They	were to see	him	beaten.

ORAL EXERCISE: Substitute other verbals in these examples; then make up other sentences using verbals as nouns, until you can choose the form you want and use it at will.

THE VERBALS AS ADJECTIVES

ADJECTIVES modify nouns. Single-word adjectives precede the nouns in the order of utterance; word-group adjectives follow them. The verbals follow this sequence rather exactly, except that the verbal **to-V** substituting as adjective follows its noun.

1) The verbal **to-V** as adjective:

N	V	D	~~A~~	N	~~AP~~
					to-V
I	have		much	work	to do.
He	has	a		proposal	to make.
Mary	got	ten	whole	dollars	to spend.

2) The verbal **V-ing** as adjective:

D	~~A~~	N	~~AP~~
The	fresh	milk	in the pantry
	V-ing		**V-ing**
The	souring	milk	sitting in the icebox
The	slowly souring	milk	
The		milk	slowly souring
The		milk	souring slowly
The	sharp cutting	edge	gashing his hand
		V-ing	
That	annoying	quarreling	coming from the kitchen

3) The verbal **V-ed/en** as adjective:

D	~~A~~	N	~~AP~~
The	new	house	across the road
	V-ed/en		**V-ed/en**
The	unfinished	house	ruined by the weather
The	burnt	child	
Two	beaten	eggs	
Two		eggs	well beaten
A	fallen	tree	
A		tree	fallen across the road
A		tree	felled by the wind

In general the **V-ing** points to a noun doing the action named in the **V-ing**: **a smiling girl, a tiring argument, a man writing a letter, a rock falling from the cliff.** In general a **V-ed/en** used as adjective points to a noun receiving the action or affected by the **V-ed/en**: **a scratched finish, a turned ankle, the emptied cans, the letter written by Mr. Lincoln.**

We must not tie ideas of "present" and "past" too closely to these forms; both refer to past, present, and future: **A student elected to this office must have a 3.5 honor-point average.**

Among the adjective-patterns which we shall treat fully in Chapter 12, there is one in which the adjective precedes its noun and the determiner if there is one, and starts the utterance. Sometimes we use a single-word adjective; more often we use a word-group adjective. The pattern looks like this:

A	D	N	V
Brutal,	**the**	**man**	**beats his children.**
Brutal and stupid,	**the**	**man**	**beats his children.**
Warm and happy,		**we**	**drove home.**

A variation of this pattern is frequent with the verbals **V-ing** and **V-ed/en:**

A	D	N	V
V-ing			
Standing by the door,		**he**	**could not be seen.**
Turning to his brother,	**the**	**dealer**	**paid out the money.**
Following a back road,		**we**	**came on a valley.**
V-ed/en			
Sent home by the teacher,	**the**	**youngster**	**went right to bed.**
Passed through the guards,	**the**	**reporter**	**went up to the fire.**
Turned on its back,	**a**	**turtle**	**is helpless.**
Caught only yesterday,	**these**	**fish**	**are fresh.**

ORAL EXERCISE: Substitute other verbal expressions for those in the patterns; then make up some sentences of your own until you have the feel of the way they work and can use them at will.

THE VERBALS AS ADVERBS

ADVERBS limit or qualify the verb or the verb-group and lay down conditions for the meaning of the whole utterance. Conditioning the utterance, an extension of limiting the verb, is permitted by the movability of the adverb and the length of some phrases and clauses which separate the adverb some distance from the verb. The meaning of a sentence is in its overall plan, not in a mere piling-up of individual words, each as self-limited as a pebble. Once the adverb falls out of finger-tip reach of the verb, its qualification spreads to the whole utterance. It is like the referee in a basketball game, who sometimes blows the whistle on a play, sometimes on the game.

When the verbals substitute for adverbs they take over either of these uses. Sometimes it is not worth while figuring out which they are doing, for you cannot affect the verb without affecting the sentence. It is worth while, however, to be able to produce a verbal at will with the intention of doing one or the other and with sufficient control to make it do what you choose. Verbals substituting as adverbs usually begin the utterance or end it, but on occasion the verbal comes before the verb or even within the verb-group.

1) The verbal **to-V** as adverb:

To-V as A_v before the pattern **N V**:

A_v	N	V	
to-V			
To make a long story short,	we	won.	
To shut off the water,	a valve	is provided.	
To let the smoke out,	the firemen	broke	a window.

To-V as A_v after the **V**:

N	V	N	A_v
			to-V
We	play		to win.
Watson	bought	the place	to keep it vacant.
We	lost,		to tell the truth.

2) The verbal **V-ing** as adverb:

V-ing as A_v before the pattern **N V**:

A͜	N	V
V-ing		
Speaking of trouble,	**the landlord**	**called.**
Granting what you say,	**my argument**	**is . . . .**
Barring accidents,	**the house**	**will be finished.**

V-ing as A͜ after the **V** in the verb-cluster:

N	V	N	A͜
			V-ing
Those boys	**smashed**	**the car,**	**driving recklessly.**
The crew	**did**	**the job,**	**working late.**
The factory	**closed,**		**causing a layoff.**

3) The Verbal **V-ed/en** as adverb:

V-ed/en as A͜ before the pattern **N V:**

A͜	N	V
V-ed/en		
The work done,	**the women**	**left** **the house.**
All told,	**we**	**had** **six dollars.**
Our money all gone,	**we**	**hitchhiked** **home.**

V-ed/en as A͜ within the pattern **N V:**

N	A͜	V
	V-ed/en	
The women,	**their work done,**	**left** **the house.**
This plan,	**all its virtues granted,**	**won't** **work.**

V-ed/en as A͜ after the **V** in the verb-cluster:

N	V	A$_v$
		V-ed/en
We	did all right,	everything considered.
The mechanics	can fix it,	given time.
The boy	straightened out,	his problems solved.

The verbals **to-V**, **V-ing**, and **V-ed/en** are instruments for putting the kind of thing a verb does within the function of the noun, adverb, and adjective. The verbals do two things at once. The verbals do not lose their verb quality; they carry with them all the verb-patterns while they serve as nouns, adjectives, and adverbs. They are still modified by adverbs—single, phrasal, and even clausal—and they take complements—nouns and adjectives—as do verbs in the verb-cluster. A single-word verbal or a verbal with all its attendants can serve as a unit in the functions of noun, adjective, and adverb.

ORAL EXERCISE: Play with these patterns, substituting other verbals and making up other sentences which match those presented.

We took up the verbals first, not because verbs are different in their change of function from the other three word-classes, but because verbs have the most elaborate and openly visible machinery for moving across classes. Their signals are obvious and open to our inspection. Aware of the verbals, we should be prepared for almost any substitution by the other word-classes. We should be ready to find nouns modifying nouns, verbs, adjectives, and adverbs; adjectives modifying verbs, adjectives, and adverbs; and adverbs modifying nouns, adverbs, and adjectives. In order to meet the burden of expression we put upon it, the language has to make maximum employment of every working unit it has. We need to know how the trick is done so that we can learn to do it at will.

Headwords and Modifiers

To see how one word-class can do the work of another, we have to go back to one of the ideas that we sketched at the beginning of our study of the patterns: the idea of the headword. In the formula **N V** we can have something simple like **Men work** with one word carrying each function. Or we can have something elaborate and expanded like **The young men in our town, who are in debt for their houses and cars, have to work day and night to pay their bills.** In terms of the pattern as well as in terms of human life, that comes down to **Men work. Men** is the headword of the noun-cluster, and **work** is the headword of the verb-cluster; all the other units are modifiers which qualify or limit in some way these two words.

For the moment we will consider the noun in the noun-group. The basic pattern is **D -A- N**. We can say **men, young men, the young men.** We can say **meat, fresh meat, the fresh meat.** We can also say **the very young men, rather fresh meat, extremely tasty dinners, usually affable clerks, quite calm expression.** We notice that **very** does not refer to **men** but to **young, rather** does not refer to **meat** but to **fresh; extremely** refers not to **dinners** but to **good;** and so on. We notice a difference between **very young men** and **bright young men,** between **extremely tasty dinners** and **good tasty dinners,** between **usually affable clerks** and **courteous affable clerks,** between **quite calm expression** and **sweet calm expression. Very young, rather fresh, extremely tasty, usually affable, quite calm** are units in themselves which can be detached as units. **Bright young, good tasty, courteous affable,** and **sweet calm** are not units; they fall apart when they are detached from the noun.

Adjectives that qualify nouns have their own qualifiers; you can split off the noun and still have a unit. In the adjective-group the adjective is the headword; in the noun-group the noun is the head. In the verb-group the verb is the head; in the adverb-group the adverb is the head.

Headword

young	men		Noun as head
very	young		Adjective as head
can	work	hard	Verb as head
quite	hard		Adverb as head
not so very young	men		Noun as head
not so very	young		Adjective as head
not so	very		Intensifier as head
not	so		Adverb as head

We have units within units. Any native speaker can slice off any complete unit by saying it with final falling juncture. We think in those units, we talk in those units, and we write in those units. The principle here involved is the principle of "immediate constituents" or "pattern-parts." It is common enough in experience: parts work together in units that are parts of other units. Take a pressure cooker, for instance, that useful instrument that keeps a housewife wondering whether she is going to have broccoli on the table or on the kitchen ceiling. The pressure cooker breaks down into a pan and a lid: the lid can be locked by a twist to the pan. The pan consists of bowl and handle. The lid has more parts: a gasket under the rim, a dome-shaped cover, a handle, a safety-valve, and a pressure gauge. Each handle is a separate unit that can be taken apart, but is not much good as a handle unless it is fixed to the pan or lid. The safety valve is a unit with several parts, and the pressure gauge is a unit with constituents which can be dismantled in an orderly sequence. There is a certain order for putting a pressure cooker together or taking it apart, and if you don't follow that order you may find yourself looking at the world through a film of mushy vegetables.

Missing the borders of units and blurring them with other units can be troublesome in language, too; it is especially troublesome in writing where the writer has in mind one set of borders but puts in signals that permit the reader to construct another. You can see what different pitch, stress, and juncture contours can do to these sentences:

The driver says the policeman is a crazy reckless fool.
The driver, says the policeman, is a crazy reckless fool.

"I work in one of the better girls' schools in the east."
"Where do you find these better girls?"

"I wonder why a girl can't catch a ball like a man."
"A man is so much bigger and easier to catch."

Each unit in English can be modified by some other unit, and each modifier is potentially the headword of its own unit. We do not think of the pattern **Prep N in the house** as being modifiable, but we can modify it and then modify the modifier: **He was in the house when the phone rang; He was almost in the house when the phone rang; He was just almost in the house when the phone rang.**

Or again: **It fell in the soup; It fell right in the soup; It fell right smack in the soup.**

ᴎ = THE NOUN ADJUNCT; D ᴎ N

WHEN we look at the English utterance in one way, it seems to be a series of noun-groups and noun-clusters related to each other by verbs, verbals, and structure-words such as the prepositions. Nouns dominate the utterance so much that some writers give the sentence over to the noun and underplay the structure-words and the delicate discriminations of pattern-signals. They end with a very muddy sentence that makes dull reading. We can never quite escape the dominance of the noun because, like Adam, we feel that we possess the world by giving names to what is in it, but we can control nouns by setting one against another. Bringing their lines of force into opposition, contrast, co-operation, and collision— especially by the substitution of nouns in the functions of other word-classes—we achieve a variety more charming than the dull march of one noun plodding after another.

We saw the dominance of the noun when we looked first at the patterns of noun-groups in Chapter 9. We had to set up two patterns for the noun-group: **D ᴀ N the young boy** and **D ᴎ N the college boy.** It would take some counting of noun-groups to tell which pattern is more frequent in use; certainly the noun is commonly used instead of the adjective to modify a noun-headword in its group. A noun used to modify another noun is called a *noun adjunct*.

Within the noun-group several kinds of modification can be applied to the head; we can say **the milk, the fresh milk, the very fresh milk,** or we can say such things as **the altogether too completely and hygienically fresh milk.** It depends on what we mean. We can modify the headword with the verbals **V-ing the souring milk or V-ed/en the soured milk,** and, by modifying the verbals we can say **the slowly souring milk** or **the faintly soured milk.** Each modifier receives its own kind of modification; the adjective **fresh** is preceded by the intensifier **very** or by the adverbs **completely** and **hygienically,** and the verbals are preceded by adverbs, **slowly** and **faintly.** When we use a noun as modifier in the noun-group, it, too, is subject to the kinds of qualification normally applied to a noun.

We can use a noun to modify the noun-headword in four ways by setting a noun directly before the headword: 1) by using the base-form of the noun D ~~N~~ N the goat milk; 2) by using the "possessive" or "genitive" form of the noun (the base-form with the ending -'s to produce N-'s) D N-'s N the goat's milk; 3) by using the "plural" form of the noun (the base-form with the ending -s to produce N-s) D N-s the goats milk; and 4) by using the "possessive" or "genitive" plural form of the noun (the base-form with the ending -s' to make N-s') D N-s' N the ladies' hats. These forms of the noun are treated in Chapter 15. When we modify any of these three noun-forms, we may use adjectives or other nouns: **the new goat milk, the farm goat's milk,** and so on. In speech we signal which noun is being modified by the way we slice the noun group into units:

D	~~N~~	N
the	/ new goat's /	milk
the new	/ goat's	milk /
the	/ new curriculum /	committee
the new	/ curriculum	committee /

One of the deficiencies of writing as a signaling instrument shows up here, for as the noun-groups are usually written and printed they could express either of the two meanings. We would like to know which meaning is intended. In speech we can indicate instantly by our pitch, stress, and juncture overlay where the meaning is sliced, but in writing we have to set each unit into such a context that it does not hover between meanings. Hence a written sentence must be more carefully composed than a spoken utterance. Somewhere, either before the sentence, in it, or after it, we have to drop the clues that make up for the inadequacy of the written line.

The noun that ends the noun-group is its headword, except in some special expressions like **Operation Iceberg** where the headword comes first. Either the modifying noun or the headword can have other modifiers; usually it is quite clear which is being modified. Sometimes both nouns have modifiers.

D				N	Modifier	Headword
a				plaster wall	plaster	wall
a			high	plaster wall	high	wall
a			fresh	plaster wall	fresh	plaster
the				garage man	garage	man
the			bus	garage man	bus	garage
the		city	bus	garage man	city	bus
an		able	city bus	garage man	able	man
a	more	able	city bus	garage man	more	able

The noun adjunct pattern **D ~N~ N** is so common and so useful that we have to consider it basic to the noun-group along with the adjective noun pattern **D ~A~ N**. Its internal mechanism is flexible and worked in by long use; since frequency breeds on frequency, we use the noun-adjunct pattern in preference to others. Thus beside **V-ed/en N, creamed cheese, chipped beef, iced cream, spiced cake, king-sized cigarettes, buttered side, phoned orders, powered mower,** and **old-fashioned girl** we have the noun-adjunct pattern, **~N~ N cream cheese, chip beef, ice cream, spice cake, king-size cigarettes, butter side, phone orders, power mower,** and **old-fashion girl.** The noun-adjunct takes the same modifiers that it does as noun-headword; it is, as we have seen, a noun-headword in respect to its own modifiers. The characteristic modifier of a noun is an adjective or another noun; the characteristic modifier of an adjective is an intensifier such as **very** or the ending **-er,** so that we say **very fresh, fresher** or **very skillful,** but not **very garage, garager** or **very bus, busser.** The characteristic modifier of a verbal is an adverb, so that beside **fresh plaster wall** and **high plaster wall** we would expect **freshly plastered wall.** Though these various noun-groups seem very similar in meaning to one another, there are perceptible discriminations among them.

Frequently in the noun-adjunct pattern **D ~N~ N** we use the base-form of the noun with the ending **-'s, N-'s:**

D	~N~	N
a	stone's	throw
a	hand's	turn
that	car's	design
a	boy's	coat

With this variant of **D ⊣⊦ N** we again have two possible meanings that can be distinguished better in speech than in writing. If we slice the noun-group by intonation after the determiner we get one meaning: **a/boy's coat/**; if we slice it between the noun adjunct and the headword we get another: **a boy's/coat/**. In the first the noun-group points to a certain kind or type of coat; in the second the noun-adjunct is "possessive"; in this case the boy owns the coat. We can distinguish **Here is a fine little-boy's coat** from **I want my little boy's coat**; we distinguish between **She looked well in her boy's haircut** and **She paid for her boy's haircut and took him home.**

Slightly less common but still frequent in this noun-adjunct pattern **D ⊣⊦ N** is the plural of the noun, the base-form with the ending **-s** or its equivalent:

D	⊣⊦	⊣⊦	N
a	communications	situations	analyst
a		heavy-weapons	expert
a		sports	enthusiast
our		rivers and harbors	policy
a		teachers	college

In the noun-adjunct pattern **D ⊣⊦ N** the noun-adjunct may be taken as a substitute for the adjective or simply as one of the things a noun normally does. The frequency of the pattern seems to favor taking it as a typical patterning of the noun, but the issue is not important. The pattern exists whichever way we take it.

ORAL EXERCISE: Make up noun-adjunct patterns using nouns in their four forms **N, N-'s, N-s,** and **N-s' (a men's college)**. Keep at these patterns until you can produce them at will.

Nouns As Verbs; Verbs As Nouns

THE INTERCHANGE of nouns and verbs in each other's positions and functions is rather free in English; it is commonest with the most familiar words, but who is to look inside each person's head and find out which words are most familiar to him? Nouns and verbs substitute for each other very simply, because each has a base-form to which endings are added: **V** is the base for **V-s, V-ed, V-ing,** and **V-ed/en; N** is the base for **N-'s, N-s,** and **N-s'.** The interchange of nouns and verbs is so common that we can set up a pattern for it as follows. (We need enter only the **N** and **N-s** forms of the noun.)

Noun-forms		Verb-forms				
		V	**V-s**	**V-ed**	**V-ing**	**V-ed/en**
N	talk	talk	talks	talked	talking	talked
N-s	talks					
N	drive	drive	drives	drove	driving	driven
N-s	drives					

Thus we get such free interchange as with the word **bully** in the following sentences: **He is a bully; they are bullies. Don't bully the child. He bullies children. He bullied my boy. He is bullying my boy. He has always bullied the other kids. Oh, he's a bully-boy!** As always, common words like **hand, face, head, finger, leg, soup, table; run, hit, smile, look,** and **dream** transfer most freely from noun to verb or from verb to noun. As verbs they take on all the modifiers and complements of the verb-cluster; as nouns they take on all the modifiers of the noun-cluster. The potential of the transfer is so general that no noun or verb is beyond its effect.

Nouns As Adverbs

NOUNS working as adverbs occur as freely in the sentence as the adverb itself—that is, almost anywhere. They can begin the sentence, precede or follow the verb, split the verb-group, or bring up the end of the sentence. They are usually nouns of place, manner, and time, but not necessarily; the limitation they put on the verb must suit the particular verb used.

Nouns substitute for adverbs:

A,	N	v	V	A,	N
N					
Sunday	we	will	go	to the zoo.	
Last year	the house	was	painted.		
No matter,	the boy	can	go.		
This way	you	can	earn		the money.
That direction	the road		is		a mess.
				N	
				a foot.	
	The car		moved	this minute.	
	The boys	will	go		

N	A,	v	A,	V	N
	N		N		
Aunt Sue	this time			scowled.	
We		have	each year	built	fifty houses.

N	v	V	A,	N	A,
			N		N
Aunt Sue		goes	home		evenings.
We	have	built		fifty houses	this year.
They		do		the work	their way.
They	'll	do		it	every time.
The party		lasted			all night.

ORAL EXERCISE: Build other sentences using these nouns as adverb-substitutes and add to these whatever others you can think of.

Adjectives As Nouns

WITHIN the noun-group we sometimes find adjectives working as noun-headwords. The determiner signals as usual for a noun, but the headword is an adjective which, if it is modified, is modified by an intensifier:

D	N	V	D	N
	A			A
The	poor	survive.		
The	very poor	pity	the	rich.
The	more able	win.		
The	wealthy	enjoy	the	beautiful.

N	V	Prep	D	N
				A
The play	died	on		first.
He	was	among	the	hardy.

Adjectives As Verbs

ADJECTIVES transfer to the position and function of verbs in the same way nouns do. The base-form of the adjective becomes the base-form of a verb and takes on the verb endings: **warm, warmer, warmest; warm, warms, warmed, warming. Mother warmed the baby's milk. The breeze cools our patio. Aspirin calms the pain. The crowd stilled its clamor.**

Adverbs as Adjectives

WITHIN the noun-group we often find adverbs modifying nouns. Occasionally the adverb precedes the noun; more likely it follows the noun.

Adverbs modifying nouns as post-modifiers:

D	A	N	A	V	
			A		
The	new	book	here	is	mine.
The		reason	why	is	obvious.
The		dinner	later	was	good.
The	last	night	before	was	cold.
The	only	way	down	was	rocky.
My		mother	especially	was	worried.

Adverbs preceding nouns as modifiers:

D	A	N	V	
	A			
Its	then	publication	was	awkward.
The	down	grade	was	steep.
The	after	effects	were	important.

ORAL EXERCISE: Try other words as substitutes in these patterns.

In the performance of nouns, verbs, adjectives, and adverbs as substitutes for one another, we have caught a glimpse of the full range of flexibility with which the language meets any need of expression. Word, word-group, phrase, and clause perform the various functions; each word-class also takes over the tasks of the others. Nothing happens by chance here; the language does not wallow around in a misty formlessness, stumbling on meaning like a blind tackle in a football game; everything is precise, ordered, integrated. Every groove of habit we follow has been worn again and again by ourselves and the members of our speech-community; we press their limits in details, but never in any large way. The penalties for pressing too far and too hard are simple and fatal: our listeners do not understand us; or they grope for our meaning and grasp it, but turn their attention from what we are saying to the way we say it. It is not a case of "anything goes." Anything goes that goes, and that is all.

✶ *CHAPTER 11* ✶

Repetition within the Patterns

WE HAVE identified the four word-classes, the four functions, and the four units which perform the functions in the six statement-patterns; we have seen the kinds of substitutions that let the units do double, triple, and quadruple duty in utterances. Still we remain tantalizingly short of the English sentence such as the ones in this paragraph, the sentence that each writer must bring to birth by wedding the spontaneous utterance of his native speech to the cold strategy of the English writing tradition. By filling the patterns we have looked at, we can produce intricate and methodical designs with words, but not quite that fluid, sensitively adjusted, ever-changing, evanescent instrument of human expression whose making is a triumph of human skill and whose reading delights the perceptive mind. Along with principles of order and of substitution, we have to examine one more general device of composing sentences, the principle of repetition.

Repetition goes by the notion that a thing that works once is worth trying again. If we put a nickel in a slot and get a candy bar out, we feel that it is worth while putting another nickel in to get another bar out. If one staple will hold a dozen sheets of paper together, two or three will really stitch them in place. If one blow of the hammer will start a nail, other blows will drive it home. We repeat for more and greater effect. In the sentence we can repeat the same words or different words in any one of the units: we can repeat single words, including markers and structure-words; we can repeat word-groups, including phrases and clauses. We can repeat in two ways: by *compounding* and by *apposition*.

Compounding

COMPOUNDING is like throwing more different items of the same kind on a pile to make it higher. It is like serving two eggs for breakfast instead of one, or three eggs, farm style, instead of two. So far we have served up one-egg sentences in our display of the patterns; with few exceptions we have used one noun as the head-word of one verb and one adjective, one adverb, one phrase, and one clause as modifier. What is the effect when we do not stop at one, when we pile up noun, noun, and noun; verb, verb, and verb; or clause, clause, and clause? We get some interesting and useful results.

Let us return to our basic sentence and see the operation of the principle of compounding. We may say **The boy loves the girl** or, without changing the pattern, **The whole family loves the girl.** That is a good sentence but often not true to life, as every young man discovers when he begins to bring his girl friends home. We may particularize the family by saying **The boy, his mother, and his father love the girl;** we replace the pattern **N V N** with **N, N, and N V N.** That is, we compound **N** in the pattern; in the same manner we may compound **V** and may get **V and V loves and cherishes** or **V, V, and V The boy loves, cherishes, and respects the girl.** We can also compound the final **N** and produce **The boy loves the girl, her young brother, her father, and her mother.** At only one point does repetition lead us into problems of selection: compounded **N, N, and N** in the pattern **N V** may select **V** as against **V-s: Eggs, potatoes, and bacon make a good meal.** There is a tendency in Modern English, however, to feel **N and N** or **N, N, and N** as equivalent to **N** in the pattern, so that the repeated nouns also select **V-s: Eggs, potatoes, and bacon makes a good meal.** It depends on what you mean.

We have a set of structure-words that we use in compounding.

Of these **and, but,** and **or** are the most common. Others of the set are **for, nor, as well as, together with, either . . . or, neither . . . or, neither . . . nor, whether . . . or, both . . . and, not . . . but,** and **not only . . . but also.** We do not always use these structure-words; often we simply say the repeated units one after the other before we move on to the next different unit, whatever it is. Any unit in any formula or any part of any unit can be repeated without changing the formula.

We can compound nouns:

N	V
The boy	came.
The boy and girl	came.
The boy and the girl	came.
A boy, girl, and woman	came.
The tumult and the uproar	died.

We can compound adjectives:

D	A	N
	sweet, fresh	milk
a	dull	day
a	dull and dismal	day
a	dull, dismal, rainy	day
a	brilliant and persuasive	argument
a	calm and considerate	attitude

We can compound verbs, verb-markers, and verb-headwords:

N	v	V
Aunt Emma		came and stayed.
Aunt Emma	has	come and stayed.
Aunt Emma	shall and must	come.
The train		whistled, puffed, and stopped.
The doctor		neither smiled nor spoke.
The doctor		smiled as well as spoke.

We can compound adverbs:

A	N	A	V	A	N	A
Later	we		knocked	down	the show	there.
Later	we	quickly and quietly	knocked	down	the show	here and there both.
Absolutely and positively	I	certainly	will not do		it	now or later.

We can compound phrases:

In the morning, in the afternoon, and in the evening we did our work.
They came by land, by sea, and by air.
Over the hills and through the woods we ride.
Among friends and among strangers alike he was shy.

We can compound clauses:

A man who knows the work, who has done the work, and who is able to do the work is wanted.
If you will get the money and if you will give it to me now, I will forget it.
He stopped and ate when he liked and where he liked.
He knew that we were coming and that we intended to stay.

We can compound verbals:

To be or not to be, that is the question.
Singing and dancing, the crowd filled the streets.
Tired and disgusted, he went home.
Being American and being patriotic, I worry about things.
We can do it, barring accidents and barring bad faith.
Either working or resting, he sulked.

We can compound markers:

He was never really in or of the group.
I didn't know who or what he wanted.
You can and should pay the bill.

When and where he stopped in the crowd, there was silence.
It is not a question of a boy but the boy.
He sends me this or that odd souvenir from here and there.

We can compound utterances and sentences:

He said that he couldn't go; he meant that he wouldn't go.
He said that he couldn't go, but he meant that he wouldn't go.
The British held one side of the channel, the Germans held
    the other, but no one held the waters between.
Come easy, go easy.

The simplest compounding is the repetition of exactly the same unit in exactly the same function. In practice we do not stop with that; we get some interesting effects by repeating the function but with other elements substituted in it. Thus in the pattern **N V**, **The music stopped**, we can repeat **N** to get **N, N, and N V: The music, the song, and the laughter stopped.** That is pretty simple and we do not stop with it. We introduce variations, letting other elements carry the **N** function in the **N, N, and N** series.

N	V
The music	stopped.
The music, the song, and the laughter	stopped.
The music, the singing, and the laughter	stopped.
The music, the singing, and the laughing	stopped.
The music, the singing, and the gay laughter	stopped.
The music, the singing, and the gay and lilting laughter	stopped.
The music, the singing, and what sounded to us like laughter	stopped.

The complete range of substitution and expansion that we have observed in this chapter and in Chapter 10 is possible within each repetition of the function. With compounding likely to occur to any unit anywhere in the utterance, we can produce complicated effects within any pattern. We can produce even more complicated effects by drawing on the full range of substitutions. We can interchange word, word-group, phrase, and clause; we can substitute nouns for verbs, adjectives for adverbs, verbs for nouns, verbals for nouns, for adjectives, and for adverbs, and so on. Any unit that can carry a function under any conditions seems substitutable within a series for any other unit that carries the function. Expanded sentences sometimes go out of control and get to the point where we wish we hadn't started them. When they do in speech we just drop them, take a breath, and make a new start. In writing we go back and revise. Free compounding and free substitution as we compound are not unusual tricks of writing. They are characteristic of our speech. Little children do it all the time.

ORAL EXERCISE: Match each of the examples with another made up as far as possible in other words, until you can juggle compounding and substitution in the series to produce any effect you choose.

Apposition

THE other kind of repetition is *apposition*. Apposition is not much different from compounding, but permits some special effects. Compounding is the creation of a series; instead of one unit performing a function we have 1 and 2 or 1, 2, and 3 or more distinct items. In apposition we have reiteration of the same item in other words. It is an aid in achieving the purpose of all speech, the exact and complete statement of what we mean. We use apposition when the first word, word-group, phrase, or clause is not explicit, not emphatic, not detailed enough for what we want it to say. We simply hit it again, and if necessary again, before moving on to the next unit in the sentence. Compounding is the addition of more items of the same kind to the first one; apposition is a deepening or widening or heightening of the first. As usual the word *apposition* is a name of no particular value unless you can perform the operation named. Apposition is something like ringing the doorbell and knocking on the door to be sure the people in the house know you are on the porch. It is like giving a nail another crack with the hammer to drive it home.

We can appose nouns **N [N]** or **N [N, N]**:

> **Joe the milkman is pretty reliable.**
> **I have just read the book "Moby Dick."**

He felt like a criminal, a regular robber.
The judge, a really distinguished man, spoke to me.
No person—no man—can talk to me that way.

We can appose adjectives **A** [**A**] or **A** [**A, A**]:

My love is like a red, red rose.
She gave him a firm steady glance.
The lake was a still, motionless sheet of water.
He had a reckless, rash career.

We can appose verbs **V** [**V**] or **V** [**V, V**]:

She screamed, shrieked, clamored.
The car skidded—slid out of control.
What he said calmed—quieted—the children.
I have written—typed, that is—all day.
Plant life can be sterilized, rendered incapable of reproducing,
    by high dosages of X rays.

We can appose adverbs **A_v** [**A_v**]:

He walked slowly, lingeringly home.
He had a roughly, ruggedly adventurous trip.
He certainly managed that slick, too smooth.
Still, nevertheless, I want the money.

We can appose phrases:

At noon, exactly at twelve, he rang the bell.
In your argument—in the basic statement of your position,
    you go wrong.
By hook and by crook he made his money.
He was always right there with coins—with nickels and dimes
    —for the tip.

We can appose clauses:

A person who works as hard as he does, who's down there
    day after day pounding it out, should get some reward.
What I want—what I intend to get—is my fair share.
When it is dawn, when the sun is just coming out of the water,
    I like to be down at the beach.
If you do—if you dare—there'll be some serious conse-
    quences.
If I were unhappy here—if I were really unhappy—I'd quit.

We can appose verbals:

> **To sleep, to close your eyes and let go, is a nice way to end the day.**
> **To have really lived—to have experienced all you can experience—is something to look back on.**
> **Singing that song, really sounding it out, she shook the rafters.**
> **Picking his way, steering carefully among the ruts, he tried the road.**

We can appose markers:

> **He's not in the group, you know—really in it.**
> **Jones was over, well beyond, the danger point.**
> **I can—must—go.**
> **When I get there—if, that is—I'll be satisfied.**
> **I don't care who, which, or what you send me.**

We can appose sentences:

> **He was flat broke. He didn't have a cent.**
> **No man was a better workman than he was; no one did a cleaner faster job.**

We can appose different units which have the same function:

> **He repeated the conversation verbatim, in the same words.**
> **They may say what they dare, nasty words maybe, about me.**
> **Not yet, not at this moment, can I go.**

ORAL EXERCISE: Match each of these examples with one of your own, using the same pattern but different words. Then invent a few for yourself just to show you can do it.

When we compound a unit in a particular function, we toss more and different items into the basket. We add one thing to another and get two; the two work in the utterance as one. We add a third and get three. When we appose a unit in a particular function, we put in more of the same, like pouring more coffee into a cup. We stiffen, strengthen, reinforce, or explain the original item; we do so, as in compounding, calling on the whole range of possible substitutions. Any unit that can be substituted for another can be apposed to it. We add one, two, or three things which fill in the suggestion implicit in the first. Apposition is a useful, a very useful device.

CHAPTER 12

Within the Noun-cluster;
Group Verbals

WE LAY a language out for examination quite differently from the way we use it in life. In our analysis of English speech as it is reflected in writing, we have taken simple elements and large outlines and moved step by step into complications and complexities. In actual talk and writing a native does not draw on a language displayed the way we have seen it; whatever language he knows, he knows all of a piece, and all of it is available to him to say whatever particular things he has to say. He has a set of language-habits of which he is largely unconscious; to communicate, he can act at will in accordance with any part of the set; it is an array of grooves among which he proceeds smoothly and automatically to express what he means.

The display we have been working with is knowledge about language; it is not language; it is not knowing the language as a native knows it. This knowledge without practice does not necessarily lead to command of language; many students of language are miserable writers. The native speaker's knowledge is a potential of action, a potential of which he is unconscious but by means of which he performs. We cannot describe or even measure his potential, because the evidence we have to go on is the residue of only a portion of his language acts. It is the sounds spoken and the words actually written. Self-inspection is some help, if the inspector knows what to inspect; but most of us are not aware of what we do when we speak, or even aware that we are doing anything of interest in and of itself. By this time we know much of what we are doing when we express ourselves. This knowledge with practice does lead to a command of language and to efficient reading and writing.

In our description so far we have looked for key patterns and key combinations of patterns, the kind that lay down the action characteristic of native users of the language. We have not covered all of them, but we have displayed enough to give a picture in broad outline of the way our language works. We have cut through a vast body of material in order to expose the living heart of the language. Sketching that for observation, we have let a good many things go for discussion later, rather than muddy up our description. When we treated the noun-group, we left some noun-groups out. When we treated the adjective phrase, we picked important phrases. We laid out basic sentence-patterns. Now we have to go back and take up some of the things we skipped. All are as important to the user of English as those we have treated, just as available when he needs them as anything we have discussed. We left them out only because we could get along better and describe the essential core more clearly without them.

The Noun-group

THE typical noun-group often is some variation on the typical patterns **D** **A** **N** this messy desk, a bright light, three blind mice; and **D** **N** **N** a tin cup. We can have **A** **N** black smoke, fresh cigarettes, green peas, fast cars. We can have **N** **N** mahogany desk, paper weight, plastic comb. We can have **A** **N** later discussion or **N** **A** discussion later, bottles here. We can have **V-ing** **N** coming events, sliding scale; **V-ed/en** **N** detached service, scribbled notes; **N** **V-ing** money coming, cars stopping; **N** **V-ed/en** name enrolled, work done; **N** **to-V** work to do, letters to write, songs to sing. And we can have variations and combinations of these too numerous to list.

Members of other word-classes can also serve in the noun-group patterns as headwords: verbs like **go**, as in **She has a lot of lively go**; adjectives, as in the **poor**, the **busy**, the **proud**; adverbs like **easy**, as in **Easy is as easy does.** The verbals can serve as noun-headwords: **to-V**, as in **To see her is to love her**; **V-ing**, as in **Frequent swimming is good exercise**; **V-ed/en**, as in **Well begun is half done.**

We can use other units also as noun-groups. We can use larger units with verbals as headwords:

Noun-group with **to-V** as headword:

> **The big to-do in the bank brought the police on the run.**
> **To make a hotrod out of an old car takes a lot of work.**

Noun-group with **V-ing** as headword:

> **Your destroying that letter was rather foolish.**
> **Those boxes being empty like that give us more room.**

Noun-group with **V-ed/en** as headword:

> **Those boxes stacked like that gives us more room.**
> **Ten letters done takes a big bite out of the work.**

We can substitute **Prep N** for noun-groups:

> **Over the hills is twice as far as through the tunnels.**
> **By the back way is best.**
> **From the credit union is the cheapest way to borrow.**
> **For you to pay now is only reasonable.**

The Noun Clause

A NOUN clause is a clause serving as **N** in the sentence-pattern. Let us review the functions of the noun:

N	V	N	Prep	N
Men	like	quiet	in	the house.
Bees	make	honey	from	flowers.

The noun combines with the verb in the pattern **N V Birds sing**; it works in the verb-cluster in the pattern **V N turn corners, paint**

the wall. The noun modifies the noun in the noun-group, N̶ N **lead pencil.** The noun follows the preposition in the pattern **Prep N by rail, for Mary, through the mail.** The noun clause as a unit—marked off by contours of pitch, stress, and juncture—functions as **N** in the sentence-pattern.

Clauses of any kind may begin with clause-markers such as **who, that, which, what, when, where, why, how, if, because,** and **since.** In speech the marker is not a vital or important signal; it is simply the lead. After the marker a plenitude of signals of order, intonation, and inflection strike the ear almost at once; the ear takes in the "shape" and function of the clause as the eye takes in the characteristic shapes and functions of motor vehicles at a glance, distinguishing between cars and trucks and between different makes of cars without the application of thought about them. In writing, this complex unity of signals is wrecked; only overt signals of form and order get through to the eye, and the marker takes on importance as the representative of that unity which escapes translation from sound to sight.

Beneath the surface variety which clauses show in use, two basic patterns of order provide recognizable "backbones" for the clause units:

1) With the marker serving as **N** in the clause pattern **N V:**

Clause-marker	V	N
who what that	came happened ruined	the fence

2) With the marker introducing the clause-pattern **N V,** but not a part of it:

Clause-marker	N	V	N
what where if although	he Joe the money business	did made comes declined	the box

It is not the internal pattern of the clause or even its marker that marks it as noun, adjective, or adverb. Almost any clause-marker starts clauses in any sentence-function. We tell a noun clause from an adjective or adverb clause by its position and relation in the sentence. We usually find an adjective clause within the noun-cluster immediately after the headword or immediately after a phrase modifying the same headword: N ⃗AC the boy who came or N ⃗AP ⃗AC the boy from the store who came. We usually find adverb clauses at the beginning or end of utterances; they limit the verb or the whole utterance: A⌄C N V N Where Joe made the box, he made a mess; N V N A⌄C Joe made a mess where he made the box.

A noun clause may take over the position and function of a noun in the sentence; a noun clause combines with a verb in the pattern **N V**, follows a verb as complement in the pattern **V N**, or follows a preposition in the pattern **Prep N**. A clause compounds with other nouns in the series **N, N, and N**; or is apposed to another noun in the pattern of apposition **N [N]**.

We can illustrate the noun clause in its various uses:

N	V	N	Prep	N
His action	settled	the matter	for	us.
NC				
What he did	settled	the matter	for	us.
		NC		
What he did	settled	what we wanted	for	us.
				NC
What he did	settled	what we wanted	for	whoever cared.

A noun clause beginning with **what, whatever, whoever,** or **whichever** exerts a limited selection when it combines as **N** in the pattern **N V**. When the clause is clearly plural inside, it selects **V** and not **V-s**:

N	V
What books he had	were very old.
Whatever people came	were relatives.
Whichever arguments he made	were answered.
Whoever make bad marriages	are sour on women.

When the noun clause is clearly singular inside, it takes either
V or **V-s**; the verb is often "attracted" by what follows it:

N	V	N
What we want	is	quiet children.
What we want	are	quiet children.
What makes her charming	is	a number of pleasing traits.
What makes her charming	are	a number of pleasing traits.
What annoys us	is	neighbors that gossip.
What annoys us	are	neighbors that gossip.

The clause is almost completely substitutable in the sentence-
pattern for the **N**; for instance, in sentence pattern TWO A: **N V
N N This calls that that:**

N	V	N	N
The boy	calls	the girl	his friend.
What you say	makes	what I have believed	nonsense.
That he had done it	made	whatever he said	what I would call a lie.

The clause substitutes for **N** in sentence pattern TWO B: **N V
N N This gives that that:**

N	V	N	N
The boy	gave	the girl	a present.
How he finished	gave	whatever he said	what its meaning was.
Whoever fails	envies	whoever succeeds	what he wins.

The noun clause as **N** in the pattern **Prep N**:

N	V	N	Prep	N
He	sent		for	what he wanted.
The reviewer	saved	the book	for	when he had time.
The travelers	drove		over	what roads there were.
The burglar	looked		under	where we kept the money.
The letter	is addressed		to	whom it may concern.

The noun clause as complement in the verb-cluster:

V	LV	N
His reason	is	that he cannot afford it.
The reason	is	because he cannot afford it.
It	is	because the store closed.
It	seems	that they are coming.

The noun clause in apposition in the pattern **N [N]**:

N	[N]	V
The idea	that you can't go	annoys me.
The notion	that crocodiles weep	is silly.
The principle	that water seeks its own level	still holds.
The thought	that there were bugs in the rug	bothered her.

There is nothing special about the noun clause within itself; it is merely a clause used as a noun wherever a noun can be used.

ORAL EXERCISE: Exercise your ingenuity making noun clauses to fit all the patterns above, until you are sure that you feel the clause as a distinct unit.

Roving Adjectives

IN order to pick up some more loose ends among the patterns of English, we go back again to the noun-cluster. The typical pattern of this cluster is, of course, **D ~~A~~ N ~~AP~~ ~~AC~~ the typical pattern of this cluster that we have been repeating endlessly.** The position before the noun and after the determiner (if there is a determiner) is the territory of the adjective, the place where the single-word adjective performs its task of limiting the noun which follows: **new books, green trees, those fast cars, a quiet afternoon.** Adjective phrases and clauses follow the noun; if there are adjective phrases, the clauses follow the phrases. This pattern, which involves something like the "modular units" used in building and in furniture, recurs in recognizable variations. We have seen how any unit can substitute for almost any other unit in the sentence; in the noun-cluster further substitutions are possible.

WORD-GROUP ADJECTIVES BEFORE THE NOUN

ADJECTIVE phrases and clauses normally follow the noun, but they are not uncommon before it.

Adjective phrases before the headword:

D	AP	N
a	by-your-leave	expression
an	in-the-swim	neighbor
an	out-of-this-world	look

In speech such adjective phrases preceding the headword are spoken with the pitch, stress, and juncture contour of a single-word adjective and are built by this contour into the noun phrase. Adjective clauses that are spoken before the noun they modify get the same treatment. In writing, these phrases and clauses are often pointed out by hyphens between the words or by quotation marks: **a between-the-acts cigar, a "between the acts" cigar.**

Adjective clauses before the headword:

D	AC	N
a	"believe it or not"	experience
a	rakish devil-may-care	expression
	hand-me-down	clothes
a	real "fill up and push back"	meal

SINGLE-WORD ADJECTIVES AFTER THE NOUN

SINGLE-WORD adjectives frequently follow the noun in the position where phrases usually occur. A current use of such post-modifiers (both adjective and noun) derives from military terminology developed in manuals and in military correspondence, where the item is named first and its distinguishing characteristics are listed after it: **rifle, automatic; landing ship, tank; landing craft, personnel;** and so on.

Single-word adjectives after the headword:

> **She gave him the cut direct.**
> **We have done this from time immemorial.**
> **We paid the money due when we got the bill.**
> **I'll see you Monday next.**
> **We made the largest payment possible.**
> **The hotel has promised the first room available.**

Single-word adjectives followed by their own word-group modifiers trail their nouns:

> **That is an argument new to me.**
> **It was some people anxious about your health.**
> **He was wearing a shirt dirty with grease.**
> **She is a woman fearful of anything strange.**
> **The negotiators sat in a room murky with smoke.**
> **He drove a car noisy as a thrashing machine.**

ORAL EXERCISE: Fit examples of your own to the patterns above. These off-beat patterns have value for your style, in that they are within the experience of the reader but just enough outside his expectation to give him the sense that you are in control and running the show.

THE ADJECTIVE PHRASE

WE may now consider some kinds of adjective phrases we have not yet looked at. The adjective phrase we took as typical consists of the pattern **Prep N man of the house, hole through the doughnut, cars on the road, fellow with the green hat, people from Ohio, evening at home,** and so on. Since **N** in the sentence-pattern stands for the whole noun cluster or any part of it down to the noun-headword itself, this kind of adjective phrase can run to some length and be quite complicated. For instance, the sentence-pattern of the following example is **N LV N He was a man with an exceedingly gentle manner that brought favorable comments from all persons whom he met.** At one level of analysis, the pattern is **N LV N +AP.** The whole adjective phrase is **with an exceedingly gentle manner that brought favorable comments from all persons whom he met.** Laying the sentence out by levels, we produce an interesting "step" pattern which brings out that each successive unit is a phrase or a clause modifying the final noun in the preceding unit; each of these nouns is the headword in a cluster of its own:

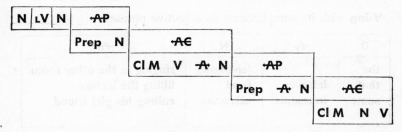

He was a man with an exceedingly gentle manner that brought favorable comments from all persons whom he met.

This is a relatively simple utterance. If you have been wondering why we have not analyzed a good normal complicated sentence, now you know.

We noted earlier that verbals used as adjectives distribute themselves pretty much as adjectives do, single words regularly before the nouns and sometimes after; phrases regularly after the noun. **V-ing** alone may precede or follow the noun: **a coming man, a man coming; a ringing bell, a bell ringing; a screaming girl, a girl**

screaming. We are conscious of a slight distinction of meaning between the two positions that keeps them from being quite equivalent to each other. **V-ed/en** also alternates between the two positions with a distinct leaning toward the place before the noun: **a tired man, a man tired; a mailed letter, a letter mailed.** We find **to-V** after its noun: **a man to admire, a letter to mail, work to do, a book to read.**

A verbal cluster (distinct from a verb-cluster) is a verbal with its complements, which are just what it would have as headword in a verb-group: **N; N N; Aᵥ; AᵥP; AᵥC.** Verbal clusters used as adjectives usually follow their nouns; if an adjective clause modifies the same noun, it follows the verbal cluster.

To-V with its complements as adjective phrase:

D	~~A~~	N	~~AP~~
a	good	road	to take across the divide
a		machine	to set ties
a	better	way	to do the work

V-ing with its complements as adjective phrase:

D	~~A~~	N	~~AP~~
the		telephone	ringing in the other room
that	leftover	food	filling the icebox
some	lonesome	salesman	calling his girl friend

V-ed/en with its complements as adjective phrase:

D	~~A~~	N	~~AP~~
the		Army	staggered by the offensive
a	Fifth	book	written in his later years
a		puppy	tied to the gate

ORAL EXERCISE: Make up some examples to fit these patterns. Play with the verbals a little; they give a genuine lift and movement to your sentences.

PATTERNS OF THE ADJECTIVE PHRASE

N	A	

N A and its modifiers:

N	A	Prep N
N	A	to-V and its complements

N	AP	
N	Prep	N
N	to-V and its complements	
N	V-ing and its complements	
N	V-ed/en and its complements	

ORAL EXERCISE: Make one to fit each pattern above, to nail this phrase down hard.

THE ADJECTIVE CLAUSE

WHEN a clause works as adjective, it usually follows its noun immediately or trails the adjective phrase. So many adjective phrases end with nouns that the hearer or reader may be in doubt which noun is being modified by the clause: **He took a course at the university that represents a new low in American education.** Which represents a new low, the **course** or the **university?** In our present educational temper it would be hard to tell which from that sentence.

When the hearer is in doubt, he can clear the matter up with a question; but when the reader is in doubt, he may have to stay that way even if he considers all the signals provided. When a reader teeters between two or more meanings unable to decide which is intended, we have a situation described as ambiguous. The state of being ambiguous is called ambiguity. Sometimes the ambiguity is serious; sometimes it doesn't really matter; but the possibility of it is always with us. Possible ambiguity is one of the prices we pay for the almost unlimited flux and flow of patterns and for the free substitution that make the English sentence a flexible instrument of expression. The chance of a conflict of meanings always lurks within a noun-cluster which has a sequence of adjective phrases and clauses, particularly in writing. The writer is often unaware that the exact words he uses to convey one meaning may just as well convey another.

When an adjective phrase ending in a noun precedes the adjective clause, the noun modified by the clause is often indicated by signals within the clause. When one noun is the base-form **N** and the other is the base-form plus **-s** or one of its equivalents, **N-s,** the choice is made by selection:

D	N	~~AP~~			~~AC~~
		Prep		**N**	
The	**desks**	**in**	**the**	**room**	**which were to be cleaned**

D	N	~~AP~~			~~AC~~
		Prep		**N**	
The	**desks**	**in**	**the**	**room**	**which was to be cleaned**

Sometimes it just doesn't matter:

> **One of those people who are always tired**
> **One of those people who is always tired**

When one noun is normally followed by **who** or **whom** and the other by **which,** the marker of the adjective clause shows which noun is modified:

> **The boy with a dog which created a disturbance**
> **The boy with a dog who created a disturbance**

> **The officers of the company which was prosecuted**
> **The officers of the company who were prosecuted**

The adjective clause nicely illustrates the danger of speaking too positively about any aspect of the utterance or sentence. We began with the noun-cluster because the elements in its are relatively fixed in the order of utterance. We have already seen the adjective clause preceding its noun: **a come-hither look, a don't-tread-on-me atti-tude, a knock-down-and-drag-out fight.** These are usually un-marked clauses.

Adjective clauses, usually with their markers, sometimes occur outside the noun-cluster after the verb or verb-group:

> **A man came in who had been waiting for several hours.**
> **That old fellow is dead who used to look after the garden.**
> **An argument has come to my attention which has been agitat-ing the whole village.**

Frequently in speech **N-'s** modifying a noun-headword will be neatly split by the intrusion of an adjective clause:

N V	D	N-'s	N
That's	the	fellow's	car.
That's	the	fellow who hit me's	car.

Did you hear about the girl who was here last night's accident?

ORAL EXERCISE: Set up some sentences in pairs where one signal or another resolves a possible ambiguity in favor of one meaning or the other. Then try to call to mind some of these out-of-position adjective clauses like those above.

Inside the Adjective Clause

In its normal place in the order of utterance, within the noun-cluster and bringing up the end of it, the adjective clause is a simple mechanism which begins with characteristic clause-markers and falls into two familiar patterns. The typical clause-markers are **who, whom, whose, which, that, when, where,** and **why.** Sometimes we have compound markers consisting of a preposition and **whom, whose,** or **which: of whom, in whom, with whom,** and so on. And sometimes the adjective clause follows the noun without any marker at all. The displays of these patterns contain brief illustra-tive clauses. Each **N** and **V** is capable of expansion into word-groups, so that very long clauses are possible.

In the first pattern the adjective clause begins with a marker

who, which, or **that** immediately followed by a verb, verb-group, or verb cluster:

N	~~AC~~			V
	Cl M	V	N	
The clock	which	struck		awakened us.
The clock	that	struck		awakened us.
The woman	who	drove	the car	was arrested.
The woman	that	drove	the car	was arrested.
All persons	who	have	tickets	may enter.

In speech, but rarely in writing, this clause occurs sometimes without a marker:

N	~~AC~~			V
		V N N		
The fellow		sold me that car		was a crook.

In this pattern of the adjective clause the noun being modified exerts selection on the verb within the clause, wherever possible, just as it selects the form of the verb following the clause:

N	~~AC~~		V
	Cl M	V	
The boy	who that	is coming	is my brother.
The boy	who that	has come	is my brother.
The boys	who that	are coming	are my brothers.
The boys	who that	have come	are my brothers.

Some selection goes on between noun and marker. All nouns take **that,** a word of all work that comes down to us from ancient times; as clause-marker it starts both patterns and offers no choice of forms. In this pattern, nouns referring to men, women, and children or anything thought of for the moment as if it were a person select **who:** nouns referring to things, ideas, or living creatures not thought of as persons take **which: Willie, who is saucy; Morning, who tiptoes across the asparagus beds. The morning, which began cold and rainy; that box which tripped me.** The alternation between **who** and **that** and between **which** and **that** is stylistically useful when an adjective clause modifies a noun in a preceding adjective clause: **a book which is on the table that sits by the front door.**

In the second basic pattern the adjective clause shows more internal variety. It begins with the markers **who, whose, whom, which, that, where, when,** and **why;** and with **Prep whom** and **Prep which.** The marker is followed by **N V, N VG,** or **N V-Cluster:**

N	AC				V
	Cl	M	N	V	
The man	that whom		we	saw	is gone.
The book	that which	I		was reading	was pretty good.
The motel	where at which		we	stayed	had terrible beds.
The hour	when at which		they	stopped the dance	was late.
The reason	why for which		help	failed to come	was not known.

This pattern of the adjective clause often occurs without a marker:

N	AC		V
	N	V	
The man	we	saw	is gone.
The book	I	was reading	was pretty good.
The woman	the boy	spoke of	did not come.
A problem	I	had heard of	came up the other day.

This pattern of the adjective clause occurs in several slight variations:

N	AC			
	Cl M	N	N	V
A book	whose	plot	I	knew
A book	whose	plot	I	had heard of

N	AC				
	N	Prep	Cl M	N	V
A book	the plot	of	which	I	had heard
A man	the wife	of	whom	Mary	knew

N	AC					
	Prep	N	Prep	Cl M	N	V
A problem	of	the solution	of	which	I	had heard
A problem	with	the solution	of	which	I	was familiar

The variety within the adjective clause is the variety of speech; the several different patterns by which we may express about the same idea give interest to our sentences and build the reader's confidence in us; he feels that our phrasing is not a matter of chance, but a courteous and thoughtful concern for his exact comprehension of our meaning; like a passenger in a car driven by a competent and considerate driver, he settles back, forgetting the mechanics of the operation, to enjoy the ride.

ORAL EXERCISE: Make up at least one example, using as far as possible your own words, for each of the clause patterns we have illustrated.

The noun-cluster, which includes the noun-group, the adjective phrase, and the adjective clause, is a large overriding framework.

Within this framework the working parts are varied and inter-changeable, but always within limits. We have not tried to test these limits by describing every change and substitution possible; we do not mean to imply that variations we have not described do not occur. To control this cluster, we need to play with it as frivolously as a puppy with a slipper, devising patterns and testing them with words, to give ourselves a larger freedom of choice than we begin with. The testing instruments we use are the mouth and ear, making and hearing the patterns, for the ultimate grammarian whose authority cannot be subverted is the muscle-sets and habit-patterns developed in the relaxed interchange of conversation.

Group Verbals

THE verbals **to-V, V-ing,** and **V-ed/en to go, going, gone** are the means by which the verb can act as noun, adjective, and adverb, performing the functions of these three word-classes while still keeping all the modifiers and complements which attend the verb in the verb-cluster. We have seen that single-word verbals per-forming in the utterance are limited in their capacity to convey meaning, as words working alone always are. We now look at group verbals in which **to-V, V-ing,** and **V-ed/en** combine with each other to achieve a range of expression denied to each alone.

The group verbal is closely related to the verb-group. In the verb-group, forms of **be (am, is, are, was, were, be, being, been)** combine with the headwords **V, to-V, V-ing, V-ed/en.** Forms of **have (have, has, had, having)** combine with the same headwords, and forms of **be** and **have** combine with each other as markers and helpers with these headwords. Thus we say **He is to drive, he is driving, he is driven; he has to drive, he has driven; he has been driving, he is being driven,** among others. We get similar combina-tions in the group verbals, with the effect of pinpointing a meaning.

Group verbals as adjective phrases in the pattern **N AP:**

With **to-V** as headword in the verbal:

> **Let's make a real effort to try to get in.**
> **The man coming to see you has phoned.**
> **He is a person entitled to receive respect.**

With **V-ing** as headword in the verbal:

> He is no man to be driving a taxi.
> Fools to have been sailing in that weather, we foundered.
> His big mouth having been making trouble, he was fired.

With **V-ed/en** as headword in the verbal:

> They were busybodies to have interfered.
> The work to be done is ready.
> The car to have been polished had never come.
> The argument being made was rather ridiculous.
> The dress having been sent, we could only wait.

Group verbals as nouns:

With **to-V** as headword in the verbal:

> Coming to work after illness is a relief.
> Getting to know you has been a pleasure.
> I never enjoy having to go out.

With **V-ing** as headword in the verbal:

> To be fishing again was a pleasure.
> To have been seeing her was more than he would confess.
> Just keeping going tired him.
> He enjoyed being talking English again.
> Having been telephoning her while she was out annoyed us.

With **V-ed/en** as headword in the verbal:

> He always liked to have done things before the rest of us.
> The country's sad fate was to be betrayed again and again.
> To have been cheated by a dumb girl was always on his mind.
> He did not like being awakened.
> He did not explain having been delayed four full hours.

Group verbals as adverbs:

With **to-V** as headword in the verbal:

> He stood by his friends, preparing to support their cause.
> The rains came, beginning to weaken the subsoil of the dam.
> The snow fell, helping to hide the drab buildings.

With **V-ing** as headword in the verbal:

He was known to be making a new model at the time.
The woman was said to have been meeting him secretly.
He held the floor, keeping talking over the chairman's gavel.
He came in excited, having been talking to the reporters.

With **V-ed/en** as headword in the verbal:

The company was known to have made some money.
The fleet was understood to have visited China.

Group verbals modifying adjectives:

With **V-ing** as headword in the verbal:

The crew was anxious to be starting home.
He was embarrassed to have been wearing old clothes all day.

With **V-ed/en** as headword in the verbal:

He felt foolish to have expected prompt delivery.
He was very eager to be signed up.
The business was too important to have been left to others.

ORAL EXERCISE: Try to match each example with another using different words.

The group verbal is probably one of the most sophisticated of patterns. There is a certain relationship between any verbal and the word it modifies, a relationship specified in the two words and adjusted by the form of the verbal—**to-V, V-ing,** or **V-ed/en.** The group verbal narrows that relationship and pins it down with a discrimination that is easier to illustrate than to explain: **He was embarrassed to wear old clothes all day. He was embarrassed to be wearing old clothes all day. He was embarrassed to have been wearing old clothes all day.** The first example is broad enough in meaning to include the other two. The second is broad enough to include the third; the third cannot substitute for either of the others, except in that narrow segment of implication which it expresses. Verbals in general give relief from the plodding dominance of the noun which our passion for naming exposes the English sentence to; the group verbals, judiciously applied where precision is necessary, pinpoint the conditions under which the "naming" is valid. The group verbals relate our statements to the flow of human existence in a changing world, to the coming into being and going out of existence of each phase of life and nature and thought in relation to the separate ticks and points of time.

CHAPTER 13

Questions, Commands, Requests, etc.

WE CAN go wrong about language if we assume that a form or pattern that occurs often is a more important unit of language than one that occurs only now and then. Any act of speaking or writing is a concentration of forces to achieve a specific purpose: to express a meaning or a set of meanings. What we hear or read is a selection among numerous possibilities. Out of a vast number of means of expression that a speaker is capable of choosing, he picks certain ones. Many things influence his choice: the kind of mind he has; the extent to which he prefers sameness or variety, the daring or the conservative; the number of expressions at his command; and the extent and range of his earlier practice. The controlling influence is, in the end, none of these. It is the burden that life lays on him as a user of the language. What he needs to say, what he wants to say, what he has to say—these decide his choice of language.

We have dealt so far with the patterns of the statement that occur most often in writing. There is some doubt that they occur most often in speech. If we could equip a house with microphones and recording machines so that we recorded every human sound made within the house, we could get an idea of the actual frequency with which language elements are used. We could let a family go through their normal lives in that house, sleeping and waking, coming and going, working and playing, and settling down at last to rest at night. Probably statements would not bulk very large in the record; questions and answers, commands and requests, exclamations, denials, sighs, and other patterned utterances like **uh huh** and **uh-uh** with no selected phonetic content would fill much of the tape.

Each person writing or speaking has behind him hours and days and years of participation in integrated family and community groups. This participation has given him a skill in language such as only professionals build up in other activities. If we judge a professional by the amount of practice he has given to his specialty, a native in a community is a professional user of language. Concert pianists practice three or four hours a day; ice skaters, ballet dancers, and tennis players may scarcely stop to eat; they attain highly developed skills. In and around these activities they practice being members of their community, largely by talking and listening. The native speaker of the language has an expertness and a virtuosity in the physical movements that produce the language; he comes up to each need for speaking with a wealth of practiced actions and a range of possibilities of action that only top-flight performers can call on in the field of their mastery.

Each speaker brings to his writing the same massive background of language, but it is not available to him in the same way. He uses writing to satisfy a more limited set of needs. English writing is not a complete transcription of speech; a great deal is left out because we have no way of representing it. Each speaker learns to write comparatively late; even the most accomplished writer never devotes the time, attention, and inattention to his writing that he gives to his speaking. Furthermore, writing is limited by taboos of various kinds; social pressures lean against the appearance in writing of many words and structures of speech that could be represented. The writer manipulates a limited system with many gaps and silences in it. Generally his skill is limited; because he doesn't trust himself to make experiments good, he works conservatively, well within the writing tradition.

We have presented a thorough treatment of the statement in terms of its six basic arrangements. These are treated at length in Chapter 9, but we will review them again here. These statement-patterns are used when we are explaining or describing something or telling a story; or, indeed, when we are offering any kind of information to someone else. These utterance arrangements are statements only when they are said with the pitch, stress, and juncture contours that also signal "This is a statement." In writing we suggest these contours by punctuating them at the end with a period (.), semicolon (;), or exclamation mark (!). A person listening to us make a series of statements may indicate his attention by movements of his eyes, head, and body, or by breaking the flow of our talk with such remarks as **Yes, um-humm, I see,** and so on. These are not interruptions; they do not break into what we are saying but help to keep us going by assuring us of his attention. A reader has no such way of participating in bringing the ideas out. The writer has to go it alone.

We review the six basic patterns of the statement:

	N	V	Comp	
ONE:	**N** **This**	**V** **affects**	**N** **that.**	
TWO: A.	**N** **This**	**V** **calls**	**N** **that**	**N** **that.**
B.	**N** **This**	**V** **gives**	**N** **that**	**N** **that.**
THREE: A.	**N** **This**	**V** **acts.**		
B.	**N** **This**	**V** **acts**	**A͜** **thus, there, or then.**	
C.	**N** **This**	**V** **acts**	**A** **so.**	
FOUR: A.	**N** **This**	**LV** **is**	**N** **that.**	
B.	**N** **This**	**LV** **is**	**A** **so or such.**	
C.	**N** **This**	**LV** **is**	**A͜** **thus, there, or then.**	

	N	V	Comp		
FIVE: A.	**N** **This**	**VG** **is affected.**			
B.	**N** **This**	**VG** **is affected**	**Prep** **by**	**N** **that.**	
SIX: A.	**N** **He**	**VG** **is given**	**N** **that**	**Prep** **by**	**N** **that.**
B.	**N** **That**	**VG** **is given**	**N** **him**	**Prep** **by**	**N** **that.**

These are skeletons of statements, not real bones around which flesh clings but more like the little stick men we draw to illustrate the positions of the body. Clothed in single words, they seem far different from the flexible line of normal casual conversation. Yet they are the essential framework of all our assertions of any matter whatever:

ONE: **Rain stalled the car.** TWO: A: **The dampness made the delay no pleasure.** TWO: B: **The driver gave his horn a blast.** THREE: A: **A man stopped.** THREE: B: **He lived there.** THREE: C: **The weather turned worse.** FOUR: A: **The man was a farmer.** FOUR: B: **He was friendly.** FOUR: C: **He was nearby.** FIVE: A: **The motor was soaked.** FIVE: B: **The spark-plugs were shorted by the rain.** SIX: A: **The motorist was offered some help by the farmer.** SIX: B: **A reward was given the farmer by the motorist.**

Clothed in word-groups, phrases, and clauses, enlivened by verbals, filled out by compounding, and reinforced by apposition, these simple structures encompass all we might have to say. They are the backbone of our expression.

EXERCISE: Make up a paragraph (not about a stalled car, rain, and a farmer but something else) to clinch these statement-patterns before we go on, and to prove that you can pack infinite riches into a little room.

The Question-patterns

As we inspect the other kinds of utterances and sentences, we can use the statement-patterns as a base to work from. Any statement can become a question or a command if we say it with the pitch, stress, and juncture contours of question or command: **The men will bring in the piano. The men will bring in the piano? The men will bring in the piano!** It is not the running line of words alone that determines the function of the unit, but the whole complex of signals working together. In the same way a typical question-pattern can be in effect a statement:

Is he a real genius? Are you tired?
Is he a real genius! Are you tired!

In speech, by controlling the overriding contours of pitch, stress, and juncture, we can convey subtle implications of doubt, distrust, irony, inquiry, interest, inquiry without interest—a wide range of suggestion that is understood by the hearer because he is capable of conveying just such suggestions himself by performing the same delicately discriminated set of actions. Much of all this escapes our writing or must be laboriously faked or explained.

"Please," said Nadine softly, making the quiet word a command by a shrug of her lissome shoulders, "let us not discuss my husband's sad death further, Inspector Knuckleknob." She spoke the next words even more quietly, with her head bowed, her hands trembling. "May we talk about—" she raised her head and gave the inspector the full treatment of a wide-eyed stare; she breathed the last word in a whisper that set off all the cartridges in his Police Special—"you?"

For questions we do have certain patterns which involve a different arrangement of units in the utterance; because they involve a different word-order, they can be transferred bodily to writing and used when they are needed. They are of various kinds. Some are holdovers from the past, and so have a standing and even a preference in writing somewhat different from their standing in speech.

We begin with an old pattern, now limited in its use. Instead of **N V** we have **V N**, a simple reversal of noun and verb without any necessary change in the intonation. We end it in writing with a question mark (**?**).

N	V	
The duke	**walks**	**in the garden.**
V	**N**	
Walks	**the duke**	**in the garden?**
Tells	**the record**	**of my defeat?**
Sighs	**the wild wind**	**lonely still?**

As we might expect, this simple old pattern is the base of our modern question-order. We find it again with that old, much used, jack-of-all-trades verb **be (am, is, are, was, were, being, been).**

N	V	
The book	**is**	**here.**
V	**N**	
Is	**the book**	**here?**

The arrangement signals the question; we can say the question with the pitch, stress, and juncture contour of a statement and it remains a question.

N	V	
That young man	**was**	**John's brother.**
V	**N**	
Was	**that young man**	**John's brother?**

When **be** is the single-word verb in an utterance, carrying the verb-function by itself, it normally follows its noun; its form is selected by the noun: **I am; He, she,** or **it is; You, we,** or **they are; The boys are; I, he, she,** or **it was; The boy was; We, you,** or **they were; The boys were.** The verb occurring before the noun selects the noun and signals a question: **Am I? Is he, she,** or **it? Is the**

boy? Are you, we, or **they? Are the boys? Was I, he, she,** or **it? Was the boy? Were we, you,** or **they? Were the boys?**

Be combines as marker and helper in verb-groups with other verbs as headwords more frequently than any other verb except **have. Have (has, had, having)** is frequent both as a single-word verb and as marker or helper. It shows more limited selection in statements: **He, she,** or **it has; The boy has; I, you, we,** or **they have; The boys have; Any N had.**

Have combines into question-patterns in two ways. In one it works the same as **be:**

N	V	
He	has	the book.
They	have	a car.

V	N	
Has	he	the book?
Have	they	a car?

When **be, have, can, could, may, must, might, should, would, shall,** and **will** serve as markers in verb-groups, the question-pattern is a simple reversal of marker and noun, from **N v V** to **v N V.**

When verbs other than **be, have,** and the modal auxiliaries are serving in verb-groups as verb-markers, they also convert to questions by means of forms of **do:**

N	v	V	
The salesman	got	fired.	
He	keeps	going.	
They	start	working	today.

v	N	v	V	
Did	the salesman	get	fired?	
Does	he	keep	going?	
Do	they	start	working	today?

The basic inherited question-pattern, a simple switching of **N V** to **V N,** is not used much with most verbs, but it is the only pattern in which we find the verb **be: He is. Is he? Have** may work according to this pattern: **He has. Has he? Have** also converts to a verb-group by the marker **do: He has. Does he have?** This is the manner of most verbs: **He argues. Does he argue?** Verb-groups change to the question-pattern from **N v V** to **v N V** (noun, verb-marker, and headword to verb-marker, noun, and headword): **He is going. Is he going? He has gone. Has he gone?** Where order mainly signifies a question, these are the mechanisms by which it works.

QUESTION-PATTERNS WITH QUESTION-MARKERS

BESIDES the questions indicated by contours of stress, pitch, and juncture **(You're coming with me? Yóu're coming with me? You're cóming with me? You're coming wíth me? You're coming with mé?)** and those indicated by the order of utterance, there are some questions indicated by special question-markers. The question-markers make up a short list: **who, whom, whose, which, what, when, where, whence, whither, why,** and **how.** They come at or near the beginning of the utterance. They may or may not be reinforced by special question-patterns of pitch, stress, and juncture; they may or may not be accompanied by reversals of order. Like questions starting with **is, have,** or **do,** questions starting with the question-markers are signaled as questions from the beginning. They fall into two groups.

One kind of question-pattern with a question-marker is based on the order of the statement; in any of the six statement-patterns the question-marker simply serves as **N** in the pattern **N V:**

N	V	
He	is	here.
Question-marker	V	
Who	is	here?
What	caused	the trouble?
Who	was	the villain?
Which	came	first?

The question-markers used in this pattern are commonly **who,** **which,** and **what.**

A second kind of question-pattern with a question-marker is also based on the pattern **N V** with **D N** serving as **N** and the question-marker used as the determiner **D:**

D	N	V	
The	ball	broke	the window.
Question-marker	**N**	**V**	
Whose	ball	broke	the window?
Which	ball	broke	the window?
What	ball	broke	the window?
What	family	lives	there?
Which	letter	is	mine?

A third kind of question-pattern with a question-marker contains a verb-group switched as we have seen above: not **N v V** but **v N V:**

N	v V		
He	has done	the work.	
He	has chosen	this one.	
He	will get	here today.	
Question-marker	**v**	**N**	**V**
What	has	he	done?
Which	has	he	chosen?
When	will	he	get	here?
Who	do	you	see?
Whom	do	you	see?
What	do	you	see?
Which	do	you	see?
Whence	has	he	come?
Whither	can	you	go?

In this pattern, when the statement-pattern is not **N v V** but **N V**, forms of **do** serve as verb-markers in the verb-group:

	N		V	
	He		told	a story.
	He		tells	a story.
	The men		went	home.

Question-marker	v	N	V	
What	does	he	tell?	
Who	did	he	tell	a story to?
Whom	did	he	tell	a story?
When	did	the men	go	home?
Where	did	the men	go?	

Questions with question-markers sometimes occur without reversal of pattern:

He has done what?   He told what?
The men went where?   He told who?
The men went when?   He told whom?
He will get here when?   He told which?

When a question begins with the pattern **Prep N** or **V-ing N** or anything similar, the question-marker serves as **N**: He tells me to do the work. With what?

			N	V	
			The letter	came	for me.
			He	thinks	she'll be ready then.

Prep	Question-marker	v	N	V	
For	whom	did	the letter	come?	
By	when	does	he	think	she'll be ready?
In	which	is	the answer	hidden?	
About	what	do	you	want	to see me?

When a question begins with the pattern **Prep D N** or **V-ing D N** or anything similar, the question-marker serves as the determiner:

Prep	Question-marker	N	v	N	V
By	which	route	did	you	come?
At	what	point	do	I	go on?
V-ing					
Driving	which	car?			

BASIC QUESTION-PATTERNS

WE can now look at the basic question-patterns arranged in the order of the six statement-patterns:

ONE: Does this affect that?
Is this affecting that?
Which this affects that?
When does this affect that?
When is this affecting that?
For whom does this affect that?
For whom is this affecting that?

TWO: Does this call or give that that?
Is this calling or giving that that?
Which this calls or gives that that?
When does this call or give that that?
When is this calling or giving that that?
For whom does this call or give that that?
For whom is this calling or giving that that?

THREE: Does this act (thus, there, then, or so)?
Is this acting (thus, there, then, or so)?
When does this act (thus, there, then, or so)?
When is this acting (thus, there, then, or so)?
For whom does this act (thus, there, then, or so)?
For whom is this acting (thus, there, then, or so)?

FOUR: A. **Is this that?**
Which this is that?
When is this that?
For whom is this that?

B. **Is this so or such?**
Which this is so or such?
When is this so or such?
For whom is this so or such?

C. **Is this thus, there, or then?**
Which this is thus, there, or then?
When is this thus, there, or then?
For whom is this thus, there, or then?

FIVE: **Is this affected (by that)?**
Which this is affected (by that)?
When is this affected (by that)?
For whom is this affected (by that)?

SIX: A. **Is he given that by that?**
Which he is given that by that?
When is he given that by that?
For whom is he given that by that?

B. **Is that given him by that?**
Which that is given him by that?
When is that given him by that?
For whom is that given him by that?

QUESTION-PATTERNS WITH TRAILERS

WE have not yet exhausted the patterns of order by which we indicate that we are asking a question rather than making a statement
or issuing a command or request. In asking questions as in any
other matters we have alternate ways of working; we have an array
of formulas from which to choose. We began with the statement
which is turned into a question by the contours of pitch, stress, and
juncture we put on it: **Your mother is certainly not any worse?** We
also have statements which we turn into questions by tagging a

question formula to the end. In either the statement or in its trailing question-pattern the word **not** or its contraction **-n't** occurs. They structure in different ways:

	V	N	Not
That store is opening tomorrow,	**is**	**it**	**not?**
	V	Not	N
That store is opening tomorrow,	**is**	**n't**	**it?**

In this pattern not the verb-headword but the marker is repeated in the trailer:

> **The cast can do that play by heart, can they not?**
> **The cast can do that play by heart, can't they?**

> **Your brother will send the money, will he not?**
> **Your brother will send the money, won't he?**

When the verb is a single word, it is not repeated in the trailer, but is replaced by a form of the verb-marker **do:**

> **Those people walk right in, do they not?**
> **Those people walk right in, don't they?**

> **That company went broke, did it not?**
> **That company went broke, didn't it?**

When **not** or **-n't** occurs in the statement, it is not repeated in the trailer:

> **That store is not opening tomorrow, is it?**
> **That store isn't opening tomorrow, is it?**

> **The cast cannot do that play by heart, can they?**
> **The cast can't do that play by heart, can they?**

> **Your brother will not send the money, will he?**
> **Your brother won't send the money, will he?**

> **Those people do not walk right in, do they?**
> **Those people don't walk right in, do they?**

That company did not go broke, did it?
That company didn't go broke, did it?

With all these instruments for posing our questions, we may always draw out an answer, but we have plenty of ways of indicating what we want to know.

Sentence-patterns with Not

WHEN we use the word **not** in an utterance, it usually denies or cancels the headword that follows it, no matter what that word may be. It cancels nouns: **not a man, not a desk, not a clock, not milk, not beauty.** It cancels adjectives: **not pretty, not red, not large, not empty.** It cancels adverbs: **not now, not usually, not quickly, not there. Not** and **-n't** cancel verbs; but when they do so, their effect is to cancel the whole verb-cluster. **Not** and **-n't** pattern in certain characteristic ways peculiar to the verb.

Again we see the use of **not** most clearly by referring to a now little-used basic pattern:

N	V		
The Duke	**walks**		**in the garden.**
N	V	Not	
The Duke	**walks**	**not**	**in the garden.**

Most verbs are not canceled this way by modern speakers and writers unless to achieve some special effect; but the verb **be,** as usual, still follows the old ways:

N	V	Not	
The Duke	**is**		**here.**
N	V	Not	
The Duke	**is**	**not**	**here.**
The Duke	**is**	**n't**	**here.**

As usual **has** (as a single-word verb) may pattern like **be**:

> **He has a chance.**
> **He has not a chance.**
> **He hasn't a chance.**

In verb-groups, **not** follows the verb-marker:

N	v		V	
He	has		got	a chance.
He	's		got	a chance.
He	is		coming	here.
He	has		come	here.
N	v	Not	V	
He	has	not	got	a chance.
He	has	n't	got	a chance.
He	is	not	coming	here.
He	is	n't	coming	here.
He	has	not	come	here.
He	has	n't	come	here.

With single-word verbs, **do** is used as a verb-marker with **not** and **-n't**, converting the verb to a verb-group:

N		V	
The Duke		walks	in the garden.
The milk		sat	on the porch.
N	v	Not	V	
The Duke	does	not	walk	in the garden.
The milk	did	not	sit	on the porch.

With the verbals, no matter what their function in the sentence, **not** usually precedes but may follow:

> **Not to see is not to believe.**
> **Not seeing is not believing.**

Not seen is not believed.
To see not is to believe not.

OTHER NEGATIVES AND AFFIRMATIVES

OTHER negative words—**no, never**—do not usually affect basic sentence-patterns. **No** usually patterns with nouns as a determiner: **no man, no young man.** **Never** precedes the noun-group: **never a busy man;** otherwise it modifies the word that follows it: **never cold, never talked, never quickly.** In the verb-group it sometimes structures like **not: has never come, is never seeing. Never** may precede the verb-marker: **never is coming.** It may occur elsewhere: **is coming home again never. No** is often used alone as a general negative: **Are you working this week? No. No** may begin an utterance: **No, I'm not working. No, I'm taking a vacation. No** may end an utterance: **I'm not working this week, no.**

Patterning in general like **no** in this use are such expressions as **yes, of course, certainly, why not? Yes, I'm working this week; why not?**

Patterns of Command and Request

WHEN an utterance begins with the base-form of the verb, we usually take it as a request or command. Often this verb is the entire utterance, but it may have any or all of its complements. It may have a pitch, stress, and juncture contour that is quite heavy on the stress; in that case we punctuate it in writing with an exclamation mark (**!**).

V	
Stop!	
Bring	me that book!
Bring	this argument to an end right now!
Halt	right now!

In this sentence-pattern of command the form **be** is used:

V	
Be	silent.
Be	ready at ten.

Verb-groups appear in this pattern of command, with the verb-markers **be, have, get, keep, do,** and occasionally others:

v	V	
Be	working	when they come in.
Have	done	with that.
Get	going	as soon as you can.
Keep	talking.	
Do	let	me have that.

Generally verb-groups with **not** begin with the verb-marker **do:**

v	Not	v	V	
Do	not	be	working	when they come in.
Do	not	get	going.	
Do	not	keep	talking.	
Do	n't	keep	talking.	

In the sentence-pattern of command we use the pattern **v N V,** the noun being the complement and part of the verb-cluster:

v	N	V
Keep	them	working.
Have	the car	washed.
Start	that thing	going.
Get	that work	done.

Some statement-patterns signify command or request, when they begin with **you:**

N	v		V		
You			go!		
You	will		go!		
You	get		moving	now.	
You	can	just	give	me	that.

In commands and requests, other elements may precede the verb or verb-cluster:

> Reader, take heed.
> Sailor, beware.
> Friends, stop and think.
> Now then, give me that!
> When you are all ready, call me.
> If you can come, let me know.
> Tomorrow or the next day, put it in the mail.
> On receipt of your orders, you will proceed to Washington.

Such expressions as **please, if you please, if you don't mind, perhaps you'd like to** mark utterances as commands or requests; they may begin or end the utterance:

> Please go.
> Pass the eggs, if you please.
> If you don't mind, come in off the porch.
> You can drop that in the box, if you don't mind.
> Perhaps you'd like to put that back where you got it.

In the commands and requests, as in most other uses of language, we have a variety of ways in which to express ourselves. Many shades of meaning are possible, from a flat order to a hesitant hinting that we would like something done. We are seldom left with only one mode of expression.

> I'd like to have that book.
> I'd like you to give it to me.
> I wish you'd call me.
> Won't you let me know when you get home?
> Let's finish this up and quit.
> Wouldn't you like to go down and see the principal, Johnny?
> Would you mind closing the door?

Some of these clearly suggest the iron hand in the velvet glove; no one misunderstands and thinks he has a choice whether to obey.

Minor Sentence-patterns

CERTAIN utterances that begin with verbs are not commands either stated or implied. There is one very common compounded pattern in which verb-cluster follows verb-cluster without any connector; it begins with the base-form of the verb:

V		V	
Come	easy,	go	easy.
Give	a little,	get	a little.
Love	me,	love	my dog.

Often the second element is linked to the first by **and** and is quite different in form. It is about equivalent in meaning to certain utterances containing an adverb clause with **if**: **If you give him an inch, he'll take a mile.**

V		N	v	V	
Give him an inch,	and	he	'll	take	a mile.
Let those people into the house,	and	they		take	it over.

There is another familiar pattern whose backbone is **the more . . . , the more . . .** or something equivalent to it:

The more you do for those people, the more they demand.
The bigger they come, the harder they fall.
Soonest started, quickest done.

Some utterances begin with **V** or **V-ed;** in such utterances the speaker is usually reporting his own actions. This is the so-called "telegraphic" pattern:

Don't know what to make of these arguments. Seems that these people want high income and low taxes. Been around a

long time, and can say that it doesn't work. Can't take in 1929 dollars and spend 1955 dollars.

Came home late. Found a note on the table. Left the package and drove back to town; had dinner with Cameron.

The whole supply of utterance patterns used in speech can scarcely be listed, because speaking is a complicated performance in which the patterned line of linguistic units is only a part. More than this, all speech takes place as part of our response to the circumstances, events, and needs of our lives. Almost any unit of language or combination of units may form a complete utterance at some time, as the pressures of living put their demand on us and create demands for expression. We should not be surprised at anything or be overcritical of what we would not ourselves say. We should not trick ourselves into mistaking for attitudes toward language what are really attitudes toward people.

Since writing is a much more premeditated use of a limited part of the resources of speech and since unstandardized speech is expressed in standardized writing, we have to build and choose our sentence-patterns with more care than our utterance-patterns. We must stick to those that are immediately meaningful and are likely to be acceptable to readers. We must remember that the reader's eye tracks our words from the left side of the page to the right, bringing him the impressions the eye can receive, and no more.

*

PART THREE

*

How We Sort
Our Words

*

$\divideontimes$ **CHAPTER 14** $\divideontimes$

Finding the Working Units

TWO LANGUAGES are not just different ways of dealing with the same face of the same world presented to all men; they are different ways of taking in the aspects of the world that have become important to two societies. Two languages are like two windows of differently polarized glass. The same beam may beat on both windows, but persons looking through the glasses see very different light. Each glass favors part of the spectrum and rejects part of it. An investigator of light looking through one glass might never suspect the existence of more than he can see. He would miss the light that came through the other and the whole spectrum of possible light that is beyond the transmission of both. If part of the range of the two polarized glasses overlapped, some of the light would be visible through both; it would not mean the same to two observers. Each would seem to the other to be describing something real part of the time and part of the time talking nonsense.

A language is not merely a way we have of talking about experiences all men have in common. It is that only in part. More than a way of talking about human experience, a language determines what kind of experiences its speakers can have. The languages of Western Europe that belong to the same family as English let their speakers experience about the same world that we do, so that it is possible for us to learn French, German, Italian, Spanish, or Russian without feeling totally cut off from what is familiar to us. When we learn African, Asian, or American Indian languages, we find ourselves in topsy-turvy worlds where things are not treated as things, where qualities may be treated as things or as actions, where time as we know it does not exist, and where whole systems of logic do not give a nod in passing to what we consider logical. Within English, different speech-communities distribute the burden of expression differently among utterance-patterns and words. No two communities see the world the same way.

Each new bit of control we acquire over language—another language of the same family, an exotic language, or another feature of our own language—is not merely a new trick of expression but a new insight into reality and a new way of imposing order on the chaos of experience. We become different men and women.

We become different as we gain command over English writing. Since our writing is a truncated system parallel mainly to the linguistic portion of the speech performance and omitting most of the rest, it puts a heavier burden on vocabulary and on patterns of order than speech does. Reading and writing (not merely for what is said but for cultivating control over writing itself) develop and even overdevelop some sentence-patterns and some vocabulary in relation to the rest of language. The effect of this emphasis is valuable, but it is most valuable when we consciously manipulate the limited linguistic system in terms of the contours of pitch, stress, and juncture, of vocal qualifiers, and of gesture. Then we succeed in saying exactly what we mean; we touch the nerve of the subject we discuss.

It is as important for us to get a clear idea of the classes of words we use as it is to understand utterance- and sentence-patterns. The syntax and the vocabulary of any language together will express what can be expressed in any other: any language can say anything. But languages differ in what they handle with syntax and what they handle with vocabulary. Languages without the elaborate expression of time our language has in its verb-system have plenty of words and constructions that can be used to express time. Speakers of English who do not exploit our verbs, verb-groups, and verbals get along by using adverbs; people who do exploit them do not rest so heavily upon adverbs. Persons who can sort and manage words in terms of what a whole class of words communicates as a class are less dependent upon the specific meanings of specific words to pinpoint what they say. They are not forever groping for specialized words that do not come; words in common use that come do the work for them well enough.

Discovering the word-classes of a language is an analysis that starts with whole utterances as they strike the ear. We begin with utterances set off by nothing more than a silence before and after; we collect and record as many as we can. Mere sorting of these brings us to shorter stretches of speech that can stand free or can be bound into longer ones; some are as short as a grunt and some are as long as speakers have wind for. Each offers a simple impression of unity produced by the composite impact of multiple signals. Order, inflection, and intonation contours slice the stretches of talk into utterance-units; within these, investigators of language know what to look for: the structure-points of an organized system. They have developed a rigorous scientific method of finding these structure-points, a method which can be applied by any investigator to any language to produce valid, verifiable results.

We dig into the utterances, cutting them into pattern-parts and units, looking for large and small arrangements of sound used over and over again. As we find these, we list them and compare them with each other, seeking units that can replace one another in all the patterns each isolated sequence fits into. When we find a number of brief stretches of sound working in the same patterns in roughly the same way, we have a class of units. In order to think about these units together as a class, we tag them; we give the class a name. We can call the classes 1, 2, 3, 4 or A, B, C, D in the order of discovery, or we can give them any other label we choose. Speech-analysis gives us phonemes, morphemes, and syntax; to deal with standard English writing, we have to translate these into letters, words, word-groups, and sentence-patterns.

The scientist tags his classes for study with numbers and letters deliberately chosen because they have no meaning. He puts these into two groups. First are the four great word-classes, alike only in that they are unlimited, open-end classes of words; you can never list all the words in any class because more are constantly being created. He numbers these 1, 2, 3, and 4. Because these classes roughly equal four of the traditional "parts of speech" though defined not by meaning but by sorting, we choose to call them here by the traditional names: noun, verb, adjective, and adverb. The structure-words, the other group, are alike in that they are limited; not many words belong to them; these words recur over and over in utterances. The scientist tags these word-sets with letters: A, B, C, D. We name these word-sets with traditional labels where we can, calling them prepositions, conjunctions, and modal auxiliaries. The others we tag with labels of our own choice —marker, intensifier, determiner, starter, pattern-filler, and so on —trying to give them names to indicate what they do in utterances. Alternate systems of analysis and labeling may be valid for different purposes; behind all, immutable and unaffected by the analysis, is the language itself.

✳ CHAPTER 15 ✳

The Four Great Word-Classes

1. The Noun

T HE NAME *noun* is an arbitrary label for a class of words, a name we use only because it links us to tradition and is easier to remember than the letter A or the number 1. A word is a noun not because of any meaning or assumed meaning; it is a noun because it displays the signals of a noun and enters into patterns where nouns are used. We have defined the noun as a word that enters as **N** into the patterns **N V men work, V N make trouble,** and **Prep N at home.** It serves as headword in the noun-group **D A̶ N this old house** and in the noun-cluster **D A̶ N A̶P A̶C that clean sheet of paper that you gave me.** It modifies the headword in the pattern **D N̶ N the glass house.** Now we have to look at the noun in and for itself, what changes in form it can undergo, what subclasses it falls into and how these are defined. And still, working as we did with the patterns, we want to isolate the class-meanings that whole sets of nouns have in common without getting caught in the specific meanings of the specific nouns—which we know or have to learn for each individual word.

SINGULAR AND PLURAL: N AND N-s

THE base-form of the noun, **cat, desk, milk, beauty, idea,** is usually
called *singular;* this name is all right as long as we do not take it
too seriously. Not all these base-forms refer to one instance of
whatever it is that is named in the word: **wheat, milk, beauty.** Most
of these base-forms can be changed into "plural" forms by the addition of **-s.** Although there are other ways of forming plurals, the
symbol for the plural noun is **N-s.** *Plural* does not always mean
'more than one'; it is well to take *plural* just as the name for **N-s,**
which is **N** modified by **-s** or by an equivalent change in form or
sound.

Our choice between **N** and **N-s** produces consistent and regular
changes in the patterns:

> **A boy   eats you out of house and home.**
> **Boys eat   you out of house and home.**

> **A cat   often brings the mouse it   catches into the house.**
> **Cats often bring the mouse they catch   into the house.**

Here, within patterns generally the same, we have a selection of
forms; the first forms said or written select those that follow. **A**
selects **cat; a cat** selects **brings** and then **he** or **it; he** or **it** selects
catches. Cats selects **bring** and **they; they** selects **catch.** This selection is a matter of class-meaning. Singular nouns are selected by
the determiners **a, this, that;** singular nouns select compatible verb-
forms and pronoun-forms. Plural nouns are selected by **these, those**
and select compatible verb-forms and pronoun-forms. The determiners **the, some, any** do not select: **the cat, the cats; some cat,
some cats; any cat, any cats.**

As we saw in Chapter 9, some verb-forms and some verb-
markers are selected by nouns and some are not: **am, is, are, was,
were; have, has; come, comes** are selected; **can, could; had, came**
are not.

We can have different patterns of selection without much difference in meaning; it is hard to see significant differences in meaning
between these sentences:

> **A**   **cat brings the mouse he   catches into the house.**
> **Any**   **mice it**

> **Cats bring the mouse   they catch   into the house.**
> **Any cats**   **mice**

Selection is a choice of forms which may or may not affect meaning. A singular noun is the unmodified base-form of the noun: **N;** a plural noun is the base-form of the noun with an added **-s** ending or one of the equivalents: **N-s.**

Regular and Irregular Plurals

We have let **N** stand for the singular or base-form of any noun and **N-s** for the plural in order not to complicate our display of the language. We have several other ways of forming plurals; several sets of nouns do not simply add **-s** to the base. They form their plurals in other ways: **man, men; leaf, leaves; memorandum, memoranda.** Even the **-s** that we attach to the base is a simplification for the eye of what we actually say: **-s** represents a hiss in **cats,** a buzz in **dogs,** two buzzes in **houses,** and so on. A display of English speech written in phonetic notation would have to employ several different symbols in place of the simple written **-s,** as we shall see in Chapter 18.

The complicated history of our language gives us the several plurals. The regular plurals which we write **-s** were developed out of the wreckage of the Old English system of endings. In the English of 900 A.D. there were several sets of nouns, each with its own way of making the plural with endings like **-as, -a, -ra, -u.** As time and change wore these endings down, most plurals drifted to two sets: **-s** or **-es** as in **cats, dogs,** and **stones; -en** as in **oxen, eyen,** and **shoon.** For a while the **-en** plural seemed likely to be an active alternate to **-s** and **-es;** some words like **child, childra** drifted to it to form **child, children.** Gradually the speakers of English settled on the plurals we now mark **-s,** and today these are regular. Old words that change their plurals today, as they do one by one, change to one of those that we write **-s** or **-es;** new words take on one of these automatically: **a Wac; several Wacs.** Several small sets of familiar words hang on to irregular plurals from Old English still.

Other irregular plurals come to us by borrowing. Since about 1250 A.D., speakers of English have borrowed words freely from Latin, Greek, and French to express in English ideas they have learned in these other languages. Today we continue to borrow words from almost any other language at will. Many of these borrowed words are used by one person only and are not picked up by anyone else; others catch on. A Latin word coming into English makes its first and strongest appeal to persons who know Latin and automatically think of the word with its Latin endings. If they use the word in English at all, they feel obliged to preserve the Latin plural. If the word comes to be used outside this narrow group, it is picked up by many people who do not know the Latin plurals and would not care about maintaining them if they did. The more generally a word of Latin origin is used, the more chance there is of its having two plurals for a while, one maintained by those who feel the Latin form should be preserved and the other by everybody else. Thus we have **curriculum, curricula** and **curriculum, curriculums.** Ultimately common use wipes out the Latin form; only a word of restricted circulation keeps it.

The pressures of common use have other effects on nouns and their plurals. The number of English speakers who know any second language well enough to know which forms are singular and plural is always rather small. One kind of Latin noun has its plural in **-a: candelabrum, candelabra;** another has its singular in **-a** and its plural in **-ae: alumna, alumnae.** Some nouns have singulars in **-is** and plurals in **-es: basis, bases.** Trying to be right about these things, even the best-intentioned fall into confusion, taking **data** (**datum, data**) as a singular, **basis** as a plural. Some words plural in Latin are singular nouns in English: **agenda.** On such words as **gladiolus** with the plural **gladioli,** the native speaker may try **gladioluses,** or he may take **gladiolus** as plural and make a new singular **gladiola,** then a new plural **gladiolas.** Or he may give up and retreat to **glads.** The more a word spreads to common use outside the group which knows and cares about its forms in the other language, the more likely it is to settle into a form that sounds singular and another that sounds plural (usually one with **-s or -es**), letting the foreign endings wither away.

Common Irregular Plurals

In the patterns we mark all nouns **N** for the base-form and **N-s** for the plural, whatever it is; we don't offer forms that force you to guess but ask you to fit words you know into the patterns. Here we offer the commonest irregular plurals. If you know them, you can skip them; if you never had to read or write them, you would not have to worry about them. All are entered in dictionaries but not always gathered together so that they can be inspected.

NATIVE IRREGULAR PLURALS

Like **child, children** we have **ox, oxen; brother, brethren. Brethren** is now used chiefly in religious contexts; the common plural is
brothers. Other familiar words form the plural by changing the
vowel: **man, men; woman, women; foot, feet; goose, geese; tooth,
teeth; louse, lice; mouse, mice.** Compound nouns with these words
change the vowel in the plural, as in **workman, workmen; Englishman, Englishmen; charwoman, charwomen; eyetooth, eyeteeth;
dormouse, dormice.** Words like **German, Norman, Ottoman,** and
talisman add **-s;** so does **mongoose, mongooses;** none of these is a
compound word. Four other common English words have two
plurals: **die, dies** (for coining, shaping, stamping, cutting, or molding); **die, dice** (for gaming); **penny, pennies** (American); **penny,
pence** (British); and **cow, cows; cow, kine** (now an archaic form).
Words like **deer, sheep, fish** make no change for the plural; **fish,
fishes** may occur.

IRREGULAR FOREIGN PLURALS

The commonest irregular foreign plurals, all of which we mark
N-s in the patterns, are:

1. Latin words:

N	N-s	N	N-s
alumna	alumnae	larva	larvae
differentia	differentiae		minutiae
	facetiae		
alumnus	alumni	locus	loci
bacillus	bacilli	Magus	Magi
cumulus	cumuli	modus operandi	modi operandi
homunculus	homunculi	modus vivendi	modi vivendi
incubus	incubi	stimulus	stimuli
addendum	addenda	desideratum	desiderata
agendum	agenda	erratum	errata
bacterium	bacteria	pudendum	pudenda
corrigendum	corrigenda	residuum	residua
datum	data		Saturnalia

N	N-s	N	N-s
amanuensis	amanuenses	metamorphosis	metamorphoses
analysis	analyses	nemesis	nemeses
antithesis	antitheses	neurosis	neuroses
axis	axes	oasis	oases
basis	bases	parenthesis	parentheses
codex	codices	psychosis	psychoses
crisis	crises	synopsis	synopses
diagnosis	diagnoses	synthesis	syntheses
ellipsis	ellipses	thesis	theses
hypothesis	hypotheses		
corpus	corpora	opus	opera

2. Greek word:

noumenon   noumena

3. French words:

madame   mesdames   monsieur   messieurs (Messrs.)

The commonest foreign words with regular and irregular plurals are:

1. Latin words:

N	N-s	N-s (irregular)
ameba	amebas	amebae
antenna	antennas	antennae
formula	formulas	formulae
lacuna	lacunas	lacunae
nebula	nebulas	nebulae
vertebra	vertebras	vertebrae
cactus	cactuses	cacti
colossus	colossuses	colossi
focus	focuses	foci
fungus	funguses	fungi
genius	geniuses	genii
gladiolus	gladioluses	gladioli
hippopotamus	hippopotamuses	hippopotami
incubus	incubuses	incubi

N-s	N-s	N-s (irregular)
literatus	literatuses	literati
nautilus	nautiluses	nautili
nucleus	nucleuses	nuclei
octopus	octopuses	octopi
radius	radiuses	radii
sarcophagus	sarcophaguses	sarcophagi
syllabus	syllabuses	syllabi
terminus	terminuses	termini
candelabrum	candelabrums	candelabra
compendium	compendiums	compendia
curriculum	curriculums	curricula
dictum	dictums	dicta
encomium	encomiums	encomia
gymnasium	gymnasiums	gymnasia
honorarium	honorariums	honoraria
medium	mediums	media
memorandum	memorandums	memoranda
millennium	millenniums	millennia
momentum	momentums	momenta
moratorium	moratoriums	moritoria
rostrum	rostrums	rostra
spectrum	spectrums	spectra
stadium	stadiums	stadia
stratum	stratums	strata
apex	apexes	apices
appendix	appendixes	appendices
aviatrix	aviatrixes	aviatrices
calyx	calyxes	calices
executrix	executrixes	executrices
index	indexes	indices
matrix	matrixes	matrices
vertex	vertexes	vertices
vortex	vortexes	vortices
genus	genuses	genera
apparatus	apparatuses	apparatus
census	censuses	census

N	**N-s**	**N-s (irregular)**
hiatus	hiatuses	hiatus
prospectus	prospectuses	prospectus
virus	viruses	virus

3. Greek words:

automaton	automatons	automata
criterion	criterions	criteria
phenomenon	phenomenons	phenomena
dogma	dogmas	dogmata
stigma	stigmas	stigmata

3. French words:

adieu	adieus	adieux
beau	beaus	beaux
bureau	bureaus	bureaux
chapeau	chapeaus	chapeaux
chateau	chateaus	chateaux
plateau	plateaus	plateaux
tableau	tableaus	tableaux
trousseau	trousseaus	trousseaux

4. Italian words:

bandit	bandits	banditti
basso	bassos	bassi
cello	cellos	celli
concerto	concertos	concerti
libretto	librettos	libretti
maestro	maestros	maestri
soprano	sopranos	soprani
tempo	tempos	tempi
virtuoso	virtuosos	virtuosi
dilettante	dilettantes	dilettanti

5. Hebrew words:

cherub	cherubs	cherubim
seraph	seraphs	seraphim

The following Latin words have a plural identical with the singular:

N	N-s
congeries	congeries
series	series
species	species

GENITIVES OF NOUNS: N-'s AND N-s'

ALL nouns except some already ending in -s may take an ending -'s which patterns in a quite different way from the plural. Nouns with -'s fit into the adjective position in the noun-group **A N John's mother** or **D A N the boy's mother.** The noun-group with **N-'s** is thus a variant of **D N N.** The -'s that we write represents a similar variety of spoken sounds as does the plural -s, though not exactly the same: **cat, cat's, cats, cats'; house, house's, houses, houses'.** Though there are irregular substitutes for the plural -s, there are no substitutes for -'s. The only variation is that when a noun already ends in -s or -es, we may stop with the first one and simply add the apostrophe. Which we do doesn't matter much; we say **the Jones' car** or **the Jones's car.** With plurals that already end in -s, we add the apostrophe: **those boys' mothers.** Other plurals take -'s: **the children's toys, the Magi's homage, a men's store.**

The apostrophe (') stands for nothing in speech; it is a signal for the eye. It occurs usually in a position before the headword in the noun-group pretty well marked off from the plural, and it is annoying and expensive to print. In present-day usage it is under attack not only from people who forget to put it in but from a number of powerful organizations concerned with printing costs. Chief among these is the United States Government Printing Office. The Printing Office has been dropping the apostrophe from place names: **Smith's Corners** becomes **Smiths Corners, Buzzard's Roost** becomes **Buzzards Roost,** and so on. Following this practice others have been dropping the mark from titles of all kinds: **Farmer's** or **Farmers' Bank** becomes **Farmers Bank; Bill's Cafe** becomes **Bills Cafe; Girls' School** becomes **Girls School;** and **Teachers' College** becomes **Teachers College.** The sound is not affected by the omission of the apostrophe.

A noun with the -'s attached to the base-form is said to be "genitive" or "possessive." Genitive is probably a better name for it, if as usual we do not try to read any meaning into the word but just take it as a name. Possessive seems to mean something too narrow for the uses of the form. The ending survives from the older stages of English when words were related to each other largely by sets of such endings; it has endured a continual slow decline in frequency since the Old English period. Two other patterns have taken over most of the load: for **D N-'s N the Government's office** we have **D N̶+ N the Government office** and **D N Prep N the office of the Government.** Choice among these three patterns is generally pretty free; native speakers may confidently depend upon the ear.

In speech the noun element in this genitive combination (the **N** in N-'s) may be a noun-cluster:

D	N	~~AP~~	-'s	N
a	friend	of my mother's		car
the	chairman	of the committee's		remarks

D	N	~~AC~~	-'s	N
the	man	who hit me	's	car

The cluster-pattern with the clause ending in a genitive is more common in speech than in writing, but it occurs.

N-'s occurs also as a noun-headword:

> **The butcher's is the third house.**
> **The definition is Webster's.**
> **He was a friend of my brother's.**

The typical changes in form which a noun may undergo appear in writing as **N boy, man; N-'s boy's, man's; N-s boys, men; N-s' boys', men's.** They combine with structure-words and patterns of order.

THE PERSONAL PRONOUNS

IN our pattern display of the language we have freely used such words as **he** and **she, him** and **her,** and **you** and **me** to perform the function of the noun. Whatever a noun can do in the utterance, one of these words can also do, though not always the same word. We may treat them as a kind of noun, a special kind different enough to be worth calling by a special name. We call them *personal pronouns,* or, for short, *pronouns.*

Most of the words in the language can be sorted into large classes about which we can make general statements that are good for almost all. But there is always a residue. Most nouns form the plural by adding **-s** to the base-form; **pen, pens;** but some nouns do it differently: **ox, oxen; man, men; alumnus, alumni.** Most verbs have four forms: **stew, stews, stewed, stewing;** some have five: **sing, sings, sang, singing, sung;** and some have three: **set, sets, setting.** Words that show some oddity in their shape or way of patterning are usually familiar words of common use that carry into Modern English some remnant of earlier stages of the language. **Man** is such a noun; **be** is such a verb. The pronouns are a fine group of similar relics.

In ancient times the pronouns fitted into the whole system of interlocking endings and changes in sound that made words work together and have meaning. As this system was eroded away, the pronouns were more resistant to change than most other words. They kept as a group more of the original distinctions in sound and form. They still keep distinctions; but change has not left the pronouns unaffected. The same forces that broke down the system as a whole have racked and readjusted the relationships among the pronouns—differently in different speech-communities. Today the pronouns are a set of separate words that fit in characteristic ways into the patterns of the modern utterance, not in exactly the same ways everywhere. We sketch here the ways of standard English writing.

The pronouns mainly serve as nouns in the sentence-patterns, but each has one or two forms which serve as determiners and fence the beginning of a noun-group: **my house, our old car.** The pronouns are rarely modified by adjectives, but they may be on occasion: **poor me.** They are seldom apposed in writing to another noun, though the pattern is common in speech: **that boy, he went right up to her.** They may have other nouns apposed to them: **I, the chairman of this meeting, demand order.** We can demonstrate their distribution in utterances by setting up two typical utterance-patterns: **N LV N Honesty is a virtue** and **D A N V N Prep N The**

young boy loves the girl at home. In these patterns we distribute the pronouns as they commonly occur.

I, My, Mine, *and* Me

We use **I, my, mine,** and **me** to represent in language the speaker of an utterance or the writer of a sentence. The person making the utterance refers in it to himself. The forms of **I** are distributed as follows:

N	LV	N	D A N	V	N	Prep N
I mine	am is, are		My young boy	loves	me. mine	for me for mine
It	is	I. me mine	mine eyes			

In general, **I** combines with the verb in the pattern **N V I go; I am going.** I, me, and mine may follow a linking verb in the pattern **N LV N It is I; It is me; It is mine.** Me and mine are used in complements. In the common speech **me** is often compounded with another noun or pronoun in the pattern **N V John and me came; I** is often compounded with another noun or pronoun after a preposition in the pattern **Prep N between you and I.** Neither of these uses appears much in standard writing. **Mine** is occasionally used as a determiner before a noun or adjective beginning with a vowel: **D N mine eyes; D A N mine old friend.** This is an archaic pattern, and rare.

We, Our, Ours, *and* Us

We use **we, our, ours,** and **us** to refer to a group which includes the speaker. **We** may refer to the speaker and one or more persons to whom he is speaking: **Catch hold; we have to move this. We** may refer to the speaker and one or more persons about whom he is speaking: **I should have called before we left without you. We** may have general or indefinite reference when we are talking about anybody, ourselves included: **We are not alone in the world.**

Kings, queens, editors, and reviewers of books and plays use **we** in writing to mean **I: We found the book lively.** A king or queen speaking today would probably use **I** unless speaking officially. It would be hard to find an editor who uses **we** for **I** in speech, even though he uses **we** for **I** in writing; many editors and reviewers these days simply write **I: I liked the book.**

N	ʟV	N	D	⊼	N	V	N	Prep	N
we	are		Our	young	boy	loves	us.	for	us
ours	is, are						ours	for	ours
It	is	we.							
		us							
		ours							

We combines with the verb in the pattern **N V We go, we are going. We, us,** and **ours** may follow a linking verb in the pattern **N ʟV N It is we; it is us; it is ours. Us** and **ours** are used in complements. In the common speech, other nouns are apposed to **us** in all patterns: **Us boys took the apples;** in careful or formal common speech, other nouns are apposed to **we** in all patterns: **We boys took the apples; They gave it to we girls.** In some dialects **ourn** substitutes for **ours** or alternates with it: **Them apples is ourn.**

You, Your, *and* Yours

We use **you, your,** and **yours** to represent or refer to a person spoken to or to persons spoken to. We use **you, your, yours** to refer to one or more people addressed as reader or readers. We also use **you** with general or indefinite reference when we are talking about anybody, ourselves included: **You can't take it with you.**

N	ʟV	N	D	⊼	N	V	N	Prep	N
you	are		Your	young	boy	loves	you.	for	you
yours	is, are						yours	for	yours
It	is	you.							
		yours							

In current standard writing, **you** is very simple: the forms **you** and **yours** pattern like almost any noun. Erosion of forms has made it a modern element in an ancient set of words. We must be prepared for alternate forms working in older ways: **thou, thy, thine, thee; you, your, yours,** and **ye.** These forms pattern as follows: **thou, thy, thine,** and **thee** are used to address one person; **you, your, yours,** and **ye** are used to address more than one. **Thou** selects special forms of the verb **be: thou art; thou wast, thou wert. Thou** also selects verb-forms with special endings: **thou goest, thou hast.** The religious group known as the Society of Friends or Quakers uses **thee** in place of **you** and **thou** in the pattern **N V** to address one person; it may or may not select: **thee is, thee are, thee has, thee have.**

N	LV	N	D	A	N	V	N	Prep	N
thou thine	art is, are		Thy	young	boy	loves	thee. thine	for for	thee thine
It	is	thou. thee thine							
you ye	are are		Your	young	boy	loves	you. ye	for for	you ye
It	is	you. ye yours						yours	for	yours

We must also be prepared for alternate forms working in different dialects; various speech-communities have carried the original forms down in different ways. In the South, **you-all** almost universally replaces **you** in the plural, with its variant **y'all.** Southerners hotly deny that they use **you-all** for one person; perhaps they don't. For **your** we often get **you-all's** or **y'all's: Is that y'all's car?** Southerners use the standard forms in writing, except to indicate local speech. In the Midland area, there are "you-uns and we-uns" dialects with complications too devious to go into here; and in the common speech here and there **yourn** alternates with **yours: Them apples is yourn.** All these variations represent various shufflings and developments of the ancient forms; none is to be sneered at by any humane cultivated person who has learned to distinguish attitudes toward language from attitudes toward the people using language, and who is sufficiently secure within himself to treat his fellow men with proper respect.

He, She, *and* It

When we come to **he, she,** and **it** and their other forms, we run into one of the peculiarities of English that give us insight into the uneasy adjustment between language and the world outside language. All the languages in the Indo-European family sort their nouns in terms of what is called "gender" into three groups, as in Latin and German (masculine, feminine, and neuter) or two, as in French (masculine and feminine). These classes are based on form and not on sex. Bantu, an African language, has at least ten gender classifications of nouns. Processes within the linguistic systems have reduced the three genders of Latin to two genders in its descendant, French, but left German with the three it began with. The same processes have wiped the gender classification right out of the English nouns, except for a few relics which hang on, as usual: **heiress, actress,** and some borrowings like **aviatrix** and **ballerina.**

Yet we still have **he, she,** and **it** in the language serving in utterances as substitutes for other nouns and keeping the distinctions in form that once referred to the gender classifications of nouns. As these words have shaken down in modern use, **he** and **she** substitute for nouns which refer to human beings, forcing us to decide whether in fact—not merely in the system of the language—we mean a male or a female. This basic decision in our use of language opens up to us the possibility of extending the distinction beyond people to animals, whether or not the noun specifically designates sex. Thus we may use **he** as substitute for the nouns **buck, bull, steer,** and **drake;** we may use **she** as substitute for the nouns **doe, cow, heifer,** and **duck.** Or we may follow these nouns with **it.** We may follow the nouns **bear, deer,** or **animal** with **it** or (when in fact we are distinguishing male and female) with **he** or **she.** For the nouns **baby, child,** or **infant** we may extend this freedom of choice to humans, using **it** as a substitute or (when we wish to distinguish male and female) **he** or **she.**

When we get outside the human race to things, like **boat, car** or **airplane,** we generally use **it;** and when nouns refer to ideas like **beauty, justice, faith,** or **quiet,** we also use **it.** When we want to use our imaginations and treat these things and ideas as if they were males or females, "personifying" them or treating them like persons, we can use **he** or **she** (now usually **she**): **I lost control of the car, and she slid a hundred feet. Faith is a gentle virtue; she steals quietly into our hearts.**

Otherwise, for all nouns and for all phrases and clauses working as nouns, we use **it** as substitute: **Give me the ball; I want it. A figure approached him; he couldn't make it out. He knew what he wanted, and he intended to have it.** We find **it** used in other ways that take it into more general use than **he** or **she:** as a starter of sentences: **It's raining. It's cold. It was only that he didn't understand.** Here **it** serves as **N** in the **N V** pattern, but not as a substitute for a preceding noun. **It** often serves as substitute for a whole preceding utterance: **I was going to have that hole dug and a crock put in, but it cost too much.**

N	LV	N	D	A	N	V	N	Prep	N
he his	is is, are		His	young	boy	loves	him. his	for for	him his
It	is	he. him his							
she hers	is is, are		her				her hers	for for	her hers
It	is	she. her hers							
it its	is is, are		its				it its	for for	it its
It	is	it. its							

In ancient times **it** had the forms **it, his,** and **him,** and so we find in the King James Bible of 1611 **The salt has lost his savor.** At present it has the forms **it** and **its**. **Its** is a relatively new form which has not pushed into the whole range of patterns where **his** and **hers** operate.

They, Their, Theirs, *and* Them

We do not carry over into the plural the distinctions between man, animal, thing, and idea or between male and female that must be expressed when the pronouns **he, she,** and **it** substitute for the base-form of the noun. **They, their, theirs,** and **them** substitute for plural nouns referring to people, animals, things, and ideas indiscriminately and have done so since the earliest times. Like **we** and **you, they** is used with general or indefinite reference when we are talking about unspecified persons: **They say that the country is a good place to live in. They're starting a new housing project on Base Line Road.** **They** is used to refer to unidentified persons involved in a preceding statement: **He didn't get the job. They thought he was too young. That company went broke; they just couldn't compete.**

N	LV	N	D	A	N	V	N	Prep N
they	are		Their	young	boy	loves	them.	for them
theirs	is, are						theirs	for theirs
It	is	they.						
		them						
		theirs						

Besides **we, you,** and **they,** a number of words structuring as nouns in every respect are used with indefinite reference: the singular words are **one, anyone, someone, everyone, none, everybody, somebody, nobody, each,** and **another;** the plural words are **all, both, few, some, many.** They do not pattern like the pronouns, and we only mention them here to exclude them. In this respect as in others, the language is not limited to one or two ways of saying the same thing, but spreads the load so that we choose among alternatives. We don't often hit off such a masterpiece as the fellow's who said, "A person doesn't like to see their mother die. I don't care who you are. We love our mothers." But there is nothing in the patterns of the language to prevent us.

We can usefully classify the pronouns among the nouns as a special subclass or kind of noun distinguished by its elaborate array of forms and by the limited way in which these forms enter into patterns. The intimacy and familiarity of the pronouns brings about their diversity; from common origins they come down to us at the center of the habit-complex of each speech-community. By the mold the personal pronouns impress early on the perceptions of the child, each community teaches him how to see himself in relation to people and things and how to relate the language to his perceptions. It is fascinating to watch an infant grappling with concepts of **me** and **you,** and fascinating, too, to watch adults teaching him by their unreflecting conversation, then muddling the matter for him when they try to help. The kindergarten teacher substitutes "**Miss Joan** wants you to do this" for "**I** want you to do this"; the baffled child can only conclude that adults are curiouser and curiouser. Pronoun use, so early learned, is difficult to supplant; the uses of other speech-communities are difficult even to hear, and the pronoun systems of other languages like Bantu and Eskimo constitute strange and unreal worlds.

INSIDE THE NOUN

THE noun is a unit in the sentence which takes on certain endings and joins with other words in patterns to make up an overall arrangement that has meaning. The sentence handles each noun in the way the post office handles a package. The post office does not care what is in the package, but the sender cares and so does the person who gets it. The package is wrapped and has stamps and an address on it to tell what to do with it. Sentences operate without much regard for the internal structure of the noun. As long as it is a noun, sentences handle it as they handle any noun. Just as a package coming through the mail can be opened and inspected, a noun can be opened and examined to see how it is made up. What, then, is the noun? What kind of package does it make up?

We can start by dividing nouns into two kinds: nouns that can be taken apart into smaller units that carry a portion of the meaning, and nouns that cannot. Some nouns like **day, hill, desk, car,** and **dish** cannot be taken apart; the word is already the smallest unit. In speech it is a morpheme, the minimal unit of syntax. Cut it apart and you get phonemes; cut it apart in writing and you get letters. The word is the package.

When we dig into the kind of noun that can be dissected, we find smaller units within it; we have to cut them apart again to get down to the letters. Sometimes these units are free forms that can appear separately like **street** and **car** in **streetcar, book** and **case** in **bookcase, desk** and **set** in **deskset,** and **know** and **how** in **know-how.** These compound nouns take a primary or heavy stress on the first unit. Not all of them appear as one word in writing; often we have to choose among three ways of dealing with them. We can write them separately, as **ice cream.** We can join them with a hyphen, as **ice-cream;** or we can run them together, as **icecream.** Dictionary writers often puzzle about entering these words. Sometimes they have a clear tradition to follow, as with **telephone girl** and **steamboat,** but with many words large groups of writers follow each of the three practices. How we write them makes no difference to their sound.

Behind the sketchy line of written English always stands the intimately grasped complex of speech-signals, so that we read written forms against our experience, innocently and unreflectingly. Compound nouns begin in the noun-group pattern **D Ｎ N** with its characteristic stress pattern: a heavy stress on the modifying noun or its stressed syllable, and a secondary stress on the headword. In the compound noun the stress is lowered to tertiary or light stress; no matter how we write it, we have a unit. We test them against the ear: **There is a gréen rôom back there; we're eating in the Gréen Roòm. There was nó bôdy in the house, and nóbòdy answered when I called. Because he stood like a stóne wâll, they called him Stónewàll Jackson.**

We have a number of compounds ending in **one: someone, no-one, anyone;** in **body: somebody, nobody, anybody;** and in **thing: something, anything, nothing.** We have a number in which the first element is a pronoun-form, and the second is **self** or **selves: myself, yourself, himself, herself, itself; ourselves, yourselves, themselves.** In the common speech we have two others: **hisself, theirselves.** These two point up the whimsy of fashion; they are made on the model of **myself, yourself,** and **ourselves,** but they have been crowded out of standard written English by the two intruders **himself** and **themselves.** Why?

Besides these compounds of free forms, we have many nouns made up of a word—usually a verb or an adjective—that occurs separately in other uses, and a bound ending that never occurs alone. A good example is **breakage** from the free verb **break** and a noun-ending **-age.** The ending is a bound form. When it is attached to a free verb or adjective, the whole unit works in the sentence as a noun. Similar endings combine with verbs and nouns to form adjectives and with nouns and adjectives to form verbs and adverbs. Such combinations produce that flexible interchange of units which permits the language to meet the needs of expression.

Verbs into Nouns

The following endings unite with free verbs to form combinations that work as nouns: **-age, -ance, -ant, -ation, -ence, -er, -ion, -ment.** It would be tempting to say something about the complicated adjustments of sound that fuse free form and bound form together; it is best, perhaps, simply to present the words as they are written. But try them against your ear.

ENDING	VERB	NOUN
-age	**append**	**appendage**
	break	**breakage**
	seep	**seepage**
-ance	**appear**	**appearance**
	comply	**compliance**
	repent	**repentance**
-ant	**ascend**	**ascendant**
	assist	**assistant**
	serve	**servant**
-ation	**combine**	**combination**
	flirt	**flirtation**
	narrate	**narration**

ENDING	VERB	NOUN
-ence	emerge	emergence
	subsist	subsistence
	superintend	superintendence
-er	buy	buyer
	do	doer
	hate	hater
-ion	abdicate	abdication
	construct	construction
	rebel	rebellion
-ment	abate	abatement
	lodge	lodgment
	treat	treatment

Language seems to go by "winner take all," so that an active principle exerts a kind of magnetism, drawing to itself elements that a historian would explain on other grounds. The speakers of a language are not historians; they take it as it comes. The pattern of word-formation by which a verb and an ending become a noun is so strong that when we have a noun with one of these endings, we freely reverse the process and form a verb from the noun. Thus from **editor** we have **edit**; from **butler,** we have **buttle**; from **sculptor** we have **sculp** and **sculpt**; and from **administration** (itself formed from **administer**), we have **administrate.**

Some verbs are converted to nouns by changes in sound. Thus we have the following pairs:

VERB	NOUN	VERB	NOUN	VERB	NOUN
advise	advice	deceive	deceit	complain	complaint
house	house	receive	receipt	bequeath	bequest
give	gift	bleed	blood	behave	behavior
				save	savior

Some verbs become nouns and undergo a change in meaning by a shift in accent:

VERB	NOUN	VERB	NOUN	VERB	NOUN
colléct	cóllect	fermént	férment	recórd	récord
compréss	cómpress	permít	pérmit	refúse	réfuse
confíne	cónfine	prodúce	próduce	reprínt	réprint
contráct	cóntract	purpórt	púrport	subjéct	súbject
digést	dígest	rebél	rébel	tormént	tórment

Adjectives into Nouns

Adjectives are converted to nouns by means of the following endings: **-acy, -cy, -dom, -eer, -ery, -hood, -ism, -ist, -ity, -ty, -ness, -th.**

ENDING	ADJECTIVE	NOUN
-acy, -cy	accurate	accuracy
	elegant	elegancy
	fluent	fluency
	private	privacy
	supreme	supremacy
-dom	free	freedom
	wise	wisdom
-eer	private	privateer
-ery	brave	bravery
	droll	drollery
	fine	finery
-hood	false	falsehood
	hard	hardihood
	likely	likelihood
-ism	American	Americanism
	national	nationalism
	social	socialism
-ist	American	Americanist
	rational	rationalist
	social	socialist

-ity, -ty	acid	acidity
	actual	actuality
	clear	clarity
	entire	entirety
	novel	novelty
	versatile	versatility
-ness	fleet	fleetness
	gentle	gentleness
	good	goodness
	genuine	genuineness
-th	true	truth
	warm	warmth
	wide	width

2. The Verb

VERBS enter into the combination **N V This car stalls, V N Stop the car,** and serve as marker, helper, or headword in the verb-group: **The boys have been gone.** Verbs undergo more changes of form than nouns, adjectives, and adverbs do, but even verbs have kept few of the endings or other changes they once had. The commonest verb of all, **be,** has the largest number of separate forms (eight): **am, is, are, was, were, be, been, being. Be** has to be treated separately. Verbs like **break** have five forms: **break, breaks, broke, breaking, broken.** Most verbs have four forms: **start, starts, started, starting;** a small group like **set** have three: **set, sets, setting;** and the modal auxiliaries like **can** have two: **can, could;** or like **must** have one.

The forms our verbs have—no matter how many—have been sifted out of a larger number they once had. Century by century the forms of each verb have been cut down, though not in the same way in all speech-communities. Different dialects starting with much the same set of forms have retained and let go different ones. The regular verb-pattern (**V, V-s, V-ed, V-ing**) has pressed all irregular verbs to join the club. Some have and some have not. In written English, some three hundred verbs which might have become modern five-part verbs like **break** have been cut down to about sixty-five; the others have gone out of use or become regular.

We have to remember the continuity of speech-communities through the centuries and the continuity of language-habits. People grow up, marry, have children, grow old, and die. Their children mature, marry, and have children; each generation hands its speech-habits down to the next, but always a minute imprecision in the transmission makes the speech of each community gradually change. Communities influence one another; dialects merge; some are passed to more and more speakers, some to fewer and fewer. Some are used at one time or place by people of prestige and power, at another by the poor and the outcast. Like people, dialects have their ups and downs. Our written language is based on the dialect of London, which became an important city and a "mother area" of English during the thirteenth century and has remained so ever since. Our writing broke off somewhat from British writing in the seventeenth century, and our spoken dialects broke off from various British dialects and took their own courses.

The same reduction of verb-forms has occurred in all dialects. Whole verbs disappear from some and remain in others; specific forms drop from some and stay in others; sounds change in different communities. Verbs leave one class and join another, stand firm, or, from different original forms, develop into those we now use. Simplification of forms shows itself in a multitude of ways; we find, within general similarity, many specific differences.

All native speakers of English naturally use the verb-forms of their own speech-communities. Generally the difference is not one of meaning, and meaning gives us little trouble. Whether we hear **He isn't home, He ain't home,** or **He an't home,** we understand well enough. Children understand a teacher's choice of forms though they speak others. They understand **They gave us those pencils** though they may repeat the utterance as **They give us them pencils.** Social attitudes do give us trouble. Each speech-community is either lurkingly hostile or openly antagonistic to forms used by outsiders. Local people prefer local ways and consider others to be foreign, "fancy," or unnatural. Educated people prefer the forms used in writing and reject others as marks of ignorance and illiteracy.

Differences in pronoun and verb usage grate more on the ear than almost any others and may be more easily drilled than any others. There is no gain in abandoning the speech of your own people, but there may be personal and professional gain in mastering other forms so that you can use them naturally and easily in the circumstances that call for them. A bagful of alternate locutions under your control is an aid to social mobility. It is worth while at least to write the forms used in writing in order to say what you have to say without stirring up hostility, unless you have some special reason for stirring it up. Learning these forms increases your range and control of language.

THE PRINCIPAL PARTS OF VERBS

COMPARED to verbs in some other languages, the English verb has so few forms that all of them can be listed together. They range in number from the eight forms of **be** to the single form of **must.** The naïve speaker, who uses language as naturally as he breathes, may never think of verbs in these terms, but if we are to understand the system of language, we must inspect the sets of units by which we communicate. We offer here the forms of current standard written English, listed as though all verbs had five parts, for economy and convenience. The "base" is the form under which the verb is entered in the dictionary.

Be, Have, *and* Do

Base	V	V-s	V-ed	V-ing	V-ed/en
be	be	is	was	being	been
	am		were		
	are				

Base					
V	V-s	V-ed	V-ing	V-ed/en
have	has	had	having	had
do	does	did	doing	done

The Four-part Verbs

Most verbs follow the pattern of this one. They have four distinct forms:

Base				
V	**V-s**	**V-ed**	**V-ing**	**V-ed/en**
play	plays	played	playing	played

Some four-part verbs change the vowel sound to form **V-ed;** some of these have final **-t** instead of **-d:**

Base				
V	**V-s**	**V-ed**	**V-ing**	**V-ed/en**
creep	creeps	crept	creeping	crept
keep	keeps	kept	keeping	kept
sleep	sleeps	slept	sleeping	slept
sweep	sweeps	swept	sweeping	swept
weep	weeps	wept	weeping	wept
deal	deals	dealt	dealing	dealt
leave	leaves	left	leaving	left
mean	means	meant	meaning	meant
hear	hears	heard	hearing	heard
say	says	said	saying	said
flee	flees	fled	fleeing	fled
feel	feels	felt	feeling	felt
sell	sells	sold	selling	sold
tell	tells	told	telling	told
lose	loses	lost	losing	lost
buy	buys	bought	buying	bought
bereave	bereaves	bereft	bereaving	bereft

Some four-part verbs change final **-d** to **-t** to form **V-ed:**

Base				
V	**V-s**	**V-ed**	**V-ing**	**V-ed/en**
bend	bends	bent	bending	bent
lend	lends	lent	lending	lent
rend	rends	rent	rending	rent
send	sends	sent	sending	sent
spend	spends	spent	spending	spent
built	builds	built	building	built

Some four-part verbs change the vowel and drop a sound to form **V-ed:**

beseech	beseeches	besought	beseeching	besought
bring	brings	brought	bringing	brought
catch	catches	caught	catching	caught
make	makes	made	making	made
seek	seeks	sought	seeking	sought
teach	teaches	taught	teaching	taught
think	thinks	thought	thinking	thought

In every age, for no particular reason, one principle of language is favored over others. The drift toward it may seem to grip the actions of most people, but if something occurs to reverse the drift, there is no reason why it cannot become a drift away again. At present the **V, V-s, V-ed, V-ing** setup dominates our verbs; we can tell how much by looking at the mistakes of children and at the way we make new verbs. A child will say **He gived me that; I runned home,** until he learns the forms **gave** and **ran** one at a time. He follows the most common pattern that he hears. He learns in time that where he can use one form **played** in the utterances **I played with Johnny** and **I've played with Johnny,** he cannot make one from **catch** and use it in the same way. People laugh at him and urge him to use **caught.** He may come up with **I catched Johnny** and **I've catched Johnny** before he gets the forms straightened out. He is always pushed by the regular verbs.

When we make up new verbs we follow the dominant pattern. Thus the invention of the insecticide *dichlorodiphenyltrichloroethane* gives us the letters **DDT** which we use as a noun: **Get me a can of DDT.** Then we use **DDT** as a verb: **I have to DDT the kitchen.** From here we follow the pattern: **She DDT's her kitchen; I DDTed the kitchen; I have DDTed the kitchen.** Even a new verb which sounds like one of the five-part verbs still follows the four-part verbs in use. We have the five-part verb **sing: sing, sings, sang, singing, sung.** The new verb **ping** does not become **ping, pings, pang, pinging, pung,** but **ping, pings, pinged, pinging.** We do not say **The ball pang on the glass** or **has pung on the glass;** we say **The ball pinged** or **has pinged on the glass.** Sometimes the reverse pull of the five-part verbs works on a four-part verb, as with **dive, dives, dived, diving,** which picks up a new **V-ed** form **dove** like **drove,** so that we now have **dive, dives, dived** or **dove, diving,** and **dived. Dive** is an exception showing a little strength in a weak counterpull.

The Five-part Verbs

In Old English there were three kinds of verbs called "weak" which have all come together in our modern four-part verbs, and seven classes of verbs called "strong" which have all come together in our modern five-part verbs. These "strong" verbs, instead of adding **-ed, -d,** or **-t** to the base to form **V-ed,** change the vowel as in **drive, drove** to form **V-ed** and change the vowel again and add **-en** to form **V-ed/en,** as **driven.** The seven classes, sadly cut down in number, are merely seven groups of irregular verbs pretty much alike within each group. We offer here a reasonably complete list of these verbs as they are usually used in written English.

You may have grown up to use other forms than these or to use these forms differently; you may say, **They give me that yesterday when I come, and I taken it home with me. I've often went there; I seen a fellow there I'm sure I've saw somewhere before.** You may make no distinction in sound between **sit, set,** and **sat;** you may wonder why all the fuss about **lie** and **lay.** These differences in verb-forms grate on the ear of people who know or who have learned the forms of standard written English; they use the standard forms (like spelling) as a crude way of sifting desirable people from the undesirable. They have been taught—and they often believe—that people who use non-standard forms in non-standard ways are illiterate. You only need to know something like this about people in order to know what to do, and there is no sense living and dressing like a cultivated person, enjoying books, music, art, and the theater if your use of non-standard verb-forms is a threat to civilized society. You ought to learn the standard forms so that you can use them at will when you write or speak to people who care about them. No one differs on many points, and you can find the forms on which you differ by testing yourself against the following pattern and then drilling the standard forms in that pattern until they come naturally and ring naturally on your ear.

N V	N V-ed	N v V-ed/en
Today I come	Yesterday I came	I have often come
Today I take	Yesterday I took	I have often taken

Possibly you say **I've seen** or **I've taken** without sounding your
v. Sound it out strong.

Base V	V-s	V-ed	V-ing	V-ed/en
abide	abides	abode, abided	abiding	abided
bite	bites	bit	biting	bitten
drive	drives	drove	driving	driven
ride	rides	rode	riding	ridden
rise	rises	rose	rising	risen
shine	shines	shone, shined	shining	shone, shined
slide	slides	slid	sliding	slid, slidden
smite	smites	smote	smiting	smitten
stride	strides	strode	striding	stridden
strike	strikes	struck	striking	struck, stricken
thrive	thrives	throve, thrived	thriving	thrived, thriven
write	writes	wrote	writing	written
choose	chooses	chose	choosing	chosen
cleave	cleaves	cleft, cleaved, clove	cleaving	cleaved, cloven
fly	flies	flew	flying	flown
freeze	freezes	froze	freezing	frozen
begin	begins	began	beginning	begun
bind	binds	bound	binding	bound
cling	clings	clung	clinging	clung
drink	drinks	drank	drinking	drunk
fling	flings	flung	flinging	flung
fight	fights	fought	fighting	fought
grind	grinds	ground	grinding	ground
ring	rings	rang	ringing	rung
run	runs	ran	running	run
shrink	shrinks	shrank, shrunk	shrinking	shrunk, shrunken
sing	sings	sang	singing	sung
sink	sinks	sank, sunk	sinking	sunk, sunken
slink	slinks	slunk	slinking	slunk
spin	spins	spun	spinning	spun
spring	springs	sprang	springing	sprung

Base

V	V-s	V-ed	V-ing	V-ed/en
sting	stings	stung	stinging	stung
stink	stinks	stank, stunk	stinking	stunk
string	strings	strung	stringing	strung
swim	swims	swam	swimming	swum
swing	swings	swung	swinging	swung
win	wins	won	winning	won
wind	winds	wound	winding	wound
wring	wrings	wrung	wringing	wrung
bear	bears	bore	bearing	born, borne
break	breaks	broke	breaking	broken
come	comes	came	coming	come
steal	steals	stole	stealing	stolen
tear	tears	tore	tearing	torn
wear	wears	wore	wearing	worn
bid	bids	bade	bidding	bidden
chide	chides	chid, chided	chiding	chid, chidden, chided
dig	digs	dug	digging	dug
eat	eats	ate	eating	eaten
forget	forgets	forgot	forgetting	forgot, forgotten
get	gets	got	getting	got, gotten
give	gives	gave	giving	given
hide	hides	hid	hiding	hid, hidden
lie	lies	lay	lying	lain
see	sees	saw	seeing	seen
sit	sits	sat	sitting	sat
speak	speaks	spoke	speaking	spoken
stave	staves	stove	staving	stove
tread	treads	trod	treading	trodden
weave	weaves	wove	weaving	woven
draw	draws	drew	drawing	drawn
forsake	forsakes	forsook	forsaking	forsaken
shake	shakes	shook	shaking	shaken
slay	slays	slew	slaying	slain
stand	stands	stood	standing	stood

Base				
V	**V-s**	**V-ed**	**V-ing**	**V-ed/en**
swear	swears	swore	swearing	sworn
take	takes	took	taking	taken
wake	wakes	woke,	waking	waked, woken,
		wakened		wakened
beat	beats	beat	beating	beaten
behold	beholds	beheld	beholding	beheld
blow	blows	blew	blowing	blown
fall	falls	fell	falling	fallen
grow	grows	grew	growing	grown
hang	hangs	hung, hanged	hanging	hung, hanged
hold	holds	held	holding	held
know	knows	knew	knowing	known
throw	throws	threw	throwing	thrown

Three-part Verbs

A few verbs like **set** have only three forms: **set, sets, setting:**

Base				
V	**V-s**	**V-ed**	**V-ing**	**V-ed/en**
bid	bids	bid	bidding	bid
burst	bursts	burst	bursting	burst
cast	casts	cast	casting	cast
cost	costs	cost	costing	cost
hit	hits	hit	hitting	hit
hurt	hurts	hurt	hurting	hurt
let	lets	let	letting	let
put	puts	put	putting	put
rid	rids	rid	ridding	rid
set	sets	set	setting	set
shed	sheds	shed	shedding	shed
shut	shuts	shut	shutting	shut
slit	slits	slit	slitting	slit
split	split	split	splitting	split
spread	spreads	spread	spreading	spread
thrust	thrusts	thrust	thrusting	thrust

Compound verbs formed from **cast,** like **broadcast** or **forecast,** may appear either as three-part or four-part verbs. The pull seems to be toward the four-part system, probably because the compounds have more than one syllable: **broadcasted, forecasted.**

THE MODAL AUXILIARIES

A FEW verbs used mainly as markers of verb-groups have only two forms; most of these are matched by a separate verb based on the **V-ed** form; this verb has only the one form. We call this set the modal auxiliaries; their use is treated in Chapter 9.

V	V-s	V-ed	V-ing	V-ed/en
can		could		
could				
may		might		
might				
must		must		
ought (to)				
shall		should		
should				
will		would		
would				

INSIDE THE VERB

THE verb is a unit in the sentence which takes on certain endings or other changes in form and joins with other words in patterns to make up overall arrangements that have meaning. The sentence handles the verb as it does the noun without much regard for its internal structure or for its individual meaning, treating one verb in the way it handles any verb. We now look into this unit to see how it is made up.

Some verbs, like **eat, drink, stand, fall, walk, drive, learn,** and **leave** are simple; they cannot be taken apart into smaller units except as phonemes in speech and letters in writing.

Many forms used as nouns are also used as verbs. As nouns they serve as **N** in the noun-cluster and as **N-s** and **N-'s: the left hand,**

both hands, a hand's turn. As verbs they serve as verb or as head-word in the verb-group: **I hand you a book; she hands you a book; she will hand you a book.** They usually take on the endings of the four-part verb. Words used as both noun and verb that take on the endings of the three-part verb, like **thrust,** or the four-part verb, like **bite,** probably began as verbs and transferred to the noun use.

Noun		Verb				
		V	V-s	V-ed	V-ing	V-ed/en
N	hand	hand	hands	handed	handing	handed
N-s	hands					
N	arm	arm	arms	armed	arming	armed
N-s	arms					
N	room	room	rooms	roomed	rooming	roomed
N-s	rooms					
N	bottle	bottle	bottles	bottled	bottling	bottled
N-s	bottles					

This transfer of function is very easy in modern English. It is a fruitful way of making individual forms do double duty in utter-ances. Without any internal change the word occurs in the position of noun or verb with the typical markers and endings either one takes on. Sometimes we are hard put to it to tell which use came first; most of the time the question does not come up. This is a free change of function.

The complicated history of English gives us a number of ways of forming verbs and a long list of words made up in the past in all these ways. The means of forming words, however, are more important to us than a list of words already formed; for as time passes, our society changes and we change with it. We meet new things and have new things to say; moreover, we are constantly losing interest in matters that once gripped everyone's attention. Person by person, community by community, we lose touch with words outside our interest and knowledge, so that much of the vocabulary listed in any dictionary is dead to us, just history. We may laugh at the Army's new words **embus, debus, disembus,** and

re-embus (for putting soldiers on and off a bus); but these words represent active use of familiar processes of word-formation that anyone can employ. If the words serve anyone but their inventors, they will be picked up by others; if not, they will be forgotten. Individually they are unimportant; quite important is the way they are brought into being.

New verbs may be identical in their base-form with the original word, or they may change their appearance by adding a prefix, an ending, or both. The German language employs one **to-V** ending for all verbs; even those formed from nouns add this characteristic ending, as in **Bad** ('bath'), **baden** ('bathe'); **Bau** ('construction'), **bauen** ('to construct'); and **Schere** ('scissors'), **scheren** ('to cut with a scissors'). English has four characteristic verb endings, **-ate, -en, -fy, -ize (-ise).** By no means must we assume that all verbs must have a characteristic mark of this kind. English also uses prefixes like **be-, contra-, -em, -en, pre-, re-,** and **un-** to make verbs.

We make verbs from nouns, adverbs, and interjections without changing the form of the original word to get the **to-V** form of the verb: from nouns, as in **contact, house, iron, place, telephone, water (to water the milk);** from adverbs, as in **to down an opponent, to up a price, to yes, to no, to ad lib;** and from interjections, as in **to hem and haw, to shush, to wow.**

We make verbs by adding endings to nouns, as in **carbonate, chlorinate, hydrogenate; beautify, classify, fishify; lengthen, strengthen; atomize, burglarize, carbonize, concertize, sermonize.** We make verbs by adding endings to adjectives, as in **blacken, harden, roughen, worsen; simplify, Frenchify; Americanize, Christianize, immortalize, sterilize, vitalize.**

We make verbs by adding prefixes to nouns, as in **acknowledge; bedew, begem, bejewel; debunk, dehorn, delouse, derail; embody, emmew; encamp, encoach, entrain.** We make verbs by adding prefixes to adjectives, as in **belittle, disable, enable, endear.** We make verbs by adding prefixes to verbs, as in **commingle, contraindicate, desegregate, disrobe, implant, maladminister, preheat, replay, unquote.** We make verbs by adding a prefix and an ending, as in **devitalize, embolden, encapsulate.** We also change the sound of a noun to produce a verb like **strive** from **strife.** Most of the verbs we make are four-part verbs, because the four-part verb is the most frequent and the most general in use.

Verb-adverb Combinations

One common way of making verbs uses a set of familiar verbs like **come, get, give, look, put, hold,** and **draw,** and a set of adverbs that have the same form as prepositions: **up, over, through, in, on, out,** and the like: **get up, give over, look on, put up, hold in,** and **draw out.** The possibilities of these combinations are unlimited; they are grasped by any speaker of English regardless of his dialect or his education. When a noun follows the verb in the pattern **V N,** the adverb may follow either the verb or the noun, giving **He put his idea over** or **He put over his idea. He saw through the difficulty** and **He saw the difficulty through** are different patterns, and not interchangeable. Since most of these verb-adverb combinations are worked out in speech and polished in conversation, their meaning is usually clear in writing, and they give an effect of closeness to speech-patterns.

3. and 4. The Adjective and the Adverb

ADJECTIVES and adverbs are word-classes partly distinct from each other in form and occurrence and partly overlapping; adverbs, moreover, overlap with some prepositions. Adjectives limit nouns; adverbs limit verbs or whole utterances. Adjectives are relatively fixed in position; adverbs, as we saw in Chapter 9, can go into almost any chink in the utterance. When a class of words like the adverbs has some forms in common with other classes, we check to see which may be most constant in performance. Adjectives occur in the noun-group in the patterns **A N green trees** and **D A N the old house.** Prepositions are constant in the pattern **Prep N in trouble.** Form alone will not tell us. Many adverbs end in **-ly,** like **quickly, hardly,** but so do some adjectives, like **lovely, manly. Hard, fast,** and **slow** are adjectives in **hard money, fast women,** and **slow train;** they are adverbs in **think hard, drive fast,** and **go slow. Quick** is an adjective in **quick look,** an adverb in **look quick. Over** is an adverb in **get over an illness,** a preposition in **get over the fence.** We say **look quick, look quickly; drive slow, drive slowly.** These short, familiar words that have to be listed among both the adjectives and the adverbs come down to us from ancient times; they are rightly used when they ring right on the ear.

THE INTENSIFIERS

SHORT adjectives and adverbs like **hard, strong, slow,** and **quick** take the endings **-er** and **-est:**

D	A̶	N
the	hard	play
the	harder	play
the	hardest	play

N	V	A̶
the boys	play	hard
the boys	play	harder
the boys	play	hardest

We may call these endings *intensifiers;* they show three levels of intensity of the quality named in the adjective or adverb. The endings **-er** and **-est** come down to us, like most, from older stages of the language when it communicated meaning mainly by means of such endings. They once were attached to almost any adjective, as **beautiful, beautifuler, beautifulest.** Modern English has developed a set of structure-words which almost exactly parallels these endings: **beautiful, more beautiful, most beautiful; quickly, more quickly, most quickly.** We are inclined to use these structure-words for adverbs and adjectives longer than one syllable; they press in on even the most familiar short words: **more brave than me, more blond than you.**

In any use the adjectives and adverbs have a little elbowroom before and after for intensifiers. If we are in doubt whether the modifier of the headword in a noun-group is an adjective or noun, we may test to see whether it can be intensified. We say **a fire department** but not **a firer department; a big department** and **a bigger department;** we say **a retail store** but not **a more retail store; a handsome store** and **a more handsome store.** With the intensifying endings we are held down to three degrees: **big, bigger, biggest.** With the structure-words marking off the space before adjectives and adverbs for intensifiers, the modern trend toward word-groups gives us almost endless possibilities of shading the force of an adjective or adverb before we reach the word itself. In that position a number of words may occur and several words may combine. We mark the intensifiers **I** in the patterns.

D	I	A̶	I	N
an		abundant		life
a	very	abundant		life
a	more	abundant		life
a	most	abundant		life
a	much more	abundant		life
a	very much more	abundant		life
a	not so very much more	abundant		life

D	I	A̶	I	N
a		pretty		girl
a	very	pretty		girl
a		pretti	er	girl
a	much	pretti	er	girl
the		pretti	est	girl
a	very much	pretti	er	girl
a	somewhat	pretti	er	girl
a	tiny little wee bit	pretti	er	girl

In writing, there has been some feeling that we should not combine **more** and **most** with the intensifying endings, but speech is somewhat freer—or more free—than writing, and the speakers of English have not hesitated to combine pre-intensifiers with post-intensifying endings for more emphatic effect: **a more wickeder woman; the most unkindest cut of all; He drove a little more faster than I could.** Adverbs are often used in this intensifying position to put other qualifications on adverbs and adjectives: **an unusually pretty girl, a really faster car.**

When the way is opened for a word to carry a function, a group of words may serve. In this intensifying position almost any word with its own qualifiers, giving up for the moment its right to be a star actor as headword, can fill a supporting part and modify another. We have merely illustrated the finely shaded discriminations of group intensifiers; they are much more extensive than the intensifying endings, limited to three degrees, could convey.

Such words as **hard, harder, hardest**—either adjective or adverb
—set a pattern which is adhered to by several irregular words.
These do not add **-er** and **-est** to the base, but switch to a different
base:

A	A$_v$	A/ A$_v$-er	A/ A$_v$-est
good		**better**	**best**
	well	**better**	**best**
bad		**worse**	**worst**
	badly	**worse**	**worst**
far	**far**	**farther**	**farthest**
		further	**furthest**
old		**elder**	**eldest**
		older	**oldest**
little	**little**	**less**	**least**

Some words still use an old form **-most** in the place of the **-est**
ending:

A	A$_v$	A/ A$_v$-er	A/ A$_v$-est
eastern			**easternmost**
western			**westernmost**
northern			**northernmost**
southern			**southernmost**
end			**endmost**
far		**farther**	**farthermost**
		further	**furthermost**
fore			**foremost**
hind		**hinder**	**hindermost**
		in	**inner**	**innermost**
low		**lower**	**lowermost**
			lowest
top			**topmost**
	under		**undermost**
	up	**upper**	**uppermost**

INSIDE THE ADJECTIVE

WHEN we dissect the adjective, we find as we did with the noun
and the verb some simple forms that we cannot cut into: **big, small,
hard, soft, green,** etc.

Many adjectives are made by adding one of the following endings to a noun: **-able, -al, -an, -ar, -ary, -ate, -ed, -en, -ful, -ic, -ical, -ine, -ish, -less, -like, -ly, -ous, -some, -y:**

ENDING	NOUN	ADJECTIVE
-able	peace	peaceable
	rate	ratable
	sale	salable
-al	accident	accidental
	nation	national
	region	regional
-an	diocese	diocesan
	Europe	European
	Nevada	Nevadan
-ar	consul	consular
	nebula	nebular
	pole	polar
-ary	function	functionary
	honor	honorary
	vision	visionary
-ate	college	collegiate
	passion	passionate
	rose	roseate
-ed	beard	bearded
	bigot	bigoted
	money	moneyed
-en	ash	ashen
	oak	oaken
	wood	wooden
-ful	care	careful
	shame	shameful
	thought	thoughtful
-ic, -ical	alcohol	alcoholic
	angel	angelic
		angelical

ENDING	NOUN	ADJECTIVE
	history	historic
		historical
	poet	poetic
		poetical
-ine	adamant	adamantine
	crystal	crystalline
	opal	opaline
-ish	book	bookish
	boy	boyish
	devil	devilish
-less	faith	faithless
	hope	hopeless
	penny	penniless
-like	dog	doglike
	fish	fishlike
	home	homelike
-ly	beast	beastly
	father	fatherly
	man	manly
-ous	bulb	bulbous
	fame	famous
	niter	nitrous
-some	awe	awesome
	quarrel	quarrelsome
	trouble	troublesome
-y	art	arty
	show	showy
	wind	windy

Many adjectives are made by adding one of the following endings to a verb: **-able, -ible, -ant, -ed, -ent, -ful, -ing, -ious, -ive, -ory, -some, -y.**

ENDING	VERB	ADJECTIVE
-able, -ible	adapt	adaptable
	define	definable
	insure	insurable
	corrupt	corruptible
	resist	resistible
	reverse	reversible
-ant	defy	defiant
	observe	observant
	rely	reliant
-ed	amuse	amused
	inflate	inflated
	insert	inserted
-ent	excel	excellent
	provide	provident
	transcend	transcendent
-ful	forget	forgetful
	resent	resentful
	wake	wakeful
-ing	dote	doting
	love	loving
	war	warring
-ous, -ious	rebel	rebellious
	study	studious
-ive	conclude	conclusive
	create	creative
	submit	submissive
-ory	contribute	contributory
	congratulate	congratulatory
	prohibit	prohibitory
-some	cuddle	cuddlesome
	cumber	cumbersome
	loathe	loathsome
-y	chat	chatty
	cling	clingy
	stick	sticky

Some adjectives based on verbs are pronounced differently though spelled the same: **graduáte, gráduate; perféct, pérfect; separáte, séparate.**

INSIDE THE ADVERB

WHEN we examine the adverb, we find some simple forms that cannot be cut into: **fast, hard, here, late, then, there, thus.**

Many adverbs are made by adding **-ly** to an adjective:

annually	**gladly**	**hopefully**
badly	**gradually**	**stingily**

Some adverbs are made by adding **-ly** to nouns:

daily	**momently**	**weekly**
hourly	**monthly**	**yearly**

Some adverbs are made by prefixing **a-** to a noun:

abed	**asea**	**ashore**
afoot	**ashipboard**	**aside**

Some adverbs are compounds ending in **-time, -ward, -wards, -way, -ways, -where, -wise:**

anytime	**backward**	**sideway**	**anywhere**
dinnertime	**backwards**	**sideways**	**somewhere**
mealtime	**onward**	**lengthway**	**crosswise**
sometime	**onwards**	**lengthways**	**edgewise**

Some adverbs have the same form as prepositions:

aboard	**before**	**in**	**since**
about	**behind**	**inside**	**through**
above	**below**	**like**	**throughout**
across	**beneath**	**near**	**to**
after	**beside**	**off**	**under**
against	**between**	**on**	**underneath**
along	**betwixt**	**out**	**up**
around	**beyond**	**outside**	**upon**
aslant	**by**	**over**	**within**
athwart	**down**	**past**	**without**

The noun, verb, adjective, and adverb are the star actors in language. They are the words we learn after we are conscious of learning words, the names for what our civilization chooses to name. These four great word-classes are unlimited; as long as new dawns bring new experiences to men and women, new nouns, verbs, adjectives, and adverbs are brought into being and have their day. Schooling exists largely to teach these words to the young; but after the schooldoors close, we go on learning them as long as we see, hear, touch, smell, taste, and think. To relate these words to each other, the patterns of English march: the patterns of pitch, stress, and juncture huddle words into related groups and keep them apart, and the patterns of order set one word meaningfully after another. To relate these words to each other, the changes in form tag them with labels that distinguish them in the patterns. These words make up the bulk of the English vocabulary. They are not, however, the language. If a monstrous aphasia were to wipe all memory of all these words out of the minds of the English-speaking peoples, so that they had to rob Eskimo, Bantu, or even Martian of their vocabularies and start over, the English language would remain the English language in its system of signals. If an aphasia were to wipe out the structure of the English utterance so that these words remained in all their multitude, there would be no English language. A language lives in its system, not in its vocabulary.

CHAPTER 16

The Structure-words

Structure-words are bits of the machinery of the language. In contrast, nouns, verbs, adjectives, and adverbs stand for the things, qualities, actions, and ideas that we think we find in the real world. In language these words are stand-ins that we can manipulate as we cannot manipulate what they stand for. We find out what they stand for and how they are related to each other only in the utterances in which they occur. Nouns, verbs, adjectives, and adverbs are surrounded in the utterances by other signals; the great word-classes are cradled in these signals, borne this way and that, brought together or separated, like fish in a running stream carried by the water. Nouns, verbs, adjectives, and adverbs are emphasized in English speech; they grab the spotlight; they hog the attention. The other signals are muted, scarcely to be noticed unless you examine language specifically to inspect them. These signals are 1) the order of utterance, 2) the clotting of words into related groups, 3) the changes of sound and form, and 4) the pattern-signaling words that we have called structure-words. Unless we have some special reason for stressing structure-words, they fall in lightly accented or in unaccented syllables.

In a conversation a noun may be used a few times and never again, a verb, adjective, or adverb once or twice, but the structure-words are used over and over and over. If we count nouns, verbs, adjectives, and adverbs as they occur, we find no limit to them; we can make more as we need them; somewhere, somebody is always creating new ones. If we count the structure-words as they occur, we soon have them all; soon we are turning up no new ones. As language changes there is a glacial change in the structure-words, a slow disappearance of obsolete forms and a slow addition of new ones; the new forms are always borrowed from the existing wordstock, almost never created anew.

Structure-words sort into sets used in roughly the same patterns for roughly the same purposes. Generally where one word from the set can be used, any other word from the same set can be used in about the same formula. We have known all the words of each set from childhood; they are the small change of language, the common words we have always with us. There can hardly be more than several hundred of them in all. We have used most of the structure-words in our display of sentence patterns; we bring them together here, as sets, to show what they are and how they work.

The Markers

FIVE sets of structure-words are important, as we saw in Chapter 9, because they fence the beginning of groups that work in the utterance as units. In speech the groups are defined by familiar contours of pitch, stress, and juncture—a complex bundle of signals that reinforce each other. In writing, most of the other signals are omitted, but the word that starts the group is a clear and sufficient indication of the kind of group that is coming and what it is used for. It triggers our muscle-memory of our native speech-patterns. These words are like road signs that tell a driver on the highway what is ahead of him and give him a chance to get ready for it. We have called them *markers*.

1. NOUN-MARKERS

THE typical marker of nouns is the determiner. In English we like to get the news about a noun-headword before we come to it, some relation of the thing designated by the headword to others of the same kind, and most, if not all, of its limitations and qualities. If the headword is to be the word **man,** the determiner begins the noun-group by cutting the particular **man** out of the general class of **men** and points squarely at him. If the headword is to be the noun **men,** the determiner picks the **men** out and points at them before the adjective comes along and defines their qualities. The simple noun-group patterns are **N** and **D N,** one without the determiner, one with it. These are the most common determiners:

The, a/an, this, that, these, those, some, any, no, many, much, more, most, both, each, either, every, neither, all, few, what, which, whatever, whichever, one, two, three, and the numbers to **ninety-nine.** In the common speech, **them** is used as an alternate to **these** and **those.**

The pronoun forms **my, your, his, hers, its, our,** and **their** are determiners also.

A determiner warns us that a noun is coming and that the span of words from determiner to noun-headword is to be taken as a unit equivalent to a noun in the sentence-patterns.

2. VERB-MARKERS

MARKERS of verbs begin the verb-group and warn us to take the whole span from marker to headword as a single unit performing the function of the verb in the sentence-patterns. The markers **be, have, do,** the modal auxiliaries, and others are thoroughly treated in Chapters 9 and 15.

Determiners and verb-markers are alike in that they point to a span of words ending in a headword; the function of the whole group, however long it may be, is the function of the headword. Three other sets of markers point to groups of a different kind.

3. PHRASE-MARKERS (PREPOSITIONS)

THE common phrase-marker is the preposition, a word which, no matter what else it tells us, warns of the coming of a noun. The preposition is often followed by a determiner; the span of a prepositional phrase can go the full length of a noun-cluster. But the preposition signals us that the whole phrase as a unit is not working in the utterance as a noun, except rarely. The preposition tells us that the phrase is a modifier; other signals tell us what it modifies and whether it is to be taken in that utterance as an adjective or adverb. Prepositional phrases are thoroughly treated in Chapters 9 and 12 under the headings Adjective Phrase and Adverb Phrase.

These are the most common prepositions:

abaft	behind	like	save
aboard	below	maugre	since
about	beneath	mid	than
above	beside	midst	through
across	besides	minus	throughout
after	between	near	till
against	betwixt	of	to
along	beyond	off	toward
alongside	but	on	towards
amid	by	onto	under
amidst	cum	opposite	underneath
among	despite	out	until
amongst	down	outside	unto
anent	ere	over	up
around	except	past	upon
aslant	for	per	versus
astride	from	plus	via
at	in	re	with
athwart	inside	round	within
before	into	sans	without

There are many word-groups forming prepositions, such as

apart from	in accordance with	in spite of
aside from	in consequence of	instead of
as to	in re	on account of
because of	in reference to	with reference to
by means of	in regard to	with regard to
due to	in respect to	with respect to

4. CLAUSE-MARKERS

A CLAUSE is a word-group containing the **N V** pattern and working in the utterance as a noun, adjective, adverb, and sometimes as a verb. Most clauses begin with a marker, a word or word-group that warns us to take the whole clause as a unit. The marker is not a very good sign of the function of the clause in the sentence. Nor is the internal pattern of the clause a good sign of its use in the sentence-pattern. The signals are more complex interrelationships of sentence arrangements. Some adjective clauses like **I read in The book I read was pretty good** are unmarked. Clauses are thoroughly treated in Chapters 9 and 12.

These are the most common clause-markers:

> **That, so that, in that, such that, in order that, lest**
> **So, as, only, like, than**
> **When, where, why, how, whenever, wherever, however, whither, whence, whereby, wherein, whereof**
> **Who, whom, whose, whoever, whomever, what, whatever, whatsoever, which, whichever**
> **If, whether, although, though, while, unless, except, notwithstanding**
> **Since, because, as, inasmuch as, whereas, seeing, being as, being that**
> **Before, after, ere, till, until, once, now, as soon as, so long as**

5. QUESTION-MARKERS

AMONG several ways of signaling questions, one is by use of a marker. Questions are thoroughly treated in Chapter 13.

These are the most common question-markers:

> **When, where, why, how, whenever, wherever, however, whither, whence; who, whom, whose, whoever, whomever, what, whatever, which, whichever**

Conjunctions

WE saw in Chapter 11 that any word, word-group, phrase, or clause that has been used once in an utterance can be used again as often as we want to use it. Any unit once used can be repeated. We can add determiner to determiner, noun to noun, verb to verb, phrase to phrase, clause to clause, and even sentence to sentence. We can add them without any special words to link them, but we have a set of words called conjunctions that we use between repeated elements.

These are the most common conjunctions:

And, but, for, nor, or, rather than, so, yet

These conjunctions operate in pairs:

Although . . . yet; as . . . as; as . . . so; both . . . and; either . . . or; neither . . . or; neither . . . nor; if . . . then; not . . . but; not only . . . but; not only . . . but also; now . . . now; now . . . then; so . . . as; though . . . yet; whereas . . . therefore; whether . . . or

Intensifiers

BEFORE and after adjectives and adverbs there is little elbowroom for intensifiers. The position before is often occupied by a set of words which define the intensity of the quality stated in the adjective or adverb or, in some cases, minimize it. The intensifiers are treated with the adjectives and adverbs in Chapter 15.

These are the most common intensifiers:

**Very, more, most, little, less, least
Quite, awfully, awful, really, real, any, pretty, too, fairly
Rather, somewhat, somehow, right, just, more or less, so**

Some words are often combined as group intensifiers:

So very much more

Before an adjective or adverb with the **-er** ending, like **better, softer, harder, stronger,** several words serve as intensifiers:

Still, even, much, some, no, away, far and away

Pattern-fillers

IN the utterance, the **N V** pattern has a dominance that extends beyond its actual occurrence, so that in some sentences that do not begin with **N,** we have to have something to take its place. By means of **there** or **it,** we get the sentence started and on its way. These words are lightly stressed. We name them *pattern-fillers*.

> **There is a book on the table.**   **There are some books on the table.**
>
> **There's a book on the table.**   **There's some books on the table.**
>
> **There was a fire at our house.**   **There were six fire trucks there.**

It serves in a similar way:

> **It is raining. It is rather warm today. It's my brother.**
> **It was a long road back. It's just that I don't believe you.**
> **It's exactly as I said before. It is unbelievable the way he beats her.**
> **It's that they won't sit down and talk. It's a long hard job to write a book.**

Starters

CERTAIN words serve as starters of utterances. The most common are:

> **Well, Oh, Now, O.K., Okay, Why, My, My goodness, Say, Look, Listen, See here**

Proposers

OFTEN we start requests with **Please, If you please, If you don't mind, If you like, If it's no trouble,** etc. We also use **let's,** as in **Let's all go together,** and **Let's us,** as in **Let's us pay for the gas, and you bring your car.**

In Chapter 15 we treated the four great word-classes and in Chapter 16 the structure-words. These are the main ways in which we sort our words and the main signals by which we recognize the sets we sort them into. One word like **like** may fall into several lists: noun, verb, adverb, preposition, and conjunction. The more common a word is, the more likely we are to give it several uses.

Thus **is** is not only a verb in its own right, but it is also a marker of verb-groups; **it, they, one,** and **you** may be definite or indefinite in their reference. **Now** may be an adverb in **See it now** or a sentence starter in **Now, look here.** In most sets and classes of words a primary group mainly carries the function of that set; but there is a "fringe area" in and out of which other words move as we want them to. Functions primarily assigned to single words are also carried by word-groups. Every twist and turn of the utterance is defined by so many signals that, if we miss part, the others are more than enough to outline the units and their functions. The result of all this is a fluid, flexible system of expression that provides the material for our creative construction of utterances serving our needs, communication between human beings in human societies.

How We Form
Our Sounds

*

PART FOUR

*

How We Form
Our Sounds

CHAPTER 17

Breaking the Sound Barrier

WE HAVE LOOKED at English speech so far in the mirror of English writing, beginning with the units of utterance and sentence where speech and writing most resemble each other. As a mirror of speech, writing is at best a distorting glass that presents subtle refractions of emphasis and proportion. It is a translation: like all translations it adds some things and leaves others out. It transmutes a sensitively modulated flow of sounds in time into a plodding line of letters and spaces on a page; for the native reader or writer it is at best a sketchy reminder of his mother tongue, a trigger to set off his memory of sounds he has made and heard throughout his life. If we wish to establish a command of English writing that will let us understand what we have to read, and write what we have to write, we need to take a square look at speech as it is in itself. From such an examination we may learn more than how the English language works; we may learn how language works and get some insight into languages other than our own.

It is not easy for us to come to grips with the system of our own language. First, our very command of English speech stands in our way. Speaking is for us a set of habits made automatic by long use. We seldom think about speaking; our minds are on what we have to say. The will to communicate that seizes the human infant soon after birth brings us to a complete control of the system so early that we have no more memory of learning to speak than we have of learning to walk, run, or eat. Hence we operate the complicated musculature by which we speak with negligence and grace; we can only inspect it by rupturing our normal easy indifference to it by a conscious act of will.

Second, we think of language in terms of writing. Our society sees it that way, thinking of English as that great body of recorded literature that fills our libraries. We think of it that way because we can remember our first painful efforts to read and write and the subsequent long years of English courses in school. Our main conscious effort applied to language has been devoted to spelling, grammar, and punctuation—not as a secondary derived record of speech but as English, the real thing. We talk mistakenly of "pronouncing letters," not of recording sounds.

These two mental sets, taking speech for granted and mistaking writing for language, stand between us and an easy consciousness of speech and what we do to produce it. Furthermore, in order to write about speech-sounds, we have to give each one a letter-value or some other mark that can be put on paper. Strange marks such as we might devise are hard to learn and hard to remember; but if we use familiar letters and add a few extra ones to them, then we have two writing systems colliding in our minds and causing confusion. Fortunately the confusion is temporary and we can get over it, for we have to use letters to represent sounds.

When we do get speech disentangled in our minds from writing so that we can examine it, we can, as natives, take a double approach to it: through the mechanisms of the body that produce it, and through the ears that hear it. Combining these two aspects of speech is not unusual for us; we do it all the time. Our minds produce a message—what we wish to say—and feed it to the vocal organs, which encode it into a modulated stream of sounds. As we speak, our ears check on what we are doing. If the code isn't the right one for the message—if the tongue stumbles and we make the wrong sounds or if we choose the wrong words—the ear notes the error, and the brain feeds back a correction. The speech-organs then break off and re-encode the message. Another hearer notes a hesitancy, a stumble, and a repetition with other sounds or other words. **When we came into the garage—no, the house—we found all the lights on. He was keam taptain—I mean team captain—**

that year. We have only to extend this monitoring which keeps us from error in speech, and make it sensitive to our normal effortless production of the right sounds and words, to discover what we do when we talk. What we do is, after all, pretty wonderful.

As we attend to speech as a code distinct from the message expressed in the code, we begin to be aware of the signals and their arrangements. We find ourselves inspecting one of the most beautifully ordered structures produced by man or nature. Within the ever-varying stream of sounds we find a limited group of basic signals recurring in patterns. These are the phonemes—the minimal sound-signals of speech. The phonemes combine into groups so that the stream of sound is not constant but blocked into segments which we call morphemes. The morphemes fall into the patterns of the utterance that we call syntax. These three ranks of signals strike the ear all at once as a single impression within a large number of variations in the stream of sound that we do not hear because we know they do not count; they have no relevance to the meaning. The whole linguistic system is attended, as we noted in Chapter 4, by a pantomime of facial expression, body movements, and gestures that reinforces the impression given by sound alone. Speech is also overlaid by the vocal qualifiers that reveal to the hearer our attitude toward what we are saying. Disregarding the pantomime and the vocal qualifiers for the sake of clarity, we shall look at these three ranks of signals, beginning with the smallest ones, the phonemes.

The Mechanics of Voice-Production

WE do not have special organs created to let us speak. We use what we have: the lips, the teeth, the tongue, the jaw, and the larynx in the throat. Each of these is a part of the basic bodily mechanisms by which we live, turned to the uses of speech. We start sounds down in the throat and modify them in the head by varying the resonance we give them. Our vocal apparatus has been compared to a musical instrument like the oboe because it works on the same principle. A column of air is set in motion in a narrow chamber by the vibration of something like a reed. The tone given off by this vibrating column of air is varied by changing its size; we change it by changing the size of the tube that contains it. A tight narrow

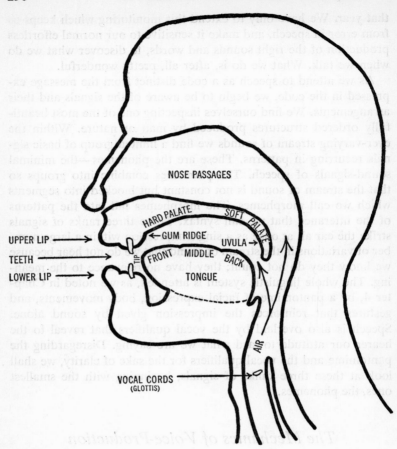

tube gives off a high vibration and an open tube with echo chambers gives off a low vibration. In a musical instrument we close and open the chambers by pushing and releasing keys; in speech we open and close the chambers by closing our lips, flipping our tongue against the roof of the mouth or against the teeth, or raising and lowering a little loose flap at the back of the mouth (the uvula) to send the sound out the mouth or through the echo chambers behind the nose. In part we also control the syllable-pulse with the diaphragm and the intercostal muscles of the rib cage. Just as the eye is a better optical instrument than a camera, so our speech-organs make up a better musical instrument than a woodwind or a horn. That is why opera singers are so highly regarded among musicians.

Let us follow speech from lungs to lips to see how it is made. The lungs are like a pair of bellows drawing air in through the mouth or nose, then pushing it out again. In English we use only the outbreath for speech. Some languages use the breathstream going both ways; we generally do not, though on occasion we may sigh, "Oh, dear!" on the inbreath. We can get air for speech in another way: people with a throat injury can have an opening made in the base of the throat to permit breathing; they learn to gulp air below the larynx and release it slowly past the vocal cords. We can also learn to explode sounds inward instead of outward to make certain sounds in other languages. Our normal way of speaking is simply to create friction or blockages of one kind or another in the outgoing stream of the breath.

Down in the throat in the larynx is a pair of membranes like curtains. These may be drawn apart to let the air flow free or drawn together so that their meeting-edges vibrate. We call these membranes the vocal cords, though they are not cords but sheets of membrane. The opening between them is the glottis. Sounds made with the vocal cords drawn open and vibrationless, like **th** in **thin,** are called *voiceless;* sounds made with the cords partly closed and vibrating, like **th** in **then,** are called *voiced*. Vowels and consonants like /**b, g, m, n, d, l**/ are voiced. We all make these two kinds of sounds, but some people cannot identify them and distinguish them from each other. A good test, if you find it hard to distinguish voiced sounds from voiceless, is to place the tips of your fingers lightly on your throat over the larynx; when you make a voiced sound, you can feel the vibration at your finger tips. Whispering unvoices all sounds without (curiously enough) disturbing the signals, since we understand a whisper as well as what is spoken aloud.

Above the larynx the windpipe is open as far as the back of the mouth, where the outgoing air meets a fork. The air may pass out over the tongue and through the mouth or it may go on up into the nasal passages and out the nose. At this fork a small fleshy flap called the uvula hangs down from the back of the roof of the mouth. The uvula, which can be seen in a mirror just above the tongue, is a very limber little point of soft flesh. It vibrates sharply when we clear the throat; it can be drawn up out of the way entirely so that both the mouth and nasal passages are open; it can be dropped down to close off the mouth or drawn back to close off the nose. Parisian French uses a vibration of the uvula to produce an /r/ sound; other dialects of French, Italian, and Scottish let the air pass the uvula and vibrate the tip of the tongue instead.

Above the mouth the nasal passages serve as resonance chambers like the body of a violin; when the mouth is closed either at the back by the uvula or at the front by the tongue or lips, the resonance is very strong. To have this resonance, the nostrils must be free and open; if they are stopped up, it is deadened and we get the effect of "talking through our noses" as when we have a cold. You can get this effect by pinching your nostrils together. Obviously you cannot talk through your nose when it is closed up, but that is what we call it. In English /m/, /n/, and the **-ng** /ŋ/ in **sing** are nasal sounds; they make the resonance chambers of the head reverberate strongly.

The mouth is a large open passage of rather complicated makeup. At the top is the palate, which is the roof of the mouth and floor of the nasal passages. Toward the front the palate is hard and bony; farther back the palate is soft and fleshy, and ends in the dangling uvula. The floor of the mouth is the lower jaw, a massive bony structure that is hinged just in front of the ears on either side of the head. The jaw swings on these hinges, so that it may be opened quite wide at the front, not so wide at the back. In a "U" around the forward part of both jaws are the teeth, set in fleshy gum-ridges. The fleshy walls of the mouth-passage are the cheeks, very limber and stretchable, so that they give with the movements of the lower jaw. The overall size and resonance of the mouth-passage is constantly changed by the raising and lowering of the lower jaw.

Fastened along the floor of the lower jaw is the tongue, a large, loose, flexible muscle that can be put into many different shapes. It can be drawn back into a compact mass or thrust forward into a snaky tip. It can be narrowed, or widened and flattened; it can be pushed up against the roof of the mouth so as to constrict the passage or close it entirely. We can think of the tongue as having three divisions: the back, the middle, and the tip. The tip, being thinner and at the place where the mouth can be opened widest, has more room to move in than the back, which is thicker, heavier, and in smaller space no matter how wide apart the jaws are held. The tongue can block the mouth at any point: front, middle, or back.

Man speaks, and in this he differs from the animals. Yet he speaks with organs that in other species give off cries only. Man speaks because he has the apparatus we have described, which is there primarily for breathing and for eating. Man speaks because, somewhere in the convoluted matter of the brain, the will to speak exists, and because the nerves that control the musculature of throat and head set going the delicate movements that modulate the vibrations of the stream of his breath.

The Phonemes
of English Speech

WE HAVE in English forty-five basic speech-signals. Of these,
thirty-three are speech-sounds that we say one after another in
line; twelve are modulations that we apply to this flow of sounds
without essentially changing them: rises and falls in pitch, rises and
falls in loudness, and cuts that we make in the line to keep the
speech-sounds clotted together and set apart. Of the thirty-three
"line" signals, twenty-one are consonants—signals made by blocking the air passage and opening it again or by narrowing the passage so that the air has to work its way through in a rasp, a buzz,
or a hiss. You can make a kind of consonant by clapping your
hand over your mouth and pulling it away, or by letting the air
escape noisily between your fingers. Nine are vowels—signals made
by vibrating the air in the open mouth cavity. Three are semivowels—signals made by changing the shape of the mouth cavity
while a sound is in process, but without closing the mouth or approaching the constriction of a consonant. The actual sound of a

phoneme may differ slightly from speech-community to speech-community; the sound needs only to be reasonably consistent in each community.

The Consonant Phonemes

THE upper teeth, the upper gum-ridge, and the roof of the mouth as far back as the soft palate are rigid and immovable; they constitute an anvil against which the tongue beats out speech-sounds. With the back of the tongue pressing up against the soft palate we make /g/ and /k/; with the tip and blade of the tongue resting against the hard palate we make /l/. Letting some air escape along both sides of the tongue-tip as it rests against the back of the upper teeth or the gum-ridge, we make /t/ and /d/.

When the tongue (or the lips, as we shall see) blocks the breath completely, the diaphragm may jerk a little puff of breath from the lungs so that the release of the blockage is slightly explosive. A sound produced by the block or by the combined block and following push of air is called a *stop*. When the tongue or the lips partly close off the passage, letting a little vibrating air through, we call the sound a *continuant*.

To make the sound of **sh** /š/ in **fish** or **shoot,** we lay the blade of the tongue against the palate and let the air whish through noiselessly; the upper surface of the tongue forms a groove. To make the sound of **zh** /ž/ in **vision,** we put the tongue in the same position, but vibrate the air going through the vocal cords. With the tip rather than the blade of the tongue resting just back of the teeth, we make /s/ in **sink** and /z/ in **zinc** with the same contrast; the air passes between teeth and tongue in a narrow slit. With the tip of the tongue thrust forward between upper and lower teeth, we make **th** /θ/ as in **thin** and **th** /ð/ as in **then.** To make the sound written **ch** /č/ in **church,** we start with the tongue in position for /t/ and ease into the position for /š/ as in **fish;** to make the sound written **j** and **dg** /ǰ/ in **judge,** we start with the tongue in position for /d/ and ease into the position for /ž/ in **vision.** With the blade or back of the tongue against the palate, the nasal passages open and resonating, we make **ng** /ŋ/ in **sing.** With the tip against the hard palate and gum-ridge, the nasal passages resonating, we make

/n/ as in **nice** and **sin.** We also use the tongue to make vowels, but more about them later.

The front of the mouth is fenced by the upper and lower teeth. We make no speech sounds with teeth against teeth (though we could) but combine tongue and teeth to make /t/, /d/, **th** /θ/ and **th** /ð/. We press the lower lip against the upper teeth to make /f/ and /v/, both continuants, for we let air through. Since tongue against lower teeth would not close the passage, we do not try to make any sound this way. It would be hard for most of us to get the upper lip against the lower teeth, since the lower teeth are usually set a little behind the upper teeth or just even with them.

The fleshy covering of the face is continuous to the front of the mouth, where there is a hole surrounded by the lips. The lips form one continuous muscle, almost round, of a type called a "sphincter." This muscle works like a rubber band or drawstring around the neck of a bag; it can be completely released to leave the opening wide open, or it can be drawn tight to close the opening. The fleshy covering of the face is elastic enough to give the lower jaw considerable freedom of movement even with lips closed, and the lips are very limber. With the lower lip against the upper teeth we make /f/ and /v/, as we noticed; with both lips tightly closed but the nasal passages open we make /m/. With both lips closed then released (often with a puff of air) we make /p/ and /b/, both stops.

Except for /r/, these are all the phonemes that we make by blocking or constricting the flow of the breath; we call them consonants. The production of /r/ is rather more difficult to deal with. It is formed in a different way in different parts of words, and it is quite different in different dialects of English. Scots trill their /r/ by vibrating the tip of the tongue strongly. The English form an /r/ by flipping the tip of the tongue to the hard palate behind the upper teeth and quickly drawing it away. To us this /r/ sounds like a /d/; we hear this British pronunciation of **very** as **veddy.** Most Americans do not close off the mouth to make /r/, but lift and curl the tip of the tongue back a little in a position near but not touching the roof of the mouth, as in **very.** Or we lift the blade of the tongue up near but not touching the palate; our kind of /r/ is more like the vowels than the consonants. Whichever way we have learned to make an /r/, that is the right one for us.

These are the twenty-one consonant phonemes. We have written

each one with a letter-value of its own, usually a letter that represents it in speech. We use special letters in phonemic notation for
/ŋ/ as in **sing**, /θ/ as in **thin**, /ð/ as in **then**, /š/ as in **fish**, /ž/ as
in **vision**, /č/ as in **church**, /ǰ/ as in **judge**; otherwise /p/, /b/,
/t/, /d/, /g/, /k/, /s/, /z/, /m/, /n/, /f/, /v/, /l/, and /r/. One
thing is hard for us to remember about these signs: the same one
always represents the same phoneme, no matter what word it occurs in or where it occurs in the word. Normal English writing has
a fixed spelling for each word even though its pronunciation varies
in the stream of speech. Through long habit we have a mental set
toward these regular spellings which makes it hard for us to read
and write a notation that disregards them. It is like switching from
a standard automobile transmission to an automatic and back; only
frequently handling cars with both kinds will train us to do the right
thing with the one we are using at the moment. A little practice
with phonemic transcription will give you readiness in its use. The
same sign always represents one phoneme, no matter how we vary
it in speech.

The Vowel Phonemes

VOWELS are sounds that are made by letting the air go into the
mouth and reverberate there. As with the voiced consonants, a
basic vibration is set up in the larynx, but there is no constriction
and no stopping of the breath. The noise that comes out of the
mouth is varied by changing the size and shape of the mouth cavity,
mainly by means of the tongue. The space involved is bounded by
the roof of the mouth or palate at the top, the teeth at the front, the
uvula at the back, and the tongue at the bottom. We change the
size of this space in two ways: by raising and lowering the lower
jaw, and by raising and lowering the tongue. The jaw, being hinged
at the back, lets the front go wider open than the back where it
moves only a little. The tongue, being thicker and wider at the
back, further limits the back opening. Theoretically we can make
more separate sounds at the front of the mouth than at the back.
In English we do not make use of the possibilities; we do make
more different sounds at the front, but the differences do not count.

The shape of the mouth provides a space like this for the vowels:

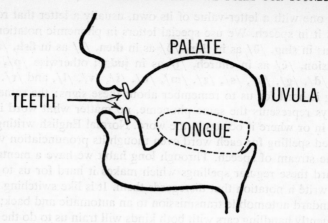

English divides this space into nine areas:

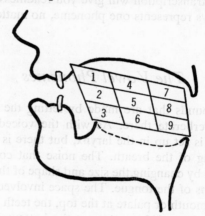

Within each sector a number of distinct sounds can be made, but the sounds made in a sector belong to one phoneme, though they may seem to the ear to be quite different from each other. It is the placement that counts. The shape of the sound is determined by the height of the tongue and the space left between tongue and palate. Sounds made in the front of the mouth are formed by the tip, in the middle by the blade, and in the back by the back of the tongue. A crest or high point of the upper surface of the tongue shapes the sound; the remainder of the tongue keeps well down and out of the way.

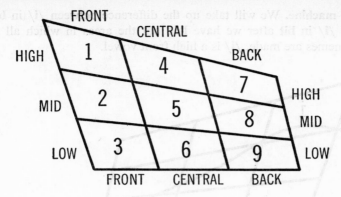

The nine sectors of the mouth cavity give us three stacks of sounds, front, central, and back, and three levels of sounds, high, mid, and low. We treat all the sounds made in any one sector as one phoneme; the sounds made in sector 1 are high front sounds; in sector 5 are mid central sounds; in sector 9 are low back sounds. Thus we can call them by name. For simplicity we will use the diagram without the actual drawing of the mouth and indicate the upper surface of the tongue by a curved line.

Now that we have mapped the mouth cavity (of all the cavernous regions of the world the most important), we can go on to examine each of the three levels of the three stacks of sounds. This map holds good only for English; another language might discriminate five or ten phonemes along the front axis of the mouth, pitch all its vowels high or low, or distinguish a set made with the nasal chambers resonating from a corresponding set made with the nasal chambers silent. Even in English other factors intrude; we make the front vowels with the lips open and the back vowels with the lips close together and rounded. But we make them in these nine sectors; all sounds in one sector belong to one phoneme.

The vowel phoneme /i/. If we say the words **beat, bit, big, bin, machine, wheel, sleeve,** we can feel the tip of the tongue in the high front area, making the sound we spell **i** as in **bit** or **ee** as in **sleeve.** The space between tongue and palate is very narrow; in this space the sound takes on a high vibration. We mark this phoneme in our notation /i/, using the letter that represents it in **bit**

and **machine.** We will take up the difference between /i/ in **beat** and /i/ in **bit** after we have laid out the areas in which all the phonemes are made. /i/ is a high front vowel.

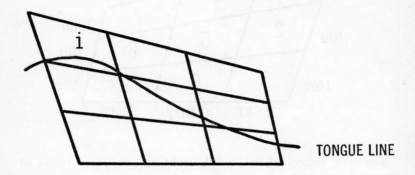

TONGUE LINE

The vowel phoneme /e/. If we say the words **bet, bait, get, gate, fret, freight,** we can feel the tip of the tongue making the vowel in the front of the mouth, but a little lower down than before. We mark this phoneme with the letter /e/, as in **bet;** it is a mid front vowel.

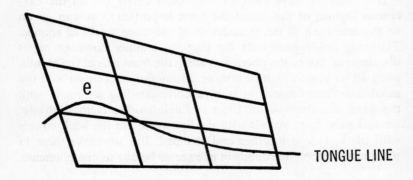

TONGUE LINE

The vowel phoneme /æ/. If we say the words **pat, man, can, fad,** and **sallow,** we feel the tip of the tongue making the vowel, still in the front of the mouth, but lower than in **bet.** We mark this phoneme with a digraph or linked **ae** /æ/; it is a low front vowel. The front vowels thus are /i, e, æ/.

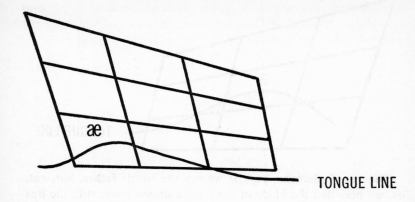

TONGUE LINE

The vowel phoneme /ɨ/. If we say the words **till** (meaning 'until,' not 'cash drawer') and **just** (**jis'** as in **jis' going**), many of us, though not all, form the vowel high in the mouth but behind the vowel in **bit** by lifting the blade of the tongue close to the palate. We mark this phoneme with a barred i" /ɨ/; it is a high central vowel.

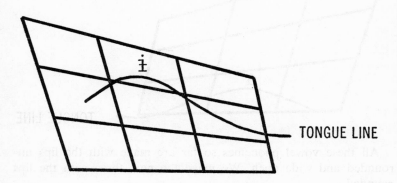

TONGUE LINE

The vowel phoneme /ə/. If we say the words **cut, but, sofa** (the second syllable), we form a vowel with the blade of the tongue drawn a little lower than in **till** and **just.** We mark this phoneme with an upside-down **e,** usually called *schwa* /ə/; it is a mid central vowel.

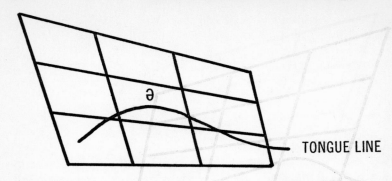

TONGUE LINE

The vowel phoneme /a/. If we say the words **father, hot, cot, ox,** we may find the blade of the tongue drawn lower still, the lips unrounded, and all muscles as lax as in **bit** and **but.** If so, we are making a low central vowel. New Englanders may pronounce **dawn** with this vowel; Midwesterners use it in **Don.** We mark this phoneme with the letter **a/a/**; it is a low central vowel.

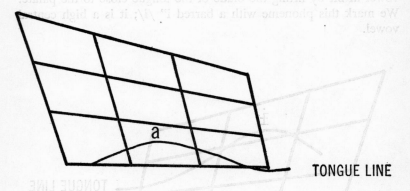

TONGUE LINE

All these vowel phonemes so far are made with the lips unrounded and wide open. We make the next three with the lips rounded.

The vowel phoneme /u/. If we say the words **food, cool, boot, book, look,** and **took,** we form a vowel at the back of the mouth by lifting the back of the tongue close to the roof of the mouth. We also round the lips somewhat. We mark this phoneme with the letter **u/u/**; it is a high back vowel.

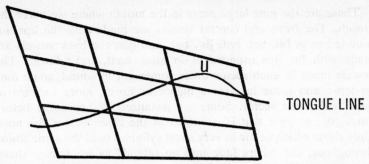

TONGUE LINE

The vowel phoneme /o/. If we say the words **stone, bone, comb, boat,** we form a vowel at the back of the mouth, but with the back of the tongue lower than in **food.** The lips are rounded. We mark this phoneme with the letter **o** /o/; it is a mid back vowel.

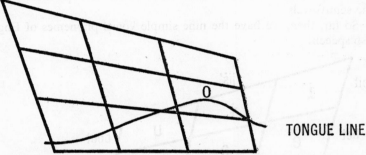

TONGUE LINE

The vowel phoneme /ɔ/. If we say the words **law, caw, gnaw, 'dawg,'** we form a vowel at the back of the mouth, with the back of the tongue drawn still lower and the lips rounded. We mark this phoneme with a reversed **c** /ɔ/; it is a low back vowel.

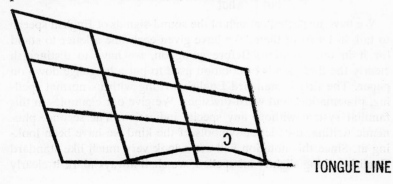

TONGUE LINE

These are the nine large areas in the mouth where we make the vowels. The front and central vowels are made with the lips unrounded as in **bit, bet, bat, jis', but,** and **got;** the back vowels are made with the lips rounded as in **boot, boat,** and **"dawg."** The vowels made in each sector differ somewhat in sound; some may be tense and some lax, some higher or lower, more forward or back within the sector. Some are nasalized if they come before /m/, /n/, or /ŋ/; that is, sounded in the chambers of the nose. Only those which occur in very short syllables hold the same sound throughout; the others fade into an offglide as we release them. Tenseness or laxness and relative position within the area are not significant in the system; but whether the vowel glides at the end or not is quite important. We do not have merely a fading or impure vowel, as in **beat, bait,** and **pass,** but a vowel followed by another phoneme before the consonant. These other phonemes are the semivowels.

So far, then, we have the nine simple vowel phonemes of English speech:

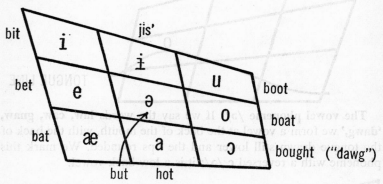

We have inspected enough of the sound-signals of English speech to talk in terms of them. We have given each one a letter to stand for it in our notation. Before going on, we have to distinguish clearly the three kinds of notation used to put a language down on paper. The first is standard English writing with its normal spelling, punctuation, and word-divisions. We give our examples in this familiar system without any special indication. The second, phonemic writing, uses letter-symbols of the kind we have been looking at. Since this notation will often look very much like standard English writing slightly misspelled, we shall always mark it clearly

by setting it off with a slant line before and after: /   /. In phonemic notation as we have seen it so far, we would treat the word
philosophy like this: /filasəfi/.

The third kind of notation is phonetic. Phonetic notation records
raw unsorted sound; it uses some such alphabet as the International
Phonetic Alphabet to show the exact location of the sound in the
mouth, and its quality. Each writer who uses phonetic notation
has to write a preface in which he explains exactly what symbols he
is employing, what value he is giving them, and what extra marks
he is using to give a fine discrimination. If you were a foreigner and
we had to indicate to you the exact sound of an English word so
that you could learn to produce it by putting your muscles and
your jaw in the right position, we would have to use phonetic notation, setting it off with square brackets before and after: [   ].
Generally we will not be using it. The International Phonetic Alphabet can be found in any desk dictionary.

The Semivowel Phonemes

THE twenty-one consonant and nine vowel phonemes we have
dealt with so far are relatively simple to understand; they are made
by certain muscles in specific positions in the mouth. We always
make /p/ with closed lips in the front of the mouth voicelessly
and /b/ in the same place but with a vibration of the vocal cords
that gives it a voiced quality. We make /i/ in the high front sector
of the mouth by raising the tip of the tongue close to the palate and
/o/ in the mid back sector by lifting the back of the tongue about
halfway in its travel. We always make these phonemes in those
spots.

The three semivowels are different. They are not fixed and static
like the consonants and vowels; they signal by movement and
change of position. With the exception of one variant, the semivowels start in one sector of the mouth and go to another; that
movement is the essence of their production. There are only three
semivowels; we mark them /y/, /w/, and /h/.

If we say the words **you, we, yeah, ye, hay, yaw,** we can feel the
semivowels in action. In most of our other examples we have found
the vowel between consonants as in **bit** and **beat.** In the word **you**
we find the vowel /u/ between two sounds that are not quite vowels

and not quite consonants. These sounds go before and after vowels as consonants do, but they don't block or constrict the mouth. They sound like vowels. The /y/ sounds like the high front vowel /i/, and the /w/ sounds like a slight tightening and extra rounding of the /u̞/. We write **you** phonemically /**yuw**/. Let us see why.

The semivowel phoneme /y/. Before a vowel as in **you** /**yuw**/, **ye** /**yiy**/, and **yea** /**yey**/ this phoneme is a movement which begins in the high front sector of the mouth and travels to the position of the following vowel. Before /i/ as in **ye** /**yiy**/, /y/ is a movement within the high front sector of the mouth, starting very high and going only a little way.

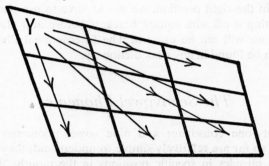

The semivowel /y/ after a vowel, as in **bay** /**bey**/, **boy** /**boy**/, **buy** /**bay**/, is a movement from the preceding vowel to the high front sector of the mouth. After /i/, /y/ is a further lifting and fronting of an already high front vowel.

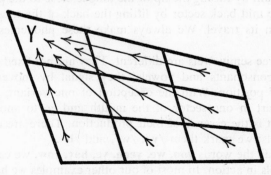

If you rest a finger lightly on the chin, you can feel the lower jaw lift and thrust a little in the production of this semivowel. It is the semivowel, not the vowel itself, which distinguishes **bet** /bet/ from **bait** /beyt/ and **bit** /bit/ from **beat** /biyt/. With a high front semivowel following, the vowel launches itself a little higher and fronter than the simple vowel.

The semivowel phoneme /w/. Before a vowel as in **we** /wiy/, **way** /wey/, **woe** /wow/, and **woo** /wuw/ this phoneme starts like the high back rounded vowel /u/ and moves from the high back sector of the mouth into the position of the following vowel. Before /u/ as in **woo** /wuw/, **wood** /wud/, **woman** /wumən/, /w/ is a movement within the high back sector of the mouth, starting very high, very far back, and with the lips tightly rounded.

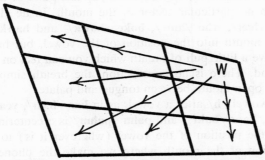

The semivowel /w/ after a vowel as in **throw** /θrow/, **house** /haws/, /hews/, /hæws/ or /həws/, is a movement from the position of the preceding vowel to the high back sector of the mouth, together with a close rounding of the lips. After /u/ as in **woo** /wuw/, **do** /duw/, and **through** /θruw/, the semivowel /w/ is a movement within the high back sector of the mouth; it is a further lifting, backing, and rounding of an already high back rounded vowel.

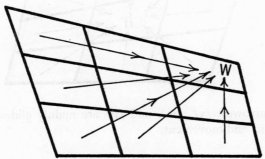

If you rest one finger lightly on your lips and another on your chin, you can feel the rounding of the lips and the thrust and lift of the jaw in the production of this semivowel. It is the semivowel that distinguishes **suit** /suwt/ from **soot** /sut/; with a high back rounded semivowel following, the vowel launches itself a little higher, backer, and rounder than the simple vowel.

The semivowel phoneme /h/. In **hay** /hey/ and **yeah** /yeh/ this phoneme is a little different from /y/ and /w/. The form these take after a vowel is a reverse image of the form they take before a vowel. The form of /h/ before a vowel is rather different from its form after a vowel. Before a vowel, /h/ is a pulse of the breath occurring in no particular sector of the mouth. In **he** /hiy/, **hay** /hey/, **hat** /hæt/, **who** /huw/, **hoke** /howk/, and **hawk** /hɔwk/ we put the mouth into the position of the vowel, but before the vowel we give a little puff of breath which you can feel on the back of your hand. There is no constriction; the breath simply blows through the open mouth between tongue and palate.

The semivowel /h/ after a vowel, as in **baa** /bæh/, **yeah** /yeh/, **dear** /dihr/, **boor** /buhr/, and **palm** /pahm/ is a centering movement from the position of the vowel (wherever it is) to the mid central section of the mouth where we make the phoneme /ə/. If the preceding vowel is rounded /u/, /o/, /ɔ/, the semivowel /h/ is an unrounding also.

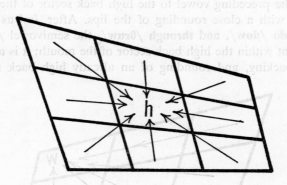

The semivowels /y/, /w/, and /h/ are mainly glides; their essence is shift and movement.

The Dynamics of Voice-Production

WITH the full list of basic sounds now in hand, we have looked separately at each of the "segmental" phonemes. They fall into three groups:

1) 21 consonants:	/p	t	č	k/	(voiceless)
	/b	d	ǰ	g/	(voiced)
	/f	θ	s	š/	(voiceless)
	/v	ð	z	ž/	(voiced)
	/m	n		ŋ/	(nasal)
	/l/				(liquids)
	/r/				
2) 9 vowels:	/i	ɨ	u/		(high)
	/e	ə	o/		(mid)
	/æ	a	ɔ/		(low)
3) 3 semivowels:	/y	h	w/		

In this chart all the phonemes are set up from left to right: front to back. Voiced and voiceless consonants are paired above and below each other. You should commit this chart to memory, so that you can write it down at will as it stands. Then it will go with you where you go and serve as a touchstone by which you can reduce any word or short utterance to its segmental phonemes.

We have considered these phonemes in separate words. Two things must have quickly become obvious:

First, when we make those words in running speech, they do not always have in them these particular phonemes we have indicated; and sometimes when we repeat a word several times in a string of utterances, it does not always have the same phonemes. When we pronounce a word separately—as a whole utterance—it is in a "strong" position; when it is isolated, it forms a complex different from the complex it forms as part of a larger utterance. Many words sound radically different pronounced by themselves: **the** in a sentence before a consonant is /ðə/ and **a (a bed)** is /ə/; when we say these words alone **the** is /ðiy/ and **a** is /ey/. The change is quite proper; it is one of the aspects of our speech that phonemic analysis exposes. Saying the same word in different utterances with different phonemes is also proper; it is another of the aspects of speech we are trying to bring out.

Second, you may have noticed that you never pronounce some of the words we have used as examples with the phonemes we have given them for illustration. Again this difference is quite proper; different speech-communities differ somewhat in their selection of phonemes for the same words. In the Great Lakes region **on** is /**an**/ or /**ən**/ and **Erie** is /**ihriy**/; in the South **on** is more likely to be /**ɔhn**/ or /**ɔwn**/ and **Erie** is /**iyriy**/. This regional or dialectal difference is another of the aspects of speech that phonemic analysis brings out.

The important thing is to face these aspects of speech, understand them, and learn to live with them, with an honest respect for the ways of other people and a continuing sense of each man's hunger and his right to be "as good as the next guy." Standard English writing disregards these aspects of speech for the most part, so that an adroit writer can be as homeless or as faceless as he wishes to be or can seem to be what he is not. Writing has a sign for each word, a set of letters that we always use regardless of strong or weak position in the utterance, of shifts from one set of sounds to another, of personal and individual differences, and of differences in dialect. We write **talk, help, palm, though, through, enough, latter,** and **ladder** without regard for the way we sound these words, either isolated or in running speech.

The eye responds more easily to a familiar grouping of letters than to phonemic symbols that record variations in the sounds of speech or of different speakers. In phonemic writing we assign a letter-value to each sound-signal and rigorously force ourselves to write that letter and no other when we use that sound. Phonemic writing is no friend to the eye. It is hard and cumbersome to write, hard and clumsy to read. Its sole purpose is to record the actual phonemes of speech so that we can become aware of the nature of speech and the way we do it. Careful phonemic notation gives us a permanent primary record of the utterance. We can inspect the notation and untangle its patterns without contamination from standard English writing. The only useful notation is the one that catches exactly the sound-signals actually used in that particular recorded utterance. Practice with phonemic notation helps us to hear not our own speech only but the speech of others. The more we practice phonemic writing the sharper our ears get, the more differences we hear, and the more problems of speech-analysis we have to face.

There are phonetic differences also between instances of a single phoneme. A phoneme can be recognizable as /p/, /k/, or /i/, made with the right muscles in exactly the right part of the mouth and yet be different in sound quality from another instance of the same phoneme apparently made in the same way in the same place. The reason is that a phoneme never occurs alone; it is always preceded or followed by another. It is affected by others and has a sound peculiar to its surroundings. Thus /æ/ in **ban** /bæn/ does not sound the same as /æ/ in **cat** /kæt/; it is nasalized because the next phoneme /n/ is a nasal. The /l/ and /k/ in **leak, lake, like, luck,** and **look** differ in these five words; they range over quite a stretch of the palate. They are front with front vowels and back with back vowels. All phonemes adjust to their neighbors in this way. An electronic voice-analyzer operating with these thirty-three sound-signaling units shows infinite variations that a phonemic notation ignores.

It is impossible for us to say the same phoneme twice even in a precisely repeated sequence in exactly the same way because of the complicated musculature we operate to make the phonemes. Large, middling, and small muscles combine to produce the sound. Each has its own rate of action. Lips and tongue are light and flexible; the muscles that move the lower jaw are heavy and strong. No weight of bone restricts the lips and tongue, but the jaw muscles have to move the heavy, hinged mass of the jawbone. Lip and tongue muscles can start for a phoneme well after the jaw muscles have begun to bring the jaw into position, and still get there first. The result is the minute differences in sound that the electronic machine records and the skilled ear hears. We cannot do the same thing twice in the same way, but the language as a system does not expect us to. Target shooting would be easier but maybe not so much fun if it were scored as tolerantly as the language scores our shot at a phoneme; we would give the same points to a shot that nicked the corner of the target as to one dead into the center of the bull's-eye.

Making a phoneme is a three-step process. There is a confused first stage in which various muscles are starting one at a time to move the different organs of speech into position for the sound. We call this the *onset*. There is a second stage when all the organs involved arrive in position reasonably together and combine to make the sound. Lips, tongue, jaw, nasal chambers, and uvula vibrate as one. We call this the *crest.* And there is the third stage, the *release,* in which the muscles, each at its own pace, abandon the sound and start toward the onset of the next phoneme. Onset, crest, release; onset, crest, release—the phonemes follow each other so fast that scientists have had to invent a "speech stretcher" to slow them down and present them in slow motion for analysis. The release of each sound is attracted by the onset of the next; the muscles letting go are drawn out of one stance into another.

Even the crest of the first phoneme is shifted toward the crest of the next, so that /l/ or /k/ is never merely /l/ or /k/ but the kind of /l/ or /k/ that accompanies the other sound; and the other sound is drawn toward the /l/ or /k/. If we say the words **hell** /hel/ and **help** /help/, the /h/ is the one that precedes /e/, the /e/ is the kind that follows /h/ and precedes /l/; but in **hell** the /l/ is the kind that follows /e/ and ends the word. In **help** the /l/ is the kind that follows /e/and goes before /p/, and the /p/ is the kind that follows /l/ and ends the word. If we say **hell** with the /l/ in **help** or **help** with the /l/ in **hell,** we make a very foreign-sounding word.

The Phonemes of Pitch, Stress, and Juncture

THE vowel, consonant, and semivowel phonemes—called "segmental" phonemes because each represents a little slice of the utterance—seemed to be the basic units of speech until a few years ago. People could hear other qualities in speech that they called "intonations" or "inflections" of the voice. For a long time no one could analyze them. But a phoneme is not a signal in itself; in itself it is only a bundle of sound-qualities that recurs. It is only one signal in a system of signals. To understand the phoneme as a signal, we have to relate it to the other signals and the other kinds of signals that work with it in the system. Our understanding of English always lacked a little until the analysts put their fingers on three other kinds of phonemes just as important to speech as the "segmental" phonemes: the phonemes of pitch, stress, and juncture.

PITCH PHONEMES

All sound has pitch and loudness. High-fidelity fans like to play phonograph records on equipment that brings out the range of sounds the human ear can hear, because the ear can respond to vibrations from twenty to fifteen thousand a second. The slow ones are the low ones. The human vocal system, like a musical instrument, makes vibrations within the range of human hearing; each human being produces his own limited span of vibrations. A small child, like a flute or small woodwind, makes a span of high vibrations; he has a "high-pitched" voice. As the child grows, his "pipes" grow and their tones deepen. Women have voices of medium pitch and men have voices of low pitch, though some women have low voices and some men have high voices. Yet all speakers of English use pitch as part of the signals of speech; that is, they use *pitch phonemes*. It cannot be "absolute" pitch that they use; obviously no particular pitch can serve as a phoneme.

Language uses relative pitch—levels of pitch related to other levels of pitch by being higher or lower. In English each person speaks the segmental phonemes—the consonants, vowels, and semivowels—at his normal level, the one best suited to the size and conformation of his throat and head passages. This is the one that comes easiest to him. This level is a phoneme. When he departs from it by raising or lowering the pitch the departure is also a phoneme, because the language uses it as a signal. In English he goes down one level below the normal tone. Above the normal tone, he goes commonly to one and occasionally to two higher levels. In our notation we give numbers to these levels, starting at the bottom and counting up. Thus we have four pitch phonemes, and we number them from the lowest up, /1 2 3 4/. /2/ is the pitch-level of normal monotone speech.

If a person raises his voice into a higher range of pitch, the habit of using four pitch-levels goes with him; he uses four intervals in the higher range. If he lowers his voice to a deeper pitch, he uses four intervals in that range. If he shifts ranges in the middle of an utterance, he uses four intervals at each range. If he runs his voice up and down undulatingly in an utterance, the four intervals undulate with it. Wherever the intervals occur within the range of human hearing, they serve as signals. They do not have to keep a certain space from each other. Any difference in pitch that is perceptible is enough.

It is hard to "hear" the segmental phonemes as we make them or listen to them, since they work by automatic habit. It is harder still to "hear" the phonemes of pitch. The vowels themselves are sounds of different pitches; the vocal qualifiers, signals of attitude, introduce confusing complexities of orchestration into the utterance. Pitch also accompanies stress. It will be enough to say at the moment that the consonant, vowel, and semivowel phonemes are overlaid with the pitch phonemes, so that each may be said at one of four levels of pitch. Of these /2/ is the normal or monotone level, /1/ is low, /3/ is high, and /4/ is very high. Like other phonemes, phonemes of pitch combine into morphemes—into morphemes of pitch.

We can inspect the pitch phonemes apart from others in a made-up passage which demonstrates one common way of saying these sentences:

3_____| 3_____||
2_____
"Did he go to the movies?" asked Jim.

3_____
2_____ \2 | 2_____||
"I think so,"   replied Mary.

4_____| _____||
2_____
"Are you absolutely certain?" asked Jim.

3,   3,
\2 | 2__ \1 | 1_____#
"Yes, I am, " said Mary's sister.

STRESS PHONEMES

ALL sound also has loudness, and some sounds are louder than others. English uses relative loudness as a signal as it uses relative pitch; again it uses four degrees of loudness. These are often easier to "hear" than the four degrees of pitch. Relative loudness is usually called *stress* or *accent* in language; hence we call these signals of loudness and softness the phonemes of stress. Three actually are degrees of stress; the fourth and least loud is an almost complete lack of stress. We call them primary, loud, or heavy stress /´/, secondary or medium stress /^/, tertiary (third) or light stress /`/, and weakly stressed or weakly accented /˘/. Consider **daily** /´ ˘/, **our daily bread** /` ^ ˘ ´/, **the night watch** /˘ ´ ^/, and **the present danger** /˘ ^ ˘ ´ `/. Normally it is simpler just to use the three marks of stress /´ ^ `/ and leave weakly stressed syllables unmarked.

Thus in English we have two kinds of syllables, stressed and unstressed; the stressed syllables may bear heavy, medium, or light stress. Dictionaries usually indicate only one or two stresses, partly because most dictionaries were written before the third stress was identified and generally accepted, and partly because most words standing alone can be marked with only two stresses at the most. As soon as we try to catch the stress patterns of running speech, we begin to hear the three degrees of loudness of stressed syllables. **Secondary** /´ ^ ` ˘/ standing alone has stress on two syllables, heavy and light; the other two syllables are unstressed. In the noun-group **secondary school** the stresses shift. **School** now takes the heavy stress; the strong stress in **secondary** drops to medium and the light stress remains light.

These unaccented or unstressed syllables in English seem like little things, but let us consider the large effects they seem to have set in motion. Old English of the early tenth century had three levels of stress: heavy, medium, and light. Every syllable received some degree of stress; the vowels in all syllables were spoken with reasonably full value, as in **pecan** /píy kæ̀n/ as against **peekin'** /píy kin/. From the tenth to the twelfth centuries certain middle and end syllables lost their stress; the old three-stress system changed to one of four stress phonemes. The vowels in unstressed syllables drifted; people began to say them with /i/ and /ə/ in the mid central sector of the mouth. The end syllables were mainly inflectional signals which depended upon clean-cut distinctions in vowel sounds to keep them apart. When their vowels all drifted to the mid-central sector of the mouth, they lost their signal value. Patterns of order which had been forming for centuries took on signal value and developed into our modern order of utterance. When the system shook down into our present way of speaking, a very limited set of inflections, **N, N-s; V, V-s, V-ed, V-ing, V-ed/en,** etc., combined with the order of utterance to do what inflections had done before pretty much alone. This little shift in the stress phonemes wrecked the old equilibrium and brought about a new one. Big consequences come from small causes.

JUNCTURE PHONEMES

A JUNCTURE is a joining or a joint, and *juncture phonemes* are joints or cuts in the utterances. They occur not within syllables but before and after them. A syllable is a unit of pronunciation with at least one sound—usually a vowel—in it. In English a syllable may be a vowel alone, like **a** /ə/ in **a bird;** a consonant and a vowel, like **the** /ðə/ in **the bird;** a vowel and a consonant, like **at** /æt/ in **at home;** a consonant, a vowel, and a consonant, like **car** /kahr/ or **fat** /fæt/. These are minimum syllables; a syllable may be no smaller. Syllables may be larger. A syllable may consist of vowel and semivowel, like **eye** /ay/; vowel, semivowel, and consonant, like **eight** /ayt/; consonant, vowel, and semivowel, like **tie** /tay/; and consonant, vowel, semivowel, and consonant, like **tight** /tayt/. In the beginning or ending of the syllable, there may be a consonant cluster, like **glimpsed** /glimpst/.

Within a syllable the phonemes "feed into" each other and attract each other, as we noted above in **help** /help/, and no juncture phoneme occurs. Some syllables feed into each other with no juncture phoneme between, as in **often** /afən/ or /ɔfən/ and **delay** /diley/. If all syllables joined this way, the utterance would be a continuous stream of sounds like toothpaste coming out of a tube. As we say the utterance, however, we clot the syllables in it by means of pitch-pause signals that we call *junctures.*

The first of these junctures is called "internal open juncture"— a big name for a small thing. It is "internal" to the utterance; it comes between the beginning and the end. It is an "opening" between syllables, a little wedge of nothing that serves only to keep two adjoining syllables from feeding into each other. If we say **Sometimes she was sad** and **She was sad at some times,** we make a minute difference between **sometimes** /səmtaymz/ and **some times** /səm + taymz/. We may hear the same difference between **nitrates** and **night rates** in He asked for the **nitrates** /naytreyts/ and He asked for the **night rates** /nayt + reyts/. We hear it between **minus** /maynis/ and **slyness** /slay + nis/. We hear it between **an aim** /ən + eym/ and **a name** /əneym/.

Like most aspects of language, internal open juncture is easier and simpler to hear than describe. It is in fact rather complicated. The phonemes that come before and after it do not feed into each other; the phoneme before it stops, as if at the end of an utterance; the phoneme after it starts as if at the beginning of the utterance. There is a minute adjustment of pitch and stress. The total effect is to give an intermittent quality to the flow of the utterances, with some syllables run together and others kept apart. We mark this juncture with a plus sign /+/ when it seems worth while to do so in an exhaustive phonemic transcription or when it seems to be the only difference between two similar expressions.

The other three junctures are "final"; they close utterances or parts of utterances. Each is a gap in the stream of speech; each involves adjustment of pitch; each is preceded by "end" phonemes and followed (if the speaker goes on) by the kind of phoneme that starts utterances. Since what happens to pitch is the most noticeable thing about them, we may describe them in terms of pitch: we mark level pitch with a single vertical line /|/, rising pitch with two vertical lines /||/, and falling pitch with a cross hatch /#/.

We hear level juncture in the utterance **I used to go to the movies:**

$$/\text{ày yúwstə gôw} \mid \text{tə ðə múwvìyz}\#/$$

No matter which pitch precedes, if it remains the same over and through the juncture, we have level juncture /|/. We may have it after **George** in **Don't ask for George** /|/ **he's left.** We may have it after **night** in **Nobody got through tonight** /|/ **the road is closed.** This juncture is usually marked in standard English writing by a comma (,) or a semicolon (;).

Rising juncture /||/ is the sentence-closing that we usually hear as "question intonation." We hear it at the end of **You're not going to send that?** It is a slight rise in pitch between the last couple of syllables or within the last. We hear it also in a series, such as **one, two, three . . .** /wə́n || túw || θríy ||/. The phoneme that precedes it is an "end" phoneme.

Falling juncture /#/ is the pitch-drop with which we end almost all statements, all answers to questions, all words or word-groups spoken alone. When we read slowly, pausing after each meaning-group, we use this juncture. It is a slight lowering of pitch, a smooth fall on the last syllable or within it. It may end an utterance on any pitch level /1 **2** 3 4/. The phoneme which precedes it is an "end" phoneme. There has been a good deal of argument about what a sentence is, and hundreds of definitions have been composed, philosophical, logical, semantic, and psychological. We have treated the sentence here as the equivalent in writing of the utterance. We know what an utterance is. It is a stretch of speech that begins in silence or after one of the three final junctures; it continues until the speaker signals its end with one of the three final junctures, but especially with falling juncture /#/. We mark it in writing with a semicolon (;) or a period (.).

The pitch, stress, and juncture phonemes of English give our speech its characteristic "tune" or intonation, quite different from the tune of French, Spanish, German, or any other language. When we learn a foreign language, the hardest thing we have to learn is to keep these intonation contours out of our pronunciation of the other language. We may learn to make individual sounds quite exactly but be very difficult to understand; if we speak with the right tune, we can be understood in spite of inadequate handling of the segmental phonemes. Our tune is difficult for a foreigner to learn when he studies English. As long as he intrudes the pitch, stress, and juncture contours from his own language, he speaks with a "bad accent" and is hard to follow.

Within the English-speaking world, different speech-communities use these four levels of pitch, four degrees of stress, and four kinds of juncture in slightly different melodies to produce slightly different accents. Some kinds of British English seem to an American ear to be surging widely up and down the range of pitches; American speech strikes the British ear as a monotone. In America, Northern English differs from Middle Atlantic and Southern dialects, and each of these differs from the others in the selection and arrangement of these phonemes. A child has fair control of intonation very young, even before he can make all the segmental phonemes in the way he hears them; he fixes them by play and experimentation. Many a youngster gets his ears cuffed for using the wrong tone to the wrong person at the wrong time. He learns. We are at one with our nation in our natural use of the tone and tune of our own home towns.

✳ CHAPTER 19 ✳

Morphemes and Syntax

WE FIND IT IMPOSSIBLE to say one phoneme alone so that it sounds right; all the familar variations a phoneme may have are assigned to it by its place in a complete utterance. Pronounced separately, it is distorted; it has the onset of a beginning sound and the release of a final sound. It is also stressed. Thus it does not strike the ear or an electronic voice-analyzer with anything like a natural timbre. About the smallest unit of speech that we can say alone with any naturalness is a syllable, probably because we are used to one-syllabled words like **cat** and **stop.** When we pronounce a syllable alone, it, too, carries heavy stress, no matter what stress it usually has in utterances.

The syllable is a working unit of pronunciation. It would be nice if the syllable as it stands were a signaling-unit of speech. Unfortunately it is not, though it has often fooled people into taking it for one. A syllable is merely an impulse of the breath something like the puff of smoke an Indian makes when he is signaling with smoke. If the Indian is to signal with smoke, he has to cut it into a series of puffs with his blanket; otherwise he has a continuous column of smoke. If we are to use breath for speaking, we have a column of outgoing air to work on, continuous in our normal breathing as long as it lasts. Each of our syllables has a vowel or vowel-nucleus

at its center (vowel or vowel plus semivowel) and is produced by
a single pulse of the diaphragm or rib-cage. Vowel seldom feeds
smoothly into vowel in English; there is usually a consonant or
semivowel at the end of one syllable or the beginning of the next,
cutting the column of air the way the Indian blanket cuts the column of smoke.

As we speak, syllables may be long or short, but length or short-
ness of syllables has no particular significance in English by itself.
Length varies with stress; syllables carrying any of the three stresses
(heavy, medium, and light) are usually overlong. Syllables that are
unstressed are usually overshort, and the vowels in them are centralized: we usually say the phonemes /ɨ/ *or* /ə/ in them, as in
American /əmérɨkən/ or /əmérəkən/.

The syllable, a mere cutting of the column of air into long and
short puffs, is too crude an entity to serve well as a signaling-unit
of speech. The consonant or consonant cluster that divides syllables
may be quite complicated to the ear, as in **capstone** /kǽpstôwn/,
but it makes one cut and one only in the flow of air. We speak by
puffs and we hear by those puffs; yet we hear the separate sounds
within the puffs with some discrimination. The phonemes combine
and separate in a system different from the syllable division, making
a rank of units we call morphemes. The morphemes fall into ut-
terance-arrangements that we call syntax.

So it is that **cat** /kǽt/ and **cats** /kǽts/ each makes one syllable;
house /háws/ makes one syllable and **houses** /háwzɨz/ makes two;
yet **cat** and **house** consist of one morpheme each, and **cats** and
houses consist of two each. A morpheme may thus be as small as a
phoneme if the phoneme is a unit of syntax as well as a unit of
sound. These words are even more complex. Said separately, **cats**
consist of several morphemes: two segmental morphemes, and a
pitch, stress, and juncture complex called a "superfix." We would
give it a complete phonemic notation as follows /²kǽts#/. This
notation exposes complexity within the syllable that makes the
syllable look about as intricate as a puff of smoke.

Dismantling speech in this manner can be a fascinating game if
you want to play it, but morphemic analysis, especially, gets complicated in a hurry—too complicated for our present needs. Much
of the analysis of English remains to be done. For us it is enough
to know what is done and how it is done, so that we can understand

how this system of speech-signals—the phonemes combining into morphemes and the morphemes combining into syntax—can be mankind's primary system of communication. Most other human communication is based on it and derived from it, and all human interaction depends on it. A language lives as long as living human beings speak it, whether it is written down or not; a language dies when living human beings do not speak it, whether its writing survives or not.

We spoke of an orderly procedure. Let us follow the analyst step by step as he digs into human speech and works out a description of it. We will then understand a little more about the relation of writing to speech and about the special problems of English writing. First the analyst tries to find a person who is as typical of his speech-community as possible. This person feels himself to be representative of his group, an ordinary type in his town, his profession, his club, his age group, or any other set of persons whose language we wish to study. The group feels him to be representative of them also. Usually they refer the analyst to him, once they understand the sort of person wanted. In time the analyst will build up a large set of records of such people and be able to check and crosscheck among them.

Next the analyst engages this person (whom he calls his "informant") in conversation and makes as complete a notation as he can of everything the informant says. Generally he begins with a phonetic notation because he does not know what the signals—the phonemes—are. He gets down the raw sounds, as they strike his ear, in a finely graded phonetic alphabet. As quickly as he can, he converts this to a phonemic notation, hunting for the signals to which people respond among those that they ignore. If he can, he records the same talk on tape so that he can play it over and over again as he hunts through it for the signals. He cannot use tape recordings alone, because tape has a dead ear; it will not distinguish **eavestroths** from **eavestroughs,** for example, and the difference is important. If the language is new to him, the analysis is an arduous process, carried on sometimes through interpreters, sometimes with no help besides a friendly attitude and a feeling of common humanity. One religious group grimly counts five dead linguist-missionaries who did not establish rapport with native informants before the shooting started. If, however, the language being studied is

English, the analyst starts with a pretty good notion of the phonemes; but he has to keep alert; any new informant can spring some
surprises on him.

Now he begins to use the data of his phonemic notation to find
the structure of the language; he looks for groups of sounds that
keep coming back together and makes a list of the groups. He is
searching for morphemes and the ways in which they combine—
the syntax. He finds that he can cut English in two directions: "horizontally"—the long way of the utterance; and "vertically"—slicing off sequences of sounds. Separating the utterance "horizontally," he takes the pitch phonemes by themselves and observes the
order they come in. He makes lists of pitch patterns: /3 2 1/,
/2 3 2/, and so on. He examines the stress patterns, watching for
the sequences they come in: /˘ ´/, /˘ ´ ^/, and so on. He lists
the stress patterns. He compares the pitch patterns and the stress
patterns with each other, to see whether they fall together by
chance or in some regular way. If he can find any regularity, he
records it.

Slicing the utterance "vertically," he cuts at first at the obvious
junctures and listens for recurring patterns of segmental phonemes,
making up a list. Then he cuts into these groups looking for morphemes that can stand alone syntactically (free forms) and for
morphemes that cannot stand alone (bound forms). Again he sorts
his materials, relating these items to the items of pitch and stress
that he has discovered, and to the junctures.

Throughout this gathering and dissection of material the analyst
tries to keep the informant talking about everything in the world
except the subject that interests both of them very much: the language. Every community has its ideas about what is "correct" and
"incorrect"; most informants will talk at length on this subject if
you let them. This talk is no more trustworthy in America than in
darkest Africa; the analyst wants to know not what the informant
thinks he ought to say but what he does say. These are often not at
all the same thing. It is a shock to discover that for what you would
write **Are you going to go?** you say /²yə gə̂nə ³gów ‖/, when you
think you are saying what you would write. The analyst is often
content merely to ask whether /kǽt/ means the same as /kǽts/ or
something different. Is there the same difference between /dɔ́wg/
and /dɔ́wgz/ as between /kǽt/ and /kǽts/? If so, he can put down
the /s/ and the /z/ as variants of the same morpheme affected by

the preceding sounds. Then how about /háws/ and /háwzɨz/? Is that the same difference again? And /líyf/ and /líyvz/?

The analyst works on into longer and more complex sequences until he has exhausted his material and discovered all the elements he can. When he has done, he has a description of that one man's speech as far as it is represented in the body of material he has collected. He can then move to a comparison of this description to others made up in the same way, noting all similarities and differences. If the language has no alphabet and no writing system, he is in a position to invent one; if it has a traditional system, he is in a position to state explicitly how it relates to speech and what the peculiarities are. By this time he is an old man who has added significantly to our knowledge of human speech and human cultures.

Dealing with a language like English with an old, honored, universal, and traditional system of writing, we find it difficult to keep in mind that speech analysis always starts with the speech of one person. It begins with a phonetic or phonemic recording of what some one person actually has said; it keeps coming back to this primary record. It must always aim to identify all the signals that the informant has used and identify these signals in all their combinations. Of course we cannot expect to pump him dry of signals in one conversation or even in many. We can hope to catch all his phonemes, but we can get only a sampling of his morphemes and their arrangements, since his selection of these depends upon what he is talking about and whom he is talking to. Behind everything he actually says is a great storehouse of what he might say and forms and arrangements he might use. We would have to get right inside his mind to know how large that store is and how available it is to him when he comes to speak. We have to take it as he gives us hints of its size and availability in his casual talk. No idea of what he should say or should have said can change the fact that he did say what he did; we have to be honest with the record; we have to stick by it.

The informant is a complex person involved in complex social situations. He speaks creatively, forming his utterances out of experience with men and things that is peculiarly his own; no one is quite like him or has quite the same relations with other people. No one has read exactly what he has read and with his peculiar reactions to it, missing what he has missed and catching what he has caught. He is unique; yet he is unique within a society. He is most like the people he has most closely associated with all his days, and more and more different from others as he has less and less contact with them.

Each unique person normally speaks with the assumption that his hearer uses the language about the same way as he does himself, responding to the same signals. In a complicated society involving many millions of people spread over a large land mass this is a dangerous assumption, but he pushes it even further. He feels that the other person *ought* to use his signals with his meanings, and he feels angry, annoyed, or exasperated when someone pulls him up short by failing to respond in the expected way to what he has said. His mental picture of his listener is an enlarged image of himself: a person with just his command of the code attending to the message. The hearer, with the same feeling that other people *ought* to use his code in his way, is angry, annoyed, or exasperated at anything that is off-beat. Speaker blames hearer; hearer blames speaker. If you think much about language, you come to realize that there must be many differences in the code used by some two hundred and fifty million people, each unique and uniquely involved in his own personal affairs.

It is not only that we have differences between people; we also have differences within the speech of a single person as he talks to various friends, acquaintances, and strangers about the matters that concern them. For what we would write or print as **What do you mean?** he may say:

/²hwə̂t dùw yùw ³míyn¹ #/
/²wə̂t də yə ³míyn #/
/²wə̀čə ³míyn ‖/

He may use any of several other variants with no consciousness of making any changes in his speech. He adjusts to the subject, the person he is talking to, and the circumstances in which he finds himself.

Exhaustive phonemic notation is the primary record; all further analysis is based on it and checked back against it. As a particular phoneme will vary in sound as it is attracted to phonemes surrounding it, so a specific morpheme differs in different surroundings. Analysis must sort the morphemes, discovering which are to be kept together and which apart, which fall into sets and which— regardless of gross differences of sound—must be considered instances of the same one. The analysis is an analysis of speech. The basic phonemic writing has to be related to our standard spelling, for each person speaking phonemes writes letters. We take this matter up in Chapter 21. Morphemic analysis leads us into a notation that makes phonemic notation look like the arithmetic of simple addition; syntactic analysis leads us into a notation as complex and difficult to master as calculus. Morphemic and syntactic analysis bring us to the spoken equivalent of the material we covered in this book in Part II: "How Our Language Works" and Part III: "How We Sort Our Words." Each person speaking morphemes in utterances writes words in sentences. Standard English writing is sufficiently morphemic and syntactic to let us talk about the larger patterns of the language in terms of words, as we have done, instead of learning to use the more precise but extremely cumbersome notation that cannot be mastered quickly or easily. We could translate this material into the corresponding analysis of speech, but for our present purposes it is not worthwhile. Our purpose is to improve our reading and writing; we need to know in general how speech relates to reading and writing, to writing and printing.

Even if we could quickly master morphemic and syntactic notation, we would have to make some decisions about the translation from standard writing to the recording of speech. Shall we transcribe into the speech of some one person? Into whose speech? Into what tone: familiar, informal, formal? Each decision leads us to a different notation. People differ, dialects differ, regions differ, nations differ. Writing evades the differences, and it is adequate for our purpose as long as we remember that the speech of each person must be related to it.

A translation of Part II and Part III into a morphemic and syntactic treatment of the speech of some one person would teach us one important thing, and that is that the differences between the speech of two persons, two communities, or two regions are not haphazard and disorganized. They are regular. The phonemes and morphemes differ, the syntax differs, and even the sounds of the phonemes differ, but always in an organized way. The way of talking of each speech-community affects all aspects of speech as a whole; the whole is systematically different from the speech of another community. Each person's speech differs systematically from another person's and changes systematically as his mood and intention change. The regularity of the differences that we hear makes it possible for us to understand what he says. If his /r/ is not the same as ours, we recognize his /r/ wherever we would use our own. If he says /páht/ or /pǽht/ where we would say /páhrt/, he substitutes /ah/ or /æh/ for /ahr/ wherever it occurs, for the most part. Once we are used to what he does we can understand him; we hear by substitution. We may find it hard to believe that he ought to substitute his sound for ours, but there it is. When we recognize that a different signal is being regularly introduced—whether it is a sound, a phoneme, a word, or a larger pattern—we can respond to it, even though we would not and could not use his signal in place of our own. We normally accept many small personal differences in speech without imitating them; it is not much more for us to accept community differences, respond to them and understand them, but without imitation.

The better we can understand our own speech and the machinery in it, the more economically we can reach a command of standard English writing. Our writing is always related to our speech; it springs from it. The forty-five phonemic signs let us manipulate on paper the forty-five elemental signals of our speech. They help us to hear our own talk and inspect it. They help us disentangle our pronunciation from our spelling, so that we don't fool ourselves into thinking that we write words the way they sound or that we pronounce the letters we write. They help us to hear our stress-patterns, pitch-patterns, and junctures, so that we know how we slice our utterances into word-groups; this grouping, so sketchily represented in standard writing, sets one word apart or tells us that strings of words are working as one.

We do not have to be rigid or overthorough in our use of the phonemic notation or too particular in trying to control all of it at once. We can leave that to the specialists. It is not easy to catch on paper all the running sequence of phonemes and the intonation signals at the same time. Even skilled analysts have to satisfy themselves with catching short stretches of talk, single words and brief word-groups. The marvelously sensitive voice spectrograph, which has been the atom smasher of speech, handles a stretch of only four or five words. The beauty of the notation is that we can use any part of it separate from the rest to dissect any aspect of speech we care about; we can focus on some one element like the vowels or consonants, or on pitch signals or stresses. We might wish to watch the /k/ in such words as **catch, pique, quay** /kíy/, **queen** /kwíyn/,

or the /ǰ/ in **judge, college, knowledge, bridge,** or **garage.** We might
be interested only in the /iy/ in **machine, peace, piece, freeze, relief,** or **quay,** in order to find out exactly how we say these words
so different in their spelling. We might merely wish to note the
variant pronunciations of **wash** /wáš/, /wɔ́hš/, /wɔ́hrš/, and
/wɔ́yš/; **push** /púš/; or /púyš/; or **laugh** /lǽf/, /lǽhf/, /léhf/,
/lǽyf/, or /láhf/. We might watch **can, can't** and **can** as said by
people from different parts of the country: **We eat all we can**
/kǽn/, /kín/; **and what we can't** /kǽnt/, /kéynt/, **we can**
/kǽn/, /kǽyn/.

We can use standard spellings in sentences where we are interested only in noting pitches and stresses; we often can use standard
punctuation when we are not especially interested in junctures. Using phonemic notation, we can dig into the shape and sound-values
of poetry more exactly than by any other method. Comparing
Ralph Hodgson's "Eve" with Robert Frost's "Stopping by Woods
on a Snowy Evening," we find that no magic creates the different
impact of these poems; "Eve" runs to front consonants and the
following pattern of vowels:

$$
\begin{array}{ccc}
\text{i} & \text{ɨ} & \text{u} \\
\text{e} & \text{ə} & \text{o} \\
\text{æ} & \text{a} & \text{ɔ}
\end{array}
$$

Frost's poem runs to back consonants and this pattern of vowels:

$$
\begin{array}{ccc}
\text{i} & \text{ɨ} & \text{u} \\
\text{e} & \text{ə} & \text{o} \\
\text{æ} & \text{a} & \text{ɔ}
\end{array}
$$

The distribution of stresses and the spans between final junctures is
quite different also. The sound-structures reverberate the meaning
of the words.

To get hold of any form of art (as we shall see in Chapter 31),
we have to understand what the artist has done to his material to
make it say what he puts into it to be said. If he uses stone, we start
with the shape the artist gives the stone by leaving part and chip-
ping part away. When we know exactly what the form is, we can
begin to discover what the form means. So with the arts like poetry
and creative prose which use language. Phonemic notation of a
poem is the most exact means available for taking the poem out of
the empty air and fixing it for study, the next best thing to total

recall. Of modern poets, E. E. Cummings has most deliberately used language the way a sculptor uses stone, and his poems are notoriously hard to read aloud. Here is a reading of Cummings' "Portrait VIII" set in phonemic notation (with vocal qualifiers omitted), but arranged to match the printed format Cummings gave it. This arrangement helps the eye, but it has no bearing on the reading.

/³bɜ̂fəlòw ³bíl³|³z

  dɨ²fə́ŋkt¹ #

   ²hùw yûwstə

    râydə wâtər smùwð sîlvər

       ²stǽlyɨn² ||

²ɨn ²bréyk²|²wə̀n tùw θrìy fòhr ²fáyv²|³pííɨnz³||²ɨts lâyk ¹ðǽt¹ #

                  ⁴jíyzɨs¹|

¹hìy wə̀zə hǽnsɨm ¹mǽn¹ #

        ²ɨn hwə̂t ⁴áy²|²wɔ̂ntə ²nɔ́w²|²íz²||

²hæ̀wdəyə ⁴láyk⁴|²yər blûw àyd ²bɔ́y²|

²mîstər ²déθ² ||/

PORTRAIT VIII

Buffalo Bill's
defunct
      who used to
      ride a watersmooth-silver
                     stallion
and break onetwothreefourfive pigeonsjustlikethat
                                 Jesus
he was a handsome man
                and what i want to know is
how do you like your blueeyed boy
Mister Death

Thus we can use phonemic notation as a tool for observation and make sure we use it as a tool without letting it run us. Without such a tool, our language seems formless, chaotic, sometimes a natural growth like a weed, sometimes a mystery. With it we expose the repetitions and regularities by which we communicate; we break the barriers of sound and penetrate to some extent the mystery.

PART FIVE

How We Write

CHAPTER 20

The Conventions of Writing

English writing parallels English speech in a rough and apparently haphazard way. For the twenty-one consonant, nine vowel, and three semivowel phonemes writing has twenty-six letters. We treat twenty of the letters as consonants: **b, c, d, f, g, h, j, k, l, m, n, p, q, r, s, t, v, w, x,** and **z.** We treat five as vowels: **a, e, i, o,** and **u.** We treat **y** sometimes as a vowel and sometimes as a consonant. Each of us is familiar with these letters in four different forms of our roman alphabet: the capitals and small letters of handwritten script, and the capitals or upper-case letters and the small or lower-case letters of print. Besides the roman alphabet we also print the capitals and lower-case letters of the *italic* alphabet, a variant of roman in which *the letters are lighter and slanted slightly to the right.* In writing or typing we usually indicate *italic* letters by one straight underline; the printer working from handwritten or typed copy sets underlined letters or words in *italic.* These are the basic alphabets we know; but any printing house which can afford a large stock of different type faces can choose among them for pleasing and emphatic impressions on the eye. Type design is an important and sophisticated form of art.

For the pitch, stress, and juncture phonemes of speech, writing and printing use punctuation marks: the period (.), comma (,), colon (:), semicolon (;), question mark (?), exclamation mark (!), dash (—), ellipsis (. . .), single quotation mark ('), double quotation mark ("), the parentheses or curved brackets ((. . .)), and the square brackets ([. . .]).

Writing and printing also use the ten numerals: 1, 2, 3, 4, 5, 6, 7, 8, 9, and 0; and a host of special marks like $, £, &, and %; but these stand apart from the capitals and lower-case letters of the alphabet and the punctuation marks. They represent unit ideas, words, or even phrases, and often stand for equivalent expressions in many languages, as 4 means **four** in English, **quatre** in French, **vier** in German, and so on. We pass over them here because we want to keep our eyes on the alphabet and the punctuation marks, the immediate representatives of speech in writing and printing. The numerals and other similar marks extend further some of the principles involved in alphabetic writing. Once we understand the relation of the alphabet to the sounds of English, we have no big problems with the other symbols that have come into use with it.

Many educated people have become annoyed with the English alphabet because it is not a very accurate representation of English sounds. They have tinkered with it in various ways—adding more letters, putting special marks on existing letters, or trading around among the letters we have to get a more effective use of them. The letter **c,** they point out, stands either for /s/ or /k/; we should use **s** in such words as **cease** and **k** in such words as **cat,** leaving **c** free for other jobs such as standing for /θ/ in **thin.** Their proposals have not caught on, because of the odd look of such formations as **sease, kat,** and **cin.** Other people have been bothered by "silent" letters like the **l** in **talk,** the **p** in **psychology,** and the final **f** in **stuff.** (But what about the **l** in **help,** which is silent for some of us and not for others?) Shortening such words by eliminating "silent" letters, they calculate, would shorten our writing about a quarter, saving a quarter of the effort we put into writing and a quarter of the cost of type and paper used in printing. None of these notions has caught on; we spell our words in the old traditional way, with such slow adjustment to the sounds of speech that the new spelling is often archaic by the time it is accepted. Disorderly as our spelling seems, we prefer it to any of the other ways that have been offered.

People with little education have conducted their own kind of

attack on English spelling. We can illustrate with a portion of a
letter sent from a junkyard to an automobile agency:

```
Dear Ser.

            [List of parts]

Pleas ship theas parts as soon as posable
this is for a 1949 chev. 4 door Style no
1208. I will be call on you again for parts.
We have opean up a rebilding shop and will
need more parts. Will you sell me parts such
as body parts.
Centril chev co hear must not stock many
parts such as body parts.
If you dont have door panel let me know what
the door will cost me
And do you have thim.
Do you have eny extery parts book you can
let me have.
Do you have most eny thang in body parts
that i might need. I know parts ar gitting
hard to git
What about olds parts BUICK parts we cant
git eny at all and PONTIC
Do your stock thim or can you git thim.


     THANK A LOT.     Your Varley Truly


          WEST SIDE AUTO SALVAG CO
                212 Gee street
                _____, ARK.

     Which was stone wrecking yard
          Just chang the name
```

The most notable thing about this letter is its irregularity. Sometimes the writer punctuates (with a period); sometimes he does
not. Three-quarters of the words are spelled quite normally: **parts,
dear, again, panel, know, might,** and **truly.** Even this near-illiterate,
no matter how little his schooling or how long he has been out of

school, originally learned his 'letters in words; and the shapes of some common words have stuck with him. He drops some final e's, as in **pleas, theas, chang,** and **ar,** but he puts others on, as in **posable, stone,** and **name.** He writes **git** and **gitting** with **i** as he probably pronounces them; **thim** for **them** may represent /**ðim**/. **Extery** for **extra** is probably close to his pronunciation, but the **l** in **Varley** (for **very**) is an intrusion. Probably some of his spellings like **Varley** are pure typing errors; we can picture him punching out his letter with one finger, painfully, and letting the errors go.

Surely no improvement in English spelling can come from the near-illiterates; yet if we sift out other factors, we may get glimpses of their pronunciation from the way they write. They write so little that they have to blunder through every word, sometimes remembering how they once learned to spell, sometimes going it blind, and sometimes hitting the wrong keys. Each near-illiterate is isolated, not only from others like himself but from the main body of readers and writers; most semi-illiterates are people of little prestige. They are in no position to influence the standards of writing; even if they could do so, they would bring about no improvement. They introduce another individual and sporadic kind of disorder. The one thing that may be said for this man is that he communicates his meaning. But a mere communication of meaning which outrages every eye that sees the writing is not enough. To be effective, writing must stay within the system and be in keeping with it.

What is the system? Where is the order? Both system and order are a little difficult to discover, but they are there, balanced between what English writing is and what it is not. In the first place, English writing is not a modern invention but a slow growth within a changing society over roughly fifteen hundred years of which only the last four hundred lie within the modern period. Hence every generation has to start with a writing system handed to it by previous generations and adapt the system to its own times and its own needs. The printing press came to England in 1476. Before that time every written communication was individually prepared by hand, whether it was a note scribbled to remind oneself or a book intended for many readers. Since that time most of what used to be written by hand has been printed; for the rest, handwriting has gone on in the old way. Though we have better pens and pencils than our ancestors had, we use them about the same way.

Handwriting always has been drawing the letters and punctuation marks on paper one by one. Its readers are people who themselves write by hand. After the invention of printing, the close connection between writing and reading was broken, though the significance of this separation was not immediately recognized. For many centuries most people read aloud, saying the words as they saw them at a speed rather close to speech. Silent reading of the kind we do now was a late development as individual readers discovered that they did not have to say the words as they saw them. This discovery set the eyes free to work in their own way at their own pace; in time it set the printers free from the manuscript tradition, as they began to print for the expert and untrammeled eye.

Early printed books were as close imitations of manuscript books as the printers could make them, for the printers were invading with their books a market dominated by the highest quality of handcraftsmanship. New processes and new inventions do not break away immediately from the ones they replace. Early automobiles were (horseless) carriages, even to the whipsockets; metal furniture was at first painted and grained to look like wood. Some time passes before new things are accepted on their own terms for their own virtues. Printing, a process in which preformed letters were set up once and used to print many copies, could reach readers far beyond those who could afford finely drawn handwritten books. It brought great changes.

Writing can be done wherever the writer can sit down with pen and paper; printing equipment is bulky and has to be kept in one place. The printer sits in that place and prints for scattered readers; his potential audience is large and widely distributed. In a country with many dialects, each with its own form of writing, the printer prefers to settle on one dialect, standardize its forms, and if possible force the users of other dialects to read this one. He prefers a form of the language that has prestige and is already widely understood. The printers of England found that the London dialect served them well, for London in the fifteenth and sixteenth centuries was, as it still is, the governmental, commercial, military, and religious center of England. Early British presses at London, at Oxford, and at Cambridge (near the universities) took over the London dialect pretty much as it was. London English, much as it was then, is the English we write today. Books and printing have carried it over the world.

Even when books were set up by hand, typesetters found that they could work faster and more accurately if they used standardized forms. It did not matter which forms they used, long or short, or what letters were in them; there was a great gain in efficiency from adopting one spelling for each word whenever it came up. As machines were developed for setting type, the gain increased; type bars could be formed more quickly, more accurately, and more cheaply if the operator's muscles habitually produced standard spellings. After the typewriter came into use, typists discovered the same thing; fingers that stumble over unfamiliar spellings fly over familiar ones. With the invention of the teletypewriter, a typesetter in one city could set type in distant cities at the same time, if he used standard forms accepted everywhere.

Thus if you have a spelling system with reasonably standard forms, with more prestige than other ways of spelling, and with many people over a wide area habituated to it, it is more efficient and more economical to stick with it than try to train skilled operators to write other forms. Habit is an enormous human investment. No matter what virtues a different system might have—it might be closer to the way we speak, use fewer letters, suit more dialects and more different dialects—it still cannot compete with one that is ground into people's minds and muscles for instantaneous response to speech. The overwhelming virtue of our spelling is that it is standardized in most respects and habitual to most educated people throughout the English-speaking world. It wins out over all comers because we have it.

We can illustrate the importance of the forms that things take when they begin by glancing at the gauge of railroads and the arrangement of letters on a typewriter keyboard. When railroads were first invented, each builder settled on a span between rails that suited his purpose. Equipment could not be used on another line; goods had to be taken off one car and carried to another. In time, connecting railroads settled on a standard gauge so that they could send freight from loading point to destination without unpacking it. Car and engine builders standardized gauges. Narrow-gauge track was used in mountainous country, such as the Rockies, and in mines or any place where the size and cost of equipment had to be held down. Standard gauge with rails 56½ inches apart was used on main lines in America and Europe; it ultimately established the length of axles, not only on railroad equipment but on streetcars, wagons, automobiles, and trucks. In Russia a wide or broad gauge was used. Broad-gauge track has almost every advantage for modern transportation. Cars are wider and roomier, more stable on their wheels, less likely to tip over, because the center of gravity is lower. But we cannot switch to it because our whole interlocking complex of transportation with its colossal investment in equipment is based on standard-gauge track. We're stuck with it as we are with our spelling, because we have it.

When the typewriter was invented, each manufacturer arranged the letters on the keyboard as seemed best to him. As the machines caught on and became widely used, a kind of professional operator, the typist, developed. Each operator had to learn the keyboard of each new machine she worked with, and a demand rose for a standard arrangement of the keys. The present arrangement is fairly good, with numbers and special characters on the top row and at the right side; but no one thought to count the frequency with which letters are used and to put the common ones where they are easiest to strike. The present arrangement gives more work to the fingers of the left hand than the right, as if a violinist had designed the keyboard. During World War II an arrangement taking into account the statistical frequency of recurring letters was worked out; it is easier to learn, faster, and more efficient. With it the typist can turn out more copy accurately and with less fatigue. But there are so many typewriters in use and so many typists trained to use them, and it would be such a large job to retrain skilled muscles in new ways, that we go on with the old keyboard.

It is the same with English spelling. Possibly a new spelling could be worked out. Yet a completely phonetic or phonemic spelling would not fit every dialect of English, even of educated speakers of English, and nothing less would bring much improvement. We would have to junk or rebuild much costly equipment and re-educate the highly skilled hands and fingers of millions of operators. We would render all previously printed material obsolete, so that it would have to be put out in the new form or left to specialists to read. We quail before such a gigantic enterprise; we find it easier and cheaper to bring up young people in the old system with all its difficulties. We suspect also, with considerable justice, that we would be running into harrowing problems that would develop only in practice. We consider it better to bear the ills we have than fly to others we know not of.

Each human society in its own portion of the globe has to take the world as it comes and make the best of it; each human being has to work out a way to live in the world as he finds it. Although some people never reconcile themselves to circumstances, most members of most societies submit to harsh realities; they develop pride in their submission and insist that all is for the best. One would expect the Eskimos to migrate en masse to California as soon as the chance offered; instead, they cling to their northern wastes and look with pity and contempt at persons who cannot take care of themselves through a savage Arctic winter. The harder a job is to do, the more pride people take in doing it—not merely passably but so as to demonstrate superlative skill. English writing is a difficult, old, complicated, and cumbersome way of writing a language down; but the difficulty has been to the educated a challenge to show what they can do. Sheer pride of mastery leads them to insist that writing be written, not merely so as to communicate meaning but so as to demonstrate a real command of its peculiarities. People who have learned to write words right demand of all expression that it be rightly written. That is a hard fact the learner has to face.

Since we are a people with a strong historical sense, we are often helped to face the present by a look at the past. Before we take up modern English writing (which embodies its history in some peculiar and interesting ways) we probably should review that history, in general terms.

1. Our writing began many centuries ago with the invention of the alphabet by some Mediterranean people, who partly perceived the phonemic principle that speech consists of a limited number of basic sound-signals used over and over in recurring patterns. Giving each phoneme they recognized a letter-symbol of its own, they produced a form of writing superior to the picture-writing, idea-writing, and syllable-writing systems then in use, superior because the symbols necessary were so few.

2. As the idea of the alphabet caught on, the original alphabet was imitated or borrowed and adapted to other languages. One form was fitted to Greek and then to Latin (but not so neatly as might have been expected). Some letters were used for more than one phoneme, and some phonemes were split among different letters. As languages changed, their alphabets changed also, but more slowly, lagging somewhat behind.

3. Besides the original alphabet which resembled our capital letters, variants were designed that were easier to write or prettier. Capitals were still used for monuments and inscriptions; in the course of time capitals were combined with the newer small-letter (minuscule) alphabets in titles and important words.

4. The uninterrupted line of alphabetic writing was divided by spaces to set off words.

5. Latin scholars and missionaries used the Roman alphabet to write down other languages including English, giving the letters as much as possible equivalent values and fitting the letters to phonemes that sounded something like the Latin phonemes. For some Old English sounds that Latin lacked, symbols from runic were borrowed, þ and ð for /θ/ and /ð/, and the 'wen' for /w/. A symbol used in Latin abbreviations, ȝ, was used for /X/, a rough continuant made by pressing the tongue close to the roof of the mouth as in Scottish **licht.** A double letter or digraph æ was used for /æ/. (We have borrowed some again for our phonemic notation.) The alphabet was applied rather loosely to different spoken dialects, so that a single set of letters was used to represent a medley of different sounds. A stabilizing factor was the universal use of Latin by the educated; Latin as they spoke it was in their minds as they used the letters to write English as they spoke it. Both languages were slowly changing.

6. In the ninth and tenth centuries during the Viking invasions of England, the English began borrowing Danish words. Earlier Old English had not been a borrowing language. These foreign words with their foreign sounds brought new problems of spelling which were resolved in various ways.

7. After the Norman Conquest of England in 1066 A.D., most educated people in England wrote French or Latin. Professional manuscript writers called scribes came over from the Continent. These scribes began to drop the unfamiliar letters þ, ð, ȝ, and wen, and substituted double letters for them: **th, gh,** and **vv.** They also introduced some French rules of spelling, putting a **u** after **g,** for instance, when it stood for /g/ as in **guest** and an **e** after **g** when it stood for /ǰ/ as in **gem, change.**

8. The letter **i** had come to stand for several sounds; it split into two letters, **i** and **j.** The letter **v** split into two, **u** and **v.** The letter **k,** which had not been used much in Latin or English, came into use, filling out the alphabet as we know it now.

9. Lecturers and preachers began to mark written texts as an indication how to set off word-groups and how and when to breathe. Scribes carried the marks into publications.

10. Early printers settled, as we noted, on the London dialect and its writing, which happened at the moment to be in a chaotic state. Until this time no one had bothered much about standard spellings. The printers used different spellings to fill out lines, following the scribal practice of keeping an even margin on the right side of the page.

11. Much early printing of English was done in Holland because the subject was religion, and Holland was one country where it was safe to print heretical religious works. The foreign typesetters did not always know English well, and they introduced some things from their own writing. They began the spelling **gh** for /g/ because they spelled /g/ that way in Dutch. Hence we have **ghost** for Old English **gāst,** which would otherwise have become **gost.**

12. The idea began to develop that words should have standard forms instead of varying from person to person, line to line, and from formal to informal spellings. Printers began to vary the width of spaces between words rather than the spellings to fill each line and make an even right margin.

13. As English entered the modern Global Period, more words were borrowed from other languages. In general, "learned" /lérnàd/ words brought in by scholars were spelled in ways familiar to the eye educated in the foreign language; common words brought in by ordinary people were spelled the way they sounded. Scholars respelled some words to show their presumed history; thus we have **debt** for Middle English **det** because it came from Latin **debitum,** and **doubt** for Middle English **dout** because it came from Latin **dubitum.** We also have **delight** for **delite** on the model of **light** and **night,** long after the original /X/ had vanished from speech.

14. The death rate in medieval and early modern London exceeded the birth rate, but the population grew from migration of countrymen to the city. The migrants fed dialect words into London English, some spelled in the London way but pronounced in the way of the dialect they came from, some pronounced in the London way but kept in their original spelling. Thus we have **bury** and **busy** spelled as they were sounded in the south of England but pronounced as they were sounded in London. And we have

such lists of words as **though, enough, rough, bough, slough,** and **through; daughter, slaughter,** and **laughter.**

15. From the tenth to the twelfth centuries the old three-stress system changed to one of four stresses. Many weakly stressed syllables changed to unstressed, and the vowels in them centralized, changing from full value to /ə/ and /i/. The old spellings continued to represent the changed sounds. Final **e** on many words remained, though no longer sounded, as in **stone.**

16. Spoken English in all dialects continued to change. In one important change of the thirteenth to the sixteenth centuries known as the Great Vowel Shift, the whole set of vowels in stressed syllables drifted: the front vowels became higher and more front and the back vowels higher, with new phonemes intervening. New vowel-semivowel combinations were created. In general the stressed vowel system was knocked into a quite different order. Some words kept the old spelling; some took on a new one. All the complications brought about by normal changes in the language were reflected in one way or another by increasing confusion in the spelling.

17. The more bizarre the spelling of English became, the more the printers, writers, and readers demanded standard forms of a universal standard written language. Printing tended to fix spelling in a single pattern. It became a matter of pride to spell each word correctly. Colonies were split between a desire to write the English way and a counterdesire to reflect the actual language developing in distant lands; in America these two desires warred and got tangled up in pro-British and anti-British attitudes.

18. In the eighteenth and nineteenth centuries the conscious cultivation of standard written English became a mark of education; spelling books and dictionaries were written to show what the standard forms were, and the schools took on the job of making sure that everyone learned these forms and used them. The changing national and regional dialects mocked these efforts, and the more distant the educated were from centers of influence like London and, in America, the eastern seaboard, the more nervous they became about the "correctness" of their English.

All this brings us about to where we are today, trying to find some reasonable way to write down what we have to say, in keeping with tradition and yet not out of contact with our speech.

CHAPTER 21

Spelling: Phonemes
into Letters

Sᴵɴᴄᴇ Eɴɢʟɪsʜ sᴘᴇʟʟɪɴɢ is fairly standard over the whole world and the speech of men and women varies from speech-community to speech-community, each speaker of English comes to use the standard spelling of words to represent his own speech. He reads words off the page in his own dialect and writes words down to stand for his own pronunciation. No difficulty rises for him as long as he can stay within eyewords familiar and thoroughly learned.

What we call "spelling" is a relation between two areas of experience and of learning in which we proceed at different rates; the differences are quite sharp today. One of these is reading—eye-literacy. Reading brings us many words that we do not hear pronounced; the better we read and the more we read, the more such words we know. Once we break out of graded readers which offer spelling-forms for the child's presumed vocabulary, we are in the hands of writers who choose the words they need to say what they have to say. We can become quite at home in an enormous stock of words that enters into our thinking and composes it; we can write those words to express our own thoughts, yet never in the daily chitchat of conversation have occasion to use them. Our thoughts fly up; our bodies remain below, and our talk can remain quite unaffected by what we know. As Franklin says, we speak with the vulgar; we read and write with the learned.

Book learning over the past five centuries has reached out to larger and larger numbers of the children of the uneducated. The mind outtravels the body and comes back stored with treasures that are pearls cast before the local swine. The situation is temporary for many youngsters as they kick the dust of Prairie du Chien, Wisconsin; Trivial, Illinois; Kanab, Utah; and Belleville, Kansas, from their feet and head out for the city, looking for other readers and writers with whom they can talk about things of the mind, other than gardens, cars, sports, women, and who said what to whom about nothing that matters. The situation is permanent for technical and professional men everywhere, isolated at tasks their learning fits them for and hungry to talk to somebody who does not have to be briefed on fundamentals before conversation can begin. Conventions of specialists surging through hotels in New York, San Francisco, Detroit, Boston, New Orleans, and Chicago are the last bulwark against professional deterioration and a sodden submission to intellectual decay. The mouth frames the words the mind knows, haltingly at first, and then breaks into a torrent of talk, the log jam broken by interest and mutual understanding. Such is the burden and the grace of literacy.

Meanwhile ear-literacy, the other side of spelling, advances at its own unrelated pace. People have always spoken words that they did not write and did not expect to read. They protect children, the other sex (whichever is other), teachers, and ministers from the more earthy part of the familiar vocabulary; they approach writing with a formality rigorous enough to keep many words that have been with us since ancient times from having any generally accepted written form, and many current words from finding one before they pass out of use. Modern writers have been more inclined to admit the reader to the intimacy of conversational usage, but still a large number of common expressions have been so well excluded from print that they are not yet recorded in dictionaries.

Every youngster enters school with a large and immeasurable store of words that he must learn to spell. Spelling lessons guide him to a written form for words that he already knows; his classes until he finishes his schooling bring him more words that he both hears and sees, and may learn to spell. A parrotlike mentality that never ranges beyond the limits of these can look like a red-hot speller and the equal in this respect to the avid and attentive reader who nails down a new word when he sees it whether he can say it or not. We can have the appearance of good spelling when the cultural environment outside of school is so limited that school alone trickles a driblet of new words associated in sound and form. Such, for instance, was the early schooling of Abraham Lincoln until he found his home in the world of books and proceeded to the study of law and on to the great debates over slavery.

Our times have brought disruptive changes to eye-literacy and ear-literacy and to the relations between them. Eye-literacy in the past was grounded in a few books read and reread until they fell apart. The printed mass-communications of our day have brought a multitude of publications to be read once and thrown away— newspapers, Sunday editions, periodicals, and comic books. A flow of words drawn at large from the vocabulary of the literate passes casually before the eye on its way to the furnace or the Boy Scout paper drive. The range is greater, but the grip of new words on the memory is minute; yet the meaning sticks—though the spelling may not—and tempts the reader to write words whose form is vague because unnoticed. Spelling seems worse than in the past because writing is often a courageous stab into the half-grasped vocabulary that made an impression on the mind without making an exact one. A well-read youngster can today be a persistently evasive "spelling problem" in a way that was rare in the days when ignorance of the forms of words meant ignorance of the words, and when the temptation to draw upon an out-of-school culture did not offer itself.

Ear-literacy has changed its scope even more drastically, not only within the lifetime of adults who remember the first crystal sets and the first words spoken over the radio but also within the lifetime of children now in grade school. The radio brought into the home outside voices talking about matters of general interest in the vocabularies of those who care about them. A tide of language beyond all previous experience flowed about the growing child. Some of it certainly stuck, but without counterpart in writing; people who speak familiarly about Freud /fr**ɔ**yd/ read his name /**frúwd**/ when they see it on paper. Like the newspaper, radio brought general information effortlessly in a form which resembled speech: the "radio voice" was a delocalized, depersonalized, stylized sonority that could confuse the tick of inconsequence with the march of time. All the events of a tortured age were enacted by puppets to background music in a Park Avenue penthouse fluffy with cosmetics, awash with deodorants, and blue with cigarette smoke. Still, radio was words, and the words brought about a new ear-literacy.

More vividly and with an actuality still to be measured, television now reaches sixty percent of the people of America; we are watching the first generation grow up with no memory of a world without it. Where radio reached the ear only, television touches ear and eye, bringing the viewer word and thing together. At first its effect seemed druglike; children squatted fascinated before the moving screen. Thinking that the children saw what adults see, adults fretted; but the bloodless carnage of horse operas left the youngsters unperturbed; the child knows realer horrors in its innocent dreams. Television punctured the empty pomposity of the radio voice and shoved it into the commercial; it brought real people, honest people, professionals of the highest skills into the presence of the child, and let them speak in their own natural voices. A child of eight is now a connoisseur of the dance from soft-shoe to ballet, of the circus, of prestidigitation, of science made homely and real by Mr. Wizard. The child has lived through "Victory at Sea," the Korean war, flood, fire, earthquake, the police dragnet and the self-adulation of the military, the scientist and the pseudo-scientist, and the medical profession. The voices the child hears have the reality of their local origins; they come from Texas, Utah, Montana, Kentucky, and New Orleans without going through the wringer of instruction in elegant diction; they take him to the streets of Brooklyn, to the uranium treasury of the Colorado Plateau, the mining towns of West Virginia, and to the obliteration of Elugalab in the far Pacific. The child meets word and thing together; he hears the word as he sees the thing. But he does not see the word. He has an ear-literacy beyond all previous imagination; he hears technical terms, place names, and historical allusions in a weather report: "Some precipitation in the Eastern Rockies. Meanwhile Hurricane Carol batters the Atlantic Coast; small-craft warn-

ings were hoisted from Cape Hatteras north, while Old North
Church lost its steeple, where the lantern was hoisted for Paul
Revere." He could see it falling.

Studies show that the children enjoy the shows the adults enjoy,
even to the late-night movies; hence they are exposed to the un-
filtered maturity of adult taste: Czech refugees on "Toast of the
Town," a passionate scene from a Menotti opera, the tragedies of
Shakespeare, the savage detraction of Berle's stooges, the sterilized
melodramatics of the operating room, the innuendo of a Broadway
play, the flying magic of Peter Pan, the roving eye of Bob Hope,
the urbane worldliness of Steve Allen, the surprise of "What's My
Line," the slick, arrogant, venal, outraged, or browbeaten faces
pilloried before a congressional committee, the flashing limbs of a
chorus, and the gowns that cling to their wearers by some internal
engineering which is all that is concealed from the fascinated eye.
The culture revealed on the screen is not that of the families which
watch; it penetrates the living room like incense borne in through
a window. And the words, the words come in in a stream, meaningful or tantalizingly on the edge of meaning, accompanied by
none of the written forms that stand for them in print. This is a
new literacy of the ear that combines with the new mass-communications literacy of the eye to make bad spellers for a while of all
who read and write.

In English, if we hear a strange word, we cannot tell for sure
how to write it; if we see a strange word, we cannot tell how to
say it. The person who does not read or write much runs out of his
reservoir of familiar eyewords rather quickly; but no matter how
highly educated he is or how well read, he still hears words he has
never seen spelled and sees words he has never heard spoken.
Even introductions to strangers force him to ask, "How do you
spell your name?" He cannot be sure that the common name /jáhn/
is spelled **John** and not **Jon** or **Jean;** that /smíθ/ is **Smith** and not
Smyth, Smithe, or **Smythe;** or that **Smythe** is /smíθ/ and not
/smáyð/. Where long habit has reduced to automatism the writing
of familiar letter combinations for familiar sounds, English writing
serves as a kind of word-picture making, something like Chinese
script but with alphabetic units constantly repeated.

The phonemic element in English spelling—and on the phonemic
element the working of the system is based—does not consist of a

standard world-wide spelling for standard world-wide phonemes. Many people think that correct spelling reflects "correct" pronunciations or that it ought to, and that faulty spelling comes from faulty pronunciations. These are people for whom eyewords perfectly spelled pop up in military regularity for mouth-and-ear words, so that the immense discrepancies between the two never become obvious. They feel that their own speech is or ought to be standard and suspect persons from other speech-communities of improper upbringing and too little familiarity with the grammar and the dictionary.

The phonemic element in English spelling varies from person to person: it is each man's or woman's use of certain letters in fairly regular correspondence to his own phonemes. The chances are that no present-day English speech, British or American, urban or rural, Northern or Southern, educated or uneducated is much closer to a one-for-one agreement between sound and letter than any other. A good phonemic notation for each person is the one that most closely records the phonemes he actually says. For each person good English spelling—as far as it is phonemic—is a regular selection of certain letters and combinations of letters to stand for his own phonemes. Beyond that, good spelling depends on a camera eye and a beartrap memory for visual forms—and a determination never to misspell a word someone has caught you on.

The phonemic core of our spelling system can only exist because most speakers of English use most of the same phonemes. They make most of the sound-signals with the same organs in roughly the same sectors of the mouth, though the specific sounds that come out differ from person to person and from community to community. Earlier we noticed our different ways of sounding /t/ and /r/. One community's /r/ will differ from another's, but some kind of identifiable substitute for /r/ will occur regularly; we can catch on to it quickly and respond as if to our own. Standard English writing will never hint of its existence. No one can predict what effect the growing eye-illiterate ear-literacy of the young will have on English spelling, but it is a fair guess that spelling will become more regular by the drift of discrepant forms into line with the phonemic core; **though, through,** and **laugh,** for instance, may become **tho, thru,** and **laff; night** and **light** may become **nite** and **lite.** Winner takes all in language; dominant patterns attract.

To illustrate the phonemic core of present-day English spelling, we have to show it in terms of some one dialect. For each writer that dialect has to be his own. The demonstration we give will be of the kind of English spoken by one person in the mid-central part of the Northern speech-area of the United States, in the region of the Great Lakes—specifically Detroit, Michigan. Each reader will have to make the adjustments necessary for his own dialect; the differences may be minute or large, but there will be differences. The phonemes and their regular spellings will be set up in parallel columns.

We take the consonants first, since they differ least from one speech-community to another. (The vowels are comparatively chaotic.) We will offer the phonemic symbol with its regular correspondences in writing.

PHONEME	LETTER	EXAMPLE
/b/	b	baby
	bb	blabber
/d/	d	dad, lady
	dd	ladder
/f/	f	fade, deaf
	ff	stiff, affable
/g/	g	go, gag
	gg	stagger
/ǰ/	j	judge
	dg	bridge
	g	gem, gin, gyroscope
/č/	ch	church
	tch	fetch, pitch
/k/	c	cat, curry, coat
	cc	occur
	k	ketch
	ck	beck, back, buck
/l/	l	lull, little, like
	ll	fall, pull, ell
/m/	m	man, mate, camel
	mm	hammer
/n/	n	now, nice, neat
	nn	tinny, tunnel

PHONEME	LETTER	EXAMPLE
/ŋ/	ng	sing, rung
	n	zinc, sunk, punctual
/p/	p	pap, pep, pop, pup
	pp	pepper, puppy, popper
/r/	r	rout, part
	rr	horror
/s/	s	such, facts
	ss	fuss, kiss
	c	necessary, cease, deceive
/t/	t	late, sit
	tt	latter, fatter, matt
/v/	v	very, vex, shiver
	vv	flivver
/z/	z	fez, zebra
	s	has, is, does
/ž/	si	vision, decision
/θ/	th	thin, myth
/ð/	th	then, swathed
/ks/	x	rex
	cc	accent
/gs/	x	exit, exactly

THE SEMIVOWELS BEFORE VOWELS

The semivowels are consistently represented in spelling before vowels:

PHONEME	LETTER	EXAMPLE
/y/	y	you, yet
	i	view
	u	use
/w/	w	win, wood, wire
	wh	when, where, why
/h/	h	help, hay, hear

For the spelling of semivowels after vowels, see below.

THE SIMPLE VOWELS

PHONEME	LETTER	EXAMPLE
/i/	i	bit, did
	y	physic
/e/	e	bet, red
	a	catch
/æ/	a	hat, latch
/ɨ/	any vowel letter in unstressed syllables	
/ə/	u	but, bud, sun
	a	sofa, about
	any vowel letter in unstressed syllables	
/a/	o	hot, sod, cot
	au	caught
/u/	oo	book, roof
/o/	o	obey, rodent
/ɔ/	au	audience, audacious

THE COMPLEX VOWEL NUCLEI

A "complex vowel nucleus" consists of a vowel followed by /y/, /w/, or /h/. The complex vowels of speech get very spotty representation in writing. Not all of them appear in any one person's speech, and those that do are sometimes represented by two letters, sometimes by only one.

SIMPLE VOWELS WITH /y/

PHONEME	LETTER	EXAMPLE
/iy/	e	we, he, me
	ee	seen
/ey/	a	fate, bane
	ay	day, way
	ai	raid, maid
/æy/		
/ɨy/		
/əy/	i	bite, night
/ay/	i	fine, nine, ride
/uy/	uoy	buoy, buoyant
/oy/	oy	boy
	oi	oil
/ɔy/		

SIMPLE VOWELS WITH /w/

PHONEME	LETTER	EXAMPLE
/iw/	u	cute
/əw/	ew	few
/æw/		
/iw/		
/əw/	ou	house, louse
/aw/	ow	town, gown
	ou	rouse, lousy
/uw/	u	brute, flume
	oo	room, roof, too
/ow/	o	go, note
	ow	know, throw
/ɔw/		

SIMPLE VOWELS WITH /h/

These vowel nuclei occur before /r/.

PHONEME	LETTER	EXAMPLE
/ih/	e	here, sere
	ee	beer
/eh/	a	bare, rare, yeah
/æh/	aa	baa
/ih/		
/əh/	er	Herbert, sherbert
	ir	fir, bird
	ur	fur
/ah/	a	far, car, barn
/uh/	oo	boor
/oh/	o	wore, forest
	a	war
/ɔh/	aw	law, paw, gnaw

The phonemic core is most consistent in the consonants, less consistent in the simple vowels, and thoroughly disorganized in the vowel-semivowel nuclei. By "consistently phonemic" we mean that, in this one person's speech, the letters seem to stand for the sounds, so that if he is given the sound of /f/, he will think of the letter f and not ph; if he is given the vowel nucleus /ey/, he will think of

letter **a** and not of **ai, ea,** or **eigh.** The large gaps come from two
factors: 1) he does not use the sound as a signal in his own speech,
or 2) he uses it but has no spelling closely or primarily linked with
it. Each speaker has a roughly similar set of sound-letter relationships, but the gaps will be different and for different reasons.

EXERCISE: Write down the letters that occur first to you for the
phonemes above. You will probably correct yourself later as your
ear is sharpened. Often it helps to have somebody else listen to you
and write for you.

It is very difficult to summarize the complex relations between
speech and spelling, but we can illustrate them from this central
list of reasonably phonemic spellings. The orderly distribution of
the phonemes in the mouth takes on an appearance of disorder,
with single, double, and even triple-letter counterparts in writing,
and some sounds with no regular counterparts at all.

Two old consonant phonemes, /θ/ as in **thin** and /ð/ as in **then,**
are represented by **th.** The phoneme /č/ is represented by **ch** as in
church and **tch** as in **fetch;** /ǰ/ is represented by **j** and **dg** as in
judge; /š/ by **sh** as in **shin;** and /ž/ by **si** as in **vision.** Before vowels
the semivowels /y/, /w/, and /h/ have regular letters, **y, w,** and **h:**
but after vowels they scarcely exist for writing, certainly not as
necessary elements in a system of signals.

The so-called "long" and "short" vowels of English writing depend on eye-resemblances only; the short vowels are not short versions of the same sound quality, as we can see by setting them
against the phonemes they represent:

	"LONG"		"SHORT"
ā as in **fate** /féyt/		ă as in **cat** /kǽt/	
ē as in **cede** /síyd/		ĕ as in **bed** /béd/	
ī as in **nine** /náyn/		ĭ as in **sit** /sít/	
ŏ as in **go** /gów/		ŏ as in **hot** /hát/	
ū as in **cute** /kyúwt/		ŭ as in **but** /bát/	
ōō as in **room** /rúwm/		ŏŏ as in **book** /búk/	

The "diphthongs" of writing are:

> **ow** as in **town** /táwn/   or **sow** /sáw/
> **ou** as in **rouse** /ráwz/   or **house** /hǝws/
> **oy** as in **boy** /bóy/
> **oi** as in **boil** /bóyl/

Writing also omits the phonemes of pitch and stress, with the result that it tells us nothing about the stress to be put upon words or the syllables in them. We read familiar words as we are in the habit of speaking them; an unfamiliar word causes us either to guess at the stress or to take the word as an eye-stimulus without making any effort to pronounce it. The native speaker comes to reading so familiar with the stresses and pitches of speech that their absence from writing causes him no pain most of the time. When he needs to, he can check the word-accent in a dictionary.

Yet with all its gaps and inconsistencies and in spite of its variation from person to person and place to place, this phonemic core of letter equivalents for speech-sounds keeps English spelling from being a list of words that each of us must learn one by one, and it sets the patterns for new formations like **radio, radar, Wac,** and **gas.** It accounts for most of the spellings of most of the words we read and write. This set of symbol correspondences has not come down to us in this relationship from the past; it is itself a product of the ceaseless change and development in speech and writing. It is the central regularity in an irregular system.

Otherwise the spelling of English words is a product of their history. Each form like **night, eight, naïve, naphtha,** and **colonel** that is now fixed and standard is a frozen record of some aspect of its past: an early stage of its pronunciation, its origin in another language, its membership in a certain class of words, an error in an early dictionary like Johnson's, and so on. The phonemic spellings with single, double, and triple letter representations prepare us for other spellings of the same sounds. Besides **e** and **ee** for /iy/ in **we** and **seen, ie** in **believe, ei** in **receive, ea** in **read, i** in **machine, eo** in **people, ae** in **Caesar,** and **oe** in **phoenix,** phonemic double letters prepare us for **ph** /f/ in **phoneme, ps** /s/ in **psyche,** and **cq** in **acquaintance.** They prepare us for the use of a letter or group of letters to stand for several different sounds, often in words that look alike to the eye: **read** for /ríyd/, /réd/ or **bow** for /báw/, /bów/. They prepare us for "silent" letters, like the **l** in **talk,** the **gh** in **through,** the **b** in **climb** and **comb,** the **k** in **know,** and the **g** in **gnaw.** A few exercises in the phonemic notation of our actual speech compared to our spelling teaches us how many carefully written letters are "silent," and how unstable individual sounds are in running talk. The spelling of many words is the spelling of another dialect than our own, a dialect of long ago and far away, a dialect that differs from word to word.

Spelling is more closely related to words spoken in isolation than to words integrated into running speech. When we pronounce a word by itself, we give it word-stress rather than stresses built into the overall stress-patterns of the utterance, and we give each sound in it a fuller treatment. We consciously pronounce it as we think it ought to be pronounced, often even saying it syllable by syllable. We are noticeably self-conscious when we say a word in isolation. Often we carry this self-consciousness over into our reading, proceeding word-by-word and producing a singsong effect quite different from the easy pace of speech. In this way of reading, each word is as good as any other, as it is in a dictionary: none steps down to lift up the others. Such reading is not very effective or clear; it is tiring to listen to because it disrupts the signals of speech. It also wears out the reader and leaves him with an aching jaw. Giving each word full value is the only way we can say it out of context, though it is still not close enough to the letters of writing to give us much help in spelling.

Good spellers have one way of saying words in isolation that does emphasize their spelling and helps to recall the standard forms of writing. Knowing which words they have had trouble spelling, they give an arbitrary sound-value to each letter in them. They thus have three ways of saying words: 1) as in running speech; 2) stressed, as in isolation; 3) stressed, with sound values for the letters in them. For **calm** they say /kálm/, not /káhm/; for **cupboard** they say /kóp bóhrd/, not /kóbərd/; and they emphasize the **g** in **gnaw** by saying /gnáw/, not /náh/. Any trick is worth using if it reminds of the silent letters: /kníjit/ for **knight,** /rìy síy ipt/ for **receipt,** and /dáy ə frǽgm/ for **diaphragm.** Where only one letter gives trouble, as in **separate,** they name the letter and emphasize it: /sep éy rèyt/. In speech **affect** and **effect** are pronounced the same, /əfékt/, but as they write, these spellers mouth them: /ǽ fèkt/, /íy fékt/. Each word we speak has so many different ways of sounding in the stream of speech that we can add one more way without trouble.

When we pass beyond the phonemic spellings into the silent letters and variant spellings, we pass beyond the help of letter-by-letter writing. A listing of the variant spellings for the sounds we speak is no use apart from the words they occur in, as we saw above with the spellings of /**iy**/. Trying to relate these spellings in isolation to the sounds they can stand for does not lead us far toward control of them. Where writing casts off from speech we have to cast off with it and deal with words as picture-units for the eye alone, rough equivalents for short stretches of speech. We already control most words this way in our reading; when we see them we know what they are and what they mean. We take each word in a lump; the eye catches its total contour without digging into the elements in it.

Taking words as eye-stimuli only and suppressing thought of their sounds, we can fruitfully bring together words that are spelled alike no matter how different one is from another in sound. Thus we can memorize together such sets as **affable, liable, pliable, malleable,** and other words ending in **-able;** at another time we can memorize **perceptible, reducible, crucible, permissible,** and other words ending in **-ible.** We memorize together **though, through, enough, slough, thorough; laughter, daughter, slaughter, laughable; read, near, fear, lead, speak, peak, leak, bean, ocean, mean; vulgar, cigar, atavar, far, war, par, gar, mar,** and other words like them. We take up all the words ending in **-ant** and **-ance** one day, and put off to another the words ending in **-ent** and **-ence.** We drill together the words ending in **-or** and get them cold before we even think about the words ending in **-er.**

Otherwise, spelling lists are of dubious value because words do not present themselves to us in ordinary life in lists, either in speech or in writing; they occur as meaning-units in connected discourse. We say them and hear them in utterances; we read and write them in sentences. We may have to develop a change of pace in our reading that lets us look squarely at the inner construction of words that have given us trouble. We discover these words when we write; a sense of disquiet tells us we are in doubt. We need to watch for them in reading and focus squarely on them whenever we see them.

No one is so secure that he spells every word he knows without a hitch; even the best stenographer keeps in her desk drawer a dictionary or a little book of twenty thousand misspelled words

and gives it plenty of use. The most accurate speller can be thrown
off stride by having to read misspellings. Reading badly prepared
copy, reading freshman English papers, learning a phonetic or
phonemic alphabet, taking up shorthand, studying French, German, or Spanish—all these can disrupt our spelling until we have
gone far enough to keep both systems in separate compartments of
the mind. We have to be alert to our confusions; when we are in
doubt about a word, we have to look it up and overlearn it until we
have it under control.

In dealing with words containing non-phonemic spellings, silent
letters, and other oddities, the grip of habit is crucial. No person
who reads and writes, however little, is free of habits of reading
and writing. All language comes down to habit actions and reactions in individual living people. Habit builds the routines by which
we live. Nothing is harder to get rid of than a habit gone wrong,
as any chainsmoker can tell you. The more you think about it, the
tighter its grip; you dislodge it best by ignoring it, by turning your
back on it, and by concentrating on an opposing set of habits by
which you perform your future actions. Only when your conduct
is automatic within new grooves do your old habits, unnoticed,
disappear.

Habit is routine; spellings are routines; misspellings are routines
by which we operate in place of the routines the situation calls for.
Otherwise, a poor speller could switch to standard spellings and go
on. Suppose one were to decide to write **esthetic** in place of **aes-
thetic, fantasy** for **phantasy,** or **sulfur** in place of **sulphur,** since
these spellings are shorter and just as standard as the others. Or
suppose he wanted to write **theater** for **theatre.** His problem is not
one of knowing the spelling he wants to substitute. He knows it.
His trouble is that he already has a habit; he may have the word
written before the thought of what he is doing occurs to him. He
must overlearn the substitute spelling by writing it often, until it is
an automatic alternative. Then gradually it will nudge the other out.

Rote learning is the means by which you set your nerves and
muscles into grooves of spontaneous action: the way you learn a
golf swing, a swimming stroke, or how to catch a baseball. It is
the way you learn all language; you pollute the whole matter and
fall all over yourself when you try to get intellectual about it. You
can't think your way to command of a language, a language form,
sound, or pattern. If you think about some form of address, like

Dear sir, How do you do, Sincerely yours, within a few minutes it seems unbelievably silly. If a person is not dear to you, why address him as **Dear**? If you are sincere, how does it help to say so? Carry on in this line of thought, and you don't know what to say at the beginning or the end of a letter; embarrassment stops you before you start. If you dwell too much with the mind on English spelling, it, too, seems pretty silly; but if you dwell long on the condition of man, a featherless biped teetering on two thin legs, digging his grave with his teeth and going yackity-yak with his mouth, all the uses of this world seem silly and the only way out is suicide. But if you trust yourself as an organism and let your body do what the bodies around it do, you fall into routines and set the mind free for more fruitful occupations. Unquestioning rote learning lets us be efficient in doing.

It is well to guard against adding new misspellings when you are learning the terminology of a new subject; it is not much trouble to fix the letter sequence of each new word when you first meet it. This is vital in school, college, or in any profession; the troublesome words are likely to belong to the vocabulary of learning that has come into English from other languages. An expert builds no confidence in himself by misspelling the terms of his specialty; he looks like a fumbler and people run from fumblers. Any misspelling once learned makes learning a double job; it has to be driven out and replaced by another.

People who have to handle other people's writing feel a permanent low-temperature antagonism to bad spelling and to those who do it. Many eminent men and women—professional authors, editors, and critics among them—have been terrible spellers. Their hasty personal letters, rough drafts, notebooks, and other scribblings often look like the letter written by the junkman to the automobile agency. Few of their erratic spellings find their way to the public which reads their published works. Sometimes they clean up their own copy before offering it, but if they do not, the marvelous professionalism of the publishing industry takes over. Typists, copyreaders, typesetters, and proofreaders take in the words as misspelled and feed out a smooth text free of irregularities. The process is efficient, as we saw in Chapter 5, but it is a costly one, consciously or unconsciously resented by every person involved in it.

Publishing houses make every effort to eliminate the need for corrections; they issue directives, style sheets, style manuals, and other pamphlets trying to persuade authors to submit copy that can be translated into type without major surgery. The costs of printing keep many works that should reach an audience out of print; to cut these costs, techniques of photocopying have been worked out that let a book be printed directly from the author's typescript. Most publishers refuse even to look at a handwritten manuscript unless it is submitted by an established author with an assured audience. Publishers do not bother much with a script that is "dirty" with misspellings, clogged type, faint print because of a wornout ribbon, erratic margins, or scribbled corrections. They push the work of preparing manuscripts as much as possible back on the writer himself. The trend is not toward an easy acceptance of irregularities, but toward a more rigid demand for a standard routinized format. All writing is largely a matter of going through routines of long habit; it is best to start early establishing the routines that pay off—not merely in money—but in acceptance among literate people as a literate person.

Most of our writing goes directly from our hand to the person who is to read it, possibly past one typist on the way. It is well to think of every reader as a potential proofreader who resents making corrections. While we are kind to our own misspellings and ready to make large allowances for ourselves, we are hawks ready to pounce on the errors of other people. In the writing of others we catch the very errors that escape us in our own. Always ready to excuse the errors of persons whose eminence puts them beyond criticism, we are savage critics of those whose knowledge, competence, and command of their subject is yet to be decided.

Businessmen, college professors, and office managers complain of the writing of high-school and college graduates, especially of their spelling as it shows up in letters of application, interoffice memos, reports, surveys, and summaries. The young person, affable, alert, and capable though he may be, is not there to speak for himself; his only presence is in his writing. Often the first eye to see his writing is that of a person hardened by years of struggling for status in the system, a secretary, an office manager, or some clerk whose only task is to receive these papers and channel them to their destination. "What do you think of this boy Earnest Endeavor?" asks the boss casually, taking the papers from her hand.

"Well, *honestly!* He can't even spell," she replies, and the shadow of the eight ball falls across his career.

The person who has drilled himself to turn out clean and attractive letters, papers, and reports has a surprising edge over his contemporaries at crucial points in his life. There is no doubt that in the organized impersonality of large corporations, government and military offices, and universities anyone whose work is not absolutely indispensable will settle down and learn to spell or he will not go far. And no man is indispensable. Executives who go into a huddle to choose the kind and quality of paper that will best carry the correspondence of the organization will give short shrift to the person who will not use that paper in a way worthy of it. When even the purchasing procedures in a corporation are considered to be a form of public relations, surely the ambitious youngster ought to consider the impact of all he writes to be part of his own public relations and develop the habit of controlling everything in it—spelling especially—as wisely as he can.

✳ *CHAPTER 22* ✳

Capitals and Other Typographical Devices

Capitals

W E USE SEVERAL different forms of the alphabet, each one of which has a set of capitals matched to a set of lower-case or small letters. These capitals represent nothing in speech; we do not represent one sound with the capital letter and another with the lower-case. Their appeal is to the eye alone. All sorts of published materials-—title pages, headlines, advertisements, signs, notices, and handbills—have a large amount of free play and artistry that seems quite individual and lacking in order. Yet the whole matter centers in the standardized use of capitals and small letters in or-dinary writing. The reading and writing citizenry has certain ex-pectations: they look for capitals in certain places and small letters in others. When these expectations are violated, the violation pro-duces a special impact. Texts printed entirely in capitals call at-tention to themselves in one way. Texts printed entirely without capitals call attention to themselves in another way. Both deviate from our standard intermixture of capitals and lower-case letters in writing and get their effects by their deviation.

Normally we begin sentences with capitals; and if quoted material of sentence length comes within a sentence, we set it off with quotation marks (". . .") and begin it with a capital. Usually we begin the first word of each line of poetry with a capital.

Beyond these simple uses several influences interplay in the modern handling of capital letters. One is a tradition coming down from very early times of beginning each important word with a capital letter. This is the sort of thing we still see in German, where nouns all begin with capitals. Early writers were not seeking emphasis by setting these words off with capitals. They capitalized the word *God* when it referred to the Christian God as a mark of His supremacy over all other deities, Greek, Roman, or Nordic. In the same devout spirit they capitalized *Almighty* and the personal pronouns when they applied to God. They used capital letters to begin the names of persons, because persons are important; and when they spoke of a person by his title, they capitalized the first letter: "Dean Johnson, this is my father; Father, this is the Dean." In the same way they used capitals to begin place names and the names of institutions. They often took ideas, such as goodness, beauty, evil, and sloth, and personified them; that is, they wrote about them as if they were persons: "At dusk, Beauty tiptoes into view." This figure of speech is outmoded today, but it occurs in a great deal of literature of the past. And, of course, they used capitals as titles and chapter headings as guides for the reader.

A second tradition is the use of capital letters to confer emphasis, to make certain words stand out to the eye and lift them to importance. "The door opened, and there stood MY BROTHER!" In modern writing we would not usually load a sentence with so many signals of emphasis, but a writer trying to give the impression, for instance, of an excitable woman's intonation contours would not hesitate to employ capitals: "My DEAR," I said, "you simply HAVE to SEE him or you won't BELIEVE me. He's ABsolutely UGLY." This tradition, like many other old things in language, hangs on among people who do not write very much; the standard English sentence seems a little dull to them, and they use not only capital letters but double and triple underlining and repeated exclamation marks to make their intent clear.

As these traditions of using capitals to indicate importance and to confer emphasis are expressed in standard written English of our day, we find them in the use of capitals in abbreviations, such as WAC, U.S.A., or AMA (American Medical Association). We find emphasis in the use of the capital letter *I* to represent the speaker referring to himself. The French, Germans, and Italians frequently jibe at the egotism of the Americans and British in capitalizing references to themselves (as they do with references to God), but probably if those languages had a one-letter pronoun referring to anybody, they would lift it to attention by capitalizing it as we do. Otherwise we find capitals conferring emphasis in the names of events, like the *Battle of the Bulge;* of eras, such as the *Renaissance* or the *Enlightenment;* of treaties and other occurrences, especially when ordinary words are used, as in *the Depression* as against *a depression.* We find capitals singling out words used in a special sense, as in *Speed kills, Flight Nine, Train 18, the Hour of Charm,* and *Brew 103.*

Italic Type

THESE two traditions are tempered by the modern practice of turning part of the work of emphasis over to italic type, to small capitals (letters with the form of capitals but only about two-thirds the size), and to bold-face type. Bold-face type has both capitals and lower-case letters; it is a little fatter and blacker than the general run of type. In ordinary typewriting, small capitals, italic type, and bold-face type cannot be put on paper; however, by underlining it is possible to indicate degrees of emphasis. We signify italic type in writing by one straight underline.

We use italic type to emphasize key words or phrases, as in "the *business* of writing for business" or in "We said that we liked the car, not that we were going to *buy* it." We use italic type to mark words that we are discussing, as in *"Garage* is a French word." We use italic type to mark letters that we are discussing, as in "Americans pronounce a *t* between vowels that sounds to an Englishman like a *d,* as in *butter;* but the British have an *r* in words like *very* and *courage* that sounds to Americans like a *d."* We use italics for titles of books and magazines, songs, movies, and art works when we mention them in a sentence, as in "We read *Gone with the Wind."* We use italics for foreign words and phrases and often for Latin and Greek words used in the sciences, though we are not consistent. In some business correspondence, capitals are coming back as a matter of convenience to the typist: it is faster and easier to

hit the shift key and go on than to backspace and type the underline.

In the general run of writing done by professional and non-pro-
fessional but habitual writers, the distribution in use of capitals,
lower-case, and italic letters is a standard interplay of these traditions. This standardization is increasing, because modern organizations—business, industrial, governmental, and educational—favor
routines wherever routines can be made to serve. There is room
for individuality in these enterprises, but not in the form of written
communications—unless it can be shown to be more economical.
The economy must be real and extensive enough to justify the train
of changes it sets into motion. These organizations are set up to
deal with package units not only of goods but, where written English is concerned, package units of meaning that can be handled by
expert operators using standard typewriters. A given office may
have its own peculiarities, but the quirks are peculiar to the office,
not to persons in the office. There is no place for the free-wheeling
individualism of the days when letters were written individually by
hand and when a thoughtful correspondent might take time to deco-
rate his capitals with whorls and sweeping loops, or go back and
underline a word two or three times. Like standard spelling, the
standard use of capitals, single underline for italics, and lower-case
letters is an organization's way of getting the unimportant routinized so that the important work can go on as efficiently as possible.
The pressure for a regularized form is not a mark of the importance
of form but of its relative unimportance. It is the package. What is
in the package is what counts.

We thus have a climate favoring standardization throughout the
workaday world, with the great mass of readers trained to respond
in a predictable way to the signals. Printers, authors, and advertising men have not been slow to see the extra impact given in these
circumstances to variation. How eye-catching is a sentence or a
title with no capitals in it at all! Or a text in italic, with the important words in standard roman! Alert people—whose livelihood depends on capturing the attention and holding it and whose minds
are wholly devoted to the problem—come up with every imaginable
variation on the standard format, in team with artists, psychologists, and public-opinion researchers. They depend as much as the
business office does on standardization and a public regimented in

its responses. If the professional and habitual writers should join in subverting the regularities of standard written English, the advertising designers would have the rug pulled right out from under them: they would have to hunt for new manners of specialized appeal. Hence the writing that seems least standardized is the one most dependent upon form, the one to which form is really important. Standardized and simplified form, though unimportant by comparison with the message, provides the best and easiest packaging device for our written communications.

$\divideontimes$ *CHAPTER 23* $\divideontimes$

Punctuation

P UNCTUATION MARKS are the silences that speak louder than words. They steer a reader's eyes through a written text, telling him how to cut the message into units and how to relate these units to each other. They are substitute signals for the junctures and intonation contours of speech, but in large part they are like type sizes and faces, signals for the eye alone, standing for nothing in speech. Of all the aspects of standard written English, punctuation shows the most variation from person to person, region to region, and from one time to another. Punctuation does not change as fast as speech, but faster, for instance, than spelling. It varies from one publishing house to another in small ways and from one periodical to another; it is the one aspect of a manuscript that the printer, copyreader, proofreader, and editor can not be kept from tampering with. Editors always assume that while an author knows the words he wants to use, he is a bumbling incompetent in punctuating and needs expert help. Authors who receive this help feel that their copy has fallen into the fingers of a madman. There is no peace between these camps.

Punctuating is something of an art, while most people think of it as a standard system like spelling. Since each person approaches his own punctuation marks in his writing in the spirit of an artist, and approaches the punctuation in his reading in the spirit of a judge applying the rules of law, some large difficulties have been created by punctuation. Courts have decided cases on the interpretation of a comma, and on the omission of one have quashed indictments; yet legal prose often looks to the layman as if it had been punctuated by blind chance with no regard to meaning. Poems have been completely altered in significance by the corrections of an editor, and in one of the earliest plays in English there is a poetical letter, an assertion of love, admiration, and respect, that is taken by the addressee to be a considered insult. A similar discourtesy results when in Shakespeare's *A Midsummer-Night's Dream,* Act V, Scene i, lines 108 to 117, Quince puts periods in the wrong places in a speech. Few sets of rules are more trusted and less trustworthy than the rules of punctuation. And no set of signals is more likely to veer out of the writer's control.

The difficulty lies in what we attempt to do with punctuation marks. We have in speech the complicated interlocking signals of stress, pitch, and juncture, which add up to what we call intonation. We have to omit these signals in writing because we have no signs for them; we have no signs because they are so basic to speech that the early analysts couldn't "hear" them. The phonemes of pitch, stress, and juncture were the last to be recognized, and there is still controversy about them among the experts. We now have phonemic symbols for them, but we have seen how these symbols clutter up phonemic notation, how slow they are to write, and how little they add to a native speaker's understanding of the text. If he can read the segmental phonemes, he reads them with a native intonation. He needs a simple set of marks that he can run into the line of text to block out larger segments and give him a hint of the way they go. The punctuation marks try to serve this function, but they are so few and they overlap so much in significance that they are likely to hint several things at once. That leads to trouble.

Modern punctuation marks were the last symbols of writing to be invented—not much before printing. They were originally a way of telling preachers and orators how to read a text out loud. Often each reader was his own punctuator. Before his appearance on the platform or in the pulpit, he marked the text for himself to guide him in his performance of it. He marked the text in accordance with a theory of oratory current at the time, setting off kinds of rhetorical units with characteristic marks. One unit was the period, one the comma, and one the colon. Part of a colon was a semicolon. We have forgotten what these units were, but we still apply their names to the marks we use. The marking got around because the texts were passed from hand to hand and copied with the marks in them. They told the reader how and when to breathe, where to pause and how long, and where not to pause at all. It wouldn't occur to a person reading to himself that he needed such marks, but in time readers found them useful. Authors and editors began including them in published texts.

Many different marks and systems of marks were used. As long as manuscripts were written by hand, there was one almost inexhaustible reservoir of forms that could be used: the abbreviations in Latin books. Because of the cost of vellum, medieval books were written very compactly, with common words represented by word-signs which consisted of key letters and a mark of abbreviation. The writing was almost a kind of shorthand. Some familiar abbreviations we still use come down to us from medieval Latin writings: e.g. (*exempli gratia,* 'for example'), i.e. (*id est,* 'that is'), etc. (*et cetera,* 'and other things'), viz. (*videlicet,* 'it is easy to see'), and ¶ (the sign printers use to show the beginning of a paragraph). In these word-signs we find the forerunners of the modern period (.), comma (,), colon (:), semicolon (;), dash (—), hyphen (-), underline (_), and other marks we use for punctuation today. As long as the scribes and copyists drew each mark with a pen, its exact form did not matter too much. But printing, with its movable types which could be used again and again and used as patterns for other type-castings, brought the beginnings of order in the appearance of punctuation marks, if not in their significance.

Printing also brought a more lavish use of punctuation marks, since they were easy to insert in a text as the type was set up. Some authors, and editors, tried to control, almost every pulse, of the reader's breath; setting off, separate phrases, from each other, as in this sentence. Even while writers were exploiting the rhetorical effect of their work and tightening their supervision over the reader's voice, some readers were discovering a new way of reading that set the eyes free of the voice, free to go at their own speed rather than the speed of talk. They began to read silently. Silent reading seems natural to us because we all do it, but it can be ranked as one of the important human inventions. Silent reading multiplies the effect of the energy the reader applies to his reading, so that he can read pages instead of paragraphs and books instead of chapters. The long-term effect of silent reading on punctuation has been to reverse the trend from full pointing of the text toward a more open, suggestive, subtle use of the punctuation marks. It has turned punctuation into a minor form of art.

Space As a Form of Punctuation

TAKEN in the broadest sense, punctuation is any trick a writer or printer uses to separate one thing from another in writing or to group related things together. In this broad sense the setting of a title or a heading in an area of white space apart from the body of the work is a form of punctuation, and we do well to think of it that way. The division of a book into chapters, each beginning with its own heading on a new page, is a form of punctuation. So is the division of a short paper into sections numbered in order. So is the indenting of paragraphs, a device which signifies that part of the discussion is over and another part is being taken up. Some typists space an extra line between paragraphs to make the division more emphatic and produce a lighter, more attractive page. Our modern way of paging a book—using Roman numerals for the preface, table of contents, and other preliminary material, and beginning the body of the work on page 1—is a form of punctuation. The arrangement of a poem on the page, with each separate line bounded by white space before and after, is a form of punctuation that guides the reader through the large blocks of meaning devised by the author. The intention is the same as the intention of the actual punctuation marks: to steer the reader's eye and, through the eye, his mind.

Modern punctuation is inclined to let space punctuate where space can do the job, for each actual punctuation mark means a stroke of a typewriter or linotype key. Thus a normal business letter (typed on printed letterhead paper to save writing the company name on each sheet) dispenses with all end-punctuation in the heading and signature. In datelines **23 March 1955** is competing with **March 23, 1955**; it saves a stroke. There is some tendency to drop the period after such titles of address as **Mr., Dr.,** and **St.;** a comma is used after the postal zone number, as in **Denver 7, Colo-**

rado, but not before it. For most typists a colon is automatic after
the salutation, even in personal letters; and if the sender signs his
title, it does not finish with a period. The typist puts her initials at
the left; if there are enclosures, she notes the number. In the body
of the letter each separate matter taken up is given a paragraph, but
here formalism ends. The discussion is direct, unpretentious, very
much like conversation; the chances are that the sender dictated it
into a machine and said what was on his mind. Such a letter might
look like this:

AVON MOTOR PARTS, Inc.

Ann Arbor, Michigan

23 March 1955

Mr Reuel Padke
1859 16th St
Greenville 9, Ohio

Dear Mr Padke:

From your description in your letter of
the 15th of the trouble you are having with
your fan, we think that the mounting bracket
is defective. We are shipping you a new
bracket (Part No 18–A 54). Since we do not
sell our products directly to the public, we
are billing you through our Greenville
distributor, Standard Auto Parts, 1918 Elm
Street.
If you have further trouble, let us know.

Sincerely yours,

Elmer Seymour
es/gbc   Sales Manager

Outside of business correspondence, this tendency to let space
do part of the punctuation can be seen in the handling of matter
quoted from another writer. Lines of poetry are set apart from
the main body:

> But I was one-and-twenty,
> No use to talk to me.

Even short bits of prose are set in from both margins a few spaces in the same manner:

> Photography today is in a peculiar transition stage, a period when old standards are being questioned and new ones are failing to meet our requirements. But to see what is and to guess what will be, perhaps we should look back a bit.

Formerly such quotations were typed with the lines single-spaced, in imitation of the smaller type used in printing, but printers now ask for double-spacing. They need the space for their own marks; besides, the double-spaced quotation is easier to read. Paper is cheap and expendable; the time and labor of the typist is costly and worth saving. This handling of quotations saves quotation marks, makes a strong impression on the eye, and it is easily reduced to routine.

It is wise for any writer to lean back from his finished work and examine its appearance without any regard to what he has said in it. Is the text pleasingly located on the page? Are the margins wide and even? Is there a good bottom margin? Are the pages numbered? Is the work, in effect, so efficiently punctuated by space as to be efficiently mastered by the reader's eye? If not, it is as old-fashioned as a hand pump, which will draw water, surely enough, but does it the hard way.

Punctuation As a System

ONCE we get into the body of a work and start reading or writing along, we meet the punctuation marks themselves. They, too, have been undergoing a gradual change to meet the needs of the silent reader. Modern punctuation, taken as a system, is not suited for the inefficient or the inexperienced reader. As a system it demands an experienced and sophisticated writing hand, and it rewards an experienced and sophisticated reading eye. In its earlier stages it was better suited to the person who plods along from word to word, framing each one with his mouth as he goes. As it has developed, it has become less instructive and more suggestive, offering signals only where signals are needed. Probably a poor reader has a harder time making his way through prose today than at any time since punctuation was invented; for him the signals are so widely separated that they do not help much, and they tend, as time goes on, to become even more sparsely distributed in the text.

To understand how punctuation works and to learn how to work it, it is a good idea to back away from sentences in the same way that a good writer backs away from the whole work, and look at their form without regard for what they say. Sentences have form apart from their meaning, form which is designed to appeal to the eye. This form alone, apart from any specific words, is significant— largely—in, through, and because of the punctuation. The punctuation is tied closely to the sentence structures dealt with in Chapters 9–16, where we displayed the structures apart from the specific words that occur in them.

End Punctuation

A NORMAL statement begins with a capital letter and ends with a period. If we use the letter **C** to indicate the capital and draw a line for the sentence, the pattern looks like this:

C _____ .

Using our basic sentence, **Boy loves girl,** to represent all statement sentences, the full pattern takes this form:

     N   **V**   **N**
C _____ .

Any question—whether the question is signaled by a question word, as in **What did the President mean by his remarks?** or by a reversal of order, as in **Did you ever receive my last letter?** or by signals of intonation, as in **They sent forty-four boxes in one load?** —is marked with a question mark at the end:

C _____ ?

A command is punctuated like a statement, as in **Please send the next shipment to me here.**

     C _____ .

Statements and commands are also punctuated with the exclamation mark, the mark ordinarily used for short utterances of intense emotional expression, as in **O my own, my beautiful, my blue-eyed!** In statements the exclamation mark is used to indicate many subtly varying degrees of emphasis. A writer uses it, for the most part, not as a visual substitute for a raising of the voice but as a means of giving some special force that might not be indicated in speech at all, as in **All our peonies bloomed this year without a bit of care!** It may simply be a means of saying that the reader should pay special attention to this statement. The mark itself does not indicate what in the statement is to be emphasized.

C --------------------------------- !

The exclamation mark is used frequently in commands; in these it seems to imply a peremptory, decisive, or authoritative tone, as in **Keep your head down!**

In straightforward writing the exclamation mark is not much used. You might read many pages of a non-fiction book and see only one or two. You might read a thousand business letters without finding one. The mark is avoided in the same way that an excess of capitals used for emphasis is avoided; the writer tries to build the emphasis into the structure of his sentences and end with a period. In verse and in experimental writing where anything can happen, you would certainly find more exclamation marks in a reach for emotional impact. In advertisements, except for those that maintain a deliberately low tone, exclamation marks pepper the page, as in **New! Now! Efficiency up, costs down! Send for our recipe book!** They seem to contribute to the general note of urgency **(Act Now!)** that the advertising agencies seek to achieve.

A paragraph containing a series of statements, a question, and an emphatic final sentence might look like this:

C ------------------------------ . C --------
-------- . C --------------------------------
-------------- . C ------------------------ ?
C ------------------------------ !

And with our modern tendency toward short sentences, that could be all the punctuation in it.

Whether to punctuate a string of sentences as one or divide them into separate units is a matter for the writer to decide. The punctuation which joins them emphasizes their relatedness to each other without creating any new relation that is not in the sentences to start with. The punctuation separating them emphasizes their distinctness without creating any division that is not built into them already. The sentences do follow each other; they are structurally divided; but they do have signals of some relation, words like **but** and **they** in this sentence and **this, that,** and so on. The question is simply which units the writer wishes to emphasize, and if the decision is to link them, how many words between capital and period he thinks his readers can handle. The decision to separate is often quite arbitrary in terms of meaning; the writer simply wishes to hold the span between capital and period within manageable limits. This era is definitely one of short sentence length.

Let us say that we have the following sequence of sentences:

C _____ . C _____ . C _____ .

The sentences do follow each other. They are structurally divided. But they do have some signals of relation.

Each of these periods represents a point both of division and of relation. Each can be replaced by another punctuation mark. A slightly different impression, suggestion, or implication will result. These sentences can be related by the semicolon (;). This mark, consisting of a period printed over a comma, once was closely related to the colon. In modern practice it might better be called a semiperiod, for the semicolon most commonly substitutes for the period. The period is a full and complete break; the semicolon, a halfbreak; and the comma, a light break. In speech any of the three junctures may occur at these points: the level /|/, the rising /||/, or the falling /#/. Any of these punctuation marks may represent any of these junctures.

For the periods we may wish to use semicolons:

C _____ . C _____ . C _____ .
C _____ ; _____ ; but _____ .

The sentences do follow each other; they are structurally divided; but they do have some signals of relation.

If the sentences are to be joined, the semicolon is a clear signal both of the division and of the relation.

For the periods we may wish to use commas, emphasizing that the sentences are not only related but that they form a series:

C _____ . C _____ . C _____ .
C _____ , _____ , but _____ .

When we have only two sentences following each other, we have more choices among the punctuation marks: period, semicolon, comma, dash, parentheses:

C _____ . C _____ .

She was wearing a new hair-do. He did not at first recognize her.

He did not at first recognize her. She was wearing a new hair-do.

We may use the semicolon:

C _____ ; _____ .

We may use a comma followed by **and, but,** or **for:**

C _____ , **and** _____ .
C _____ , **but** _____ .
C _____ , **for** _____ .

When the second sentence begins with **however, yet, nevertheless, consequently, therefore,** and similar words or word-groups like **in addition, on the other hand,** and **as a result,** we ordinarily use a semicolon after the first sentence and follow the introductory adverb with a comma:

C _____ ; **however,** _____ .
C _____ ; **yet** (with or without the comma) ___ .
C _____ ; **therefore,** _____ .
C _____ ; **in addition,** _____ .

We may use a dash:

C _____ — _____ .

He did not at first recognize her—she was wearing a new hair-do.

We may use parentheses:

C _____ (_____) .

He did not at first recognize her (she was wearing a new hair-do).

One of the points at which modern punctuation is in flux is an overlapping between semicolon and comma. As the semicolon has become more and more a semiperiod, the comma has come to span larger units within the sentence than used to be the case. The skilled silent reader does not need his sentences as closely punctuated as they used to be. Hence, when two sentences are quite short, modern British and American writers are coming to use the comma where older readers and writers would expect and even demand a semicolon:

C _____ , _____ .

He did not at first recognize her, she was wearing a new hair-do.

This is what we call an emerging or developing usage. Formerly, if an author wrote it, the publishers changed it to a semicolon. Then gradually it began to appear in print—an indication that the proofreading eye was no longer drawn sharply to it. Probably more are still corrected than get by; this use of the comma seems to occur much more frequently in letters and other personal papers than it does in print. It is a usage to watch, because at present a great issue is often made of it, yet it makes its way at the expense, mainly, of the semicolon. Keeping a close eye on points of change like this one is an excellent way of becoming sensitive to what authors think they are communicating by the signals they use.

Internal Punctuation

WITHIN the sentence the most common mark which occurs is the comma. A writer puts a comma in wherever he feels it necessary; that is, he uses it wherever he feels that the sense of his sentence will come more sharply to his reader with a comma than without it. It usually marks one of the three final junctures; unfortunately for those who move their lips as they read, it may represent any one of the three. The author puts it in where he feels that the eye, not the tongue, needs a guide. Formerly a good rule to follow would have been: when in doubt, put it in. Today a good rule is: when

in doubt, leave it out. The modern reader expects a more open
punctuation; he wants major groups defined, but, as we shall see in
the chapter on reading, he does not want the page cluttered up
with marks that tell him what the running line of text by itself tells
him. Often we put commas in as we write (saying our words aloud
as we set them down) but take them out as we revise, because then
we are more aware of the reader and his needs. The reader needs
the larger, not the smaller, elements of the sentence set off; he does
not want the sentence sliced too thin. Hence we use the comma to
emphasize any sharp turn the sentence seems to be taking that is
not clearly indicated by the group markers alone.

Still, there are some regular uses of the comma. It is used to set
off an introductory adverb—word, phrase, or clause:

> **Still, there are some regular uses of the comma.**
> **Towards evening, cows wander home.**
> **Whenever the wind comes from the west, the waves take a
> few more bites out of our shoreline.**

In these examples, the main **N V** pattern is preceded by a starting word, phrase, or clause. We often omit the comma, but when
it is in, it signals a particular kind of variation from the normal
N V N sentence pattern, and thus serves as a guide to the reading
eye.

The comma is used to point out the elements in a series. Whether
it is a series of words, phrases, or clauses, or any combination of
these three, the comma steers us through it. No law says we have
to use a comma here, but it is a help. The comma is often omitted
before **or** and **and** in a series of words, but it is just as often used.

> **Men, women, and children ran out into the streets.**
> **Men, women and children ran out into the streets.**
> **He had some books, what looked like a small chest of draw-
> ers, and a stack of letters on his desk.**
> **After he had come into the room, while he was speaking to
> the hostess, but before he had greeted any of the guests, he real-
> ized that he should not have come at all.**
> **They were never certain what they were quarreling about, why
> they had developed this tendency to bicker, or where it was tak-
> ing them in their relations to each other.**

Here we come to one of the uses of the semicolon where it is not
a semiperiod but more like a comma. When there is a series of

units long enough to have commas within them, we use a semicolon
to keep the larger units distinct:

**I am sending you a large box, which I picked up in Japan;
some chopsticks, elaborately carved, from China; and a cotton
dress, your size, that is a native costume often seen in the Philip-
pines.**

The manner of punctuating a series is one of the two most important aspects of the punctuation of running discourse, because, as
we saw in Chapter 11, repetition is the chief architect of complexity in Modern English. Any element or any part of an element that
is used once in an utterance may be repeated. Where we can use
one noun, we can use any number of nouns in series; where we can
use one verb, adjective, or adverb, we can add another or a string
of others. We can do this by the simple addition of other items referring to different things, as we throw things in a pile to make it
bigger, and that is compounding. The normal expectation of reader
or hearer is that the units of the basic sentence-patterns will follow
each other in order:

D ⫫A̶ N ⫫A̶P ⫫A̶C̶ V (or VG) A̸ (or A̸P or A̸C)

The normal flow of the basic utterance is from determiner to adjective to noun. When we use two or three determiners, two or
three adjectives, or two or three nouns, we interrupt this flow and
raise questions in the mind of the reader: Where is this structure
going now? What is its ultimate shape? How much of a deviation
from the pattern will it offer?

The speaker signals these turns in the structure by his intonation
—by the familiar signals of pitch, stress, and juncture. Lacking
these signals, the writer has to rely on punctuation. Anyone reading an unpunctuated sentence can puzzle it out in the old, old way:
he can insert his own punctuation, trying different ways of splitting
up the line of words until he feels that he is close to the writer's intention. That is a slow and somewhat irritating way of proceeding
through a piece of prose, especially irritating when the puzzle
seems to have occurred in relatively unimportant matter. The
reader expects to be steered through any unexpected shift in structure. Repetition, common as it is, always is a variation on the patterns we expect.

For this reason a writer is wise to take special care with the punctuation of elements which occur in a series, whether they are words, phrases, or clauses. He should make certain as far as he can that the reader is guided over the aggregation of repeated elements and back to the main line of the sentence again. The more formalized and more reduced to routine his punctuation of a series, the better. The patterns are really quite simple. They can be visualized at a glance:

C _____ 1, 2, and 3 _____ .

When the repeated elements have commas within them:

C_____ ___ , ___ , ___ ; ___ , ___ , ___ ; ___ , ___ , ___ _____ .

In using punctuation a writer cannot take corners like a playboy in a convertible, coming up to them at full speed and whipping around into a new direction. He is more like the driver of a bus, who must take every turn slow enough to keep his passengers from falling into the aisle.

The other kind of repetition—apposition—falls in with a number of expressions that take their punctuation marks in pairs, one before and one after. Apposition, as we saw in Chapter 11, is not the addition of items within the same general class of words, phrases, or clauses to make a pile; rather, apposition is a kind of repetition that is like another blow of a hammer that drives the nail home. The second item is in the same class as the first, and it has the same referent. The second pins down the first a little more fully or more accurately. When an apposed element is punctuated, it is set off by a pair of marks—as in the first sentence in this paragraph —unless the end of the expression marked off is the end of the sentence. In that case the period often, but not always, takes over. The general term for these set-off expressions is "parenthetical expression," because *parenthesis* means 'putting something beside or in something else.' Parentheses interchange with a pair of dashes and a pair of commas.

Apposition occasions one use of punctuation marks that closely parallels intonation. This similarity occurs when a writer must decide from his speech whether or not to punctuate apposed elements. If he does not use falling juncture before and after the ex-

pression, he does not set it off. If he precedes it and follows it with
falling junctures, he sets it off. Whether he uses commas, dashes, or
parentheses depends on the separateness he wants to indicate. If he
wants the reader to read a pause before and after, he punctuates;
if he does not want the reader to read a pause, he puts no punctuation marks in. In some sentences the general structure leaves him
no choice, but most of the time he must indicate how he wants the
sentence to be read.

Let us consider some examples:

> **My brother Charlie has come home.**
> **My brother, Charlie, has come home.**

> **Public officials who are always on trial for their political lives
> rarely are able to maintain independence of judgment.**

> **Public officials, who are always on trial for their political lives,
> rarely are able to maintain independence of judgment.**

> **Public officials—who are always on trial for their political
> lives—rarely are able to maintain independence of judgment.**

> **Public officials (who are always on trial for their political
> lives) rarely are able to maintain independence of judgment.**

Obviously the punctuated sentences are different from the ones
that are not. The relationship in **my brother Charlie** is close; the
whole unit functions as **N** in the pattern **N V**. In **my brother, Charlie,** the name **Charlie** is a detached unit, set off in speech by junctures and in writing by commas. The commas may be called signals
for pauses, but they are more than this: they are instructions to
the reader's eye to take the expression between them as a whole
and relate it as a slightly detached whole to the rest of the sentence.
In the third sentence all the words before **rarely** are closely integrated into one functioning unit. In the three variations on that sentence the words between punctuation marks are set apart, and they
are to be read as a separate unit.

These units whether closed or open—unpunctuated or set off by
a pair of commas, dashes, or parentheses—are always words,
phrases, or clauses in the noun-cluster or in the verb-cluster; or
they are elements dislodged from their usual place in these clusters
and inserted elsewhere. Except for the appositives, they are adjective or adverb units. The appositives are simple repetitions used to
drive home a point not sufficiently stated by the first element:

> **He met a man—the man—at the appointed time.**
> **He staggered—stumbled, rather, or was tripped—and fell into the street.**
> **We had read that book Jane Eyre before they showed the movie.**
> **We had read that book, Jane Eyre, before they showed the movie.**
> **Send it to us at once—today, if possible—for processing.**

Appositives always occur within a sentence, since the appositive always follows its antecedent.

Adverbial elements—words, phrases, or clauses—may be closely joined or set apart from the words or phrases they modify. We noted in Chapter 9 that adverbs are free-wheeling elements in the sentence, likely to occur at any chink between other elements, and especially likely to occur at the beginning or end. Any loose element that begins a sentence is likely to be followed by a comma or dash, but the capital letter overrides the beginning mark of the usual pair:

> **At the signal, he released his hold and threw the line free.**
> **Although the letter had not come, he put the call through anyway.**

Such an element at the end of a sentence is preceded by a comma or a dash, but the end-of-the-sentence punctuation mark overrides the second mark in the usual pair:

> **He came by every day, just as the sun was rising.**
> **He came by every day—just as the sun was rising.**

Parentheses used to set off loose elements always occur in pairs. They are not overridden in the beginning by a capital or at the end by an end-of-the-sentence punctuation mark. They do not often occur at the beginning, but they are common at the end:

> **He always sent flowers (when he had the money).**
> **He always sent flowers, when he had the money.**
> **He always sent flowers—when he had the money.**

We noted that a reader can make his way through a series, even when the commas are left out, though there are some series that cannot be resolved by any reader. These elements that may be either closed or loose must be marked or left unmarked by the writer, because the differences in meaning or in implication is a matter for him to control—often on the basis of knowledge, information, or intention that no one else can have, since it does not appear otherwise in the writing.

Closely joined adverbial, adjective, and appositive elements—those not set off by any marks of punctuation—are often called *restrictive* when they are approached by way of their meaning. Those set off by commas, parentheses, or dashes are called *non-restrictive*. The signals, however, are junctures before and after non-restrictive elements in speech; commas, dashes, or parentheses before and after them in writing. Say the sentence as you write it, and listen for the junctures. You, as the writer, are the only person who can make the decision to set the element off or leave it unmarked.

Closely joined (restrictive) patterns:

C --- .
C ----   A -- , ------------------------- .

Loosely joined (non-restrictive) patterns:

C ---------- , ---------- , ---------- .
C ---------- (----------) ---------- .
C ---------- — ---------- — ---------- .
C ------- , ------------------------- .
C ------- — ------------------------- .
C ------------------------- , ---------- .
C ------------------------- — -------- .
C -------------------- (------------).

In normal running prose we find the period to be the basic end mark, with the semicolon as its most frequent substitute when we want the reader to separate sentences as one closely joined unit. In the same way the comma is the basic interior punctuation mark, though with some tendency to encroach on the semicolon when the units to be joined are short. The comma is used to mark any turn in a sentence that might be confusing, to set off the units in a series, and to set off separately interior units that must be taken as a whole a little apart from the words they modify. In this last use the parentheses and the dashes—usually in pairs—substitute for commas.

Why not get by with periods and commas and abandon the semi-colon, dash, and parentheses? Obviously the period does not sepa-rate and join at the same time the way the semicolon does; there is a use for the semicolon. As for the commas—in a sentence that has commas in all three uses we can get more definition and clearer understanding by using parentheses or dashes simply by contrast. Balancing all these marks so that they help the reader's eye through a line of writing is a minor form of art, though an important one.

Punctuation is an art form made even more expressive, though perhaps more complicated, by some other quirks. We have not touched on the colon, which in running prose has a limited use as a substitute for the period. It warns us that the words which follow are in some way an explanation or illustration or spelling-out of what has gone before it. We might have put a colon after the word **period** at the end of the second sentence above, if the sentence had not already been long enough. The colon may be followed by a capital letter or it may be followed by a lower-case letter:

> **I have only one thing to say. You must return that book.**
> **I have only one thing to say: You must return that book.**
> **I have only one thing to say: you must return that book.**

> **They brought only the barest necessities with them. An ax, a gun and ammunition, and some dried food, hard on teeth and taste both.**
> **They brought only the barest necessities with them: an ax, a gun and ammunition, and some dried food, hard on the teeth and taste both.**

In running prose, also, the dash has other functions: it substi-tutes for the colon in such sentences as those above, and it substi-tutes for the comma in its use to mark off turns in the sentence-structure that might be confusing. Some people employ the dash in this use to give an impression of speech, with its quick starts and turns of expression. The dash comes close to being interchangeable with the comma—but held back, by most writers, for the sharper switches of structure and meaning.

Punctuating your writing is no push-button matter, where you hit the right button and get a specific, predictable reaction. For each of the divisions we wish to make in a sentence, we may choose among several marks. In place of the period we can use the semi-colon, the colon, the comma, or a dash. In place of commas we may use parentheses or dashes; and in a series where we already have commas, the semicolon. Much depends on which marks we use before and after. Much depends upon the extent to which we can use space to keep similar units together and different units apart. A great deal depends on how far the sentence-structure itself is clear and unequivocal; the simpler and more familiar the patterns, the fewer defining marks we need. Finally, the choice is also affected by the care with which we choose the order of our words to bear clear marks of their function in the sentence. The whole aim of punctuation is to lead the eye of the reader across the page with the fewest possible hitches. When a reader wishes to change marks or add them, we may take his interference as a sign that the signals we intend are not being received. If we lose the attention of the reader, we lose all.

Formal Punctuation

SOME uses of the punctuation marks are matters of visual form only, with even less regard to the pitch, stress, and juncture patterns of speech than the ones we have discussed. Sometimes, if we try to read them as "pauses," we find these uses conflicting with the others, as in the case of the commas around the year in a date or around the name of a state following a city, as in **January 25, 1955,** or **Terre Haute, Indiana,** in running prose. It is not any January 25 or any Terre Haute we are talking about; the year and the state are closely joined, restrictive units. Custom—which is to say the publishing industry—demands commas at these points.

The marks used in formal punctuation are the same as before: the period, comma, semicolon, dash, and parentheses; and in addition there are the single and double quotation marks, the ellipsis (. . .), the square brackets ([ ]), and the apostrophe.

QUOTATION MARKS

WE use quotation marks around quotations when we wish to indicate that we are giving the exact words of a speaker or writer. We mentioned earlier a growing tendency to indent passages of quoted matter without any other identifying marks, even when the quotation is rather short. When we run them into the text, we need the

marks. These marks are usually inclusive: they go outside other
marks, even when it doesn't seem to make much sense to put them
outside. Printers think they look prettier that way. Thus we have
the following patterns:

> "C _____ ," he said, " _____ ."
>
> He said, "C _____ ."

Printers feel that a semicolon occurring between two quotations
looks prettier outside the quotation marks:

> "C _____ ." "C _____ ."
>
> "C _____ "; " _____ ."
>
> **"Lift up your hearts and sing." "Music is love in search of a word."**
>
> **"Lift up your hearts and sing"; "music is love in search of a word."**

Even when only one quoted word ends the sentence, the quotation marks go outside the period:

> C _____ " _____ " and " _____ ."
>
> **He used such terms as "outrage" and "crime."**

If the whole sentence is a question or exclamation, the question
mark or the exclamation mark is outside quoted words at the end
of the sentence:

> C _____ " _____ "?
>
> C _____ " _____ "!
>
> **Did not Walt Whitman write: "I too am untranslatable"?**
>
> **Enjoy your friends and "gather the love out of their hearts"!**

Note, however, that a question mark or exclamation mark remains
inside the final quotation mark when such a mark belongs to the
quotation:

> **Did you ask, "Who has done his day's work?"**
>
> **Pay attention to the "endless unfolding of words of ages!"**

Most publishers use double quotation marks for the general run
of quotations; for a quotation within a quotation they use single
marks:

> **He said, "C _____ , ' _____ ,' _____ ."**
>
> **He said, "C _____ , ' _____ .' "**

Botkin says, "The New Regionalism grew out of the new 'renascence of wonder,' which is retrospective."

Poe wrote: "In Heaven a spirit doth dwell 'whose heart-strings are a lute.' "

When we have a quote within a quoted quote, we use the single mark again:

He said, "She said, 'He said, "We said, 'No.' " ' "

And so on.

Some publishers who begin with the single marks can be ignored, since they oblige themselves to go over all copy and convert it. Of course, some writers of fiction use no special marks indicating quotations at all, apparently without confusing anybody except the unhappy proofreader who is accustomed to the marks.

THE PERIOD

GENERALLY, we use the period after abbreviations, such as **Mr., Dr., Mrs., Mt., pct., Pa.,** and **R.I.** When one letter stands for each word, we used a period after each, as in **a. m., p. m.,** and **i.e.** In our age of alphabetical agencies in government and public life, these periods may be left out of familiar abbreviations: **A. A. A.** or **AAA, W. A. C.** or **WAC, E. T. O.** or **ETO.** Oftentimes the names of such agencies are made up with the idea of creating a pronounceable word out of the initials, especially by the military, as in **SPARS** (from semper paratus, 'always ready,' the motto of the U.S. Coast Guard), **SHAEF** (Supreme Headquarters Allied Expeditionary Forces, in World War II), **CINCPAC** (Commander in Chief, Pacific Theater). There is also a tendency to drop the period after familiar abbreviations such as **Mr** and **Dr,** especially in business correspondence; but if you have once learned to put these periods in, it is not easy to drill yourself to leave them out. Be consistent in using or omitting periods in abbreviations.

THE COLON

THE colon is generally used after headings, and it is from this use that the practice arose of using a colon to end the salutation of a letter (as in **Dear Mr. Sommers:**). Formerly this use, considered dignified and restrained, was confined to letters addressed to persons with whom the writer was not on familiar terms. With the coming of the typewriter, fingers that were in the habit of striking a colon in business letters went on striking it for all letters, so that there is no real consistency in familiar letters; the salutation may close with a colon, a comma, or a dash. Politer forms of address have a way of spreading into general use and crowding out more familiar forms, and we could guess that the colon will, in the course of time, eat up the comma and dash—at least in typewritten letters.

As for headings other than salutations, the colon seems to be losing ground to space. When the heading is centered, the colon is not used; even when the heading is placed at the left of the page, the colon is often omitted. What readers expect is not that one or the other will be used, but that whichever practice is followed is consistently followed. A series of such headings should all be treated the same way.

The colon is often used to precede a quotation where a comma or even a dash might occur: **General MacAuliffe answered with only one word: "Nuts."**

THE COMMA

THE comma is used in dates to set off the year, and in geographical designations to set off the county, state, nation, or even continent.

> **On January 25, 1955, he died.**
>
> **He was obviously a resident of Plainville, Boone County, Kentucky, U.S.A., North America, and he liked you to know it.**

When the "military" form of the date is used, no commas occur:

> **On 25 January 1955 he died.**

The comma is used in names, when the last name is given first, so that it can be put into an alphabetical list:

Adams, John	**Madison, James**
Jefferson, Thomas	**Washington, George**

When an indication of family succession, a title or degree or honor follows the name, a comma sets it off:

Herbert Hoover, Jr.	**Sewell Avery, Chairman**
Henry Ford, II	**Earnest Endeavour, Ph. D.**
George John Miller, Esq.	**Sir Hubert Wilkins, K. C. B.**

THE DASH

ABOUT the dash there is not much to say. In writing, it is simply a line dashed with a pen; in typing, it is a double hyphen; and in printing, it can be as short or as long as the printer chooses to make it. It substitutes for the period on occasion and for the colon; in most of its uses it is about equivalent to the comma, and in some situations a pair of dashes are equivalent to parentheses. Some people write a dash after a period, colon, semicolon, or comma, sometimes for emphasis, sometimes for dignity, sometimes for informality. Since it is hard to tell which of these emphases is intended, the proofreader's eye gleams at the sight of a dash used this way, and he gets out his blue pencil—with not much change in the effect when he is done. The one formal use of the dash which remains standard appears at the end of an incompleted utterance as the signal that the speaker was interrupted or broke off. The dash in this usage occurs with and without final sentence punctuation:

> **"Please, please—!" she began.**
> **"Where shall I—?" she asked.**
> **"If I come there, I'll—"**

THE BRACKETS

Two kinds of brackets are commonly used, curved and square brackets. The curved brackets are, of course, the parentheses. Most matter tucked into the running line of discourse is set off with parentheses, but people who put parenthetical matter within parenthetical matter either put parentheses within square brackets: [_____ (_____) _____] or square brackets within parentheses: (_____ [_____] _____). It does not matter which way you do it, but being consistent does help the reader.

For most insertions, side remarks, added information, and the like, parentheses are used, because they are on all typewriters and are most convenient. The eye is expected to pick up this information without taking it as a part of the main line of the discourse. The insertion could also be put between dashes and read the same way. The fact that it is in the line at all makes it part of the discourse. Writers often play with the ambiguity of this situation, giv-

ing essential information as if it were an aside, often giving it
special emphasis by setting it apart:

He entered the Army very young (14) and left it very old (78).

The point is in the inserted numbers; the sentence is not much
without them.

This device carries us again from writing as a close rendering
of speech to writing as a set of signals for the eye, and it sometimes
results in a quite unspeakable prose that can scarcely be read aloud
and understood by a listener. "Let me see it," he says in dismay,
unable to unravel the thread of the sentence. It is a trick much
used in *Time* and in magazines that accompany pictures with extended comment.

**Caracas (pop. 87,000), the balmy capital (average tempera-
ture 70°), is the national show window.**

**Highly educated (Groton; Harvard, A. B.; Yale, Ph. D.; Sor-
bonne, Doctor ès Lettres) Professor Earnest Endeavor set about
making some repairs to his domicile (a two-story frame house,
with attic).**

Square brackets have a very precise use in careful writing, and
a person who is unacquainted with their use may well miss the
whole point. We are in an era when writers who quote other writers
are expected to quote them exactly, letter by letter and punctuation
mark by punctuation mark. The borrowers are expected to quote
another author in his own terms, giving his meaning and not their
own. They are expected to give enough of the text so that the
original author's meaning is clear, though they may omit anything
that does not bear on their point. They are faced with two problems. The first occurs when the original author is individual, eccentric, foreign, or old-fashioned in his spelling or punctuation. If
so, the borrowers may have to indicate in some way that the oddities are his and not their own. They can stand off the printer or
proofreader by writing *stet* ('let it stand this way') in the margin,
but they still have to face the reader. For the reader they write *sic*
(a Latin word meaning 'so' or 'thus') in square brackets to indicate
that the oddity is in the orginal work.

We saw some karaboo [sic] at a distance.

**Her stomick [sic] being somewhat queesie [sic], she desired
to rest.**

The other problem is one of compression and focusing on the point. The original author may have named a person earlier in his paragraph but not in this sentence. The quoting author inserts the name at the proper point:

In the original text:

Henry Poole was then sheriff, as he had been for many years. This overbearing, brutal man was reputed to be of the opinion that wealth can do no evil.

In the quoted form:

This overbearing, brutal man [Henry Poole] was reputed to be of the opinion that wealth can do no evil.

Square brackets are used in quotations for any comment, information, correction, or insertion by copying authors:

Then, said Hurley, "we recognize that it is essential that we send them to the expert [i.e., the psychiatrist]."
He came there with [text blurred] and his brother.
We had no sooner kindled a fire then [than] we where [were] saluted with a rain storm witch [which] put out our fire.

This kind of meticulous accuracy may seem extreme, but it is only fair to the person being quoted. Yet its whole point may escape the reader who does not understand this use of square brackets.

THE ELLIPSIS

THE ellipsis is a series of three dots used in quotations to indicate that something is being left out. The punctuation of a sentence containing ellipses must be in accord with standard practice. If another mark is needed to supplement the ellipsis, that mark is included.

Mr. Haredale grasps the cord of an alarm bell which hangs within his reach, but he succeeds in sounding it only once or twice.
Mr. Haredale grasps the cord of an alarm bell . . . , but he succeeds in sounding it only once or twice.
Mr. Haredale grasps the cord of an alarm bell . . .

The ellipsis also substitutes for the dash as a sign of an incomplete statement either in conversation or running discourse. In the latter situation the writer simply says enough to start the reader's imagination, then stops:

If these remarks are true, our future will be . . .
The voters go to the polls tomorrow, and they will elect . . .

THE APOSTROPHE

THE last two marks we ought to speak about, the apostrophe (') and the hyphen (-), are really more matters of spelling than of punctuation, but since they are not letter marks, we treat them here.

Like most other things in English writing, the apostrophe shows its history in our present uses of it, and in our difficulties also. Its first and basic use was as a sign of omitted letters in the spelling of a word, and we still can use it almost at will to show that we are leaving out letters that are ordinarily written:

I don't s'pose there's fishin' allow'd.
He always said lit'rature and hon'rable.
Po' li'l chil'

An offshoot of this use of the apostrophe is our present way of spelling the **N-'s** form of the noun. About the year 1600, people thinking about this "possessive" form decided that **-'s** was a contraction of the pronoun **his;** they thought that **John's book** came from **John his book** and that **the man's hat** came from **the man his hat.** When they wrote formally, they actually wrote **his** out as more elegant and correct than the **-'s.** The **-'s** form of the noun was a natural development from one of the Old English cases. If any letter was omitted, it was an **e,** not the first two letters of **his.**

About the same time, the apostrophe came into use in the plural in such words as **folio's** and **hero's.** In this instance of **-'s** the apostrophe was a sign of an omitted **e.** This usage, which for a while was fairly common, has largely passed away, but it leaves us with some oddities of writing that we persist in.

In standard English writing we use the apostrophe for most possessives but not all, for some omitted letters but not all, and for some plurals but not many. Still, all the former uses of the apostrophe hang on in the writing of some people. Persons who do not read much or write much employ the apostrophe in non-standard ways: they use it with all "possessives," and they use it as a sign of the plural. Their variations do not usually go outside the range of what was formerly accepted usage. It seems to be as hard for the writers of English as a whole to give up old habits as it is for an individual.

Nevertheless, modern standard employment of the apostrophe is quite simple and can be learned as easily as any of the word-pictures we learn to spell.

We use the apostrophe with a set of old and familiar contractions but not with others where you might expect it. We use it in combinations of forms of the verbs **be (am, is, are, was, were, be), have (has, had), do (do, does, did),** and the modal auxiliaries with **not.** We have no contracted form of **am not** (except **ain't,** but you know all about **ain't**). **Is not** becomes **isn't, are not** becomes **aren't, was not** becomes **wasn't, do not** becomes **don't, will not** becomes **won't,** and so on. We also use the apostrophe in combinations of the personal pronouns **(I, you, he, she, it, they)** with forms of the verbs **be, have, shall, will,** and **would.** We thus have **I'm, I've, I'll, I'd, you're, you've, you'll, you'd,** and so on. Similar contractions that we make in running speech get no such reflection in writing; these do. Once taboo in formal writing, these contractions are appearing with increasing frequency in books and magazines whose authors reflect an urbane conversational tone.

We add **-'s** to the base form of the noun to produce **N-'s,** and we add the apostrophe alone to the plural form of the noun **(N-s)** to produce **N-s':**

N	N-'s	N-s	N-s'
boy	boy's	boys	boys'
child	child's	children	children's
woman	woman's	women	women's

We do not form plural nouns in standard written English with the apostrophe. We do not form the possessives of the personal pronouns with the apostrophe. The fact that we once did both of these things causes some people to go on doing them now, and, of course, people who do not read and write much find it hard to keep in mind that the apostrophe is used with nouns but not with personal pronouns. Thus we have **man's** (and **men's**), **cat's, person's**—usually before another noun in the familiar pattern **N-'s N:**

D	N-'s	N
the	man's	hat
the	cat's	meow
a	boy's	book

N-'s	N
John's	car
Mary's	purse
trail's	end

But we have	his	hat
	its	meow
	his	book
	her	purse

	my	car
	your	box
	their	business
	its	end

And we have	The book is mine
	his
	hers
	ours
	yours
	theirs

It offers a special case. We recall that the old possessive of **it** was **his,** as in the Biblical **The salt has lost his savor. His** lost ground as the possessive of **it,** and for a while **it** was used: **Did it hurt it finger?** Then **its** was formed on the analogy of **his, hers,** and **theirs.** From the very beginning, usage wavered between **its** and **it's,** because the new form was created after the **N-'s** form had become standard. There is another **it's,** the contraction of **it is** or **it has. Its** and **it's** sound exactly the same, but they are used in different structures:

N	V
it	is
it	has
it's	

N	N
its	business
its	end

We seem to have come full circle: proofreaders, once quite successful in keeping **it's** out of print except as the contraction of **it is** and **it has,** are missing it, and we find it fairly often in newspapers, weekly magazines, advertisements, and even, now and then, in books. Some things never die.

We use the apostrophe with plurals of letters and numbers treated as nouns and with words treated as words:

He does not dot his i's.
In the early 1950's
Too many and's and but's weaken writing.

We use the apostrophe with plurals of capital letters used as names of college degrees, agencies, bureaus, clubs, etc.:

He has two Ph. D.'s.
There are three AAA's.
He gave me four old PMLA's.

THE HYPHEN

THE hyphen (-) has two uses which are like two sides of a coin. It tells the eye to take words together which are usually printed apart, and to separate parts of words—syllables—which are usually printed together. It is a sort of marker that tells the reading eye how to slice the line of the sentence into meaning-groups—especially when the grouping or separation is outside our normal expectations. It is thus a way of getting around the difference between speech and writing we have mentioned before: we speak in whole connected utterances, but we write in words whose boundaries are traditionally established for the eye. In its first use, the hyphen leaves these boundaries intact so that the reader is not confused, but it minimizes them, building the words before and after into a single functioning unit. In its second use, the hyphen merely defines syllable-boundaries in terms not of speech but of writing, without destroying the unity of the whole word.

Rules for the use of the hyphen in running discourse and in lists of words commonly hyphenated have their value, but they may obscure for us the fact that, like most punctuation, handling the hyphen is an art. It depends on the writer's developing a sharp sense of the reader's needs where the reader can effortlessly grasp the relations of words and where he needs a bit of extra help. It helps, for instance, for us to use a hyphen to separate a prefix ending with a vowel from a word beginning with the same vowel, as in **re-elect, re-emphasize, co-operate,** and **pre-eminent.** It helps the reader when we separate any combination of letters that may confuse the eye, as in **eel-like** and **fall-line.** And it helps for us to separate the prefix from a following word when the combination may be taken for another, as in **re-creation** and **recreation, re-cover** and **recover,**

re-form and **reform.** When we use a prefix before a word beginning with a capital letter, it helps to set it off with a hyphen, as in **pro-Labor, anti-Communist,** and **ex-President.**

There are many other places where a hyphen eliminates a hitch in the reading by showing the reader how to group a phrase. When word-group modifiers precede a noun, we can show their relationship with a hyphen, as in **a green-topped metal desk, a fast-breaking electrical storm, wind-tossed hair, night-blooming cereus, red-lead paint.** Longer groups may be joined: **a pay-as-you-enter proposition, a devil-may-care look, a stay-at-home existence.** Even longer groups may be joined: **a pay-your-money-and-take-your-choice attitude; a sentimental, I-can't-give-you-anything-but-love attitude.** In these larger groups we find the hyphen and the quotation marks, single or double, capable of doing the same grouping with the same result: **a sentimental, "I can't give you anything but love" attitude.**

Compounds involving **self-** are often hyphenated: **self-control, self-liquidation, self-development.** Numbers from twenty-one to ninety-nine are hyphenated: **a hundred thirty-three.** Fractions are usually hyphenated: **three-fifths of a pint, five-eights, nine-tenths.**

Various publishing houses have their own standard practices and can be depended upon to go through copy and convert it. The proofreaders, as usual, can be depended upon to feel that they know better than the authors what guidance the reader needs. Perhaps they do.

The main use of the hyphen in dividing syllables rises from the desire to keep a reasonably even right margin on the page. When copy is prepared simply to be read without further resetting, a word may begin on one line and be finished on the next. Ordinarily only longer words are split; some words like **rhythm** and **women** should not be split and a word like **water** seldom is. A danger lies in hyphenating words at the ends of lines in manuscript. If the copy is retyped or even set in print, the operator may carry the hyphen along when it should be dropped. Confusion is eliminated by never splitting words at the ends of lines in manuscript, and some publishers advise authors to avoid line-end hyphenation. The long and confused history of English sounds and spellings makes the division of words into syllables rather chancy, even for experts in the matter. The dictionary makers' habit of peeking at each others' books has had good results in syllable division: most dictionaries agree on the division of most words, and writers and publishers generally follow the dictionaries. Syllable division, like spelling, is reasonably standard; unlike spelling, its problems can be avoided by the writer and left to the printer.

The shape of modern punctuation marks has become quite standard. No matter how fancy the type is, the marks look pretty much alike in all fonts and are all familiar. Handwriting is more fluid than typing or printing, and there is more variation in the shape of marks; any handwritten symbol that is like one of the punctuation marks is converted to that mark in print. Any dot becomes a period, and any dashed line a hyphen or a dash. Any upright curved line becomes a curved bracket, and anything that looks like a comma becomes a comma. Thus we have marks appearing in print that seem to follow no rule, like the single curved bracket following numbers in a series, as in 1), 2), and 3). And of course the marks have been carried over into the various fields of learning like mathematics and chemistry—as far as they serve—and other marks are added to fill common needs. Nothing general can be said about these; if you know the field, you know the marks and how to use them; if you do not know the field, explanation does not do much good.

These dozen or so marks of punctuation used in standard English writing overlap in their uses and are somewhat confusing to learn, but they are sufficient for what we ask them to do—or possibly a little less than sufficient, so that we may look for changes to occur among them. Changes are in progress. As the comma has been withdrawn from close punctuation of word-groups, it has edged into the uses of the semicolon in spite of the resistance of custom. We see here again practices frequent in language and writing—in the phonemes and morphemes and in the alphabet—the maximum employment of commonly recurring materials which have no meaning in themselves, but find their place and meaning within the total pattern. We cannot understand the uses of the comma without reference to the period and the other marks or without reference to the forms and arrangement of the words and the balanced distribution of capitals and small letters. The sentence, like the utterance in speech, is a structural unity with all its parts related to each other. Logic might demand that we give one task to one mark and stick to it, but efficiency of communication demands that we split the burden and distribute it widely, so that the mark most apt and expressive in the circumstances can be used. Effective punctuation lies somewhere between two extremes, between a cut-and-dried routine and a blind peppering of the page with periods, semicolons, commas, parentheses, and other guides to the reading eye.

The Arts of Reading and Writing

*

PART SIX

*

The Arts of
Reading and
Writing

CHAPTER 24

The Structure of the Book

T HE BASIC GERMINAL idea of the twentieth century is the concept of structure—the idea that vast and apparently confused entities consist of a limited number of basic units in an orderly system of arrangements. This idea has contained the expanding universe and it has penetrated the atom. The idea of structure is the prime modern principle of analysis in the arts and sciences. As we human beings crowd each other more and more on this teeming planet (we increase in numbers at the rate of a hundred thousand every single day), structure is the principle on which we build our lives and our means of living.

We are system builders; by organization of physical resources and of human beings in larger and ever-larger systems we make room for each other and provide a living for all. We feed millions where thousands once starved, we transport millions where thousands once walked, we house millions where thousands once slept in the wind and the rain, and we cut down the effort that each single individual once expended for far less than we get. The problem of a young person today is not how to fend for himself but how to find and keep a place in one or another of the vast business, governmental, service, or educational systems—how to find a beneficent organization and how to grasp the idea of structure, how to penetrate structures with his mind, and how to put that knowledge to work.

All the patterns by which society exists are possible because men and women can talk to each other. Let us never underrate conversation, for it is the cement that binds single persons who would be helpless by themselves into groups that can cope with the harsh but fruitful world we live in. Most of the clans, tribes, and nations in the history of the world have had no other means than speech and the memory of speech for preserving past experience and applying it to what faces them. Language was one of the first structural systems by which the human race, sparsely distributed on this planet of overwhelming vastness and indifference, could pool its efforts in its struggle to keep alive and discover some meaning in existence beyond mere survival. But talk is limited in time and place; a stream of sounds is paced to the large and small muscles of the vocal system, it is heard within earshot, and it instantly dies away. It limits the size and complexity of the groups which must depend upon it.

Early man groped for a way to extend his will beyond the range of his voice and to store his experience beyond the capacity of his memory. He tried pictures and picture writing, ideographs, and syllabaries. He built great empires on the organization of people and human resources that these devices made possible—the Egyptian, the Babylonian, the Inca and Aztec, and others whose ruins humanize the waste places of the earth. The line to our kind of complexly integrated societies of modern magnitude begins with the invention of the alphabet, takes a large jump with the invention of the book, but really advances with the invention of movable type used for printing multiple copies of individual texts. Each age, improving on what it received from earlier times, has contributed to efficient organization of the writing that carries all the disciplines of science, technology, human relations, and human expression of our own world.

The book as we know it—separate pages bound at one side and otherwise free—is as central to reading and writing as conversation is to language itself. Prehistoric men tried various writing materials —stone, baked clay, and wood—before they settled on thin sheets of vellum or paperlike fibers. After they hit on thin, flexible sheets to carry their writings, they glued them together—end to end—in a continuous line as long as the text required and wound the ends on sticks to keep them under control. Anyone who has tried to find his place on a long microfilm or on a tape recording knows the difficulty these rolls caused. Cross reference is impossible, because the matter you are not reading is wound up on one stick or the other. Still, a library of scrolls was an advance over a library of stone or clay tablets; it contained the records of society, even if they were hard to get at. Whoever then thought of cutting the scroll into sheets and pasting the sheets together at one edge invented the basic form of modern records and the basic tool of modern intellectual life, because the book that resulted permitted the reader to hold his place in the text, mark it, and find it again. He could start reading at any point, stop, jump to another section, turn back, compare and relate materials within one book or in many—in short, he could use the book for cross reference. In the multitude of experiences that men have recorded, order and meaning can be found only if they can be related and compared. The book itself could be enclosed in a stiff cover, marked, and stored in a little space where it could quickly be found again.

With printing, the final basic invention, the making of books was taken from individual hands. Identical copies could be prepared, and these could be widely distributed wherever there were men to read.

We came into the present age with the book in hand to teach us the value of multiplied copies and easy cross reference. Our society has experimented endlessly with these fundamentals. We have torn books into sheets and the sheets into cards, applied photographic and machine techniques, keyed the sheets and cards with slots that activate electrical fingers and eyes. We have enormously increased the speed and efficiency of finding, in a mass of matter, related information that can be related to other information. Ours has been called the iron age, the statistical age, the electronic age—even the aspirin age—but it is certainly the age of maximum exploitation of cross-indexing, the technique that pulls order out of diversity.

As an instrument to be taken into the hand, the book has set the form of notebooks, daybooks, journals, telephone directories, magazines and other periodicals, pamphlets, comic books, and newspapers; any of these can be flipped open at any page or read through from beginning to end. Internally it has set many patterns of our intellectual life. The table of contents is the model of the subject indexes of our libraries, and the index at the end has set the pattern for the crossfiles within them. Numerals for chapter headings give us the order of large blocks of material. The order of the alphabet is the order of lists, dictionaries, guides, telephone directories, encyclopedias, reference works, and license plates from A to Z and from AA to ZZ. Roman and Arabic numerals, together with capitals and lower-case letters, permit a clear array of classifications. The format of the book is parent of them all.

The sum of the developments in writing and in the book is a sophistication and economy that make no concessions to bunglers. Modern writing for publication is prepared for a sophisticated reader. A writer—even a writer who thinks he is writing down to his public—assumes that his reader is qualified to read. He assumes that his reader is 1) a native speaker of the language; 2) experienced with books and able to use their apparatus—table of contents, preface, introduction, appendices, and index; 3) at home in the culture of Western Europe and America and reasonably well-informed about it; 4) conscious, at least in general terms, of the political, economic, and intellectual history of Europe and America, and conscious—though in perhaps even more general terms—of world history and our place in it; and 5) efficient in reading, with a complete and automatic response to the signals of print. All readers are not that good, but writers make no concessions to the ignorant. They try sometimes, but while a writer can temper what he has to say about his own special field of interest, he has to assume that otherwise his reader is someone much like himself with a trigger response very much like his own to what is on the page.

The structural nature of language and the related structures of writing are central to the existence of our society. In this book we have sketched the structural relations of language; we have looked at language from several angles. We have discussed language as it relates to the other patterned activities of human society, especially our own English-speaking community. We have examined language as an orderly system of habits in the individual speaker, and we have touched on the way he has learned these habits. We have displayed the English language as it works—a system of units in structural arrangements—when its speakers use it to say what they have to say. We have seen how the smallest units—the phonemes—combine into patterns which themselves are units in larger patterns—the morphemes—and how the morphemes combine into patterns of syntax. Finally, we have sketched the relation of speech—a modulated stream of sounds produced by human muscles and emitted in sequences that have length in terms of time—to writing, a line of letters on a page, a line that has its length not in time but in space. We have related the complex performance of speech—aimed at the ears, the eyes, and the sympathetic muscle-memories of the listener, participated in by the listener as he hears what is said— to the more isolated performance of the writer composing in private for the eyes of persons who are not present and whose responses he can only estimate. We have so far provided the tools by which any reader can deepen his knowledge of language and writing and enlarge his experience by his own observations. What remains now is for us to apply this knowledge to the specific problems of reading and writing for the efficient and economical improvement of both.

✳ CHAPTER 25 ✳

The Way to Read by Structures

T HE PERSON WHO READS and writes well and effectively is in his way an expert, just as the person is who listens attentively and retentively and who speaks his mind precisely. He is an expert in the skills that of all accomplishments are most demanded and most rewarded in our society today. The grease in the complicated gears of our highly organized technological society is effective reading and writing. Any young person who dreams of a better-than-average career, or hopes even to hold his own in the stern competition for place and pay in American institutions, had better look to his reading and writing. No matter what his field—law, engineering, business, medicine, pharmacy, government, the arts and sciences— he will be more master of it and master of his own career, the more he gives thought to the control of the marks he puts on paper and what they mean.

Ordinary native speakers of English have a high basic aptitude for self-expression which they can cultivate into expertness. How well they learn to read and write depends more upon their interest and their practice than on any natural gifts. There is not room for many of us in the big league of highly paid professional writers, but there is need throughout the nation for many more competently literate persons than all the schools can produce. Doctor, lawyer, merchant, scientist, soldier, sailor, flyer, teacher, secretary, stenographer, clerk, and housewife—all are better and better rewarded if they add to their professional skills an equally professional competence in imparting and receiving ideas through paper and ink. They add immeasurably to their quality as human beings and as citizens through the wonderful world of books which an easy and enjoyable literacy opens for them. As Doctor Samuel Johnson said two centuries ago, any profession that supports numbers of people is within the grasp of an ordinarily intelligent person. You don't have to be a genius to read and write well; you do have to give it your full mind, you have to study and observe reading and writing, and you have to read and write as a matter of habit.

The Attack

THERE are certain matters of "attack" that distinguish a good reader from a bungling amateur. When he picks up a book or an article, he does not simply start at the first word and read doggedly on to the last. He wants to know first what there is in it, and especially what there is in it for him. He knows that printers, editors, and writers take great care to set up the whole book and each page in it so as to tell him these things quickly and easily. In a book there is usually an introduction or preface, and there is always a title page and a table of contents. In a periodical there is usually a page "About this issue" or "Our contributors," which discusses the writers and what they have to say. He turns to these first, to see whether he wants to go to the effort of reading on. At the beginning of each article there may be a subtitle or heading which gives a fair notion of what the article is about. One glance may tell him whether to stop or go on.

The table of contents of a book is an outline of what is in it, a gathering-together of the main headings which are scattered through the book. In this book this important table supplies a guide to the matters discussed. The preface gives the authors' point of view and aims. Prefaces and introductions that come before page one are numbered with small roman numerals. These essays are written after the book is finished and before it goes to press; though they come first in the book, they are the author's last word on the subject, and should be taken as such. The final section in a book is the index, a handy guide to the various items—men and women, books, words, and other things—touched on in the discussion. Indexing is a trade performed by skilled analysts or by the author (or his wife) to make the book more useful. The preface and table of contents are most useful to the reader before he gets into the book; the index can be useful to him before, during, and after his reading. The text of a book is designed to introduce the reader to the subject as the author sees it; it moves from point to point by building each explanation on what has already been explained. The reader needs to go through this process only once; when he reaches the end he is in command of the subject and sees it as a whole. Yet he cannot keep in mind all the items that went to build that whole or all the details about these items. The index, alphabetically listed by subjects, saves him much shuffling of pages; it steers him quickly to all the places in the book where he can recapture the detail about any matter afterthought tells him to check. It is also useful to a person who wants to know whether certain specific matters are treated in the book, or whether certain authors are cited or quoted; the index guides him to what he wants to see and saves him from plowing through the whole book. Like all other aspects of modern printing, indexes have a standardized form. The titles given to subjects interlock with the great subject catalogs, indexes of periodicals, and bibliographies (lists of books arranged according to what they are about) in our modern libraries.

Publishers of books and editors of magazines have to keep attracting readers in order to stay in business. They use every trick of art, design, and typography to catch the passing eye and give the impression that they are offering something worth looking into. Book publishers cover the enduring but often drab covers of their books with dust jackets. On these jackets the publishers often squander big type, expensive art work, and four-color pictures, luxuries they cannot build into the books themselves without pricing them right out of the market. Publishers of paper-bound, pocket-sized books glue this jacket fast and use it for the actual cover. From the jacket you can often get a good notion of what the book is about—though the pictures, comments, and quotations from the book often serve as an elaborate come-on and don't have much to do with the text. Frequently the jacket of a book gives a fair notion of its subject, its treatment, and its relation to other works in the field.

Periodicals may be issued every week, two weeks, month, or every three, six, or twelve months. They include comic books; picture magazines like *Life* or *Look;* general magazines like *The Saturday Evening Post* or *Collier's;* women's magazines like *McCall's;* men's magazines like *Esquire* or *True;* journals of opinion like *Harper's, The Atlantic,* or *The Reporter;* reviews like the *Saturday Review* or *The New York Times Book Review;* and a host of special trade, technical, and professional journals of all kinds. Of these the comic books and picture magazines make the strongest visual impact, and the general and men's and women's magazines not much less, in their effort to catch the eye and hold it until it is moved by interest to read on.

Titles, pictures, and subheads give some notion of what is in the articles or serve as come-ons. The other publications may assume that their readers begin with an informed interest, and they may bolster the text less elaborately with these aids; but it is quite rare for the reader to have to read blindly into an article to see what it is about. Some periodicals like *Woman's Day* depend on selling each copy of each issue on the stands; others like *Collier's* depend on both newsstand sales and subscriptions, but many publishers rely mainly on subscriptions and sell only a few copies in the stores. With current issues, the reader has to pick the magazine up to know what is in it, but back issues of most periodicals are analyzed and their contents indexed in *Reader's Guide to Periodical Literature* or in *International Index to Periodicals.*

It is often worth noting whether the pages of a magazine are numbered separately for each issue. If so, then the table of contents of that issue is the only guide to what is in it. If the pages are numbered right on through a volume, from the first issue of the year to the last, then the last issue of the year has a combined table of contents and often an index for the whole year. *Collier's* is numbered for each issue; *Consumer Reports* is numbered through the year, and, furthermore, it has in each issue a cumulative index for the year so far. All these aids can be very useful, and the expert reader pays attention to them. Many magazine articles are reissued in brief form in digests of one kind or another such as the *Reader's Digest,* but the digesters often treat these articles with a high hand;

if you want to know what the author really intended to say, you have to dig up the original publication. Doing this a few times when a digested article catches your eye may startle you somewhat and weaken your faith in the digests.

All these matters of "attack" represent both a widening and a narrowing of the reader's interest. Expert readers read widely from habit; as they grow up or grow older, they extend their reading into new and more meaningful areas, moving from the comic books and picture and general magazines into the journals of opinion and the reviews. In the periodicals of limited circulation rather than in the ones that sell to millions, the thinking people of the nation and the persons in positions of responsibility discuss important matters. There they don't have to please everybody; and, especially, they don't have to please advertisers, so that they can bluntly raise issues and discuss them with something like the freedom they have in books. Widening experience in this way does not necessarily mean cutting off old interests; you can still sit down with Pogo or Superman without feeling you are slumming. You simply include the periodicals that the educated read.

The expert reader's attack on a specific article is a progressive narrowing from the general to the particular, even before he tackles its text. He begins with a rather broad knowledge of men and their subjects, and of magazines and their "slants"—a knowledge built up by reading. He cases a particular issue to see what it may have for him by checking on the authors, reading the headings, and looking over the pictures. He may glance at a few paragraphs to see how they go. Then he turns back to the first page and launches on his reading. Having exploited all the tricks of display and typography that our sophisticated printing industry offers him, he is prepared to dig into the actual work of the writer. He expects the experience to be a pleasure.

The Efficient Reading Eye

THE efficient reading eye is not, as you might think, a young, alert, athletic, twenty-twenty eye, able to distinguish each curlicue on each letter or able to read a street sign a block away, but an old, lazy experienced rounder of an eye that can only occasionally be bothered to draw anything into sharp focus. A good reading eye need not be any great shakes as eyes go; compared to a poor reading eye, it might score low on many visual tests. It has only one virtue—the ability to carry the written message from page to brain with ease, efficiency, and speed.

We may compare these two kinds of eyes to two persons at a dance. One, a comparative stranger, is alert to every detail; he notices the decorations, the older men and women chatting along the walls, the orchestra and its leader. He glances attentively at every girl; he notes her face, her figure, and her dress. He takes the measure of every other male. At the end of the evening he is full of impressions; he has had a busy, exciting time; he is tired. But who is the mother of which daughter, and which young men are engaged to which girls, and who is merely around for the dancing —these are the things, the important things, that he can only vaguely know.

The other person, the man about town, lounges at the doorway detached from it all. The decor of the hall, he knows, was left over from the American Legion dance of the week before, touched up here and there with something less patriotic and more festive. He recognizes Melissa Melish by her blue dress; it is the third time she has worn it this year. Seeing Melissa, he hardly needs to glance at the young men about her; that gang has been surging through these dances all year. Angela Angle is dancing for once, he notices; he recognizes her rigid back and hesitant steps without seeing her face. As usual, Daddy-o Daring and Sue Scramble are cutting a few jitterbug steps in the corner; with a rapidly beating fan Sue's mother is signifying her disapproval. He knows every relationship; he scarcely needs to glance at anyone to identify him—surely one does not stare at old acquaintances and friends. He nods to a passing couple. It is the old, old dance; he has seen it all before. He stops to look squarely at only one person—the stranger in the hall, who is in the corner of everybody's eye. He wants to be sure to recognize this fellow when their paths cross again.

The efficient reading eye is one that knows relationships, not one that pauses over each isolated detail. It is a casual eye that saves itself effort by dealing in groups and masses, patterns and forms. It is a searching eye that gives close attention only where some irregularity or unfamiliarity interrupts its progress. It is a relaxed eye that some people develop early—as early as seven or eight, as early as the third or fourth grade. It is an eye that some people cannot develop by themselves, and hence one that some never develop unless a chance occurrence shows the way. The difference between efficiency and inefficiency cannot be a matter of vocabulary, for efficiency in reading comes to many children before they can possibly know the printed form of many words. Command of vocabulary is a result of efficient reading, not a cause of it; it comes with much reading. Many ear-minded folk with extensive vocabularies in speech never become good readers. To see where efficient reading comes from and how it comes, we have to consider the way eyes look at print and what they see.

We all know something about how the eye is built and how it works. We know that seeing, in spite of the way we talk about it, is something that happens to the eye rather than something it does, because of the peculiar properties of light. Light falling on an object is partly absorbed and partly reflected; it bounces. Bouncing, it strikes the eye, which is like an extremely efficient camera, very sensitive in adjustment. The light passes through a lens—which adjusts in focus and in size of opening—and falls on light-sensitive cells at the back of the eyeball, making an upside-down image which is transmitted to the brain. Except for a small "blind spot" directly behind the lens, this battery of cells is most sensitive to color at the center, most sensitive to light around the edges. These cells demand a certain fixity between eye and object; either the eye must move with the object, or both must be still. If one moves without the other, the eye sees nothing clearly until the motion stops. Yet the cells seem to go blind if they hold an image too long; recent tests seem to indicate that they vibrate minutely; when we give the object a corresponding vibration, it cannot be seen.

The eyeballs are moved by muscles in the eyesocket, so that we can shift our eyes without moving our heads. The eyes move easily because they are lubricated by a slippery fluid; when we blink we cut off most of the light, secrete more fluid, and distribute it over the exposed front of the eyeballs. Even tinier muscles within the eyeball change the size of the lens opening, stopping it down for brighter light, opening it for dimmer. Other minute muscles change the depth of the lens, so as to give a sharper focus when it is desired, or so as to bring objects at different distances into focus. Focusing is an effort, especially on small objects; when we bring one thing into focus, we permit other things around it to remain blurred.

Following a narrow line of black print across a white page does not come naturally to us; we have to learn to do it. We work better with objects that are as high as they are wide, or at least offer more height to the width than a line of type offers. The eye has to distinguish the line we want and ignore the lines above and below; and it has to be motionless in order to see the print. As it moves, whether from letter to letter or word to word, it receives a blur; hence its motion is a pause, then a jerk to another pause, another jerk, and so on. Naturally the more the eye takes in at each pause, the fewer motions it has to make to travel the line. Each motion is an effort, and very many such motions are tiring.

The stop-and-go travel of the eye across a line of print is called the "saccadic movement" of the eye, and it has been much studied. Investigators of reading have mounted cameras in position to photograph the eyes as they read, where they pause and how they move, but no one has devised a means of telling just what it is the eye sees when it stops and looks, except by relating the number of pauses to the number of words. Various means have been tried to cut down the number of separate moves the eye makes on each line, in an effort to reduce eyestrain. We do know that efficient readers make fewer pauses than inefficient readers do and therefore see more words at once—how sharply is another matter.

We may draw some parallels from automobile driving, where the same difference between gross and fine movements of the eyes is involved. Certain accident-prone drivers are puzzling cases. They go along, alert, tense, gripping the wheel, eyes on the road, seemingly in command of the situation. Still they crash. Expert drivers tend to be relaxed and to hold an easy grip on the wheel. They do not keep their eyes on the road, nor do they keep them focused on what is before them. Rather they keep them unfocused, unless they have cause to identify an object looming up ahead. They scan the roadway, glancing from one side of the ribbon of pavement to the other. When an object comes toward the road, it appears at first as a moving mass some distance ahead. This mass in motion in the field of vision catches the driver's eye; he focuses on it and inspects it. An expert driver is seldom conscious of the cars or drivers passing him, unless they deviate from what he expects of them. He knows that when you look closely at one thing you cannot see others in the field of vision; hence he looks sharply only at what is out of line with what he expects.

The expert reader uses his eyes in a comparable way. He can focus down on one letter or one word when he has reason to do so, but for the most part he depends upon his "field vision" rather than on close inspection of individual objects. His eyes make fewer pauses in the line and focus much less frequently on what they see. They sharpen up, apparently, only for those words or letters that offer something unexpected; otherwise they take in a succession of total impressions not very clearly defined but each quite satisfactory for the purpose.

We can also find some clues in the experiences of expert readers with motion-picture films designed to improve reading speed. These films present a text line by line, somewhat in the manner in which we read it. Part of the line is photographed in sharp focus and part left dark or blurred. After an interval the clear segment moves on and shows another part of the line. Beginning films offer the line in three segments; advanced films show it in two equal halves. As the student moves through the series of films, he sees longer segments of the lines for shorter and shorter times. The object is to make him grasp groups of words quickly rather than one word at a time.

Whatever help these films may be to poor readers, they give an expert reader a rough time. He finds the segments either too large or too small. Either his eyes pick up part of the words exposed, or they stumble at the end, hungering for more words than he can see. The regular one-two-three or one-two sequence of line sections collides with his way of diving the text; far from helping him in his reading, they interfere. They leave him with eyestrain and a headache.

What kind of machine does help an expert reader increase his speed? It is a very simple little invention that draws a curtain down the text at a constant speed. At first the whole text is exposed; then the moving curtain cuts it off line by line. The expert reader, left to deal with each line in his own way, often finds himself keeping several lines ahead of the black-out no matter how fast the thing goes. This machine can push a good reader up to a phenomenal rate of speed. The record is a rate of 8000 words a minute, hit by a student with rather poor eyes who dazzled his instructors and himself at once.

The efficient reader is not necessarily a fast reader, though as the experience with the reading machine shows, he can be pushed up to high speed. The efficient reader is one who takes from the page about what the writer put there for him to read, and takes it with a minimum of effort. He divides the work of reading between his brain and his eyes; he lets his eyes do as much of the work of reading as he can. He trains his eyes, as a routine, to take in large blocks of matter at once by submitting to the writing system which has been developed through the centuries to serve just such eyes as his. He knows that writing is not speech, and he does not try to deal with it as if it were speech. The speaking voice limits the reception of the hearers; they have to take the sounds at the rate they are offered. The signals of print are all on the page at once; if the eye could bring them all to the brain, the brain could handle them all at once. The efficient reader leaves to his eyes all the work he can get them to do, letting them carry to the brain the widest span of related words they can handle at each pause they make along the line. He is capable of speed. More importantly, he can change his pace, scanning easy matter but bearing down doggedly and slow on difficult matter that comes hard. Speed in itself means nothing.

Efficient reading cannot depend upon vocabulary, because some children achieve expertness before they can have a large vocabulary of printed words. It does not involve looking sharply at a word, moving to the next, focusing on that, and to the next. Such repeated focusing is desperately tiring to the eyes. Efficient reading involves seeing segments of the line, and seeing those segments not very sharply. It is a relaxed, easy, rhythmical shifting of the eyes along the line with a minimum use of the small muscles that tire so easily. It is a pleasant occupation, and those who can do it enjoy it. It can be learned, for efficient reading is primarily an efficient use of the eyes and does not demand great intellectual capacity. Anyone can do it.

The Signals of Print

A LINE of print is not very high. You might expect that it would make no difference how you look at it, whether at the lower or upper part. If you read letter by letter in the manner of a semi-illiterate puzzling out a newspaper, holding his finger under each letter as he spells out the words, it probably doesn't matter. But if you read words or groups of words at a single fixation of the eye, whether you read the tops of the letters or the bottoms makes a great deal of difference. If you slide a card down over a line of print, uncovering the letters bit by bit, you find that you can make a reasonable guess about the words well before you wholly uncover the letters. If you slide a card up over the line of print, you find that you have to uncover almost the complete letters to read any words. The upper shapes are more distinctive. The letters **b, h,** and **k** have their long strokes to the left of the space, **d** has its long stroke to the right, and **f, t,** and **l** have their characteristic shapes centered. The small letters and **p, q,** and **g** have distinct upper contours. Hence the vision should rest high on the line.

Most of the words we read in most prose are quite familiar, and many of them are short. Certainly the structurally important words which are repeated again and again are always familiar and should give us no trouble. We should not have to focus on them, or even look squarely at them in order to identify them. They are part of our normal expectation. Even writing that uses many specialized words cradles them among words that we know by sight and that we do not need to linger over. We may need to train ourselves not to give them more attention than they need, but to take them within larger wholes in a single inclusive glance. We can depend on them to be there and to have their familiar shapes—especially their familiar upper contours. We look at the upper half of the line, far enough into it to take several words in at a glance, and no more sharply than we need to in order to identify the commonly repeated words. Then we shift the eyes and take in another group of words, shift again and take in another.

When we begin to read by structures we see punctuation marks in an entirely new way, not as signs for "pauses" but as interrupters of the line of print that tell us what to take together and what to separate. They do not ordinarily set off short groups, but longer ones, unless the writer specifically wants a single word or group of words set apart from those before and after. We note that printing makes each punctuation mark part of a group-signal that is obvious to the eye. The period, for example, unless it ends a paragraph, never stands alone; it is followed by a space and a capital letter. The dash is higher than the comma and is centered in a fairly long blank space. The semicolon in its two main uses is perfectly predictable: in the one, it ends the same kind of complete sentence or utterance-group as the period. In the other, it sets off groups arranged in a series—not short groups but longer ones with commas within them—and it is a raised dot over one of the commas. The colon occurs where the sense of the sentence warns of a period, but some word or group of words in the sentence backs up the colon in warning that the next sentence is to be taken as a spelling-out of something in the first. The colon is a period with a dot over it. We note that commas, dashes, and parentheses run in pairs before and after a segment of a sentence. We learn to take the punctuation marks within their environments, associated with the sentence-structures whose limits they signify.

Within the larger groups roughly cut off by punctuation marks, we use the structure-words as signals of speech groups that are spoken together and must be seen together. No more futile advice could be given to a reader than to pay attenion to the big words and let the little words take care of themselves. The "little words" are crucial to the meaning; they guide the eyes as substitutes for the complicated patterns of intonation that tell the ear and the brain how to hear speech.

It may help to review briefly the four systems of signals that make up the structural patterns of English speech. First is the order in which we say the words, the order of utterance, which appears as word-order in written English. It makes a great deal of difference which comes first in English; **houseboat** is not **boathouse.** Second, there are the signals of pitch, stress, and juncture that clot the utterance into word-groups that are meaning-groups. Since the line of print cannot show these intonation contours directly, the marker which begins the group serves as a kind of road sign and warns of the kind of group which follows. Third, there are the structure-words which relate the nouns, verbs, adjectives, and adverbs to each other in the patterns. Fourth, there are the inflections, the changes in sound and form that distinguish **drive** from **drove, man** from **men, house** from **houses,** and **go** from **goes, went, gone,** and **going.**

The English language today gives its big play to the nouns, verbs, adjectives, and adverbs, because they receive the strong and secondary stresses; we speak them more loudly than we do most of the structure-words. Stressed words or stressed syllables are overlong as we say them; unstressed or lightly stressed words and syllables are overshort. Changes in form show up mostly in unaccented syllables or in the boundary between syllables. The order of utterance seems so natural and inevitable to us that it was scarcely noticed as an integrated system of signals until very recently. We have to pay close attention to this order so that we can use it in our reading. Because the nouns, verbs, adjectives, and adverbs are overobvious in English, the structural signals which cradle these words in the utterance and relate them to each other in the patterns are much less emphatic and much less obvious. Yet, since the nouns, verbs, adjectives, and adverbs have no meaning except in the patterns, the important reading clues in the patterns are these four kinds of signals that define the patterns and give them their meaning. We might better say, Take care of the little words and let the big words take care of themselves—you can't miss them anyway.

The structure-words which are most important in reading are the markers—the words which start meaning-groups and warn us how to take the group as a unit in the sentence. There are four sets of markers. Two of the sets warn us of an oncoming headword and tell us to take the whole group in the sentence in the function of the headword. These are the determiners which point to noun-headwords, and the verb-markers that point to verb-headwords. The third set is the prepositions, which tell us that the whole phrase following has its own function apart from any word in it. And the fourth set is the clause-markers, words like **who, what, as, since, when, where, that, if,** and **although,** which tell us that the whole clause following has a function in the sentence apart from any word in it. Groups marked by these sets of words are so common and so often repeated that they establish our habit-reactions and let us cope with the unmarked phrases and clauses which also have to be taken as unit-groups in the sentence. The expert reader using these markers builds speech-patterns into the line of print and reads what he sees in his own dialect as he normally speaks and hears it. His reading is simpler, easier, and more meaningful than the reading of a person who reads by letters or by separate words.

Some people jump from word-reading to pattern-reading rather quickly once they know it can be done, just as some athletes score victories soon after they learn better ways to run, bat, or throw. There is, however, an orderly step-by-step procedure which can be followed from the one to the other. It requires only an easy text with no unfamiliar words in it, a pencil, a quiet place, and regular, day-to-day practice. You have to expect a little disruption of your ability to read in your usual way, and some lag in the replacement of old reading habits by new ones. If your reading is at all slow, if your eyes tire from reading, if you have difficulty getting through reading assignments, or if you often do your assignments without much notion of what you have read when you are done, you have nothing to lose and much to gain. Reading by structures is a way of yielding to the language and meeting it on its own terms, and it gives superior comprehension. If you are interested in speed, it permits somewhat faster reading.

First, take a familiar, easy text and read it through so that you know what it says and eliminate comprehension as a problem. Then, read the text aloud, slowly. Speak it the way you would normally talk, saying word-groups as groups and clauses as clauses. As you read, mark a slant line at every natural pause in the sentence. Many of these pauses will occur after nouns. Thus you will be setting off noun-groups (**D ᴀ N**) and phrases which begin with prepositions and end with nouns (**Prep . . . N**). You will also be cutting nouns from verbs or from verb-markers. Be sure also that you place a slant line after each verb-headword, so that you are also setting off verb-groups. Now go back to the beginning and look at the text you have marked. Speak it again, aloud, and correct any marks that you have put in at the wrong places. Most of your groups should be only two or three words long.

As you read the text again, try to look at the center of each group and see the words between slant lines as a whole. Look at the upper contours of the words; let your gaze rest a little high on the line. Try not to focus on any particular word but see them all together. Then quite consciously move your gaze to the center of the next group, using your slant lines to guide you. Don't try to be too rigorous; if your eyes want to take in two groups, let them. Then move your eyes along again. At this stage you may have to force yourself not to revert to word-by-word reading. Go on to the end, and then start over. Continue this way until you are thoroughly—not just a little—bored by the whole business. Then drop the matter until later, or until the next day. Repeat this whole procedure with other easy texts until you can see the groups as groups even without your slant lines.

Photographic studies have been made of poor readers by mounting a camera behind the text and taking pictures of the eyes as they move. These pictures show that the inept eyes make many pauses in the line—as many as there are words or more. In addition, these eyes regress; they go back and pick up words that have been missed. Or, rather, the reader's brain loses the thread; he forgets what he has read and goes back to check up. The better reader makes fewer pauses in the line; he does not have to go back, because he is letting his eyes group the words before they get to the brain. The brain, instead of dealing with a number of small bits of information, has to handle fewer but related groups.

The next step is to read aloud, using the eyes in a somewhat different way. Instead of looking at a small group and saying it, pick up with your eyes the longest stretch you can, look up and away from the book, then say what you have seen. This is what speakers do who are speaking from a prepared text to an audience. They do not mumble what they have written, with their eyes down and the top of the head toward the audience. Keep pushing for longer and longer segments—whole lines, if possible, or even whole sentences running to two or more lines. Be careful to speak in your usual conversational tones, without the "reading monotone" that is so boring to listen to. Practice this. After a while you can stop saying the words aloud but form them silently, so that you can practice anywhere. Note that this exercise is designed to keep your reading actively related to the way you talk; do not worry if you have heard that it is wrong to form words with your mouth as you read. The fastest and most expert readers still make muscle-movements of throat and jaw as their eyes scan the page. The reason for reading aloud is to enlist the aid of the muscle-memory of the language in finding the groups.

We now can consider what it is the eyes see as they rest so lightly on the page. They are taking in structure-groups, but we must remember that they are taking in a wider span than we are prepared to use. They see more at the sides, but as we have concentrated on the meaning-groups, we have ignored this overlap. The overlap at the sides of the eyespan is essential to good reading, because the good reader knows more than what he has just seen and what he is seeing. He also has a good idea where he is going, because the first word after the structure-group comes into his field of vision. It is usually a structure-word, and most often a marker—therefore perfectly familiar. The field of vision overlaps at the left, so that the reader still sees the last word of the last group. It is no wonder that the expert reader makes few regressions. He knows right where he is all the time.

Since many sentences begin with a determiner, the first element is often the noun phrase, **D -A- N,** or any variation of it: **The best way . . . , This superior method . . . , Most English sentences . . .** , and so on. But what follows? After any noun we have a number of possibilities.

D	-A-	N	Prep	N		
This	superior	method	of study			
			CIM	N		V
This	superior	method	which	the	work	demands
			V			
This	superior	method	makes	studying	easier	
			v	V		
This	superior	method	can	make		
			V-ed/en			
This	superior	method	introduced by the French			
			V-ing			
This	superior	method	involving a new approach			
			to-V			
This	superior	method	to do the work			

There are other possibilities. These samples are enough to show the way in which the person who reads by structures treats the sentence somewhat like a chain of sausages, cutting it into word-groups joined at what we may call "points of choice." A point of choice occurs at the end of each meaning-group; at this point the sentence may take any of a dozen different turns. The turn it actually takes will be clearly marked by the opening word of the next group; the general pattern and its probable span—the reach to the next point of choice—is sketched out. The reader may take one, two, or three of these spans at one fixation of his eyes; since the structural relations between words and word-groups establish their meaning, he lets himself be steered and guided by these relations. When these relations are unclear as they often are, he goes along until he meets the signal that unravels them. Often the exact sense of the first part of a sentence depends on what follows, and no plodding rereading of the first part will unscramble it. The expert reader reads by wholes; he looks for wholes, larger and ever-larger wholes.

The person who reads by patterns, lightly scanning the line for its structural signals, puts out much less effort than the person who moves his eyes from word to word, and he gets more for his work. The method works just as well with difficult matter as with easy; but until you have this method firmly established as a habitual approach to the printed page, you had better confine it to regular practice with stories and light articles that give you no special problems with words. Here, as always in language, when you wish to make a change, you do not start clean and free of interferences. You already have a set of habits; these habits, whether they have served you well or poorly, have been your equipment for the job. You don't simply decide to get rid of them and then watch them disappear. You can only dislodge them by another thoroughly learned complex of habits that gradually eases into their place and takes over the work. Pleasant practice with enjoyable writing, such as you can pick up on any magazine rack or find in any library— regular, repeated practice—will strengthen the new habits and strengthen them better the less you dwell on the old habits.

The Happy Efficient Reader

READING by structures gets at two troublesome problems that do not yield easily to any correction. The first of these is the problem of the reader who, ignoring the "little words," takes from the page not what the writer intended but something else entirely. Seeing words that he recognizes like **business, profit, enterprise, way of life, success, socialism, public welfare,** and so on, he does not take from the page the writer's relations of these words to each other and the meaning the writer intends. He lets these words trigger his own ideas and his own prejudices; he comes up with the same ideas that he brings to his reading. Instead of reading from the text, he reads into it what he assumes the writer will be saying, so that he ends, in effect, where he began. He misses the writer's careful qualifications and balancing of ideas and replaces them with banalities dredged from his own mental sets. Such a reader is not the one best beloved by writers. The writer gives thought to making his text a corridor through which the reader must proceed to certain ideas; he does not intend it to be a springboard from which the reader jumps into his own uncontrolled reveries.

Reading by structures gives the reader the same key words embedded in patterns that control their meaning in this text. **Business naturally seeks a profit, but it is more than enterprise; it is a way of life whose success is a kind of socialism, since its real end is the public welfare.** This sentence is not the obvious one we would expect from that particular list of words—at least in our times. Its specific meanings are produced by the patterns; if you miss the patterns you miss the meanings. The person who reads by structures does not miss the pattern-meanings; he picks those up with his eyes, and as he picks them up he surrenders to the writer's intention and takes the writer's meaning from the page.

A second problem yields in time to reading by structures rather than by letters or words. This difficulty is most discouraging to people who have a great deal of reading to do, want to get through it, and get it done. It is a sort of hypnosis that comes on the reader as he reads; he looks up from the book he has passed his eyes over and suddenly realizes that he hasn't the slightest notion of what he has just read. All is gone. He starts resignedly turning back the pages to find the point where his brain left off while his eyes went on. This annoying experience—this inability to attend—certainly takes the pleasure out of reading and has been known to drive quite intelligent people out of college.

We may refer again to the parallel of automobile driving, where a similar thing happens. A conscientious, reliable, alert driver at the wheel of a car which holds, perhaps, every person in the world who is dear to him—his wife and children, his sweetheart, his parents—suddenly comes to himself and realizes that he has been careening down the road at high speed, but he cannot guess how far he has traveled since he was last conscious of what he is doing. He is lucky if he comes to before the car drifts out of its lane into the ditch or headlong into the oncoming traffic. This effect is commonly known as "going to sleep at the wheel," and we assume it to be responsible for many accidents that we can find no rational explanation for. It occurs to salesmen, truck drivers, tired businessmen, and bright young men and women whose pride in their ability to handle their cars is otherwise justified. It is a harrowing experience, even if you survive it.

Modern students of traffic problems see this now as a form of hypnosis rather than a true dozing off. It is true that some drivers do go to sleep at the wheel, if they are tired enough to go to sleep anywhere. But a driver can go into this suspension of faculties and come out of it within seconds—even before his car begins to drift. Various remedies are prescribed: stopping every so often for coffee, playing the radio, having a passenger talk or argue, opening the windows, getting out and running around the car. A driver who succumbs to this trance would be better advised to check on his use of his eyes. The long, endlessly unrolling ribbon of the road hypnotizes him; if he lets himself stare at it, the effect will sooner or later get him. Expert drivers do not look at the road directly; they scan it, moving their eyes from side to side, from point to point away from the onrushing surface. They do not "look" at anything most of the time; they depend, as we noted before, on their "field vision" rather than on "point vision."

The reader who suddenly realizes that he has no notion of what he has been looking at is suffering from a similar hypnosis; while it may not cost him his life, it certainly costs him effort and time fruitlessly expended. He can get up and walk around, drink a cup of coffee, or do something else for a while, but his best course is to check on his use of his eyes. Reading by structures, using the field of his vision and the widest spans possible within it, relieves the eyes from the strain of reading and frees the brain from this letter-and-word hypnosis. The expert reader like the expert driver can go on indefinitely; he may get tired muscles, but they are not in his eyes. They are in his back and where he sits. That is where they belong.

Reading, when you come right down to it, is not an intellectual matter. It does not depend on intelligence; some very stupid people read rather well. It depends on a set of habit-responses to signal-stimuli; the stimuli differ for different readers, depending on what they have learned to respond to. The semi-illiterate who knows his letters responds to letters. Taking them off the page one at a time, he tries them out against the sounds they may represent until he finds some word-pattern they seem to fit. There is a story about a farmer who looked at a freight car and read the legend on its side: *Capacity, 80,000.* "C, a, cay," he said, "p, a, pay. Cay, pay, City, 80,000. Why that's durn near as big as Decatur!" Reading by letters is a painful process, subject to many errors. Most poor readers read by words, taking them off one at a time and fitting them to sound-patterns of words, but the patterns are of words in isolation, in stressed position, not in the stream of speech. Seeing each word is effortful and tiring, because the words must be related to each other within the brain. Fitting the words together is a process of trial and error which often sends the inefficient reader back to see whether he has the right words in mind. It is an exacting mental exercise, and a tiring one.

The person who reads by patterns, however slowly he chooses to go, takes the words from the page as they sound in the stream of speech; he reconstitutes the stream of speech from the signals on the page. He thus brings to bear on his reading all the complex reinforcing signals of speech, so that the trigger-signals of the page, to which he responds as directly as the semi-illiterate responds to letters, stand for slices of utterances, often very large slices. His habit-responses to these stimuli are no more intellectual than the habit-responses to letters. His eyes are released from fine motions and delicate adjustments to minute shapes; they are relaxed, and he is relaxed. Reading-hypnosis is no threat to him. His native intelligence may well remain what it is, but his broader experience with printed texts makes him familiar with many more printed word-pictures, for most of which he already has sound-counterparts in his speech. Since intelligence tests rely heavily on verbal manipulations, and since we often mistake sheer verbalism for intelligence, he may seem to have improved in intelligence from his reading, and perhaps he has. If so, then a person can be made brighter by being taught to use his eyes more efficiently. Probably the most we ought to say is that efficient habits of reading permit him to operate up to the level of his intelligence, whatever it is, without basically affecting his wits. In any event, efficient reading habits fit him better for life in our world of books, magazines, newspapers, mimeographed and duplicated matter, advertisements, signs, symbols, and other stimuli to behavior.

CHAPTER 26

The Way to Write by

Structures

WRITING IS NOT really a language problem, though it may seem like one; it is a kind of "handling activity" related to language. The objects that we handle when we write are mostly word-signs built up by combining the twenty-six letters of the alphabet into groups that we set off from each other by spaces before and after. We may be sure that our ability to write will never outrun our command of our native speech. As the little girl said when her father read aloud to her a list of words from the dictionary, "I guess I know lots more words than I know how to read and write." She also knew lots more structures than she knew how to read and write, but, like most people, she took the structures for granted and worried about the words. The word-signs are fairly easy to learn, as long as you have had experience with the sound-patterns they represent; almost anyone can take down a list of isolated words, as they are read aloud, accurately enough so that someone else can read them. That is a far cry from writing sentences which express meaning. There are vocabulary problems involved in writing, as we shall see in Chapter 27; and there are problems of spelling the words, but the real problems of writing are structural and must be approached through structures.

When you sit down before a blank sheet of paper, pencil in hand, with something to say, you may sit there a while before you venture to make the first marks on paper—even though you could reach to a telephone, call up the person you are addressing, and launch into what you have to say. You are stalled by a mild anxiety neurosis caused by the cold, impersonal, inhuman situation, so different from the warm, personal, human interaction of common talk. Compared to what you do when you talk, writing is an extremely simple, almost primitive activity. Writing is merely the conscious fitting of twenty-six letters and a dozen or so punctuation marks to utterances you have been making all your life, and would be making at the moment if you had before you the audience you are writing for. The problem does not lie within the writing, but between speech and writing. Speaking is a set of habits so thoroughly learned that we act without being conscious of them. Writing is a process that could be habitual but is not, a process that must be consciously directed step by step.

This is not to say that consciousness is a bad thing or that there are no times when we must pick our way carefully as we speak. Circumstances change for us. From the easy familiar chitchat with our family and friends, with whom it is difficult to say anything disastrously wrong or anything that we cannot repair, we move through a whole range of situations in which we have reason to think before we speak. In any contact with strangers we watch our words, and when we deal with people on whom we particularly want to make a good impression, our language itself—not merely what we say but how we say it—becomes a matter of concern to us. With teachers, employers, lenders, the parents of our friends, ministers, important or eminent people of any kind, or with people who have or may have power to help or harm us, we become conscious of our "grammar," and it is wholesome for us to do so. At first this consciousness makes us stumble—it is like trying to think about how we walk as we walk—and it is agonizing for us to hear ourselves. Only repeated experiences in these situations give us confidence and teach us to keep a relaxed control over the manner as well as the matter of our speech while we seem to be our own natural selves.

Most of our writing, except for easy, informal letters to our friends, is like our conversations with strangers and important people. It demands that we keep in mind the impression we make in our use of English as we write. No matter how long or how often we write, we can never be free of the likelihood that our control of the language itself may waver and make us seem to say what we do not mean in a way we do not intend. We can never quite let down our guard. On the other hand, we have a better chance to be sure of ourselves than we have in speech, where we can listen to our own mouth betraying us, unable to stop it. We have time and opportunity as we write and after we write to put what we have to say into the form that best gives the impression we want. This consciousness is an essential part of writing, and a good thing in itself.

The self-consciousness that paralyzes hand and brain when we look at a blank sheet of paper is not a good thing. It takes the pleasure out of writing, making it a burden; it eats up time and consumes energy. It results from the great gap between our easy command of our native speech and our halting, haphazard control of its writing system. It makes us produce, with great effort and agony of spirit, primitive sentences that are childish in form and manner; it makes us reach wildly beyond our grasp for big, "literary" words that are just a little off key. It makes our punctuation look as though we had thrown the commas, periods, and semicolons blindly from the other side of the room. It makes our writing a mess that does not convey our meaning or honestly represent us for what we are. This kind of self-consciousness is a bad thing. The only cures for it are knowledge and practice in the light of that knowledge.

The knowledge that bears upon this problem is knowledge about language. We have in this book gathered together a good deal of information, much of it only recently explored by researchers, about how our language works and what we do when we use it. It falls into three main divisions: the way our language works in our society, the way it works in ourselves as a set of learned habit-patterns, and the way it works within itself as an interlocking system of forms, word-classes, and patterns. We have related all these aspects of language to the system of English writing. We have aimed at a general orientation which is very valuable in itself as a humane understanding of the basic instrument of human interaction, and which also may be applied to the practical problems of reading and writing. In our display of the language in Chapters

6–16, we exposed the mechanisms by which the language works. The objective of this display has been to bring to the focus of attention the patterns which we learned so young that we manage them almost instinctively without any great awareness of them. The exercises which accompanied the display were intended to enforce these patterns on the conscious mind, and then to drill them "below" the level of consciousness, so that they become available in a new and different way.

All the knowledge in the world about language will not help your writing unless you write, unless you find and make opportunities for writing. In this we are, in a sense, victims of our age, because there have never been so many means offered to the person in school and college for avoiding the need for writing. Objective tests, true and false questions, mimeographed sheets with blanks for only one or two words to be filled in, graphs, charts, movies, and other teaching aids directed to the ear and eye have cut down the number of situations which compel a student to take his pen and set his thoughts down on paper. Thus the burden falls upon each to propel himself, to write on his own. Nothing can make him do it except an active sense of the value to himself of the command of written English, both as an individual and as a member of a literate society. We have tried to make these values obvious.

The kind of writing we normally think of is directed to readers. The writer has something to say; he puts it down on paper for someone else to read. Reading audiences are hard to catch, and readers are hasty and indifferent anyway. Of a writer they demand skill which he is trying to build up, skill in fitting his expression to their understanding. The writer knows it is well to seize every opportunity to write for an audience, just as a speaker does well to speak to an audience every time he gets a chance. He can learn to measure responses. But this kind of writing must be bolstered by another, by writing that is done for no eye but his own.

It is easy to overestimate the value of writing for other people to read as a means of learning to write. One real objective of all our study and practice is to be able to lay out on paper, plainly and clearly, what we have to say to the people we want to communicate with. Writing for other people means always performing in public; it is like practicing on the tuba in the city park. We would prefer a little more privacy for our flat notes. We are self-consciously aware of the eyes of the world upon us, and we never really give way and see how loud we can make the thing blow. For practice we need to withdraw to a place where we freely can try out the range of our instrument and our command of it. When we are learning to write we need privacy most of all, a withdrawn place where we feel no self-consciousness and no embarrassment about our ideas or how we express them. We need a place where we can "finger" our instrument, the language.

The writer must be shameless. He cannot worry about what his grandmother, his father, or his maiden aunt may think of his writing. He must put down what he sees and feels and thinks as it comes to him. He must be honest. He must share his integrity with the page so that his writing is an extension of himself. He must be willing to refute the judgments of all other persons, of all nations in all times, if it is his sober considered judgment that the facts are as he sees them. He must use his reason, knowing that he may be in the end as wrong as the conceptions he denies.

Thus the writer needs a notebook, a private drawer in his desk where he tosses odd sheets, and a regular habit of writing for no eye but his own. Privately, by himself, he singles out the aspects of language that he wants to learn; on these he "runs the scales" somewhat as a musician does, trying out his skills in public only at intervals. He learns to use his pencil to see what he can do with the language, to see what kind of sentences he can build, what kind of pattern-substitutions he can make to express the same idea, and what kind of changes are brought about in the idea by a difference in pattern. He needs to develop the habit of using his pencil to search out his own thoughts, refine them, develop them, clarify them, and get them down on paper. He needs the habit of using his pencil to find out exactly what it is he thinks about what he thinks about.

Weekly writing is not enough. The practice must be daily, or close to it, for a pile of writing done at one stretch will not teach half as much as a little bit done day by day. The mind goes on between stints of writing, working over the material for next time. Going to the desk day after day, with only a limited time to work, the writer forces himself to get that first line on paper, to break that cold grip of paralysis and free himself from it forever. By holding himself to short bits, he learns to get into a subject, deal with it, and get out of it.

Learning to write is like learning to drive a car. You could start out across the country and end your trip very little more in command of your car than you were when you began. If you take the car to a deserted suburb, start it, drive it a block, and stop it, start it and stop it, practice left turns and right turns, back up, park it, and pull away and park it again, you will put yourself into a state to learn something from a good long cross-country run. By getting the measure of your vehicle, you dispose of your fear of it. It is the same with writing: short bits done at frequent intervals teach the shape and nature of written discourse, and give you the feel of it in your hands. If you ever get this feel, you never lose it.

Writing for your own eye alone, for a short time and at frequent intervals, you set yourself two kinds of exercises: you pose problems of structure and solve them, and you pose problems of idea and solve them. When you are working with structures, you make or choose sentence patterns and fill them with the words that fit the patterns. You might set up a paragraph made up of each of the six basic statements, and try to write a paragraph, like the sample on page 210, using all of them. Or you might set up a simple sentence pattern and introduce every possible variation into it:

1)	**N**		**V**		**N**
2)	A̶ **N**		v **V**	**D**	A̶ **N**
3)	**N-clause**		v v **V**		**N**
4)	**N**		v v **V**		**N-clause**

You could concentrate on the noun-cluster or on the verb-group, using a variety of markers and helpers with the different head-words. You could play with adverbs, phrases, and clauses. You could take a sentence from some article—one that appeals to you because of its form—and use the same structure with totally different words. This manipulation, by making available for your writing the structures that you use so easily in your speech, gives you a nice, tempered sense of their expressive quality.

When you are working with ideas, you come at writing problems from another direction. Here you take elements from your experience and try to put them into words. You can begin quite simply with items you have observed. What is the view from your window? How does your desk look after you have worked at it for a while? Describe a jackknife, a cigarette lighter, a comb, a typewriter eraser. How did a particular rain come? What was a specific bus ride like? Describe the feeling of sunlight on the back of your hand. What was your snap reaction to a stranger's voice? Keep these essays simple, and try to get each one into a single paragraph. Do not reach out for vocabulary; use the words that come to you. Use common, familiar words for reasons we will explain in the next chapter; never send a man out to do a boy's work. Don't worry about your vocabulary while you are writing; everybody knows plenty of words.

From these exercises you may move to somewhat larger problems and begin to use writing to discover a little about yourself, noting down briefly what you have seen, thought, or felt since your last stint of writing. You can write sketches of your friends or your teachers, comments on your reading, reactions to events you participate in, always keeping them short—on a page or so if you can. Here is where many beginning writers have learned to have some fun. One reluctant draftee who got into the Marine Corps discovered his vein of caustic humor in a series of short sketches of his service. A Korean veteran found himself writing a daily page which made up a history of his military career, caught while the memories were still sharp and before the flavor of his experiences had blurred into vague impressions. A hotrodder wrote an essay on converting an old Ford into "a glamour girl," and launched on a dictionary of hotrod terms when he found that this paper was meaningless to outsiders. He did not get far with it, but that does not matter. What matters is that he discovered for himself a segment of experience, and of language to match, where his own knowledge outran anything he could find in print. Each writer drifted where his own interests took him, finding out for himself who he is, what he knows, and what he thinks.

A somewhat more difficult structural exercise is to combine a chosen form with a chosen subject. You can set up a series of sentence-patterns to serve as the vehicle for an experience, thought, or an observation. You may not move freely in your expression; the pattern sets bounds within which you must move. You must weigh your thought against the form it is to take.

Such exercises serve the writer as quick water-color or pencil sketches serve the painter, or as a piece of soft stone and a knife carried in the pocket serve the sculptor. You practice manipulating your language, as a ballplayer handles the ball or the swimmer romps in the water, with no object except the control of your material. You get the feel of it into your fingers, so that when you have something to communicate you do not begin by floundering ineptly, stalled by inexperience. The words come to you as you need them, because you have established the channels by which they may come.

Probably the most strict and rigorous structural exercise you can take on is the writing of verse, for you put new and even more binding restrictions on yourself. These are the bonds of rhythm and of rime. You proceed by settling on a line of a specific number of syllables. The most common number of syllables in a line of English verse, and probably the easiest to begin with, is ten. The next most commonly used number of syllables to a line is eight. Between these two you can set up any number of patterns that serve well in practice; two lines of ten syllables each, with the last words of the lines riming (**thing, bring**); four lines of ten syllables each, with the second and fourth riming, or with all four riming (**through, too, few, you**); or four lines, the first and third of ten syllables, and the second and fourth of eight. Your first efforts will not amount to much, but the restrictions will force you to consider your words in a new light.

This kind of practice is common to many disciplines; by setting restrictions within which you must operate, you cut down on the formlessness of undirected practice. Soldiers have their obstacle courses, and football players practice running and wheeling through a cluttered field; surgeons drill their fingers by tying knots in surgical thread through a small opening and out of sight, against the day when they will have to slip two fingers through a narrow incision and cut off a flow of blood. Such practice creates the expert, the person who proceeds confidently to his work because he has taken the measure of himself and his material and knows what he can do. When you were a little child this kind of "pattern-practice" gave you command of your language. Applied with persistence and imagination, pattern-practice with the structures of written English will give you the same sure control of your writing.

✳ **CHAPTER 27** ✳

Thirty Years to a
More Powerful Vocabulary

Learning English words is quite a different matter from learning the structures of English. There are far more words to learn, particularly in a society like ours which is changing rapidly in almost every aspect and constantly adjusting its vocabulary to match and express the changes. The various speech-communities within the English-speaking world do not share all the same words or use them in the same way. No matter how many nouns, verbs, adjectives, and adverbs we know and no matter how many senses we know for these words, there is always a multitude that we have never seen or heard and a multitude of different meanings attached to them. About the structures of English, on the other hand, the speakers of English are in substantial agreement. Most of us know most of the structures of English and have known them from childhood. Words and their meanings are like the sands along the beach, easily tossed about by winds and waves; the structures are like the rocky backbone of the continent whose alterations have to be measured in centuries.

Popular books like *30 Days to a More Powerful Vocabulary* or *Increase Your Word Power* fool us in two ways: they give us the notion that there is something deficient about our vocabulary and lead us to think that a few more words tossed into it will fix everything up. Studies of the vocabularies of business executives show that they score about as high, for instance, as college professors; and it is probably true, as some people suggest, that you can pick the better of two mechanics by giving them a test on the terms used in their trade. The better mechanic will have a more precise and more extensive knowledge of the language of his trade. A big vocabulary is not a road to success. There is no evidence that the vocabulary comes first. The expert has a big vocabulary because he is experienced and competent.

Command and range of vocabulary and command and range of structures seem to result from two different kinds of ability, separate though not wholly unrelated to each other. In a group of people selected at random from the whole population according to their aptitude for learning words, a few people would come low on the scale, most people would group at the center, and a few people would place high, regardless of where they live, what their education or state of wealth is, and what the color of their skin. Some people, no matter who or where they are, love to learn the names of things; some learn enough to get along and quit. A hill boy from the Cumberland mountains may relish every local term for farm tools, animals, flowers, trees, and for minute changes of the weather, even without any formal schooling. He may be a walking treasury of words that have never qualified for the dictionary, though they go back to Middle and Old English in a line of descent as honorable as any. A fairly well-off city boy, not much of a word lover but apt at making structures convey his meanings with common familiar terms, can get by with far fewer words quite well. Neither would ring the bell on a standard vocabulary test.

Persons with high I. Q.'s know more words than persons with low I. Q.'s, but that is not surprising, because an important part of the test on which the I. Q. is based is itself verbal. City people show up with higher quotients on these tests than country people, the children of the well-to-do come off better than the children of the poor, and whites do better than non-whites. An only daughter of well-to-do white city dwellers shows up best of all. Small wonder, since the tests are made up by well-to-do white city dwellers and favor their vocabulary. If she were tested on the vocabulary of the poorer non-white country people, she would run a sad race.

No successful means has ever been worked out for measuring a person's total vocabulary, but there has been a good deal of loose talk about vocabulary size. An ordinary person in any society knows about as many words as any other ordinary person in any other society; a gifted person knows more, and a less gifted person knows fewer. The ordinary person in any society has about the same control of structures; the more gifted control more, and the less gifted control fewer. Those gifted with words and those gifted with structures need not be the same people, for structure and vocabulary together express meaning; when you fall short on the one, you lean more heavily on the other. Modern scholars have the uncomfortable suspicion that the ordinary person in any society knows thousands more words than he has ever been given credit for, and that he adds to this store at a rate faster than has ever been calculated. As long as he moves in society he continues to add to his store of words. He probably increases at the fastest rate while he is young—simply because he starts out with none, and because all education is a learning of names for whatever the society finds worth naming. While a youngster is increasing his knowledge by reading, by taking courses, or by putting himself in the way of experience, he cannot fail to increase his vocabulary.

The English language uses many words of foreign origin. Before the eleventh century, English made new words out of native roots and stems, largely by combining materials already in use in the language, because the English-speaking people were relatively isolated on their islands. The Norman conquest which brought French rule to the English began a contact with other cultures which has never ceased. When two speech-communities meet in any kind of regular contact—in trade, in war, in day-to-day interchange of any kind—they trade words. When one society has prestige of any kind over another, the greater flow is from the respected group to the other. When any language is considered worth learning by another people—for its elegance, for the knowledge expressed in it, or for favors to be earned through knowing it—it forms a kind of mine of words to be exploited by the people who see its value. Thus the English-speaking people have borrowed freely from the French, Latin, and Greek, and at particular times for special reasons from

German, Italian, Spanish, and most of the languages of the world. Borrowing is the respect that our people have paid to the accomplishments, the prestige, or the power of other nations.

All languages borrow. All languages have within their vocabulary many alien words; English does not differ from other languages in this respect. Since the eleventh century the English-speaking people have preferred to borrow. They came into the modern Global Period of the language with no deep-seated or effective prejudice against borrowing. At all social levels, in all occupational groups, and in all intellectual disciplines the speakers of English drew from strange lands and peoples, from strange cultural complexes, and from strange systems of thought the words that seemed useful. They have borrowed with a more or less imperfect understanding of the other societies and languages, so that often the use of a word in English has little to do with its use in the language it came from. They have borrowed into living and compulsive structures of thought and language that have always put their own stamp of meaning and form on the borrowings. Only words of limited use keep their original sound and meaning; once a word catches on and becomes public property it assimilates to English and loses its foreign quality. Thus we cannot distinguish between native and foreign words in use; only the etymologist, patiently checking the history of the word, can tell its origin. Still, the origin of a word has little to say about its present use. A word is, after all, only a slice of an utterance, a sequence of sounds whose meaning is a part of the total meaning of the utterance. All English words in general use are English, regardless of where they came from or when they came. They submit completely to the intentions of the English speech-communities which use them.

English is interesting, however, in having a "léarnèd" vocabulary which is associated mainly with writing and mainly borrowed from Latin, Greek, French, Italian, and German. Educated men and women, set apart from the uneducated by their interest in the arts and sciences and linked by this interest to the educated people of Europe, have an "international" vocabulary which is used, only slightly nationalized, in all the modern languages of Western Europe. As these intellectual disciplines advance, their practitioners (often without much actual knowledge of Latin or Greek) dip into the dictionaries of these languages for roots and stems that they can build into new forms of rather special meaning. Thus we have the "Schenectady Greek" of the electrical and electronics industry and the fancy new coinages of nuclear physics. This "vocabulary of learning" has to be mastered by anyone who wants to understand the arts and sciences: art, music, literature, the criticism and study of art and literature, the physical and biological sciences, the social sciences (anthropology, sociology, economics, history, education, and government), and all kinds of technologies. The prestige of these studies rubs off on the words used in them. Thus we have the peculiar notion that there is some special value in knowing and using "big words" for their own sake. We think we can take a short and easy way to education through word study and vocabulary building, whether or not we know anything about the arts and sciences in which those words are used.

The hard fact is that we talk as we live. Our vocabulary is not a dress that we put on our thoughts to make them socially acceptable. It is something more integral to our thinking. It is a private set of symbols that represent, for each of us, not things in the real world itself but the aspects of the world as we see it. We manipulate these symbols within the structures of the utterance; as long as we are talking to ourselves or within small groups, we can give them any meaning we choose. Thus children who play together often evolve a private language that sounds like gibberish to outsiders; thieves, lawyers, musicians, doctors, and used-car dealers, too, have special jargons that serve communication within the group without tipping off its secrets to the general public. The specific meanings we give to words are private. The meanings are always tied to the emotional circumstances we associate with our learning of the words. Since the normal use of language is in conversation, our employment of these private symbols is always a public matter. When we talk, we talk to other people; we have to come reasonably close to their meanings for our words in order to be understood. A constant cross-checking goes on within each speech-community in conversation, and this give and take of common talk keeps our private meanings for words pretty close to the meanings generally current in the whole group.

Mankind does not create a word and then look about for a meaning to attach to it. A human being is a living, growing, developing organism acting and reacting within total situations, themselves also always in flux. Each person comes to each new situation triply armed: with his own individual personality and character, with his experience in the world and in human society, and with the inherited fabric of his native language. As a person he has a running flow of unexpressed perceptions that are entirely his own. Some of his perceptions have come to other people and have been expressed in words; some of his perceptions could not have come to other men and women because the state of human society did not give rise to them. As John of Salisbury said in the twelfth century, we are pigmies standing on the shoulders of giants; we can see farther than they because they have lifted us up above their level. Each person, as an individual and as a member of human society, is experiencing beyond his own previous experience—often beyond the recorded experiences of other men.

Each person is pressing the language in two ways: he is pressing his own previous expression in language and he is pressing the previous expression of all dead and living users of the language. As far as he can, he uses the inherited vocabulary, nudging its range of meanings into a little wider compass; when that fails or when his knowledge of the inherited vocabulary fails him, he creates a new form to carry his new burden of meaning. In either case his private coinage must meet the public test; if other speakers have the same experience and find his term for it the handiest one to use, then it lives on. The experience may be too private to be communicated and may not be generally repeated. It may be only individually and not generally new, so that terms for it already exist. It may have been related, in ways he has not foreseen, to the general experience of men and women and expressed in familiar terms. Time may have shown it to be merely a partial observation of a whole new set of perceptions. If so, his term may last a while and pass out of use. In any case, vocabulary follows experience; it does not precede it.

Vocabulary building is a long process along two parallel lines. It is in one sense a slow maturing within a society, so that you learn its beliefs, customs, and concerns; and you learn the terms applied to what its necessities make it care about. In the other sense, it is an endless manipulation of these terms in language, of making and hearing utterances, of testing terms in structural patterns, so that you have a fair knowledge of the range of contexts in which each one occurs. This is the dual exploration by which children grow up into their parents' world, as the expanding reach of their senses brings more and more data to their brains. "What's this? What's that?" they ask, touching, handling, listening, and pointing. Their inquisitive minds take the proper order for vocabulary building—first the experience, then the word for it. In the endless chatter and inventive word play of children, the terms find their places in utterances. Children will use and overuse a word to the total distraction of adults, testing its reach in the language system. Their innocent acceptance of the relation between word and thing is wholesome for vocabulary building; children take concepts as given to them, directly and without subtlety. The unlettered adult continues this same uncritical association of word and thing. "Why do you call that thing a ratchet?" "Because that's its *name, stupid.*"

Words follow experience. Without experience to tie them to, words are sheer empty verbalisms, sounds without sense. One good way to learn words is to put yourself into the situations where they are used and in the company of the people who use them, so that if you hear a term that is obscure you can ask how it is used and what it means to its users, like a child endlessly inquiring, "What's this, and what is it for?" In a garage you learn the parts of a car and their function; at an airport you learn about an airplane; you learn the vocabulary of art by contemplating works of art and seeking the answers to the questions they raise among artists and critics of art. You learn about drama by going to plays and joining in the talk in the lobby between the acts; you learn about music at concerts, by playing an instrument, by listening to records. You learn the vocabulary of philosophy by facing the problems of philosophy: what is existence, what can we know, and how can we know it?

The way to build your vocabulary is to build your experience, moving much among men and women and taking interest in their interests, with a courteous grave inquiry like that of a child. Before this flattering inquisitiveness the crustiest characters melt; the sailor displays his lines and nets, the mechanic explains the mysteries of a torque wrench or a stroboscopic timer, the scholar takes you through ancient manuscripts and shows you the brilliant illuminations or the rabbit drawn whimsically into a margin. In response to this inquisitiveness factories conduct guided tours, and museums lay out in displays the step-by-step creation of an etching or an epoch of civilization. Object and word go together; to put the two together for the inquiring stranger, a cook, baker, or candlestick-maker will pause in the day's occupations and explain what is what in his line of work. To put object and word together, the picture magazines run photographic essays, often of some grandeur, like "The World We Live In" series in *Life;* and "how-to-do-it" experts publish books and articles telling the novice what is involved in carpentry, bricklaying, or ceramics, and how to do it himself. It is a rare craftsman who brushes off a courteous interest in his craft.

The vocabulary of an educated person must go beyond this naïve sense of the relation of words to things. Words are symbols in language, not for the real world but for our ideas of the world; that is, they stand for concepts. They stand for thoughts, not things, even when they seem to have direct reference to objects. In language they sort into classes—into nouns, verbs, adjectives, and adverbs in English—and then they impose their class-meanings upon our perceptions, so that we see the world in the terms that our language permits. Other languages permit other perceptions; it is possible that if we are ever to get an accurate or complete representation of the world in language, we shall have to develop a super-language of languages, able to draw on the perceptions of all. In the meantime we get by with the perceptions our own language permits, classifying the events of the real world as well as we can within its framework. Our words stand for concepts that our people have developed; which word stands at any one time for which concept is determined by the utterances the words occur in. Our civilization is an elaborate structure of thought based on the relations between concepts; our arts and sciences are ordered statements of these relations. Scholarship as we know it is a professional search for new relations and systems of relations unperceived before.

The various intellectual disciplines that we study in college or out make heavy dependence on words because each one is a system of concepts expressed in words. In art, anthropology, chemistry, physics, biology, law, sociology, history, medicine, and in linguistics, we search for units that have not been perceived before; and when we think we see them, we give them names. We search for new relationships, new arrangements, and all kinds of manifestations other men have missed, and we give them names. Think of words like **gas, vitamin, phoneme, anesthesia,** and **allergy** as representing discoveries made by men whose minds looked into the world and found something new. These men chose or made up words that would let them talk about their discoveries. At the same time the investigators are looking at existing concepts to see whether they are real. Thus **ptomaine, phlogiston, ether,** and **rheumatism** have been examined and found to be grab-basket names for things that should not be classed together or names for things which seemed at first to be real but turned out in the end not to be.

When a student takes an introductory course in psychology, sociology, or physics, he spends a good deal of his time learning words, but not for the sake of his vocabulary. These are old studies in which a good deal of the basic thinking has been done before our time. We have to learn the basic concepts and their names so as to get quickly over what is known and on our way to the frontiers, where the line between what is definitely known and what is definitely not known is a shadowy half-world of the dimly perceived, the half-understood, and the tantalizing fragment.

We learn the basic jargon of each field. We must keep in mind that the persons in the field think that real perceptions of the way things are and work lie behind the jargon and are represented in language by the jargon. Otherwise, we are likely to think that a cute chatter made up of the terms is genuine knowledge. Scientists try to teach us their terms by putting us through the experiments, but we often come to the courses so full of popular misinformation and half-truths and so familiar with the sounds of the words, that we think it is all old stuff and we have nothing to learn. The problem is worse, perhaps, in psychology and sociology, since terms like **stimulus** and **response; personality, mesomorph,** and **other-directed; psyche, libido,** and **inferiority complex** are kicked around so much in public we forget that they have ever been precisely related to careful observations anywhere. As always, experience must come first, then a vocabulary that lets us talk about experience. A big vocabulary is a by-product of maturity.

Taking your body to where things are done is a good way to learn, and to learn words, but it has limitations. This is a big world full of societies of unmeasured antiquity and unimaginable complexity; so many things are going on that even a confirmed globetrotter cannot look at all of them. Man is distinguished from the beasts by his ability to remember and record his experiences. Our society keeps its records in books; the people concerned with each part of human activity keep the records, many running back several thousand years. We can buy these books and own them for ourselves, or we can read them in libraries. The books can carry us where our bodies cannot go; the wonderful world of books is one we can travel without leaving our chairs. As single persons tied to our daily responsibilities and limited to a short life, we cannot get far beyond what our own five senses bring to us—what we can actually see, hear, touch, taste, and smell. With books our horizons stretch to the limits of the universe, over the whole span of recorded time, and into the minds of men of all eras and all countries. In our daily lives we meet the common run of men and women, but through books we can become acquainted with select men and women, brilliant minds, daring and inventive discoverers, persons whose good or bad qualities have raised them to special eminence. The experiences we get through reading are just as real and just as much a part of us as those we get through our senses. The words we learn from reading—even if we have never heard them spoken and don't know how to pronounce them—enter our minds as honestly and as vividly as those we hear spoken in conversation.

When we say of a person that he is "well-read," we are saying something nice about him; we are giving him a title of respect. We do not mean merely that he has handled a lot of books of any kind; we mean that he has read books on many subjects and that the books have meant something to him. They have given him knowledge, and he has transmuted the knowledge in his own mind into wisdom. He knows a great deal, and he has thought about what he knows. He can enter into conversation with experts about their specialties. They recognize at once that he is using their language in their way. He understands how they feel about their work. But he has not read so as to become a bright and universal conversationalist; he has read for his own needs, his own development, and his own better knowledge about human beings in the world they live in. Of course he has a big vocabulary, and he uses it to think with, not as words only but as the tools of thought. There is no other worth-while use for a big vocabulary.

Standing in a library and looking at the thousands or millions of books, a youngster thinks: "How can I ever read all these?" Of course he cannot read them all. They are not all there for him, any more than all the bread, pies, and cakes in a bakery are all for him. The library serves many needs; it tries to have some books for almost everybody. The staff hopes that it can serve him by having all the books that he needs, or by telling him where he can find the books it does not have. His next question is, "Where shall I begin?" Of course he is not beginning; he already has a good deal of reading behind him. What he means is probably, "Where shall I start now to read the books that will be of the most use to me?" That question can be answered: start by reading the books that writers read.

What are those books? To begin with, there are six: the Bible, the plays of Shakespeare, Bulfinch's *Mythology,* Homer and the Greek plays, and Ruth Benedict's *Patterns of Culture.* Each person trying to become educated should own these books and have them on his own shelf, along with a good dictionary or two. He cannot know these six books too well. They are valuable to him because they are well-known, especially to people who write, so that other books are constantly referring to them. The human weakness that we have noticed before—our way of assuming that everybody knows what we know, except for the particular thing we are trying to explain at the moment—makes writers assume that everybody knows these books so well that it is safe to echo them, cite them, and reflect them in their writing. When Sigmund Freud, the great student of sick minds, thought he saw a complicated reaction of a son toward his father, a mixture of love, hate, and jealous competition for the affection of the mother, he cast about for something to call it. He chose a name from the Greek plays, the name of a king who had killed his father and married his own mother. He called it the Oedipus complex, confident that other people, too, knew the plays and would get his point.

Long before the Authorized Version of the English Bible appeared in 1611, the people of England had sneaked their translations and passed them from hand to hand. They read them in secret, often in great danger, hiding them from outsiders and poring over them by candlelight behind locked doors. The Bible meant to them the ordinary person's assertion of his right to know at first hand the word of God. The Roman Church published a Catholic Bible in English, the Rheims-Douai Version (1580–1610). From that time on, the English-speaking peoples have known and loved and studied the Bible. Both versions were quite beautiful in their phrasing, and so not only the Bible stories but the very twists and turns of language used in their telling have entered into our way of talking and writing and have become part of us. When William Jennings Bryan said, "You shall not crucify mankind upon a cross of gold," arguing merely about a gold standard for our money, he was talking to people who could be stirred deeply by the reference.

Therefore, if for no better reason than to understand what you read, you need to know the Bible. You cannot know it too well.

About the same time, William Shakespeare was writing his plays. Even then the English-speaking peoples knew that they had something good. The plays have been acted and re-enacted, published and republished ever since; like the language of the Bible, the language of Shakespeare has become part of our heritage. For three and a half centuries, educated people have known them so well and have assumed that everybody knows Shakespeare so well that they freely quote, cite, and refer to the plays in their writing. You should buy those plays and read them, and you should do more; whenever any group of actors, no matter how good or bad, puts on a Shakespearean play in the movies, on the stage, or over television you should be there to see and hear them as dramatic performances, so that you can hear the living words of Shakespeare as he meant them to be heard—spoken by living men and women before an audience. You cannot know them too well.

Thomas Bulfinch's *The Age of Fable* (1855), often given the title *Mythology,* contains much of what we have left of the Classical tradition. Once all educated men and women knew Latin, and many of them knew Greek. They started the practice that still goes on of referring frequently and easily to Venus and Adonis, Aphrodite, Jupiter, Juno, Theseus and the Minotaur, Diana the Huntress, and Hercules the strong man. Bulfinch gathered all these myths up into a kind of dictionary and told them in brief and interesting form. Even if we know no more of Greece and Rome than we learn from Bulfinch, we at least know precisely what is being referred to when someone cites or quotes one of the ancient tales.

Homer's two rousing good stories about the Trojan War have been loved and read, quoted and translated since at least eight hundred years before Christ. Technically they are epic poems; but for our purpose, which is to understand better what we read, we can treat them as novels. The *Iliad* tells of Paris and Helen, Hector and Achilles, the siege of Troy, and the battles around the Greek beachhead before the city. It is still considered (especially by soldiers) the greatest war story of all time. The *Odyssey* tells of Odysseus' (Ulysses') ten-year struggle to get back home to Penelope in spite of battles, monsters on land and sea, and luscious and loving ladies who just liked to have him around. You can get these books in good, cheap, modern translations; they are interesting in and for themselves and they make good reading; more important, they are known and loved by authors who freely refer to them and assume that they can use them to make their points clear. They are keys to better reading.

The Greek plays of Sophocles, Aeschylus, and Euripides, which date from about 300 B.C., have been studied with few lapses since that time because of their deep insights into the acts and motives of men and women in trouble. In present-day terms they are good psychology besides being good drama; modern authors know them well and draw on them for references. They are still being acted in college, on Broadway and in the commercial theater, and on television. They have been used in operas. We have many good translations of them. They are quite short and easy and interesting to read, and they will leave you somewhat more civilized; the value in them which concerns us here is that they bring you better informed to other reading and better able to cope with it.

Ruth Benedict's *Patterns of Culture* (1934) is a book that introduced the general public to the work of cultural anthropologists. It is a beautifully written display of the patterns of conduct within which members of human communities live, illustrated by the Pueblo culture of the American Southwest, the evil-magic-dominated society of the Dobu people of the Pacific, and the Kwakiutl Indians of the Pacific Northwest, with their wacky economic system that seems like a travesty of our own. From these groups Miss Benedict draws wise and penetrating extensions to the more complex society we live in. Sometimes called "cocktail anthropology," *Patterns of Culture* has become widely known, and it has introduced a general audience to the concepts of anthropology without swamping them in detail. Knowledge of it gives you a "stance" from which to cope with other modern works of history, economics, and sociology. You can get it in a paper-backed edition.

These six books can lead you to other books which give you a general cultural background. They touch all the arts and sciences at many points. You could find most or all of them on a list of ten best books such as people often make up, or a list of fifty or a hundred. (If you could carry only ten books with you to a desert island, one of the ten should be a notebook with blank pages in which you could set down your own thoughts.) People often find it worth while to find a list of a hundred great books, and systematically stock their shelves with them in preparation for those long winter evenings when no company comes, the television breaks down, and there is nothing to do but read. You can find such lists in a book which is surely the reader's best friend, *Good Reading,* a volume published by the New American Library as a Mentor Book at fifty cents. The latest edition is a handy guide to more than 1250 books arranged by subject, with a comment on the nature and quality of each one. With this volume in your hand, you can read your way into any subject, from the older, standard books to the latest works just out.

The road to a big vocabulary is a long one, occasionally hard enough but pleasant and rewarding. It is not worth taking if you only want to dazzle your friends in conversation; people don't dazzle easily and they expect to have their say, too. If your aim is to walk the earth as an educated man or woman, at home and at ease with modern civilization, able to learn and teach as all educated men and women must, able to express yourself in terms that your hearers can understand and respect, then this is the road. Go through your days with an alert, sympathetic, inquiring mind, letting the people you meet teach you what they know; use your private hours to extend your acquaintance with men and affairs through reading. In thirty years or so you will have a more powerful vocabulary, and it will be where power must be to be of use to you—in your mind, available and at your command.

✴ CHAPTER 28 ✴

The Structure of Usage

THE SPEECH that comes most naturally to us is what we learned when we were young in the unforced conversations of childhood and youth. As our interests and associations widen, we cut off some associations; we talk more to some people, less to others. Our personal relations, our group memberships change; but we can always be sorted on the basis of geography, sex, age, education, wealth, occupation, and interests. The sorting must be done on other grounds than language. If we are talking about "educated" and "uneducated" English, we have to choose some objective standard of education, and then firmly record the language of those who pass the standard, whatever it is, as "educated." If we want to distinguish the usage of women from the usage of men, we have to start with obvious physical sex-membership and go to the study of language from that. To say of a woman, "She talks like a man," is to express an interesting opinion, but if she is a woman she talks like one; we have to record her speech-habits with those of other women, whatever they are. The speech of all communities is in flux. Changes always begin with specific persons; if we cross people off simply because their usage is different from what we expect, we falsify the record. We get into a circular argument; and when we argue in circles, we get confused.

Spoken usage in America is complicated because our history and our society are complicated, and because Americans won't stay put. We would expect to find a sharp line between the United States and Canada along the political boundary, but actually there are more striking differences within Canada and within the United States than between the two nations. We would expect to find great differences between the speech of the educated and the uneducated —on the European pattern—in any one area. There are no important phonetic or phonemic differences between these two groups in the Northern and Midland areas; and in the South, where the differences are systematic, uneducated speech is close to cultivated Midland. Everywhere we turn, the facts of usage surprise us. Californians consciously avoid expressions that they think are Southern, but California speech is full of Southernisms that nobody identifies as such. It is hard to make general statements about usage in America that will guide a person who wishes to change his speech to an acceptable standard that will help his career. For many years the American Dialect Society has published lists of dialect words garnered in various parts of the country; readers of the lists from other areas have checked off large sections of the lists as perfectly familiar since childhood. The still incomplete surveys of the *Linguistic Atlas of the United States and Canada,* using a checklist of some three hundred items, show local and educational differences of usage, but they are not always the ones the casual traveler would expect. How is a young man or woman on the make to know what is correct and what is not?

No one can package the language and hand it to you in a bundle, so that you can be sure of saying the right thing to the right people at the right time and place. The more one knows about language and about English, the less inclined he feels to try it. Only a confident person who takes his own speech as a standard and all deviations from it as errors or a person whose ear is deadened to the actual words and ways of American speech would try it. The advice is mainly negative: don't say this; avoid that. Such people are to be heeded, for they often have a keen sense of the niceties of writing and of formal speech; they represent, furthermore, a kind of taboo-tradition in our society which is very influential among people who teach and write. You will have to weigh their comments against your own sense of fitness, trusting in the end to your own ear. You should never brush off any person's critical comment on your use

of language; the fact that your manner has called attention to itself
is important to you; it is a kind of feedback from your audience.
It does not give you much of a standard to go by; your standard is
something you must work out very laboriously for yourself. No
one can hand it to you fully formed.

Some general guides give you help in orienting your own speech
to the various groups you mingle with and the circumstances you
get into. One is knowledge of the geographical divisions of the
great American speech-community. It is well to know that people
speak differently in different places, and that they are often quite
hostile or suspicious toward an obvious outsider. Knowing this,
you can walk soft and speak courteously when you notice that other
people's speech differs more than slightly from your own. Your
dialect may excite humor (if you are from Boston, Brooklyn, or the
deep South), suspicion (if your speech is obviously citified and
you are in the country), hostility (if you are from the North, from
New England, or New York), contempt (if you are in an area
which has absorbed large masses of poor immigrants from your
state), or respect (if you happen to use a cultivated Eastern speech
in the West, or a Tidewater Maryland or Virginia dialect almost
anywhere). Your use of any American dialect may stir any or all
of these reactions in Canada or in Europe; on the other hand, if
your speech is identified in the United States as Canadian, you may
benefit from the fond family-feeling many people in the States have
toward Canada. Any outsider whose speech is noticeably different
has some difficulty in making himself felt as an individual; the reactions he provokes are directed less to him than to an imagined
stereotype.

Within each geographical area, large or small, the typical speech
of some groups bears considerable prestige. The speech of other
groups calls little attention to itself and provokes few reactions,
either favorable or unfavorable. The speech of still other groups is
considered bad, ignorant, illiterate, and slovenly. No matter what
the speaker says, whether it is wise or foolish, graceful, apt, pun-
gent, or stilted, he is not judged by it but by a snap reaction to his
dialect. This sort of judgment, though it seems to be based on language and directed at language, is a reflection of complicated reactions of groups to each other, based on their real or imagined
ways of making a living and their ways of life. The attitudes are
those of insider to outsider, with the outsider taken not for himself

but as a representative or stereotype of his group. The whole business is irrational and in its expression rather crude.

People who commonly and habitually associate with each other form a community within which the network of conversation is close-knit. In each group are some people who never willingly have much to do with outsiders, and some people whose intercourse with outsiders is easy. There are all shades of differences between these extremes. Some people are proud of their group membership and make a point of it, some take it for granted, and some make as little of it as they can. This shading-off within groups is common to all, not just to a few of them. Some people are defensive in the presence of outsiders, some take outsiders for granted without much emotional reaction, and some are aggressive. It depends on situations, personalities, and experience.

Language is only one aspect of the crisscross of influences that tie people together into a community and give them a sense of oneness with one another. Other things like dress, manners, possessions, church membership, social clubs, businessmen's organizations, and union membership shake down into a loose uniformity, so that the insider has a number of clues by which he can detect and isolate the outsider. As you travel through a city and its suburbs, you notice that even the choice of plants and flowers runs by neighborhood, so that a two-stem birch clump looks out of place in a three-stem birch-clump subdivision. People sort themselves by neighborhoods, finding a place to live where other people of about the same general status and income and often of the same race, religion, and politics live.

In familiar places and in the company of people like ourselves, we find a security even more real than what we get from newer and more luxurious possessions. We like to be in company where we know the signals; we want our children to be like ourselves, just as we want our neighbors to be like ourselves. We buy a pleasant house at a price we can afford out at the edge of town, where other people's cars are not too much older or newer, bigger or smaller than our own, and we hope that things will pretty much stay put. They will not stay put. The city grows out and beyond us: our neighborhood loses its identity; it begins to deteriorate. Some people sell and move on out to better houses; those who are left peer through the curtains at moving vans unloading the goods of strangers coming from an even less desirable neighborhood further in or, even worse, from out of the state. The immaculate housewife of German descent watches the Poles move in; in their turn the Poles stare at Kentucky and Tennessee women sitting immobile on their porches in the sun, or listen to the excited, exciting chatter of Yiddish. Poles, Midlanders, and Jews see the first Negro families moving in, as each group in turn makes a little more money and finds in the new neighborhood something better than it has known before. Change comes, whether we want it or not.

What happens in housing also happens in the trades and the professions. The older, settled inhabitants once had the best places, and each wave of new people started at the bottom. A small, well-to-do educated group set itself apart from the rest of the population, practiced medicine and law, ran the businesses, and did the teaching. It sent its children to a few select schools, mainly in the East, where they received their education in a dialect which was itself a mark of education. Skilled craftsmen learned their trades locally by apprenticeship; solid citizens and self-respecting, they spoke the local dialect. Below them were the great mass of the unskilled, a hodgepodge speaking common English or any of a dozen different kinds of broken, foreign-flavored dialects. However divided these three elements were within themselves, they were sharply set off from each other by differences in dress, manners, housing, income, church or parish affiliations, foods, table manners, entertainments, and all the other things that people do in company with their equals and apart from their superiors or inferiors. Each element found some ground for a fierce pride that permitted it to face the others, however much the ideal ladder of success led from the unskilled to the skilled and on to the professional, ruling, and employing group at the top.

Today the proportions and the relations have changed. The vast need of our technical culture has made room in the professional and technical fields for thousands where there were hundreds before, and these have been drawn from the children of the skilled and unskilled workers. Government and business requirements for management have multiplied in the same way, and have been filled by upgrading. The proportion of skilled to unskilled labor has changed so far that skilled labor now predominates; every year there is more need for skilled labor and less for the unskilled, so that the slash in this group is one of the most dramatic of our age. As each person moves up in the economic scale, he changes his wants, his customs, his dress, and his entertainments in some rough adjustment to the group he enters. The upper groups are enduring an upsurge of outsiders that swamps the original happy few.

Normally any element in the population educates its children to carry on as their fathers have, but the school system tries to satisfy the needs of the community by educating for the opportunities that develop. During the great tide of immigration the task of the schools was simple Americanization, and it was met by the primary schools. Since 1900 the great pressure has been for functional literacy and vocational training, so that the youngsters out of school could enter the skilled trades and the sales and minor executive jobs that were opening for them. These needs have been met by the high schools. Primary schools and high schools are mainly local, and so most children are educated at home.

At the same time a vital need has arisen for people to fill professional, technical, and upper managerial positions. Beginning with the Morrill Act of 1862, which established an Agricultural and Mechanical College in each state, higher education has also become more local. Land-grant colleges and universities have provided higher education for thousands of young people in their home states; normal schools and teachers colleges trying to prepare enough teachers for the ever-growing school systems—but never quite keeping up—have brought higher education to the cities and towns. In the Depression of the 1930's, when older institutions where students lived on campus were being cut down or just holding on, city colleges were set up in many places to educate young men and women who lived at home and rode the streetcar or bus to their classes. Today about half the college students are in public institutions not very far from their homes; a very large number of students at these are the first in their families to go beyond a grade or high-school education. The story is very similar in Canada. Besides the older schools and colleges in Ontario, Quebec, and the east, there are colleges and universities from Nova Scotia to Saskatchewan and Vancouver.

We are now putting more students through college than we used to put through high school. If you are in college now, the chances are that your parents had a high-school education or less, and their parents had a grade-school education or less. You are in a minority if your parents completed college, and in an even smaller minority if your grandparents did. Once most students "went away" to college; today if you are attending college outside your own dialect area, you are again in a minority. If you go on to graduate school, you will probably be taking another step beyond the education of your parents. If you belong to the "skilled labor" force, the chances are that your father did not; if you take an executive position in business, government, or industry, it is probably a better one than your father had; and if you are a teacher, doctor, lawyer, engineer, scientist, social worker, in upper management, or an officer in the Army, Navy, or Air Force, you are probably moving in a world your parents did not reach or even expect to reach, a new person in whatever milieu you attain; you are likely to have a higher relative income, more possessions, more "expectations," and a higher status than you can find in your family tree.

We have to set this upgrading against what we know about the stratification of language within each geographic speech-community in order to see what it means to usage. In each community there is a cultivated speech used by educated people whose interests and professions or other occupations put a great burden on their ability to read and write. They cultivate literature and the arts, they read widely, and they concern themselves with the interests common to educated people everywhere. They take their language to be the standard for the community, and to some extent it is accepted as standard even by people who do not use it. Generally they have a college education or its equivalent in self-study; generally their work demands a precise command of a large vocabulary and a considerable amount of writing. We call their speech cultivated, standard, or educated English.

At the other extreme is a common or folk speech used by people who, whatever they do for a living, do not read and write much, and do not have to rely on precise language in their work. These are the multitude of ordinary people. They are farmers or farm hands, day laborers, small storekeepers, or the like; they have no great intellectual pretensions, and they have often quit school at the end of the eighth grade or before. They are not particularly concerned about language, or even overconscious of it, except when they are among the educated. They seem to accept the prestige of cultivated English, and they expect their children to learn "good English" in school; but in fact they consider good English to be full of big words, overinflated, and unnatural. They don't particularly like to be with educated people; they feel out of place, and they begin to watch their manners and their language, or break out in open exaggerated opposition to the practices of the cultivated.

The sound of educated English stirs in them something less than admiration. It is the language of the big shot, the shyster lawyer who gets them off but strips them of their possessions, the judge who browbeats them, the teachers who flunk them out of school, the doctor who parks his fishtailed Cadillac in the driveway, the social worker who pries into their personal affairs, the shavetail M. P. who locks them up for wearing battle dress in the rest area, the general who whizzes by in a jeep throwing mud in all directions, the snotty salesgirl in the department store, the credit manager, the employment man—educated English is the language of all who push them around, take their money, dole out charity, and try to make them feel like two cents while they are doing it, with looks and comments on their clothes, their manners, their housekeeping, and their talk. Educated English is the contemptuous, audible, universal sneer of the haves for the have-nots.

Between these two extremes and shading off into them is what we might call popular speech—the language of persons who have a high-school education and hold down a host of middle jobs— skilled and semiskilled labor, sales, and minor executive positions. They are clerks, storekeepers, foremen, office managers, and the like. They associate rather easily with the educated and uneducated alike; they have had enough schooling so that they are not particularly impressed by higher education or hostile to it; and they have good enough jobs so that they are secure within themselves. They are not much driven by ambition; they are not very competitive or defeated in competition; they tend to be work-centered; they are competent in their trades, but they don't care for too much responsibility. They don't want the boss's job because they don't want his worries; they often refuse advancement.

Once the users of common or folk speech were the most numerous in our society, and the users of cultivated English were a small and rather jealous minority. The upgrading we have been describing has made serious inroads on the users of common English; skilled and semiskilled laborers now actually outnumber the unskilled, and the proportion of youngsters going beyond the eighth grade is building up. The common laborers in our society—the dishwasher, the plowman, the ditchdigger, the cotton-picker, the janitor—are coming to be machines. Men and women are being crowded up and away from the crude application of muscle to things; even at work they have to be people: they have to have some of the knowledge that can only come from literacy. A more startling and upsetting aspect of upgrading has been in higher education and in the professions for which higher education prepares us. The nation's need for teachers, doctors, lawyers, engineers, scientists, technicians and for people capable of management in industry, business, and government increases year by year; every year the call comes for more trained and educated persons than all the schools, colleges, technical institutes, business colleges, and training programs can supply. Once there was a very small, tight, select group of the elite, mainly composed of the children of the elite themselves. Now the cultivated, professional, and educated segment of our society has grown into a sizable mass, recruited at large from the users of popular and common English.

There has always been "social mobility" in America, summed up in the familiar phrase, "from shirtsleeves to shirtsleeves in three generations." The cultivated group, conscious that its real quality lay in many intangibles beyond money and power, could hold the newcomers off until it could be seen whether they were going to hang on or subside into the poverty from which they came. The cultivated could reject the father whose speech and manners were crude, and accept the children whose speech and manners fitted them to belong. The new mobility is not an overnight matter of making and losing money; it is a permanent uplift because it is based on years of education and on sternly tested proficiency in positions of responsibility. The new invaders of cultivated society are up to stay; their invasion is one of the important aspects of present-day life.

Let us consider the real substance of the cultivated or educated element in society, disregarding geographical differences. These are the people who read and write; they are the lovers and owners of books; they preserve the written tradition. They organize and staff the libraries and museums. Whether they are rich, well off, or quite poor, their money and their interest support the author, the artist, the musician, the architect. They own and read good books; they buy record collections, paintings, statuary. They are the students of history, science, and literature; they are the playgoers, the concert audience. They are the teachers, the doctors, the lawyers, the politicians and statesmen, the managers of business and government.

While the cultivated are not all good men and women, not all virtuous, not all honest, still as a class they have been responsible for the continuity of our intellectual life. As long as they exist, our arts have a tradition, and works of art have a home and are protected. The learning of the cultivated provides standards against which what we think and do in our own times can be measured, so that we face the changing world informed and strengthened by the intelligence of our ancestors right back to the beginning of writing and the first written records. The cultivated once formed a very small class of people who defended the tradition of our civilization from the crude, ignorant, unthinking mass of day-to-day livers that had to depend on mouth-to-mouth transmission of limited, local human experience. Naturally they thought well of themselves, and they stood in self-conscious detachment from the mass that would rather burn books than read them, stable horses in a cathedral, or tear down an opera house for a parking lot.

The sudden augmentation of the cultured element of our society by local, mass, higher education has caused great strains and tensions within it. Like any other self-conscious group, the cultured element identifies its members by their conduct, manners, interests, and speech. In the past its members grew up largely within the tradition or came from elements in the society which knew of the tradition and respected it, so that they were fairly easy to bring into line. Today the newcomers enter the cultivated group as adults after spending their youth and adolescence among the speakers of common and popular English, where the whole structure, not merely of language but of manners and conduct, is noticeably different. In their college education which introduces them to the tradition and to the intellectual life, they stay among people like themselves, and their teachers are largely people like themselves.

These newcomers are not set off from the mass by their manners or their speech, only by the knowledge, the competence, and the interests which they share with the cultivated everywhere. They use the vocabulary of learning in the sounds and structures of popular and common English. In casual talk they are hard to distinguish from the ignorant and indifferent (if not hostile) majority. And they, too, are confident, self-conscious, self-respecting, and sophisticated possessors of the intellectual tradition of our civilization, relaxed in their possession of the tradition because they have earned it. The situation leads to clashes, regrettable because they are unnecessary and temporary, because their children do not go back; they grow up within the tradition.

We have to face a current disorder in standard cultivated English speech—the language of the educated. It has more differences within it than ever before. It has geographical differences because colleges and universities are scattered all over the continent. It has apparent social-class differences. Young people first use the common English of the uneducated in the primary schools and up to the eighth grade, then the popular English of the high-school crowd. In college they augment this popular speech with vocabulary and structures which they pick up from their teachers and their books, but they do not abandon their native speech; their language remains local in sound and structure. Some deliberately give up the speech of their youth for what seems to them more correct—since everybody hounds them to be correct. Many more of them deliberately go on talking as they always have, feeling that their real identity is with the people from whom they came rather than with the consciously superior groups with whom they now move by right of their learning and professional careers.

There is now no longer one right way for the educated to speak, but many right ways; the language of the educated is being enriched immeasurably from the popular speech of Americans, becoming more like general American speech and less distinct from it; it is being established on a broader base and on the usage of a larger selection of the American people than ever before. Modern educated English in America offers a wealth of alternative expressions that educated speech formerly did not permit; but there is a crossfire of hostility rising out of the fact that every speaker of English naturally assumes that his English is good English and that the English which varies from it is bad.

Written usage is a quite different matter, because most writing is done by the educated, whether they have a high level of formal schooling or a high level of informal self-study. The uneducated don't read much, and they don't write. Written usage is much more universal than spoken usage for a number of reasons. It does not closely represent the actual sounds we speak; the words are written about the same the world over. The vocabulary of writing, where it differs from local usage, is common to all educated people concerned with the subject. Where usage is national, regional, or local, the fact is obvious; the reader detects an unfamiliar expression or an unfamiliar significance for a familiar word; if he is wise he treats it very gingerly until he finds out what the author had in mind. Different subjects demand different treatment; writers reaching for different audiences have to respect their readers. The writer has to be somewhat less honest than the speaker in deliberately slanting his writing for the kind of reader he wants to reach. He writes quite coldly and formally, for instance, for college professors on a subject like literature, history, or government. He writes informally or familiarly for college students on a subject like athletics or campus politics. Written usage is a matter of controlled art and artifice, aimed at contributing to a desired impact or impression.

Usage, written or spoken, is structured like any other aspect of language, but the center of the structure for each is himself. To determine how we are going to speak or write, we have to examine ourselves and decide what kind of people we are. Each has to consider his career as a whole, where he began, and where he expects to end. Each has to consider his birth and his upbringing and the kind of people he likes best and wants to associate with. He has to decide where he wants to make himself felt, in familiar local surroundings or among strangers in a different part of the country, possibly among a quite different class of people. He has to decide on the source of his strength and his self-respect, whether it lies in his pride in the people he belongs to or in the learning that has separated him from them.

In the end the best course seems to be to root yourself firmly in your own ground, to try to develop manners of speech and writing that reflect your native dialect without overemphasizing it, that are equal to the subjects which you have to talk or write about, and that are familiar to most people—so that you cover, without affectation, the widest possible range of readers or hearers. No one, as we said before, will package the language and hand it to you. You have to develop the habit of observing speech and writing as different people and different groups and classes use them, so that you can pick your own way. It is a process not of giving up locutions but of enrichment, of adding alternatives, so that you move easily in any company you want to keep.

CHAPTER 29

The Dictionary

ANYONE WHO READS and writes needs reference books: a good modern encyclopedia, a good modern atlas, a good modern cyclopedia of names, an up-to-date almanac, and a good modern dictionary. He can also use some good books of these kinds which are not so modern; and he should think twice about throwing out what he has to make room for something new. It is a lucky person who can find among his father's books any edition of the great *Century Dictionary,* the Merriam-Webster *International Dictionary,* or the Funk and Wagnalls *Standard Dictionary.* It is a fine thing to have the thirteenth or fourteenth edition of the *Encyclopaedia Britannica,* old as they now are, or some travel-worn copies of Baedeker's *Guides* to European countries or cities. If he should come on a copy of Fowler's *Dictionary of Modern English Usage,* any of the Oxford *Companions,* or Mencken's *American Language,* he should hold on to it as a pearl beyond price. Breathes there a man with soul so dead that he can throw out the back files of the *National Geographic Magazine?* He should have his head examined.

These works are what we call "standard." They are productions a cut above the general run of such works; they also represent a heavy investment that should not be dumped as long as you can manage shelf space for them. Whether you have them or not, you need a kind of book which we have called "good" and "modern," that accurately fills in information accumulated since the great reference works were last thoroughly edited. You also need handier guides than most of those we have mentioned, books you can carry around without help. Particularly you need a recent edition of a first-class one-volume desk dictionary that you can keep handy and even lug with you where you go. The newer American dictionaries are more than wordbooks; in this they differ from British dictionaries, and the advantage is mainly on our side. The desk-sized dictionary published in the United States is a much more useful book than you might expect from its name; it substitutes in many ways for the atlas, the cyclopedia of names or biographical dictionary, and even for the encyclopedia.

Dictionaries have long been considered by the self-educated (and what education in the end is not self-education?) the finest single instrument for cultivating the mind. Joe Curran, the tough president of the National Maritime Union, who has contributed much to the self-respect and well-being of the American merchant sailor, once remarked that he had built his career on two books: *Robert's Rules of Order* and a dictionary. In the union hall, surrounded by sea lawyers, he had to become a parliamentarian quick on his feet in order to hold his position. Once he came into conflict and conference with the trained legal minds of the shipping interests, he found himself assailed by coldly precise language with plenty of traps in it for the ignorant. Probably he oversimplified and overstated the matter, but in one way or another he built up a command of vocabulary equal to the needs of his office, and he gave credit to the dictionary. One wonders which one.

We noted earlier two ways of building vocabulary. One is to put your feet down on the ground and let them take you where words are used. The other is to put your body into a chair and your feet up and let books carry you where the body cannot go. In either circumstance you ought to give alert and retentive attention to any word or any combination of words that puzzles you, and reach for the dictionary to see what it stands for. You should let the person or book tell you, if possible, what the word means, exploiting every signal that will give you a clue. Words have meaning in actual use, not dried and hung on hooks in a wordlist. Many capable readers give an unknown word or an off-beat meaning three free throws before they turn to the dictionary. Then they look it up.

This delayed and selective use of the dictionary means that you have to be alert; you have to know when you see a word that you don't understand and that your lack of understanding is important to the meaning. There is no use wasting time on non-recurring vocabulary; the words and meanings you need to know are those you have to live with. Often you can go a long way on an intelligent guess. If you can, do so; any hour you spend in conversation with experts or curled up with a good book is worth several spent chasing words in the dictionary. There is no security like getting your knowledge straight from those who know rather than secondhand.

For many of us, dictionaries seem like monuments and public buildings; they are there, and as far as we know they have always been there. Unless somebody has taken the trouble to orient us and make them come alive, they do not seem to have much personal relation to us. Yet they exist only to serve our needs. The dictionary helps bridge that gap between the personal, local, short-term use of language and the general, universal, permanent language and literature of the English-speaking peoples. Bridging that gap is education, and we spend our lives at it; the dictionary is there to help.

The modern dictionary has come gradually into being during the last five or six centuries. If you have ever studied Latin or another second language, turning your book into a "trot" or "pony" by writing in key words between the lines, then you know how dictionaries began. In the Middle Ages when most books were written in Latin, some readers inserted easier Latin or English words, sometimes in ink, sometimes just pressing the paper with a sharp point in a sneaky way. These interlined additions were called "glosses"; they proved so useful that they were collected into lists called "glossaries."

About 1500 the first glossary was printed, a wordlist with an English word followed by a Latin equivalent. During the next century (the sixteenth) the Island Period of English ended and the Global Period began, as Englishmen broke out into a wider world. One mark of the expansion of interest is a number of English-French, English-Spanish, and English-Italian wordlists—the first foreign-language dictionaries. During the seventeenth century, as a number of writers tried to "enrich" English with Latin and Greek loan words, other writers tried to help the reading public by publishing lists of hard words with their meanings in common English.

The first English book to bear the name "Dictionary" came out in 1538; it was a glossary of hard words.

The first three centuries of English dictionaries produced such books as any educated but untrained person might write today for people who don't understand the hard words in their reading. In the eighteenth century, dictionary writers (technically known as lexicographers) became professional; they took on additional tasks that demanded considerable study. They began to set up their books to answer such questions as these: Of the several ways of spelling a word, which one is the "right" way? How do you divide the word into syllables? What is its history; what form does it originally come from, and what changes has it been through? What evidence in quotations justifies the definition of its meanings? We find a printed form in books, but how do you say the word? Dictionaries which tried to answer these questions were expensive to produce, but they were better than the older ones and soon crowded them out.

The first of this kind was Nathaniel Bailey's *An Universal Etymological Dictionary* (1721), which laid the basis for all subsequent unabridged English dictionaries. Using it as a starting point, Samuel Johnson prepared *A Dictionary of the English Language* (1755), a work of great merit. Moved by patriotism to provide a dictionary containing words and meanings of American origin, as well as the basic English vocabulary and more accurate etymologies, Noah Webster devoted twenty-eight years to the preparation of *An American Dictionary of the English Language* (1828). This monumental work, the last of the great dictionaries prepared by one man without the financial support of a publisher, immediately gained the reputation of being the best available. Already famous for his Spelling Book, originally issued in 1783 and destined to sell by 1900 a total of at least seventy million copies, Webster became even more famous as a dictionary maker. The words *Webster* and *dictionary* became synonymous.

The spelling book and the dictionary were and are the two inescapable basic tools of American education. The dictionary is a much more important tool of education in the United States than in any other nation in the world. The business of producing dictionaries is also a larger, more competitive, and more profitable one than elsewhere. The reasons lie in the nature of the population and

the ideals which stir Americans to provide more and better schools
for their children. These matters we have already discussed, but it
is not out of place to repeat several of them. Our population now
numbers over one hundred and sixty million. To the few million
original English-speaking settlers have been added many more millions of others who have had to learn English as a second language
and to teach their children to speak and write it as their native
language. Most of these newcomers have sought to upgrade themselves and their families. The schools have accepted the challenge,
the greatest one ever imposed upon a school system. Yet the
schools serve only partially in this undertaking. Self-education is
also a vast enterprise. The one indispensable language guide is a
dictionary, the one reference work found in nearly every school-
room, business office, and home. The supplying of this market offers challenges to businessmen, challenges to furnish this necessary
language tool at a low price and with the highest scholarly integrity.
The best current English dictionaries are American in origin because competition has steadily raised the sights of the publishers.

In the eighteenth century the dictionary developed as a commercial venture when a group of booksellers underwrote the cost
of Johnson's *Dictionary*. As the dictionary becomes more expensive to produce—and the money is mostly spent before anything
begins to come in—the actual writer becomes less and less a free
agent. Publishers decide to enter the field; they put up the money
and look around for an editor. The editor hires a staff and goes to
work. The publishers promote the book and take whatever profits
come from its sale. Therefore they want a book that will sell; they
indicate to the editor what kind of book they want. They control
the advertising. New dictionaries become somewhat like new cars,
with changes enough to meet competition but no more changes than
necessary. Dictionaries grow larger because the number of entries
becomes a selling point. Dictionary wars develop, with competition,
price and throat cutting, litigation, claims of authority and counter-
claims of greater authority.

Through this commercial rivalry the form of the modern American dictionary developed, and with it the pattern of modern American dictionary publishing. Webster employed Joseph Worcester to
prepare an abridgment of *An American Dictionary,* and thus in
1830 came into being the first reputable desk dictionary based upon
a larger work. Worcester went on to compile *A Universal and*

Critical Dictionary (1836) to compete with Webster's big book. For the next forty years the Webster interests (owned after 1847 by Merriam) and the Worcester interests fought for a growing market, each bringing out successive improvements, and each trying by selling campaigns and legal action to squeeze the other out. Other publishers entered the field—Century and Funk and Wagnalls in particular—eager to share in the profits of a stable and extensive market. Today a number of large publishing houses either have dictionaries of their own or serve as selling agents for others.

Most publishers do not depend upon a single dictionary but blanket the market with a whole string of books of diminishing quality and price. Merriam-Webster has the longest history; basic to their string of dictionaries is a large "unabridged" reworked at intervals: 1864, 1890, 1909, and most recently 1934. The latest one is the *New International,* Second Edition, with some 600,000 entries. For economy the plates from which the *International* is printed are kept unchanged except for minor corrections; new words are run into supplements. The company expects to give birth to a newer *International* about 1960. Similar "unabridged" dictionaries are the *Century Dictionary* of 1889 and 1909, still the grandest American dictionary ever produced, and the Funk and Wagnalls *New Standard* of 1893 and 1915, which claims 458,000 entries.

Based on the *International* is Merriam-Webster's desk dictionary, the *Collegiate,* with 125,000 entries. The Fifth Edition was first printed in 1936, two years after the second *New International.* The *Collegiate,* too, was economically updated by the use of supplements; but the company, lulled by lack of competition, kept it substantially unchanged until 1949. After the sudden appearance of a strong contender, *The American College Dictionary* (ACD) in 1947, Merriam sold out the remaining copies of the Fifth Edition through department stores and brought out a revision called the *New Collegiate.* In addition to this entry in the field of college and desk dictionaries, Merriam also produces school dictionaries of inferior quality and even a *Pocket Webster* which sells among the quarter books on newsstands.

Funk and Wagnalls maintains a similar string of books based on the *New Standard;* the latest thorough reworking of the *New College Standard* appeared in 1947. It has 145,000 entries. There are various others: the *New Desk Standard* with 100,000 entries and introductory material of use to secretaries and office workers; the *Student's Standard* and the *Desk Standard,* which make thrifty use of older editions by the addition of supplements of new words; and the *Standard Junior* to fit the schoolboy's allowance. The *Century* has not altogether died, for the Century materials were available to *The American College Dictionary* put out in 1947 by Random House (textbook edition by Harper) and to the *American Everyday Dictionary* and the *American Dollar Dictionary*. The *ACD* was edited by Clarence Barnhart, one of the ablest living lexicographers, who then prepared for Scott, Foresman and Co. the *Thorndike-Barnhart Comprehensive Desk Dictionary* with some 80,000 entries and a pocket Permabook *Thorndike-Barnhart* with 37,000 entries which sells at the newsstands.

When somebody says "according to *Webster* . . . ," we may well ask which *Webster* because of the complicated enterprise (some say chicanery) of the dictionary business. Just as the word *dictionary* passed from the title of a particular book to a general name for all such books, so the name *Webster* or *Webster's* entered the public domain quite early in the United States as a synonym for *dictionary*. Furthermore, since copyright to a printed work expires in twenty-eight years (with possible renewal for another twenty-eight), the normal habit of lexicographers of working with one eye on the competitor's product is lifted into the opportunity to steal a whole book. There is also more than one way for the copyright holder to milk his old plates when he brings out a new edition. He can go on printing the old book at a lower price and under another name, or he can sell or lease it to somebody else and sit with piously averted eyes while it rampages as an amazing bargain in the low-priced field.

Merriam, having purchased the copyright to Noah Webster's *American Dictionary* from his heirs, fought again and again in the courts to keep the name *Webster* as the company's private property. In 1917 Merriam came up with a partial victory: a federal court ruled that other publishers using the Webster name on a dictionary must print this warning: "This dictionary is not published by the original publishers of Webster's *Dictionary* or by their successors." By the use of microscopic print in advertising and by depending on dictionary buyers' not glancing at the title page, other publishers managed to nullify the decision pretty well. *Webster* continued to mean *dictionary* to the general public. The name *Webster* in the title has meant prosperity to publishers of some unworthy dictionaries, and its absence failure to some worthy ones. Free right to it has been worth fighting for.

In our lifetime the largest publisher of *Webster* dictionaries outside of Merriam has been the World Publishing Company, a concern which also prints many versions of another work in the public domain, the Holy Bible. World dictionaries and Bibles of all shapes and sizes flood the bookstores, drugstores, and department-store bookshops at prices ranging from forty-nine cents up. By various devices of bookmaking, titling, and promotion, World, concentrating on the low-priced market, placed a *World Webster* of some sort in most American homes. By nearly every standard of lexicography and scholarship these were pretty poor books; one entry described a character in a novel thus: *"Moll Flanders,* a notorious English courtesan of the reign of Charles II; she was a woman of great beauty and accomplishment." One redeeming feature of these inexpensive books was a plain uncluttered page on which the words were defined so simply and so clearly that anyone could read the definitions and understand them. Even college students with bright new desk dictionaries have been known to sneak a look at an old *World Webster* that has always been around the house, confident that it would not swamp them with bigger problems than they brought to it. The editor, an Australian, included for the American housewife a generous measure of Australian Bush slang to widen her cultural horizon.

In 1941 World decided to put out a revision of one of its popular dictionaries. It hired one of the best lexicographers, Joseph Friend, and built up a staff. In 1951 *Webster's New World Dictionary of the American Language* came out in a two-volume Encyclopedic Edition. For this book World successfully asserted its right to the use of Webster in the title. World issued the one-volume College Edition in 1953; the title pages of both editions are free of the disclaimer. When in these days we say "according to Webster . . . ," we should qualify: *Merriam-Webster* is one kind of book, and the *Webster's New World* another and not necessarily inferior kind. But you can consider it likely that any *Webster* bearing the forementioned warning on its title page is an outdated and highly suspect book.

It is almost a relief to turn from the sometimes noble, sometimes

sordid hoo-raw of commercial dictionary publishing to a more enduring and important line of lexicography. About 1850 a group of
British scholars proposed a dictionary of the English language
based on historical principles and on the best linguistic scholarship.
The idea was to give the complete history of every word entered:
its entry into the language, its source, its various spellings, its relations to words in other languages, and its meanings discriminated
carefully and backed by dated quotations. The work was begun at
Oxford University. It was immediately discovered that much of the
evidence lay in libraries in unpublished and often unread manuscripts. The Early English Text Society was organized to edit and
publish the manuscript evidence. Volunteer workers all over the
world undertook to read and cull out on slips all English words in
the sentences where they were used; some six million of these slips
were then worked over by the editors. The first fascicle (a group of
leaves bound together) came out in 1884 and the last in 1928. A
one-volume supplement was issued in 1933. Known today usually
as the *Oxford English Dictionary* (*OED*), this collaborative work
of ten massive volumes is the greatest dictionary in any language.

The *Oxford English Dictionary* was followed immediately in
1934 by the *Shorter Oxford* in two volumes, and there is also a
Concise Oxford. The *OED* was not intended to be a finished product but an essay at recording continuing investigations. In the direct
line of linguistic studies, the general treatment of the language in
the big book was to be bolstered by studies of specific periods and
areas. The first of these, *A Dictionary of American English on Historical Principles,* edited by Sir William Craigie, was published by
the University of Chicago in 1944 in four volumes, and a two-
volume *Dictionary of Americanisms,* edited by Mitford M. Ma-
thews, came out in 1951. Dictionaries of Older and Later Scottish
are in progress, and at the University of Michigan (to which the
earlier files of the *OED* have been moved) the first fascicles of the
Middle English Dictionary, edited by Hans Kurath, have been
printed.

These books are important and you can buy them or use them
in libraries, but they represent something more important. They
are products of the scholarship of thousands of language specialists
scattered throughout the colleges and universities of the English-
speaking world. More important than the books are the articles and
notes which appear in scholarly periodicals recording the docu-

mented investigations of experts into the English language. Most important to all lexicography are the experts themselves, teachers and scholars whose brains and experience are available for the making of dictionaries. Files and permanent staffs maintained by commercial publishers do not necessarily lead to superior dictionaries. The staffs brought together for particular projects and dissipated again when the work is done are free to apply the most modern developments, and they have the resources of the whole scholarly world to draw on. They are not hampered by previous investments in type or plates; they are not tied to tradition; they tackle the problems with fresh minds and with the disciplined devotion to scholarly standards which marks their professional life. They want good dictionaries for their students; they realize that only commercial publishers can put up the money (which runs these days to a million dollars for a college edition); and they set to work to see that each new book is the best that can be done.

From this sketch of dictionary making we can see something of the real nature of a dictionary. No one book can be a "supreme authority" on every word or usage in the English language. The claim of authority is an exaggeration, and those who make it are not the working lexicographers but promoters eager to recover their investment and begin to count the profits. The dictionary is not even about speech; it is a record of words that have appeared in print; it tells something about how they have been spelled and what they have been used to mean. Making a dictionary is such a long and difficult project that it is a little out of date even before it gets into print. The book is limited in size whether it runs to 20,000 words or half a million; the treatment of each entry must be brief. The editors must decide what words to put in and leave out, which spellings, pronunciations, and meanings to put in and which to leave out. Is a word or meaning so old that it can be dropped or so new and probably temporary that it can be ignored? How much of its history is significant to the modern reader? Each decision is a compromise between the desirable and the possible. The result is an essay in history, in only a limited sense an authority.

Any influence that tries to set a book or a man up as an unquestionable authority is a hindrance to a full intellectual life; we ought to have such an ingrown alarm system to alert us as the scientist keeps always fully charged; his statements only hold for the evidence that has been observed. He leaves himself an out in case new evidence turns up that forces him to go back and reconsider everything he has said. "Guess those sheep have been sheared," says a man walking along a country road. "Looks like it from this side," says the cautious scientific spirit. Studies of sound and meaning have already outmoded the treatments of our most respected dictionaries and brought about much more realistic and useful books than older ones; their full effect is still to be seen. We use the dictionary of today as we heed any older and wiser head: as a guide to be trusted as long as it really seems to know what it is doing, a guide to be questioned when common sense and experience tells us that the advice is no good.

The most immediate and frequent use of a dictionary in reading is to check up an unfamiliar word or meaning after exploiting every structural signal and every clue of context. Reading varies from a romantic novel in which exotic words are used to give a generalized feeling-tone (**kraal, jalousie, assagai, spoor;** the **space-ghouls** and **psychotherms** of science fiction) and need no looking up, to a poem in which each word bears its exact share of the meaning and must be exactly grasped. Somewhere between these two falls the Latin-Greek vocabulary of cultivated discourse, sometimes laid on brazenly for the effect rather than the substance of erudition, and sometimes as carefully chosen as bits of glass in a cathedral window. The dictionary should be handy but not leaned on; it is best to read quickly and alertly to the end of a section or chapter, trusting to the author to make himself generally clear. A second reading picks up what is unfamiliar, but if the matter is scientific or technical, it is best to turn in another book to the chapter covering the same material. Some writers are so clumsy that plodding over their limping prose is hopeless. Still, you may be left with a residue that sends you to the dictionary.

A thorough acquaintance with your own dictionary is essential. Different dictionaries present word-meanings in different orders, and your object is to get quickly to the meaning that you need. The order followed in the Merriam-Webster dictionaries is historical: the oldest meanings are presented first. Unfortunately some of these may be archaic or obsolete; you will have to jump them to get the living senses of the word. (*Obsolete* in a dictionary means no longer used by anybody, but found in older literature; *archaic* means passing out of use but not quite dead.) To avoid the bodies of dead meanings, most dictionaries list definitions in the order of currency, giving commoner senses first. *Winston, Funk and Wag-nalls,* the *ACD,* and the *Thorndike-Barnhart* do it this way, with some loss, because the development of the meaning-range of a word is part of its meaning. The *Webster's New World* uses a modified historical order, giving older senses first as long as they are living and current today and tacking obsolete and archaic meanings on at the end. You should scan the whole list of meanings in order to fix the word in your mind in its semantic range, then pick the one that fits the structure of the sentence and the other words in it.

Language in use, as we have seen, is a dynamic form of action by which whole utterances are produced; writing is a form of action correlated to speech. In utterances and sentences all the elements are held in suspension until the end releases the meaning. The whole sentence assigns meanings to the words in it, generally giv-ing each word a meaning picked somewhere within the range of the past use. Dictionaries try to present that range in reasonable completeness as briefly as possible. Dictionaries operate by a con-vention that a group of other words, which may be substituted for the word you are looking up, has the same meaning. Thus for **father** we find 'male parent'; but if we substitute **male parent** for **father** in **My father sent me home,** we get **My male parent sent me home.** Who would say that? It sounds like a Martian talking by the book. One dictionary printed in 1834 met this problem by not defining at all; it gave the word in quotations which illustrated its use.

There used to be an ad for bouillon cubes which took some liberty with fact and showed a whole living steer being compressed into a single cube. The entry in a dictionary has the same relation to the word as a unit of living expression; it is condensed, com-pressed, and quite dead. Yet it gives the essence of the meaning; and where in your reading you encounter a word without previous experience with it, the dictionary may patch up the hole in the sentence well enough to get you over it. We ask of the dictionary treatment that it be accurate, as complete as possible, and so clearly expressed that we can turn quickly back to our reading with what we have learned.

Dictionaries differ in their accuracy and their completeness, but they differ most in the clarity of their expression. The phrasing of the definition is the point at which the dictionary, as teacher, stands between scholarship—what is known about the word by experts—

and the puzzled reader seeking information. Defining must walk between two extremes of futility: the concisely erudite and the concisely oversimplified. The dictionary writer is a scholar who has to master his material in the language of the specialists, if he is not actually a specialist called in to do the vocabulary of his field. He may define **manatee** as 'an aquatic herbivorous mammal,' an expression structurally simple and verbally exact. From the reader's viewpoint, this may be an invitation to look up two or three other words after **manatee.** This same editor defines **combine** as 'combination' and **combination** as 'a combining'; then to clarify he adds, 'a union or aggregate made by combining persons or things together so as to effect a purpose,' repeating **combining** and using the words **aggregate** and **effect. Effect** is a troublesome word which is not distinguished from **affect** in sound in common speech and often not in meaning. Yet the language is exact, if you know it. Even a simple word like **come** can be translated into hard words: 'to move hitherward; approach . . . ; to appear or arrive . . . ; to issue as by birth, emanation, development.' The same dictionary, the *New Collegiate,* defines **pedant:** 'one who makes a display of learning either in ostentation or in unduly emphasizing minutiae; a formalist or precisionist in teaching or scholarship.' It stabs itself with that one; you might describe these definitions as little notes from expert to expert; you have to know what they are about to know what they are about.

The other extreme of futility which awaits the maker of definitions is oversimplification, the use of simple structures with words so common that they need discrimination. Thus **machete** is defined as 'a large, heavy knife used esp. in Latin American countries as both a tool and a weapon.' How large and how heavy? If you have never seen a machete, you would like to know. This is a main vice of the cheaper dictionaries; they seem to define without informing. Desk dictionaries are reasonably free from this fault. The need to omit increases as the space decreases and shows up not merely in unintelligibly compact treatments but in the omission of entries and of meanings for words entered.

One point at which the scholar whose main business is teaching can bring his experience to bear on dictionary writing is here in the phrasing of definitions. Any staff which is properly financed can gather the facts which the theory behind the dictionary demands and present them accurately. But scholars drawn directly from the classroom temper their information to what they know their students can take in; they bring a special gift to the reader: concise, clear definition of entries in words he already knows. Thus **manatee** is defined as 'any of several large, plant-eating aquatic mammals living in shallow tropical waters near the coasts of North and South America and West Africa. . . .' **Conjecture** is defined as 'guesswork; inferring, theorizing, or predicting from incomplete or uncertain evidence.' A **reprobate** is 'a depraved, vicious person.' A **retinue** is 'a group of persons in the service of, or in attendance on, a person of rank.' A **pedant** is '1. a person who lays unnecessary stress on minor or trivial points of learning, displaying a scholarship lacking in judgment or sense of proportion. 2. a narrow-minded teacher who insists on exact adherence to a set of arbitrary rules.' The definition for **come** begins: 'to move from a place thought of as "there" to or into a place thought of as "here." '

This treatment of hard words explained by easy ones came into modern dictionaries most notably in the *Winston's Simplified Dictionary* of 1926 and is continued in the *ACD, Thorndike-Barnhart,* and the *Webster's New World.* The definitions in the preceding paragraph are from *Webster's New World Dictionary; Winston* is briefer, more compact, a little more crowded, but neat. *ACD* is a little less rigorous than *World* in staying within the vocabulary of common use, but still understandable without a great deal of chasing up other words, with a style terse, clipped, and clean.

Quite apart from simplicity, though not from clarity, is another quality that definitions may or may not have, the quality of "grace." Grace is rather difficult to define, but we find a touch of it in the definition of **pedant** above. It is an aptness and charm of phrasing that comes into the dictionary when the definer is not merely a "useful drudge" but a lover, cultivator, and manipulator of words who can turn off a striking phrase. Samuel Johnson had grace and Noah Webster had it. Johnson's grace was baroque: Webster's spare and strict like a New England church. The *Century* dictionaries had grace; obviously their authors were literary men and stylists. If you have the *Century* at hand, you look at it first, for the fun of it. Grace lights up the *Winston,* in which we find under **geocentric theory:** 'the theory held by ancient philosophers, that the earth is the center of the universe and of divine solicitude.' Grace is a constant satisfaction in the British *Wyld's Universal* and in *Webster's New World,* whose editors were creative writers and stylists before and after they turned their hands to lexicography.

One of the early discoveries of language study was the remarkable continuity of words. Completely new formations are so rare that we can trace most modern words back through centuries of continuous use; sound-changes are so regular that we can build up within a language and between languages whole families of related forms. Dictionaries began early to include these word-histories in their entries; it has often been thought that knowledge of word-origins is a key to the "real" or "correct" meanings of words in modern use. We have seen that a word means what its users take it to mean; its "real" meaning is the sense it has in a specific utterance. Nevertheless the history of a word tells us much about its range and deepens our sense of what we can do with it. Only the cheapest dictionaries, therefore, omit these word-histories or etymologies; desk and unabridged dictionaries include them.

This old aspect of language study, etymology, has a wide appeal, for the love of words as words is widespread; we are still very close to the name-magic which is a primitive response to words. Etymology is thus one of the best established studies with more solid information stored than the more modern study of structures has. Etymology is a collaborative effort among language scholars everywhere, each publishing a bit of historical lore that goes into the common treasure, correcting earlier guesses, pinning down origins, filling in gaps. Only a dull graduate student in English has not settled some problem left dangling in the *OED* or added some new information. In such well-supported enterprises as the *Middle English Dictionary* the advance is massive. The knowledge is public, and all language scholars are trained to handle it.

Thus the difference between first-class dictionaries in the treatment of word-histories is a matter of presentation, except that later books will pin down a few details unknown to earlier writers. In most desk dictionaries the etymologies are given but in a perfunctory way. Only the *ACD* and *Webster's New World* differ significantly; the *ACD* undertook to reappraise and modernize all etymologies; then, impressed by the length of the entries necessary for all this, the editors set out the information in a shorthand (*t.* for *taken from; g.* for *going back to;* etc.) with a key on the bottom of the page. The result is a set of technical-looking notes. *Webster's New*

World gives space to a full treatment of native and foreign words in the light of recent studies, carrying them back, where possible, to Indo-European roots and down through their changing forms in English to the point where the definitions of current meanings pick up the story. In the Merriam-Webster *New Collegiate, Winston,* and *Webster's New World* the etymologies come before the definitions; in *Funk and Wagnalls* and the *ACD* they are printed at the end of the entry.

The handling of pronunciation is another matter on which dictionaries differ. British dictionaries give British pronuncations of the so-called Received Standard; American dictionaries give American pronunciations with an occasional stab at important British differences also. Earlier American books took the cultivated speech of New England as a standard, ignoring or merely sketching the pronunciation of other identified dialects. The *Merriam-Webster* dictionaries, *Funk and Wagnalls,* and *Winston,* all with a heavy investment in this tradition, still favor New England pronunciation; the *ACD, Thorndike-Barnhart,* and *Webster's New World,* mindful of some eighty million Americans living west of the Connecticut River and north of the Ohio (the largest body of English-speaking people using one reasonably consistent dialect), use "General American" as their base. These books treat New England, South Midland, and the Southern and Western dialects as variants, and lump North Midland into General American. Present scholarly knowledge of American dialects far outruns anything that has got into any dictionary, because this is a rapidly developing branch of language study.

All the dictionaries indicate pronunciation by respelling entry-words in a different alphabet. The *Merriam-Webster* treatment is old-fashioned, dating back to a period when phoneticians were riding high. We have noticed before how delicately attuned a phonetician's ear can become to finely discriminated sounds; this alphabet and its diacritical marks treat each word as if it were to be spoken separately and slowly by a cultivated New Englander much influenced by the spelling. It ignores the overshortening of lightly accented syllables and the overlengthening of syllables bearing stress. It is cumbersome and unrealistic, and it is unacceptable to modern speech analysts. *Winston* generally follows *Merriam.* The Funk and Wagnalls *New College Standard* gets along with little respelling; its "Emphatype" system of pronouncing uses small capitals and underlining such as newspapers with a single font of type have to get by with. It brushes off modern linguistic scholarship to pursue a more eccentric line.

The *ACD, Thorndike-Barnhart,* and *Webster's New World,* besides trying to base their pronunciations on those used by most Americans, show some reflection of the phonemic principle. They respell words in simple alphabets that are not hard to grasp. The *ACD* and *Thorndike-Barnhart* borrow the symbol /ə/ from the phonetic and phonemic alphabets to represent the centered vowel in unaccented syllables; *Webster's New World* uses /ə/ in the same way and also borrows /ŋ/ for the final sound in **sing** and **wrong.** For other sounds requiring special signs the three dictionaries use double letters which are mainly quite familiar. They illustrate pronunciations with key words that permit speakers of various dialects to work in terms of their own sound-systems and come fairly easily to a general notion of how a word is said in their speech. All the dictionaries print the International Phonetic Alphabet (IPA) and relate it to their own respellings in the preface, but none has risked introducing this or a genuinely phonemic key. Possibly Merriam, now preparing a new *International,* will feel brave enough to go phonemic.

Ease of reference is another aspect of dictionaries that makes one more useful than another. The handiest system is a single alphabetical listing with an adequate treatment for each item; abbreviations, geographical names, foreign words and phrases, given names, and synonyms and antonyms run right in with the basic wordlist. *Webster's New World,* in an effort to make each entry as self-contained and self-explanatory as possible, uses perhaps the least cross reference; it has a separate listing only for colleges and universities, arranged, unfortunately, by states. If you don't know what state Baylor University is in, you had better look it up in the *New Collegiate,* where the listing is alphabetical. *ACD* offers only in its trade edition a separate listing of given names; in its place in the textbook edition sold by Harper are listed colleges and universities. These, too, are arranged by states. *Thorndike-Barnhart* offers a single inclusive alphabetical listing. *Funk and Wagnalls* lists abbreviations and geographical names separately; *Winston* runs abbreviations into the main list, but has separate listings for persons, places, and foreign words and phrases. Merriam-Webster, using separate listings except for foreign words and phrases, requires a great deal of cross reference; all this, with the big words in the definitions, makes a foray into the *New Collegiate* quite a treasure hunt.

When you buy the latest printing of a dictionary, how up-to-date is it? There is really no way for the casual buyer to tell, since promoters have charge of selling the books, and there is no sign that the ethical level of the dictionary trade has made any substantial rises. Everybody claims to have the latest, and only *Webster's New World* does not announce itself as the supreme or absolute authority or something like it. Three factors which the publishers are very cagy about announcing determine the actual up-to-dateness of these books: 1) the date of editing of the basic book or the last thorough revision of it; 2) the date of the last thorough re-editing of the dictionary, especially if it is an abridgment; 3) the extent of updating that is actually done during re-editing and in successive printings. All the publishers maintain standing type and correct obvious errors between printings; they introduce death dates of defunct celebrities and to some extent follow the newspapers as persons and places come to public attention.

Merriam-Webster revises the *International* at about twenty-five year intervals; the last major re-editing was issued in 1934. Between times as successive printings come out, new words are entered in a supplement bound in with the old wordlist, but separate. Funk and Wagnalls handles the big *Standard* the same way; the last major re-editing came out in 1915. The *New Collegiate* and the *New College Standard* are abridgments of the big books—that is, selections of the material in them. To the extent that they rest on the big books, they cannot be up-to-date; to the extent that they depart from them, they may well be. Each major editing job is dated; it represents the theory of its period and lays down the ground rules by which the permanent staffs proceed until a new revision brings in new ideas and sets new rules. Before 1949 the *Collegiate* was updated by supplements. This practice was first challenged by *Winston,* which introduced simplified defining in 1926 and kept its plates open not merely for corrections but for new words, new definitions, and redefinitions. It was an excellent book for that day, prepared by a distinguished staff. The *New Collegiate* was issued in 1949 with the obvious mark of the *International* on it. Criticized severely for its definitions of linguistic terms (substantially the same as in the *Collegiate* of 1936), the Merriam editors quietly redefined some terms and entered others, so that in printings since 1951 their treatment in this field is unsurpassed. The *New Collegiate* now makes a direct exploitation of the files being built up for the next *International,* with new words and new treatments entered at each printing. Funk and Wagnalls first issued the *New College Standard* in 1947 with its eccentric system of pronunciation; it runs new words into a supplement still.

The *ACD* came out as a totally new book in 1947, prepared by an able editor and a staff of linguistic scholars. *Webster's New World* came out in 1951 and 1953—a new book brilliantly edited on modern principles. The *Thorndike-Barnhart* came out in 1951, also a new book—too limited in the wordlist for general use but modern in treatment. These three books embody modern developments in language studies in their basic handling; they are in keeping with the views of language which we have presented here; they are much less "bookish" in their approach than the others, frankly accepting English as the instrument of expression of a whole nation communicating within itself.

There is a difference between an aggressive updating carried on by an alert staff and a perfunctory inclusion of enough new words to justify a new copyright. As far as one can tell at the moment, *Webster's New World* and *Thorndike-Barnhart* each has an excellent editor and sufficient staff to make each new printing a substantial improvement over earlier printings, with new entries and new senses for old entries following close on their introduction into the national vocabulary. *World* is away in advance in handling word-groups and current idioms. The Merriam-Webster *New Collegiate,* after a disappointing beginning and handicapped by archaic notions of language which put a strait jacket on its development, is now accepting the challenge of a changing language. The next edition of the *International* may well find itself based on the *New Collegiate,* where experiment and adaptation is in the end less costly. Updating in the *ACD, The New College Standard,* and the *Winston* at present seems comparatively minor.

Editors wisely give a great deal of thought to the introductions in their dictionaries, but readers unwisely give little attention to them. Each includes a guide to the book which should be read with care. The *Merriam-Webster* guide to pronunciation though somewhat old-fashioned was for years a classic. *Winston* offers a neat description of the language; *Webster's New World* a history, description, and analysis which is excellent though quite technical. *World* also includes a good brief history of dictionaries. The *ACD* offers a group of essays on etymology, pronunciation, and usage. *Winston* is the most truly encyclopedic of all these books, with color plates, charts, and tabular treatments of various matters, and even an atlas of the world with a number of maps in color. Obviously there is a great deal of useful matter in these books besides the wordlists (as we show in the chart below); just as obviously it is skipped by most readers, who pick the book up and flip it open to a particular word. Who reads the preface to the dictionary? Only the wise.

In the following display of the dictionaries we have discussed, the six books are lined up from left to right in the order of their overall quality and utility as we evaluate them. *World* seems definitely superior on most counts, with *ACD* a close second choice. Both are excellent books. If neither is available, the *New Collegiate* is the next choice; then *Winston* and finally the *New College Standard*. These books all run around five dollars without thumb-indexing; about six dollars with it. If you can only spend three dollars for a dictionary, the *Thorndike-Barnhart* is the only lower-priced book worth having. It is well to budget a dollar or two a year for dictionaries and add a new one now and then as some new effort is made to apply the latest linguistic theory to illuminating the written or printed word.

A steady, thoughtful employment of a good dictionary to steer us over the rough spots in our reading is a good thing, just as any persistent effort to learn about language and its working is good. A notebook at hand to enter puzzling words and their definitions can aid persons for whom writing helps to fix information in the mind, but can handicap persons whose memories abandon responsibility for what is committed to paper. Each of us proceeds most safely and most successfully in his own way to convert words casually encountered into useful instruments of his own thought and expression. No one should allow himself to be panicked into a desperate and hasty effort to "build vocabulary" by trying to pack words into his head.

Our relations with words are somewhat similar to our relations with people. The world is full of people we do not care about be-

SIX COLLEGE AND DESK DICTIONARIES

	WNW	ACD	NCD	WSD	FWCS	T-B
Entries	142,000	132,000	125,000	100,000	145,000	80,000
Illustrations	1200		2300	3000	1000	750
Pronunciation	x	x	x	x		
New Words	text	text	text	text	x	text
Abbreviations	text	text	x	text	x	text
Places (Gazetteer)	text	text	x	x	text	text
Persons (Biographical Names)	text	text	x	x	text	text
Foreign Words and Phrases	text	text	text	x		text
Synonyms and Antonyms	text	text	text	text		text
Preparation of Copy	x	x				
Guide to Usage	x	x				text
Spelling	x	x	x			
Capitals	x	x				x
Punctuation	x	x				x
Signs and Symbols	x		x	text		
Weights and Measures	x		text	x	text	
Given Names	text	x (Trade ed.)	x		text	
Rhymes			x			
Letter Writing						x
Forms of Address	x					x
Colleges and Universities	x	x (Coll. ed.)	x			
Description of English	x					x
History of English	x			x		
History of Dictionaries	x					
Chronological Table			x			
Atlas				x		
Table of Alphabets	x	x	x	x	text	
Color Plates					x	
Number of Pages	36; 1724	40; 1432	22; 1174	20; 1276	18; 1406	32; 869

In the chart "text" means that the matter is handled within the main wordlist or dictionary proper, x means that the items are given a separate treatment before or after the main wordlist. The final line gives the number of pages of introductory matter, followed by the number of pages containing main entries.

cause they do not touch us in any meaningful way. We recognize a good many people in the situations where we meet them: they ride the same buses with us or shop in the same stores, but we would not know them elsewhere. We call a smaller number of people our acquaintances; we speak to them, do business with them, and interchange some slight effect upon one another. Then there is our circle of friends and relatives with whom we have direct interaction and about whom we care. A person can make his way gradually from the mass of utterly unknown persons into the passing and barely noticed throng, into the broad circle of acquaintances, and so into the intimacy of friendship or family relations. Or a person unknown one day can move directly into close personal contact on the next; an example familar enough is what we call "love at first sight." It depends, as we say, on the situation.

Something like this happens with words. Riffling the pages of a dictionary, we find it full of words that we do not care about and probably never will. We brush a good many words somewhere in our reading or our experience; our only real chance of meeting them is to read over the same pages in the same book or a similar one on the same subject. Always around the fringes of our memory such words linger; we know them because we recognize them; we have seen or heard them before. We could not quite say what they mean. A smaller number of words have meaning for us in sentences that have meaning as a whole; a person may read **the several states** without ever coming to grips with the meaning here of **several,** or **taking for granted** without a distinct notion of what **granted** might mean by itself. This is our "recognition" vocabulary; it consists, in part, of words we say or write in set phrases that come to mind as a whole. Then there is a smaller stock of words that we could in a pinch define. This is our "recall" vocabulary, the words we habitually speak or write. Like persons, words may make their way gradually from beyond our experience and interest into the recognition vocabulary and then into the stock of our active expression; or they may come directly and suddenly into frequent use in our speech and writing. It depends on the situation.

Vocabulary building was summed up in a famous epigram by Francis Bacon: "Reading maketh a full man, writing a profound man, and conversation a ready man." Bacon did not think of poring over a dictionary as a way to build a man, perhaps because dictionaries were not much in his day. Reading stores our minds with words in contexts; the earlier we begin reading, the more words we come to know. As we have pointed out, experience also stores our minds with words in contexts. Each word stands alone when we first grasp it, but time shakes it down in our minds with other words so that our sense of its relationships widens. It enters families of sound and meaning and takes a place in each family which no other word quite shares. Here the dictionary is of use because it gives us concisely the areas in which the word has meaning faster than its normal random occurrence gives them. It thus lets time begin its operation a little earlier; the earlier we can fix words within our span of attention the better. But we have to let time have its way with us.

We let time have its way by not pressing matters. It is best, therefore (in spite of all contrary advice), to speak and write the words that come spontaneously to mind when the mind is on a particular subject. A word can come to mind without actually occurring to us; we get so far into a sentence and then hang up; we know there is an exact word, but it won't come. Better wait. If we reach in the dictionary for some new and only half-understood word, we may use it in some off-beat way, so that we either don't convey anything or we raise a smile—which is in some ways worse. In the private leisure of writing we have a larger "recall vocabulary" than we have for speaking, because we have more time to dredge words up from the deep recesses of the memory. In speech or writing we do well to depend on the words that come by themselves and do not spend much time riffling through a wordlist for a fancier vocabulary. We can sound like fakes when our thoughts wear somebody else's clothes.

Writing makes a profound person—if we write much for our own practice, satisfaction, and self-discovery—by letting us discover who we are and what we know. Part of what we know is the words that have filtered into our store and have lain in the mind long enough to be at home there. In vocabulary building we are always working like squirrels for the need to come, putting fresh green kernels away while we live on the harvest of other years. When someone commands us to write, we face the test, provided for only so well as we have provided for ourselves in all our lives up to the moment. We can't save the situation by a wild dive into the dictionary.

Conversation makes a ready man because the interchange of

talk is the life of language. We began with conversation, and we will end with it. As we enter upon new experiences and tackle new subjects, we need to talk so as to fix the terminology in our memory and our muscles. We need to put ourselves in the company of people who are also interested in these subjects, and join in the conversation. The talk forces us to put to use the words we have met; the reactions of companions give us a quick test of how well we have grasped word-meanings. That is why college life with all its distractions is a good situation for learning. Where else will you find people interested in a step-by-step introduction to a subject? Out of college, people are either well past the preliminaries and no longer interested in anyone else's halting first efforts, or they do not know anything about the matter and do not care.

Your dictionary serves effectively as a guide and companion to your experience and your reading, stabilizing new words in their relations as you take them in. It should be a companion in a real sense, with you and at hand wherever possible. In your talking and writing, the dictionary also has its value but not as an original source of new words. It can police your use of words, telling you whether the word that occurs to you is actually fit for what you want to say; and it can tell you how to spell the word. It cannot feed you a supply of apt terminology that will make you a fascinating phrasemaker. If anything can do that, it is last year's, last month's, last week's, last night's reading of some significant book or article. The dictionary can be the reader's constant guide but merely the writer's occasional friend.

✳ CHAPTER 30 ✳

The Language of Business

NO MATTER what career a young person in school or college chooses for himself today, he can be sure that one part of his career will choose him. Set his sights as low or as high as he will—day labor, semiskilled or skilled labor, white-collar work (clerical or executive), teaching, art, writing, music, law, medicine, engineering, science, social work, national defense, government—it does not matter. Sooner or later the American business system touches every man and woman, and each has to deal with it. Even early marriage no longer removes women from contact with business, for in the management of family finances women control most of the spending for consumer goods. Many married women hold jobs until they have children, and again between children. Women retire as mothers in their forties and turn to outside work to fill their lives; chances are that they will outlive their husbands by seven years, during which they have to manage their own affairs. No matter what we do or how we live, we spend a good part of our lives doing business.

This is an era in which business means organization—the organization of people, machines, materials, and finances toward one end, one purpose. That end is efficiency, doing the work as quickly, cheaply, and effectively as it can be done. Almost two hundred

million people now live well on a continent that once barely sup-
ported four or five million Indians in hardship and peril. Most
Americans live in cities which can exist only because life in cities
is highly organized; it is not magic that brings the people to their
jobs in the morning and home at night, that stocks the stores with
food and clothing, provides the coal, oil, gas, and electricity for
heating the houses and cooking the food. It is organization. Every
day the ordinary American is affected by dozens of organized activities that have been developed from very small beginnings over
the last three centuries, each one there and functioning as long as it
is efficient and because it is efficient. Let it lose its efficiency, and
it is soon disintegrated and swamped by some other organization
that is more efficient.

The whole business runs on money. What is bought is bought
with money and what is sold is sold for money, whether it is a
piece of land, something grown, mined, or manufactured, or the
services of someone's hands or brains. Artists paint for money,
writers write for money, doctors doctor for money, soldiers fight for
money, churches tithe for money, charities solicit money, governments tax for money. Everybody takes his pay and turns around
and pays again. Money is the blood of the system. You might
dream of a self-sufficient life, like Thoreau's at Walden Pond, growing your own food and making your own clothes; but somehow it
seems a fuller, richer life to get into the flow of money deep enough
to get by, and take money into your hand and pay it out like the
others. And so you get a job and take your check like the rest. The
money depends on business, not merely what we think of as buying
and selling, but business as a way of life.

Business touches us all. If you have anything to do that is like
anything done in business, it is done best the business way. If you
write, you write fast and well with a typewriter—the basic business
machine. If you count many small and simple figures, you do it
best with an adding machine; if you count in large, complicated
figures, you do it with Univac or something like it. If you handle
money, as in a charity or a tax office, you do it the business way
with business machines. If you handle people, as in a university or
an army camp, you use personnel records and an IBM machine;
you "streamline your procedures" to increase efficiency and save
money. You mechanize, mechanize, mechanize, whether with self-
opening doors or with self-loading ships, self-operating elevators or

self-tripping timers. You may not call in the businessman in person except for his advice, but you carry on the most humane and humanitarian activities most efficiently and most cheaply his way. You save your own hands and brains for what is important for you to get done, whether it is putting out a college yearbook, searching for a rich man to endow an art museum, or computing the statistics on a polio serum adminstered to second-graders in school.

If money is the lifeblood of business, the nerve is language. Every business suffers in one way or another from disease in this nerve. Every corporation, no matter how successful it seems, confesses itself to be in trouble in its communication in one of three aspects. One of these is passing the word from top to bottom and bottom to top. A person afflicted in the same way would be slow to feel pain in his hand and slow to pull his hand away. The second is passing the word among units at the same level—from person to person, office to office, from branch to branch. A person afflicted in this way would not be able to let his right hand know what his left hand does. And the third is passing the word from the organization to the outsiders—to other organizations and to the public. A person afflicted in this way would strangle on his own words, with intelligence shining in his eyes and a stammer coming from his mouth. A person afflicted in all these ways would be a spastic, and a community of such persons would be a mental hospital. Business has outgrown its nervous system—communication. Business is still growing, and is looking rather desperately for ways of improving the flow of information without which it cannot thrive.

Thus the administrator, sitting in his office, writes a memorandum that flutters from desk to desk among his subordinates, signifying nothing. The research laboratory submits reports that only the person who wrote them can understand. In a public utility an order goes out setting up a new procedure; on the basis of that order, five different powerhouses set up five different procedures. Thus in the Army Ordnance Corps one department consigns to the junkpile surplus switches which another department has on order and cannot get. Automobile dealers report defective brakes on a new car and continue to correct the same defect on the next year's model. A union goes out on strike to correct an abuse which has kept its men sullen for years but never was mentioned to top management by the personnel director. Thus American business in general has had to confess failure in its fantastically expensive effort to "sell" the "business point of view" to the American public. Thus the U.S. submarine service enters World War II with torpedoes that submariners know won't track down a target and won't explode if they do. "Now hear this—" says the loudspeaker. Is anybody listening? No. Nobody listening.

However bad this news is to the nation at large (the mere thought of its cost in money is appalling), it can be good news to the intelligent student in college. If communication depends on language, then a failure in communication is a failure in the use of language. Somebody doesn't get the word. The student in college is in a good position because he is in a position to learn. The college may or may not be able to teach him the knowledge that is important in his field, and that knowledge may or may not still be worth something when he gets out. The college can give him something that will stay with him the rest of his life, whatever he does and wherever he goes—a command of his language. Then when he speaks or writes he communicates what he has to say in such a way that it is heeded. Then he will be of value to business, and it will have a place for him. Business is the interaction of human beings; the means of their interaction is language. If the college student will put his mind to it, he can develop a control of English that will serve him well in business.

The language used in business depends very much on what it is used for: who originates the communication, what it is about, and whom it goes to. There is of course a kind of communication which is largely mechanized and consists of the forms that accompany people and things through the organization, such as orders, invoices, and trace slips of various kinds for things; time cards and personnel records for people. If we think of a corporation as a living body, then this is the "autonomic nervous system" which keeps the heart beating and the lungs pulsing even while the conscious mind sleeps. Girls with machines take care of most of it; machines will soon handle all of it.

Then there is the communication that passes upward from small shot to big shot, from workman to foreman, from foreman to manager, from manager to superintendent, and so on up. This is like the sensory nervous system in a living body that tells the brain what the limbs are feeling and how they are doing. It is a flow of information, often from the less articulate to the more articulate, and usually from the more specialized person to the less specialized. The person who originates it is concerned with a specific problem which may be a small thing in itself but is what occupies his time. It often passes through very sluggish channels, partly because the person who originates it is inept at saying what he means and partly because each person who gets it has many things to think about. It could be the report of a testing laboratory on a product or material the company is thinking of buying. It could be an appeal for promotion. It could be a summary of a recommended change in method, a report by a salesman or a sales manager. Its direction is upward, from the less important person to the more important.

Inability to do the writing for this kind of communication can nip a promising career before its starts. Like most upward communication, it must be formal, relatively impersonal, and relatively respectful. By formal we mean that it imitates the tone which has been established in the organization for this kind of message. It must be clear, brief, factual, and definite. It ought to be honest in what it says, and what it says ought to be on the subject. If the writer has any side remarks to make on the way the company is run, he should save them for his wife. Upward messages should be written in the consciousness that they will fall in with other communications of the same kind from other persons or units on the same level. The writer probably knows more about this particular matter than the reader; he should make a point of telling the reader what will get the point across. Where he cannot avoid the jargon of the expert, he should translate it. If graphs, charts, or pictures will make the point easier to grasp, he should include them. "Brief me," says the boss. Well, brief him. If you do this job well, you may move up with your message to that heaven of all specialists—a job where you no longer do the work but direct the people who do it.

Flowing from the top down, from big shot to small shot, is the communication that gets things done. It is like the efferent nerves in a living body that move the limbs at the command of the brain. This flow of command moves generally from the more articulate to the less articulate; the person who originates it usually has more education, more experience, and more varied experience than the person who receives it. It seems easy—just tell them what to do and let them do it. But the transmission line is like a funnel; more can get in at the top than can get out at the bottom. The matter varies. It could be a simple order to start up the machines. It could be a directive to do a certain task in a certain way, but the directive may vary from assigning a man to his job for the day to setting a policy for a department, branch, or agency. This kind of communication must bring about exactly the kind of action that the originator intends and not something else.

Inability to do this writing can keep an otherwise competent man in minor positions throughout his life. The writing that goes up can assume that the reader is able to handle the language of the educated and can appraise the message on the basis of a more general grasp of the situation than the writer has. The writing that goes down must assume that the reader, whatever his special competence may be, knows less about the whole situation than the writer, often has less education, and needs to be addressed in simpler English. The writer must not only have a general knowledge of people; he must know specifically what he can say to each person or group of persons and how he can say it. If he wants a specific electrical device designed, he does not necessarily have to know much about electricity, but he does have to know the crotchets of electricians. He must put his instructions in their terms, or they will come up with something he can't use. If he is setting a sales policy, he must know his salesmen and how to address them. If he is changing the workload for the men on the assembly line, he must make clear that he is not attempting a "speed-up," or he will spend some uncomfortable time with the shop stewards while the line sits idle. He must put his directives in terms of the men they go to, or they will be non-directives.

This kind of downward communication has more to do with a young man or woman starting out on a career than you might think, for there is a line of promotion in large organizations in what we may call "staff" work. The head of an office or of a concern does not sit down at a typewriter and peck out his instructions. He dictates them and turns them over to his staff, a group of people he has drawn together because they are capable. They know him and what he wants, and they know how to get it done. An executive in a large organization does not move alone through his business day. No matter how much he likes to "get out into the works and talk to the boys," he is always at least within telephone call of his staff, who are his real eyes and ears. Chief among these is his secretary, usually a woman but not always, who sets up his schedule, filters calls and callers to him, buys his tickets and makes his res-

ervations, sees that a car meets him at the station and takes him
back to it, and incidentally writes his letters and speeches from his
instructions. Backing her up are his assistants to whom he delegates
anything they can handle. She, too, may have her assistants. Competent people for these jobs are so rare that executives scrabble for
them, bribe and steal them from each other. A person with a delicate sense of language, who can phrase instructions and orders so
that the receiver knows what is expected of him and can act on it,
can move in the shadow of the executive and build up experience
for his own advancement.

It was probably while the secretary was sick that the general
editor of one of the dictionaries we have discussed sat down and
typed out an order which was posted on a photostatting machine.
The machine had just been introduced to eliminate the typing of
passages which illustrate the uses of words. It photographed them
on 3 x 5 paper. The memo went something like this:

NOTICE TO EDITORIAL AND CLERICAL PERSONNEL

1. The operation and utilization of this machine shall be
under the cognizance of the supervisor of clerical personnel.

2. Utilization of this machine for company business shall
take precedence over non-editorial purposes.

3. Editorial and clerical personnel having matter of their
own to photograph will consult the supervisor of clerical personnel. . . .

And so on, through about twelve points. Visitors being shown
through the plant did not usually have time to read to the bottom.
Possibly the editor was depending on the high educational and intellectual level of his employees, but the point of the memo was
quite simple and could have been simply expressed:

1. The head clerk is in charge of this machine.

2. It is here for company business but employees may use
it for their own work when it is idle.

3. If you have anything to photograph, arrange it with the
head clerk, and she will see that its gets done.

Within any organization there is also sideways or horizontal
communication, which goes on between persons or units working

together on common problems, though on different aspects of them. Rank or status is not much involved; the persons are pretty much on a level. They may work side by side at a machine; they may be in charge of comparable offices, laboratories, departments, or branches. The company expects them to co-operate; as the little boy said, "Nobody talk big, nobody talk little, everybody talk medium." Each person involved is a specialist who knows his own job but often little about the others. The communication is thus normally from the specialist to an outsider who is a specialist in another field. Examples would be departments of Design and Engineering. Design works out a model which Engineering has to put into production, preferably without buying a plantful of new machine tools. Engineering defines the limits of its equipment; Design goes over the model and brings the parts within the range of the machines. In the same way production, packaging, and shipping departments have to work together.

This sideways writing is a real test of skill. It varies as the people vary, but it always involves explanation. Since no one can order anyone else to do anything, the writer has to make clear what is to be done, why it has to be done, what the issues are, and which are important. He has to let it be known that the necessities are not personal; it is the nature of the work or the material or the equipment that dictates what has to be done. He has to indicate he is not trying to run the other fellow's job, that he has tried everything possible to keep difficulties down, and that he is open to suggestions. Often the matter is extremely technical, but it must be sufficiently translated so that the specialist who has to pick it up from there knows what is involved. The person who has bolstered his technical education with a mastery of the language has an edge over the specialist who has not.

Finally there is the communication that passes from the organization as a whole to the outside—that vast area of contacts now known as "public relations." Here the organization faces its suppliers, its employees, its customers, and the community at large. Here, like a nervous lover, the organization tries to establish an image of itself that will be attractive, that will have dignity, and that will win and keep friends. To this end it builds an attractive plant—or at least an attractive façade—with a green lawn and a fountain, if possible, with ducks in it. It sets up impressive front offices in which an atmosphere of dignified calm approaches rigor mortis. It hires specialists in packaging to package its products, artists to design its letterheads, and public-relations men to make sure that it supports the right charity drives, athletic teams and leagues, and other community enterprises, so as to join the effort without seeming to take it over. It tries to be lovely to look at, friendly to live with, easy to do business with. To this end it organizes its communication.

An organization presenting a unified face to the world cannot set up a single office to handle the matter and let every other employee be as hairy-chested as he likes. Its contacts with the public occur at all levels and at every point. Telephones jingle on every desk. Letters come and go from every office dealing with purchases, production, sales, adjustments, and the thousand issues that come up in any complicated endeavor. It soon becomes obvious which people in which offices can be trusted to write letters. They are not specialists in letter writing but persons who know the work and understand the problems and can interpret to others in some kind of gracious way. These chances of any employee to be, for a moment, a representative of the whole outfit come as unexpectedly and as often as spring rainfall, and each is a small opportunity to grow a little bigger in stature and influence in the enterprise.

Possibly the touchiest of all the outside relations of a big organization is with its own personnel. Each employee has only one foot planted in the business; the other is outside groping around for something solid to stand on. Each person is seeking something for himself—a job with another concern, a better job where he is, more pay, more dignity, more status, a better living, or a better way of life. The personnel department must see that he finds what he seeks within the organization, if it can be provided. Most of the labor force has a dual loyalty—to its union as well as to the company; an employee is most productive when he can feel that these two loyalties are pulling together toward a common end. If the two are divided and resisting each other, then each employee is split right down the middle; if he is forced to a choice, he will go with the union. Therefore, the people in charge of personnel must approach the staff as outsiders and must understand the needs and drives of men and women at work.

Several things of importance are here for the young person looking for a career. Personnel relations—often miscalled "personnel management"—is a growing field in large organizations as more and more concerns discover that friction between a man and his job is a costly waste. Personnel relations is a practical art for which some people are gifted and some are not, and those most likely not to be gifted have trained too narrowly for specialized work and have slighted literature, art, psychology, and social studies in their education. This cuts two ways. It is no great blow to be shut off from work in the personnel department itself on account of a barbarously narrow training in engineering, chemistry, or business administration. It is a blow to be cut off from advancement because a narrow interest in a specialty has unfitted you for a supervisory post. A concern that will hire you to do a job for which you are trained would prefer to have you grow up, out, and away from that job, but personnel studies demonstrate fairly well that if you promote a specialist to manager you may ruin a specialist and not get a manager. It is easy to develop some breadth of outlook in school or college, but hard to develop it in the day-to-day pressure of a job; if you cannot develop it, you stay in the same bottom job where you began—at close to the same pay. Industry is full of arrogant young technicians and disgruntled older ones, still sweating it out where they began.

The public relations of a large organization involve all its contacts with its customers and the public at large. The customers are hidden until they are discovered in the public at large, so that the simplest form of public relations is the avoidance of unnecessary friction. The picture editor of a newspaper made this point clear. He listened to an exasperated desk man explain to a woman by telephone that her tip on an accident had come in too late to win a prize; somebody beat her to it. "Madam," he said, "you did not get in first; you do not get the money, and that's that!" He banged the receiver. "Do you know who you were talking to?" said the editor. "Oh, some dame. . . ." "For your information," said the editor, "that was a *former* reader of the *Times.*" Every concern has some employees who should be locked away from telephones and typewriters; they have to be very good at their specialized work to stay on.

The "institutional" side of public relations is the creation of the image of a concern which it wants to present to the public—usually the image of a good citizen. It is as if you added up all the people in the organization as citizens concerned with health, schools, recreation, government, and public welfare generally, and take over as an organization a concern for their concerns. A big organization has a great deal of weight; its citizenship is a matter of delicate negotiations, careful scrutiny of projects and appeals for money and services, and constant watchfulness for the effect of rejection or approval. It commits a little and then a little more, and then, when the project is obviously going to be a success and everyone connected with it is going to look good, the company plunges and puts it over.

Closely allied to this institutional public relations is advertising of the product, which can range all the way from the sleazy come-on of a streetcorner pitchman to the sober statement in a medical journal of the properties of a drug. This is the only kind of public relations that all the people in the enterprise do not participate in. It is a specialist job. In spite of the number of experts involved in it and the money spent on it, advertising is not yet well understood. We can see that in the mass it does influence people and it does move goods. What ad in which medium is best for each item is hard to say; as a result, advertising is wasteful, like a blind man sowing clover seed by hand on a windy day. It seems to cry out for some of the citizenship in institutional promotion. Not surprisingly in its vast range from responsibility to empty dishonesty, advertising reflects the morals of the multitude that engages in it. The fact that the same concern can advertise the same drug with the cynicism of the pitchman and the scrupulousness of the scientist certainly raises some questions of ethics; and we may well wonder as consumers what image of us lives in the murky minds of the advertising experts. Still, it is a specialist job, and the young person whose writing will help or hinder his career in fields that are mainly not writing need only know that it is part of the public relations of business, a part that will not involve him except as captive audience.

We may now look at a typical corporation and see the place of written communication in it. This is a corporation, located in southern California, which manufactures civilian and military airplanes. It is a growing concern with large contracts for airliners and larger contracts for jet bombers and fighters.

This aircraft company is typical; we mention it not because it is special—which it is—but because it represents present-day business. We could take an automobile factory with its ceaseless inflow of materials and outflow of finished cars and trucks, or a building contractor with its giant trenchers, bulldozers, and earthmovers to prepare the ground and its army of skilled and unskilled workers who may put housing for thirty thousand people in a cornfield, build factories for them to work in, or thrust a shimmering tower of glass and aluminum toward the sky. We could take a steel company with its iron and coal mines, ships and trains to carry the ore, blast furnaces and foundries, fabricating plants making partly finished bolts, sheets, and slabs of steel of special formulas for everything from needles to machine tools. We could take an oil company with its wells, refineries, and chemical plants, its gas stations and tire factories. We could take a university of fifteen to fifty thousand students, with its libraries, classrooms, laboratories, atom smashers, and even farms and airports. We could take a shipyard, a government bureau, a philanthropic foundation like the Carnegie or Ford, a branch of the Armed Forces, a labor union. It is the same story in each: elaborate organization of diverse elements to accomplish a common set of purposes, and an elaborate spread into sidelines unexpected by the founders of the enterprise. Modern organizations are like many of the people in them: they didn't plan to end up where they are or doing what they do.

Except for a battleship, the big modern bombing aircraft is about the largest and most complicated machine built by man. In the ten years since World War II came to an end, each military aircraft has become about ten times as complicated as the World War II model; it is bigger, faster, heavier, and more costly to build and to maintain, since ten more years of experience has gone into the design and building of it. Yet each one—Sabre-jet, helicopter, and Strato-bomber—is obsolete when it goes into production; the day and almost the date when it will go out of production can pretty well be guessed in advance. The paper work involved for each one, gathered together, would make a pile almost as high as the plane itself. Because of the interdependence of every element on every other element in a plane, each must be planned with respect to the others; each has its number and paper to correspond to that number in the records. Somewhere there is an exact description and probably an exchange of notes or letters in which its shape and function were worked out. Because an aircraft is seldom "frozen" during production, newly designed elements are slipped in here and there, until the last completed plane of a specific model bears little resemblance to the pilot design for which the production line was originally set up. Complication on complication, the modern aircraft in itself is no greater marvel than the intricate modern organization that produces it.

To see the place of language in aircraft production, let us divide the whole enterprise into two parts, external and internal. Between the company and outsiders there is a host of contacts: purchase, sales, and maintenance, among others. The company must buy what it needs—in part, raw materials; in part, semifinished materials like sheet aluminum and preformed girder stock; and, in part, finished components like instruments and control mechanisms. It must also buy tools and machinery and sometimes whole factories. A modern company depends so much on its suppliers that it looks on purchasing as a form of public relations; it must be a good, reliable, honest buyer, exactly describing its needs and responding to suggestions for substitutes or improvements. Second, it must sell its products, and in the air world this means selling to persons using many languages, not only English, German, French, and Spanish but Arabic, Chinese, Japanese, Amharic, Hebrew, and several others. Third, it must keep its products in the air as long as the owners want to fly them. Purchasers of the old Ford Trimotor still feel that it is the best cargo-carrying aircraft for short hops over rough terrain, still use it, and still write in from Cleveland, Ohio; Brazil; and perhaps even New Guinea for parts. Yet Ford went out of production on this plane many years ago. Battered old Lend-lease craft from World War II still lumber over distant continents and seas with Ethiopians, British Indians, and Chinese pilots, not to mention the British, French, Americans, Germans, and Italians who still make a living with them. The maintenance department must respond to inquiries couched in many languages and must offer the sum of the company's experience with its planes translated into the same languages. Technicians who can translate—let alone give clear instructions in English—seldom hunt long for a job. Every need anyone feels in regard to purchase, sales, or maintenance is expressed in writing and must be dealt with in writing.

A company building large passenger and transport planes for civilian use, and the same planes plus fighters and bombers for the military, does not ordinarily do business with individuals either in buying or selling. It deals mainly with other large organizations like itself and with governments. It does not have full control over its own actions; it cannot get high and mighty and say, "Take it or leave it." It does not even have full control over its own correspondence. It has to be multilingual. If it is addressed in French, it replies in French, not English. More difficult than this, it has to observe protocol; that is, it has to address each system in terms of the system, and each person in the other system in terms of his place in it. It has to have an internal system of its own which it can equate to the other, so that in a touchy case it can assign a vice-president to reply to letters from a vice-president, or ask its own very top man to communicate with a general, an admiral, or a Minister of Foreign Affairs. In most cases, before these very high-level heads are permitted to bump together, a crisscross of low and middle-level correspondence has cleared the ground and defined the issues to be settled.

Ordinarily, when two business systems have to deal with each other, they fit together pretty well because they understand each other—both are in business to make a profit. There is a natural symbiotic relationship between them; one thrives with the other. But when a concern does business with government, one does not necessarily thrive with the other, for only one is concerned with profits. When the product is matériel for war, the other agency— the government—is committed to waste. It cannot set out to fly its aircraft as long and as cheaply as it can; it has to have the craft capable of the highest speeds, the longest flights, and the most integral efficiency. To be caught with the second best can mean death, not merely to men and women but to the nation itself. The end and aim of all the aircraft is destruction—if it does not ride to flaming disaster in the sky, it rots to surplus and the junkyard, while other, newer, better aircraft take its place. Thus the government which is pinning the very life of the nation on its purchases must interfere in the corporation at every level; and in every contact or conflict the government has the final word. It lays down the specifications, inspects the work, guards the production and its secrets, and tests the product. Every communication that passes between the company and the government must be "according to regulation," often secret, often on forms provided by the government, and always through channels determined by law.

Every internal element in the corporation is under the eye of the Armed Forces and must justify its actions to the government. We may distinguish four of these elements: Research, Design, Production, and Testing. Research has its eye on the future: impossible speeds, fantastic heights, unimaginable destruction. It must determine the effect of cosmic rays on high-altitude flight; it must fling shuddering experimental airframes against the leaden wall of air. It must discover the potential and limitations of the human body in flight, and devise ways to bring its crew to earth alive with or without the plane it flies in. Design, working a little closer to today, must translate present knowledge into blueprints for tomorrow's flight. Production must convert yesterday's blueprints into today's power plants, armament, controls, and airframes. Testing must torture production models beyond any stresses produced in flight, so that flyers can sit their seats in confidence as they ride the skies. Each department must be in constant communication with the other, with the cold eye of the military overlooking all. The flow of reports, instructions, requests, and answers is colossal; there must be a record of everything, and every record must be as clear as it can be made.

A modern aircraft is a complex product of many men and many minds, each a specialist at his own task. It involves mechanics, hydraulics, electronics, ballistics, physics, chemistry, geography, meterology, astronomy, physiology, psychology, and even psychiatrics and medicine. There must be communication between these specialties; each must in some way reach out to comprehend others. But through channels only, and to control the channels the aircraft industry has "security"—a means of making sure that no one man knows more than he needs to know in order to do his work. The highest security involving experimental and classified materials is itself a secret matter.

Plant security goes by levels: one man may have security clearance for his own department only, another for several departments, and another for the entire plant, depending upon his responsibilities. A man's clearance is indicated by a security card and by a badge with a color bar which shows whether he is salaried or "on the clock"; he may have two badges, one for where he belongs normally and the other for where he is permitted to move around. Thus in the plant no man looks first at a stranger's face; he glances at the badge to check status and security clearance. Some groups have clearance that admits them to just about everything: supervisors, engineers, schedulers, etc., and the technical writers. These have to cross all specialities and nose into everything.

The supervisors and the technical writers are important in industry today, and they will be more important in the industrial world which will face young men and women now in college. In a specialist world they are generalists; they cut across trades, professions, and disciplines. They have to have that keen understanding of human beings which is native to a few people, but which comes to most of us as the result of study and reading—reading of literature, history, philosophy, psychology, sociology—and of an acquaintance with the arts. They have to have alert open minds, quick understanding, and broad interests. They have to be able to move in on a specialty and master it in the jargon of the specialists, then turn around and express in ordinary English the gist of what they have learned. Supervisors become more important as industry becomes more highly organized, and the technical writers become more important as the products of industry become more complicated, as doorbells, automobiles, washing machines, ships, and aircraft become more complex and involve more diverse components. Each of these constructions must have its instruction manual—a clear guide to dismantling it, fixing it, and putting it back together. This is the real McCoy among "How-to-do-it" books, and technical writers are the cream of the "How-to-do-it" experts.

We may follow a technical writer through a small part of his day to see how he fits into the industrial picture. He approaches a line of partially finished airframes to check on one little thing. In the belly of a fighter plane is a set of holes into which supports may be screwed for carrying loads—an extra fuel tank, a rocket-launcher, a parachute drop. Over each hole a small plate is fastened with screws to maintain the smooth skin of the plane in the stream of air. This plate goes with the plane everywhere; when it is not covering the hole, it is fastened to a frame member inside with the same screws. The question is where.

The technical writer knows from the blueprints, but he has to put the location in the manual, and he wants to see how to get at it. He crawls into the fuselage beside a riveter who glances at his badge and then gets back to work because the badge is ambiguous; the wearer could be anybody or nobody, but he has overall clearance. The writer looks for the screw holes, but he does not find them. He introduces himself and asks; the riveter does not know: he rivets for a living. The writer asks the leadman, the foreman, the superintendent. Nobody knows. He sighs and goes back to the blueprints. The blueprints have been revised by Engineering Orders; as each production change is introduced, it is recorded in an E. O. bearing a change-letter, A, B, C, etc., then AB, AC, AD. These nearly completed airframes are up to their sixtieth production change: there may be twenty more before the first ship is completed. He begins with the sixtieth set and works back through them, looking for the location of the storage holes for the cover plates. At fifteen he finds them. Somebody failed to carry them over to sixteen, and they dropped from the record. Now they will have to be put back in. He makes a note for the draftsmen and goes back to his job of writing the manual: "These cover plates must be stored with their screws . . ."

Obviously it is not the main job of the technical writer to keep some mechanic on Okinawa from standing around with a set of cover plates in his hand, wondering what to do with them. His task is writing the manual. He has to be free to nose into the whole written story of the aircraft, and free to question any of the technicians who have designed it and put it together. He is a gatherer of relevant information, and a translator; what he learns must go into the book in common English that can be understood by any craftsman. He works a little sadly because of the production changes. The technical writers begin to lay out the manual according to a standard form when the plans are delivered and when the first airframe begins to take shape on the line. Almost immediately, as Design begins to feed in the latest developments of Research, the production changes start to come through. Components change —a new airspeed indicator, a new shape for the tail surfaces, a new pilot-ejection mechanism. Finished work has to be pulled out of completed units. The writing staff works on, keeping up as long as it can, but sooner or later it must stop—in order to have the manual completed when the planes are ready for delivery at, say, eighty production changes. The staff gives up at the fortieth or fiftieth, conscious that part of its work, at least, will be obsolete before it is done, and that the manual will have to be followed by a supplement of corrections.

Who are these technical writers? Where did they learn their trade? Like many people in modern industry, doing work that often did not even exist when they were in school or college, they "drifted into it." A former pilot who tried school teaching, office work, and selling before he drifted back into the building of the planes. An electronics specialist whose gift for making complicated things clear pulled him off the bench and into the office, a college instructor who took one last look at an English class and went out looking for a job, a mechanical engineer, a salesman—almost anybody with an intellectual bent and an inquiring mind and with that one necessary quality in modern business organizations, the habit of reading widely and writing constantly with craft and care. No illiterate specialist these, but citizens of the air world and of the universal Republic of Letters.

Let one of them speak for himself. "When I came into this business, everything was hydraulics, and hydraulics are complicated. Now we still have hydraulic mechanisms all through the plane, but they're triggered by electronics. The planes go so fast that human reflexes are too slow: electronics respond instantly and correct themselves. At the speeds these planes fly, the forces are so great that you have to have power controls. Power controls have no 'feel'; they're as dead as an electric light switch. So you have to build machines that put the feel back in. All this machinery adds weight, so you have to miniaturize—cut everything down in size, make it smaller, lighter. Then you have to protect the pilot. These jets are sturdier than piston planes, because they're simpler, in a way. They'll take a lot of pounding. Even so, they put a terrible strain on the pilot, on his blood and his guts.

"The human brain is a very complicated instrument in a fragile body, and you have to do what you can to bring each one back. So the next step is still ahead of us: replace the pilot with a mechanical brain that is expendable. You don't have to bring it back. That means guided missiles. We're not building them now, but we've got to. That brings in the physicist and the meteorologist. Will the machine work the same at ground level as at forty thousand feet? Will it take in weather information and correct itself according to the winds, moisture conditions, and icing the way a pilot does? The hydraulics man says, 'I don't know anything about electronics; that's his business.' The electronics man says, 'I don't know anything about meteorology.' The meteorologist says, 'I'm a weather man. I just feed the information to the fly boys and let them figure out what to do with it.' Somebody has to learn hydraulics, learn electronics, and then go on and learn meteorology and any other -ology that comes into it. I think it's the most exciting thing I ever got into, and I can't see where it's going to stop."

"And that isn't all. Every business is up against the same thing. Look at your washing machines—they run themselves. Your flat-irons keep their own heat wherever you want it. Look at your television. Radio was complicated enough; now you've got television, and color is coming in. A black and white tube costs twenty dollars, say—a color tube about a hundred and seventy-five. Look at your automobiles, with automatic transmissions, power steering, power brakes, power seats, and automatic dimmers. Ships with automatic pilots, trains that stop if they run a block signal, lawn mowers that hunt around for the long grass to cut. We've got big computers here, but when we have anything really complicated to figure out, we send it to places like MIT, Wayne, and Harvard, where they've really got machines that think, big enough to fill up a whole building. Even looking at where we are today, it's hard to see where we're going to be tomorrow.

"And we do it all with language. If you tie up our communications, we're sunk. Everything stops until you get it going again. And you can't leave language to the other fellow. You've got to do it yourself. Everybody's got to do it.

"Another problem I can foresee is that I see more and more terms being used which I never heard of, for example **enthalpy** ('heat content'). Pretty soon I can see where only engineers of like interest will be able to communicate with each other; and if my argument is correct, then in the near future it would appear that engineering progress is going to rely entirely on the technical writer or editor or abstract writer to translate many of the highly scientific pieces of writing into something comprehensible to interested parties in other allied fields."

The technical writer, like the supervisor, is not a special breed of person. He is the ordinary business person with ordinary writing responsibilities lifted to the nth degree. He is one who patiently cultivated his ability to take in information from writing and put it out again in writing while he was learning his own specialty, whatever it was. Most cultivators of language tend to be lovers of words; they like the feel and savor of words. The technical writer, like the poet, is a patternmaker more than a mere wordlover. He uses various technical vocabularies, but they are known in advance to his readers. He does not look for ways to get around using a single term for an object like a condenser, a rheostat, a turbine, or an afterburner. That is its name, and he sticks with it. He tries for a plain style, though not necessarily a simple one, for he has to deal with an organized complex of things in an organized complex of language that fits it. His tools are the commonest patterns of the common speech, and the inflections and structure-words that build those patterns. Anyone can see his problems who has tried to put together a knocked-down cabinet or build a boat from a kit, and has had trouble figuring out from the instructions which parts go together first. The technical writer must show how to find out which mechanism has failed, how to get into it, how to detach it, how to find the trouble, and how to fix it. Then he has to tell how to work the unit back into place, how to connect it, and how to ease it back into operation again. To do all this, he has to play with the sentence so that it tells in order what has to be done in order.

The technical writer has to weigh the values of the most familiar words, so that he does not use one when he means another. Let us say that two relays, A and B, operate simultaneously. The chances are that his readers will not recognize the word **simultaneously** in print: he must be sure that a tired airman working with stiff fingers on a cold desert base will make no mistake. Should he say, "If the coil of relay A is energized, the coil of relay B is energized," and add, "at the same time"? Or should he say, "When the coil of relay A . . ."? Or would it be better to say, "As the coil of relay A is energized, the coil of relay B is energized at the same time"? Both **if** and **when** are ambiguous; they may set up the wrong notion too well for "at the same time" to correct it. He may "try it out on the dog," as they say, by handing it to one of the boys on the line to read. He feels some urgency because if those two relays are hooked up wrong, an aircraft representing a million dollars or more of the taxpayer's money may go up in smoke.

The technical writer must sharpen his ear for the common speech, that part of the language that is understood by everybody, educated and uneducated, from any part of the nation. **Carry** in the South may mean 'take,' as in **I carried my girl to the movies** or **Carry me back to Old Virginny.** In the North it may mean 'lift and bear from one place to another,' or 'support.' Can he stay within a range of meanings that is shared by both? He must, to avoid mistakes. He must watch pronouns. A sergeant told a private, "This is a hand grenade. You just pull this pin and throw it. Go ahead and try it." An explosion injured both men. The private

asked, "What happened? I threw the pin just like you said." The
technical writer must especially watch the names of the various
parts and elements. Nomenclature is very important. The same
name must be used throughout the entire manual; otherwise complete confusion results. Many times there is a close similarity between names; for example: **secondary relay, secondary bus relay,
secondary bus control relay, secondary bus power relay,** and so on.
The technical writer must consider the physical movements involved in the work; he cannot define a procedure that only a con-
tortionist midget with four hands could carry out.

Every advance in technology and in business methods increases
the burden on language in business and the responsibility of those
who use it. Automation in manufacture replaces muscles with
brains; every workman becomes a supervisor; every supervisor, a
director. The human element is reduced in quantity and increased
in quality; the marvel of humanity is that it rises by sharpened
use of language to meet every need. Any person who takes a responsible position in the world of modern business moves away
from direct contact with things into the management of men and
women whose actions he must direct by language.

A business executive addressing an "Industrial Liaison Sym-
posium" at MIT stated the case for technical writing in terms of
cold cash: "The technical report—as a means of transmitting information internally or to the public—is an increasingly important
item in company operations. To maintain the competitive advantage derived from competent technical reporting, management
should recognize, encourage, and plan for the writing activity at
all levels, from that of the individual engineers through the various
stages of review and editing to printing in effective format."

The business of writing for business is everybody's business.
Business writing must be clear, factual, honest, and accurate. Only
the advertiser can play fast and loose with language, hinting at love
that will come if you use a certain toothpaste, calling on "medical
science" to justify smoking a certain cigarette, wearing a certain
girdle, washing with a particular soap. Every other kind of business
writing must honor the facts, or business cannot run. Language is
the nervous system of all organizations; it cannot be handled too
well. Like all other uses of language, writing for business must
be prepared for; at the moment of writing you have to go forward
on what you know. If your writing fails, the failure is only the end-

product of all you have done or not done, through all your life, to communicate with other people in terms that they can understand. The place to start is where you are, reading the books and magazines that the educated read, and writing at every odd moment for that most critical eye—your own. Then you will meet the tests of your career, serene and ready to bring all your powers to bear.

CHAPTER 31

The Language of Literature

IT SEEMS a long way from the workaday language of business to the language of creative writing, but the technical writer who has to play down vocabulary is closer to the poet than you might think. Consciously or unconsciously he has to depend on structures to convey his meanings, for common words can only be given precise significance by arrangement with other words in patterns.

Like other modern arts, poetry, drama, and creative prose penetrate the community far beyond the circle of people who enjoy them directly. It is the same thing with sculpture, painting, and architecture. Modern sculpture explores the expressiveness of shapes applied to solids, even to the extent of depicting motion in stone or metal. Although the expression is too daring for the general public, designs based on modern concepts of sculpture give form to sport cars, dishes, and silverware. Modern painting, despite public apathy, explores the expressiveness of colors and of shapes arranged on a flat canvas; advertising, design, interior decorating, and even high fashion in clothes imitate modern art at a distance and are accepted by the public. Modern architecture shocks with its search for ways of enclosing space for human use; it scares off the public, but it influences building construction so that a person who runs from a solid wall of glass will go home and put in a picture window. Literary works which seem strange and unreal to the public break ground for expressive devices that creep into popular books, magazines, newspapers, and advertising prose.

The only difficulty with all this is that educated men and women —most of whom are only a generation or two from the less educated and hardworking general run of people—go for the second-rate in art, music, architecture, and literature as bees go for a field of clover, and get very high and mighty before first-class artistic productions. Like the housewife who passes up Roquefort cheese for domestic Blue, or the car buyer who prefers juke-box gaudiness to grace in a car, they like semiclassical music, "realistic" and sentimental painting, "modernistic" ranch houses, and television dramatizations of "'Twas the night before Christmas." They mutter "I don't know anything about art, but I know what I like and I don't like this," unaware that they are really saying, "I don't know anything about art and I like what I know—which is nothing." To take their proper place among the cultivated guardians of our civilized heritage, they need to learn to take good artistic creation straight.

We are in a remarkable state in regard to the arts. We ride our civilization at top speed like drivers on the Pennsylvania turnpike, over a four-lane road that levels mountains and plains alike. We stop at well-designed resthouses that serve our needs and please the eye, not too conservative and not too modern. The road itself is honest functional design for a motor age; the roadside buildings are a little less honest, but the proportions are good and the colors and forms are good. Wherever modern design can be thinned out to the public taste, the effect is pleasing. But wherever there is space for a painting on the walls—a spot where a creative artist might speak honestly to his fellow men—there is a sentimental daub that says exactly nothing to anybody. It seems to have been painted by a barn painter who has come inside for the winter. We fade out in the pinch. It is bad enough for us to do so, but to do it on the showplace highway of the nation makes us look to the visiting world like clay-footed, mud-souled slobs. It is hard to believe that that is what we are.

The problem is not our lack of innate artistic sensibility or our indifference to what our fellow men are trying to say to us, but that, like the low man in a chain of command, we fail to get the word.

We don't get the key to what is going on. Give us that, and we have strength and wisdom enough to stand up to a work of art. We have to be taught to see what is in the work and how to get it out before we can learn to give ourselves freely and humbly to the work in honest contemplation, and get some of the enrichment that is there. We will not all respond with the same vigor to the same works of art; we do not abandon our own personalities and our preferences for some things over others, and we do not have to, but we need to see the work clearly in its own terms. Then, when we know what is there, we can accept it or reject it. We learn not to ask the question "Do I like it?" until we know for sure what is there to be liked or disliked.

The first question is the basic question: how is it that there is a "language of literature"? How can we take the speech that we normally speak—to order bread with, tell our thoughts with, stir passions with—the speech that comes to us without reflection and without premeditation, that serves to carry on the normal business of our lives—and use it as the material for a form of art? How can this be done?

Each artist has to start with a material, something workable which is the vehicle for what is to be expressed. The painter's material is some sort of pigment suspended in a fluid which can be depended upon to evaporate, leaving the ground, colored stuff clinging to a surface. The sculptor's material is a malleable earth like clay or a solid substance like wood, stone, metal, or plastic. The musician's material is sound, sound made by a membrane stretched tight, a reed vibrating in a tube, a string drawn tight over a hollow box, or the vocal organs of a human being. For each artist the nature and range of what he can express is defined by the material. Of the many things he might have in mind to say by means of the material, he is limited by what it can express. He cannot go beyond this; he is fenced in. How, then, can language serve as one of these materials?

You have to have a theory of what art is, and a good simple one is this: art is a means by which a person can take an emotion from inside himself and get it out of himself into an object. It need not be an emotion that he actually feels as he is getting it out—though it might be—but it must be one that he has inspected until he knows what it is like. He puts this into an object, the shape of which will be determined by the material he chooses to work. It could be a statue, a painting, a song, a symphony, a poem, or a novel. He gets the emotion out of himself into the work, where it is available for the contemplation of his fellow men. They can look at it, feel it, hear it, or read it.

Contemplating the object, other people recognize the emotion and draw it out. This contemplation is their share of the marvelous process by which they, too, get out of themselves and achieve an understanding of an emotion that is somebody else's. They feel their way into it. They do not need to feel the actual emotion in the act of contemplation, feeling sad at a sad play, for instance, though they may. The essential is for them to recognize it in the work and inspect it. We have said "an emotion" for the sake of simplicity; the emotional life of any person is extremely complicated, and therefore the expression of even the simplest work of art is many-faceted. The work of art is a human being's statement of what it means to him to face the world as he sees it, but it is an indirect statement carved into some kind of material. How can language be one of these materials?

An artist is drawn to a material because he likes something about it—its look or its feel or its weight. He may like its history, as the sculptor Leonard Schwartz showed when he carved figures of men, women, and children in fused, burnt bomb-rubble that he found in the weathered cellar-holes of blasted French houses. We can always take such a material and examine it for itself, carrying our investigation of it with scientific tools beyond the impression it conveys to our senses. The granite used in statues offers to our sight and touch a tight granular surface of a distinctive hardness. It has mass; it has weight. Under the microscope it is a concretion of different crystals; the surface is an organization of these crystals. Probing into the crystals themselves, we find ourselves on a quite different level of organization. Molecules organize themselves to form crystals; different molecules in different arrangements produce different crystals.

Going beyond the crystals to the molecule, we find a level of organization, this time of atoms, which resembles neither of those we have passed through. It has its own special nature. In our time we have adventured within the atom and found there a constellation of entities to which we have given names like proton, neutron, and deuteron. The difference between atoms lies in the number and organization of the entities that make them up. At each level the substance is formed of units in arrangements; the substance is the arrangement and the units. Each level is absolutely different from the others; its units are the organized structures of the level next beneath. In the same way we can break down the sounds of music as they strike the ear into vibrations and into the wave lengths, and so on. We can dig into the painter's pigments the same way.

Any substance that has a nature and a structure of its own can be used by the artist as a material for an art form. We can use language as a material for literature because, like granite and sound, it is an organization. It is an arrangement of separate elements, an arrangement on different levels, but with this difference: all its levels of organization are presented together; we hear them all together. The texture of language is the fabric of all the units in all their arrangements at all levels of organization at once.

In the organization of language as we have described it, the level comparable to the weight, look, and feel of granite is the unit of the whole utterance—in writing, the sentence. The utterance exists in its organization; in language we understand whole utterances, not parts except as they form portions of the whole. As we noted before, **That girl is pretty** is an utterance the whole of which gives **pretty** its meaning. In **That girl is pretty fat,** a different whole gives **pretty** a different sense. In **That girl is pretty fat in the head,** the utterance assigns a new meaning to **fat.** The overall arrangement is *syntax,* and the working units of syntax are the segmental morphemes and the overriding morphemes of intonation. A segmental morpheme may be equivalent to a word as written like **die** or to a part of a word; **undying** has at least three morphemes in it: **un-, die-,** and **-ing.**

Below syntax, the morphemic level (about equivalent to the molecular level of physical substances) consists of the internal structure of the morphemes. This level is different from the syntactical in its elements and their organization. The sound-units within the morphemes are the phonemes, of which, as we have seen, there are forty-five in English. If we want to dig into the phonemes, which are the "atomic" units of language, we find that they, in turn, are structures analyzed out of raw sequences of speech sounds. Each is a sort of "chord," a bundle of distinctive features that set it off from other phonemes. When we get down to the raw data of sound as it is heard by a recording machine, we are at the lowest stratum of language, though we can, if we need to, dig right on down to the sound-waves themselves. Or, as we saw in Chapter 4, we can widen our analysis of speech to the two other structured systems which accompany any normal utterance, the vocal-qualifiers and the patterned motions and gestures characteristic of each community of speakers.

We have, then, ascending levels of language structures—the phonetic, the phonemic, the morphemic, and the syntactic—each having many units, each unit highly organized, and each level quite different from the level below. We have a substance with a nature and a structure of its own. Since any such substance can serve as the material for an artist to work with, it is clear that language is by its nature capable of serving as the material of literature. To get this far is only to get a very slippery grasp on the answer we seek, and so we must go on to what the artist does with language which is equivalent to the shape the sculptor carves into stone. We are still a long way from a poem, a short story, a play, or a novel.

If language is a structured substance, a literary work is a structure of structures, put into writing to make it permanent. There are great literatures in the world which have never been written down, being handed from mouth to mouth for generations, with the additions that each age chooses to make. To have a work of literature, we must have other patterned organizations "wrought into" the ordered structures of language. Instead of a casual flow of talk, spontaneous and quickly forgotten, we have carefully planned and designed sentences set into precise relationships with each other.

Here the key to literature lies, as far as literature is a special molding of the language we speak. Every act of speech is a creative act, though not necessarily an artistic one. It is possible for a chance utterance to have the form of art, as driftwood sometimes resembles a piece of sculpture, but artistry is an assertion of conscious will. Thus we have aphorisms and proverbs which we treasure like bits of driftwood found on the beach, because sometime, possibly even centuries back, someone hit on a nice form for what he had to say. "A stitch in time saves nine." "Many hands make light work" or its opposite, "Too many cooks spoil the broth." We have Nathan Hale's "I regret that I have but one life to give for my country," and Franklin D. Roosevelt's "The only thing we have to fear is fear itself." "Man works from sun to sun; woman's

work is never done" is a rimed sentence often used to prod tired
husbands into helping with the dinner dishes. These proverbs have
the form of art, but most of them probably fell into that form by
chance.

An artistic act is an act of will; the artist deliberately imposes
another organization on the innate organized structures of the
material, another whole. In literature this whole is a structure of
structures, an organization whose units are themselves literary
structures. Since the levels of language organization already strike
the ear in a single complex impression, they merge with this literary
overpatterning in an even more highly organized, tenser, and
denser unity.

We might as well start with poetry, where we can see this organization cleanest and clearest. A short poem is about the most
condensed kind of literature, with at least four overriding literary
structures combining to form an integrated complex. The same four
kinds of pattern seem to compose the main systems of patterning
in larger and longer works, like stories, plays, and novels, but less
obviously and more diffuse, harder to see. These are the kinds of
patterns you have to use if you are going to write literature; they
correspond to what the sculptor has to do if he is going to work in
stone, regardless of what in particular he wants to say. The sculptor picks up his chisel and takes a whack at the stone; the author
picks up his pencil and begins to fiddle with words.

A poem is basically a fabric of utterances, but because it is
written, it is a fabric of sentences. The first pattern we may consider is the arrangement of sound. The sounds in a poem do not
fall by chance as they do in speech; they are selected. The poet's
problem is to pick the word that says what he means and has the
right sound for his pattern. In English he may watch three places
in the word, using either exactly similar or somewhat similar
sounds. He may alliterate the beginnings of words:

> Western wind, when wilt thou blow,
> The small rain down can rain?

He may use similar vowel and consonant sounds within the words:

> Better to walk forth in the murderous air
> And wash my wound in the snows; that would be healing;

Because my heart would throb less painful there,
Being caked with cold, and past the smart of feeling.

JOHN CROWE RANSOM

Here the poet has related in sound **healing** and **feeling, walk** and **wash** (and in some dialects **throb**), and **snows** and **cold.** He may also rime the ends of words as **air** and **there** in the lines above, and, again, **healing** and **feeling.**

FIFE TUNE

One morning in spring
We marched from Devizes
All shapes and all sizes
Like beads on a string,

But yet with a swing
We trod the bluemetal
And full of fine fettle
We started to sing.

JOHN MANIFOLD

In these lines you get all the correspondences of sound, and you see that sound patterns play all through the lines as well as at the ends. In our time poets write two kinds of poems, one in which the poet sets up a pattern in one stanza and writes all the rest of the stanzas to the same pattern or something near it, and the other in which the sound-patterns play irregularly and subtly as the line of the thought flows. It depends on what he has to say. We also get slant rimes, sounds which are near to the others, but a little off: **love, prove; lover, over; up, step,** and so on.

I like to see it lap the miles,
And lick the valleys up,
And stop to feed itself at tanks;
And then, prodigious, step
Around a pile of mountains. . . .

EMILY DICKINSON

Every sentence in a poem also has a rhythm created by the poet's intent. There is rhythm in every utterance of man. Upon this native rhythm the poet imposes a structure of rhythms that derives from his idea of the whole he has planned. An instance is the serene terminal repetition in a beautiful stanza from "Stopping by Woods on a Snowy Evening":

> The woods are lovely, dark and deep.
> But I have promises to keep,
> And miles to go before I sleep,
> And miles to go before I sleep.
>
> ROBERT FROST

Or this:

> And twelve o'clock arrived just once too often,
>   just the same he wore one grey tweed suit, bought one
>   straw hat, drank one straight Scotch, walked one
>   short step, took one long look, drew one deep breath,
>   just one too many, . . .
>
> KENNETH FEARING

Rhythm is repetition and recurrence; things keep coming back. In a sense the poem is like a turning wheel: the same spokes circle around and come back but not to the same place, for the turning of the wheel has moved it on along the ground. There is rhythm in breathing and in the heartbeat, in the coming of light and dark, and in the passing of the seasons; there is rhythm in every vibration, in a line of trees, and in a picket fence. Human beings respond to rhythm, and so all the arts, from music to architecture, play on people by playing on rhythm. The rhythmic beats in poetry are syllable beats.

An utterance is structured, or we cannot understand it. It fits into the pattern of things we say in our society, and it has an internal patterning of its own. In a poem another syntactical structure is imposed on the normal syntax of the sentence; sentences are built to have within them certain sound and rhythm patterns, and still come to the end with full meaning. It is not enough for the sentence in a poem to express a thought; it might better be said to compress the thought. A sentence in a poem is smaller on the outside and bigger on the inside than a typical utterance, more efficient, more tense; and its shape determines and is determined by the other sentences in the poem. In the following stanza by a minor modern poet, the first sentence sets the pattern of inversion for the second:

> All too meanly and too soon
> Waxes once and wanes our moon;
> All too swiftly for each one
> Falls to dark our winter sun.

That is, life is too short. Many modern poets tend to make each sentence in a short poem equal to a stanza; then in the following stanzas they work subtle variations on the pattern set up in the first. The poet differs from the technical writer in several things. Where the technical writer tries to discover the normal expectations of his readers and stay within them, the poet studies these normal expectations in order to weave around them. You must watch him, for he is trying to keep you, the reader, off balance. He knows what word, what sound, what rhythm pattern you expect him to use, and he keeps dangling it before you, sometimes giving it to you, sometimes not. He would probably hate himself in the morning if he gave you part of the poem so baldly that you could go on and complete it for yourself. He plays with you like a winsome girl with her boy friend: she's going to give him a date, but she's going to make him work for it, and like it. Where the technical writer tries to organize a sentence that matches the organization of some mechanism that you can take in your hands, the poet tries to organize a sentence that matches a thought in his head that you cannot know except through the sentence. Where the technical writer tries to stay within the language of common speech, the poet weighs each word for its suggestions, for its quality of carrying more of the meaning than anybody ever expected it to.

Finally, there is a structure of imagery. In normal speech, whenever we are trying to make something clear, we are likely to do so by relating it to what the hearer already knows. "What is a half-track?" he asks. "Well, it's a sort of a truck, but it's like a tractor, too. In place of the rear wheels it has caterpillar treads like a tractor." "What do you mean by caterpillar?" "Crawling over the ground instead of rolling like a wheel." In poetry these comparisons are condensed and related; they hang together; they form a separate and distinguishable structure. What we call imagery is not different in its nature from the comparisons by which any speaker explains the unfamiliar in terms of the familiar, nor is it different from the transfers in meaning that keep our vocabulary enveloping new things and new ideas. The words **spaceship** and **airship** have come far from the first small floating vessels that the Anglo-Saxons called a ship. We have here the stuff of poetry and art, but it is not art. It is not organized; it is too chancy. The order that constitutes literature is not a product of chance.

The following tight little wedding song derives as much of its meaning from its interplay of structures as from its vocabulary. The poem is not in the wordlist: **a, all, and, any, at; bed, beget, both; come, conscious, content; dance, dancers, dark, death, deep;** and so on. Nor is it in the sentences alone, in the rhythms alone, or in the sounds. It is in all of these together.

BRIDAL COUCH

Follows this a narrower bed,
Wood at feet, wood at head;
Follows this a sounder sleep,
Somewhat longer and too deep.

All too meanly and too soon
Waxes once and wanes our moon;
All too swiftly for each one
Falls to dark our winter sun.

Let us here then wrestle death,
Intermingled limb and breath,
Conscious both that we beget
End of rest, endless fret,

And come at last to permanence,
Tired dancers from a dance,
Yawning, and content to fall
Into any bed at all.

DONALD J. LLOYD

No doubt there are more than these four literary structures in the unity that makes a poem. Sound—the order of phonemes; rhythm—the order of syllable beats; syntax—the order of form-classes; and imagery—the order of likenesses: these are the most obvious arrangements of language that make up a poem or, indeed, any work of literature whatever. No one has yet succeeded in drawing a clean line between poetry and prose. There are simply degrees of diffuseness of these structures. Each work is a construct whose total form and aptness for its burden of expression lies in its internal thrusts and tensions. A literary whole is something like an iron truss bridge spanning a stream. There is a material in the bridge—steel or iron—of a characteristic toughness and hardness. Each piece in the bridge has its own shape and strength, fit for its own share of the load: the whole bridge supports itself by the pull and thrust of its parts. Without that material organized in that way, the bridge will not stand. Paper bridges collapse.

When an artist chooses his native language as the vehicle for what he has to say (or is chosen, for he often has to write whether he wants to or not), he explores its possibilities, acquainting himself not merely with its patterns and its vocabulary but with the specific utterances that are associated with specific human acts. He must know what people actually say in the midst of life. As a painter exploits the range of color or as an actor notes the unpremeditated gestures of men and women as they go about their affairs, so the writer has to tune his ear to the impromptu and deliberate speech of people living their lives, whether they are standing on their own ground among their own people or moving diffidently in strange situations among strangers, and whether they are merging sympathetically with their fellows or detaching themselves from the hands that reach toward them. To the limit of his sensitivity he absorbs the stream of human speech in all its random disorder. By practice and discipline he learns to create lifelike pseudo-utterances that he can manipulate in writing, in the strict and purposeful structure of structures that make up a poem, a short story, a play, or a novel.

What is it, then, that the artist puts into the work of art by imposing his order on the material? It is his awareness of the world and the people in it. As artists differ in the efficiency of their organization of the materials they work with, so they differ in awareness. One artist's awareness may be minute or grand, specific or general, completely or incompletely available to him as artist, but it is all he has to constitute what he says. Organized and projected beyond himself into the work of art, his private and unique awareness—his vision of men and the world—is presented in the only way it can be presented for the inspection and enrichment of his fellow men.

Some large claims have been made for this factor of awareness. Shelley called poets "the unacknowledged legislators of mankind."

Others have called them teachers, and some have called them prophets. In a famous lecture to the undergraduates of Oxford, Gertrude Stein said that the function of the artist is not to be a prophet, for no man can look into the future. The artist is no visionary, though at times he may look like one. Instead, he is contemporary. He is sensitive to the turns and tempers of his own times, the tides of *now*. Most people—especially young people—are not contemporary; they are enveloped in the past and wrapped in it. They hide their faces and turn away from the present; when they must, they deal with it in terms of old modes of thought and old patterns of action. Therefore when the artist, aware of the present and sensitive to it, presents his peculiar and unique insight organized into a structuring of the material of his choice, his service to the public lies in part at least of acquainting it with its own times.

Let us look a little further into this factor of awareness. Unique, personal, limited by the fact that the artist is one short-lived human being, it is presented in art in terms of human response—in terms, that is, of emotion. No man can be universally aware of the temper of his times, of the traditions of his people, of the records of civilization, or of the resources of the language. He cannot express beyond his taste and his choice of what is significant to him. Yet there is a rough consistency in what the artists of an era, tutored in part by the artists who have gone before them and in part by each other, can perceive in life and present in their works. The consistency is very rough, but it permits us to think of them together and speak of an era as "classic," "baroque," "romantic," or "modern." To this consistency of style and outlook has been applied the word *idiom*. In one sense, each artist has his own idiom, his way of saying what he says. An age has its idiom. Usually the public is learning to grasp one idiom while another is unfolding before it. That is why we can make out better with older books and the modern ones that tag along after them than we can with the new works of first-class adventurous writers. The old books have created their own audience; by just being there they have taught people to read them.

What, then, would constitute the idiom of our own times? We can catch a glimpse of its raw materials from some things in print that a literary artist is aware of as he writes today. He sees in the New York *Times* news reports phrased in words like those which are italicized; the Army is planning an *airlift* using *fixed-wing planes* powered by *jets* and *piston engines,* and *rotary-winged planes*—*helicopters* or *whirleybirds. Genocide* is frowned upon at the *U.N.* The United States Marines, true to their traditions, have consolidated their hold on *Jane Russell Hill* in Korea. Admiral King records his failure to *liberate* a *doodle* left behind at a meeting by Stalin; *pre-owned televisions* can be purchased; and *subteen-agers* constitute an alarming proportion of *juvenile delinquents.* We pick up a clipping from a newspaper. Its headline is QUEEN OF VET BALL, and it bears the picture of a pretty young woman. She is a laboratory technician in a drug company; more interesting than this, she turns out to be an Apprentice Seaman in the United States Naval Reserve.

Another clipping, this one from Jane Lee's column in the Detroit *News,* says in part:

> DEAR JANE: My husband is in the service, and I am home because I am about to become a mother. Every night I write to my husband. I mail these letters every morning at 8:55 in the same mailbox just before I go to work. My husband claims that my mail has been postmarked any time from 10:30 a. m. to 4 p. m. Also he claims the zone mark is different every time. From this he thinks I must be running around. Now it has gotten to the point where I either must explain the postage marks or have a divorce on my hands. Where can I find out exactly what the postage markings mean and how the mail is stamped? I don't believe my husband really wants a divorce, but I know unless this is settled it will lead to one.
>
> GRATEFUL

To this sad note Jane Lee replies:

> The Post Office informs me that the number appearing on the postmark of a letter has nothing to do with postal zones. It is merely the number of the cancellation machine through which your letter happens to pass. The time of cancellation may vary from day to day due to the volume of mail. If the mail is heavy, it will take longer for your letter to be canceled than it would on a day when the mail is light, even though your letter is picked up at the same time and place every morning. Perhaps it would help if you were to clip this and include it in the letter you write to your husband tonight.

Here is the age-old problem of a husband away from his wife in wartime and doubtful, as he broods alone, of her love and faithfulness to him. The terms this problem is embodied in are postal machines and postal zone numbers and letters mailed by a pregnant young wife on her way to work. This distracted young woman takes her problem, not to her minister or her parish priest but to a faceless name in a newspaper, to a woman who makes a business of benevolence, picking it up at nine in the morning and dropping it at five at night. Who is this woman? Who knows? What are her qualifications? Who knows? Jane Lee is a copyrighted name, and when one Jane Lee quits her job, another Jane Lee silently takes her place. All these, too, are of our time. It is not merely A-bombs and H-bombs whose mushroom clouds pollute our skies and rack our seas and cities, but the texture of intimate personal relations woven by our times that creates our idiom, the matter of our living artists.

This matter, brought into the order our artists impose upon it, will find its presentation in the language of our literature. The whole enterprise is possible because each element finds its place at some level of organization in some kind of structure. Language, the material of our literature, is a structured system. Because our society runs on ideas in human heads, language participates in all the structured activities of society, and in some ways perhaps even constitutes them. Society is a cluster of human responses expressed in language—political, economic, technological, religious, and philosophical systems so vast in relation to the individual and so intimate in their effects that they are almost like natural forces and seem, like the physical world itself, to make up the absolute conditions of his being. They make up the everyday world. The chances of time, circumstance, and need bring them into his range. Out of the multitude of impressions that impinge upon him, each person selects and reacts as his nature permits.

The artist—particularly the writer—is all open to these impressions, as Danae to the stars; he is a sensitive receiving organism. His character lays its own pattern on what seems to be random and fortuitous. Language, the material of the writer, is available to him because the patterned elements that make it up give it a nature and a structure of its own. The artist, submitting to his language, shapes it into the organization, into the structure of structures that makes it the vehicle for what he desires to present by its means. What he presents is experience passionately grasped, emotion objectified in a written work for the contemplation of other men and women.

We have literature as an art form because its material, language, is one of the most complex structures known to man and is a participant in all the structures within which he lives. It is a substance having its own inviolable nature and its own descending levels of integrated organization. It is a substance as real as granite, as real as the sounds of song.

People who love literature and value it for the human understanding they get from it feel pretty sick about the competent technician who does not like literature and does not read it. How can he be a responsible citizen and an enlightened companion, they ask, if he has shoved his nose down a technical groove and never lifted his eyes to what it means to be a human being in this troubled world? How can he pretend to be educated if he is not well-read, if the only intellects he has met are the ones who walk the same streets with him instead of the vast company of great creative minds he could meet in books? How can he get out of himself into a broader comprehension of other men and women if powerful works of art have spoken to him and he has not had wit to hear them? How can he be civilized without literature?

CHAPTER 32

Working Your Way
to a Style

Lᴇᴛ'ѕ ꜰᴀᴄᴇ ᴛʜᴇ ᴛʜᴏᴜɢʜᴛ in the beginning: If you had the finest command of written English, you might still be so dull that you would interest no one—except for one thing: a dullard cannot command written English and remain a dullard. A command of writing can not only make a person seem more interesting; it makes him more interesting. Our problem is not that we are uninteresting but that we are inarticulate. Children who are wholly or partly deaf cannot hear the whole range of speech-signals; and because they cannot hear, they cannot imitate. They are dull, listless, uninteresting, often hostile and unruly. If the deficiency is so slight that it is unknown, they fall back in school and are thought stupid. Let a good teacher get hold of them, fit them with hearing aids, teach them to lip-read, and before long their real natures come out and their real capacities come into play. You have nothing to fear about your worth as a human being; if you can learn to express yourself, you set your real self free.

In the eighteenth century, education worked so as to give most educated men and women an adequate command of English. In their writing—of which we have a great deal—they stood forth pretty much as they were because they were articulate. If they were dull or brilliant, their writing showed it. They backed into a command of English by not studying it, by taking it for granted. They went through a rather dreary discipline of studying Latin. Most of them never really got a good grip on Latin; they read it with a grammar in one hand and a dictionary in the other, painfully writing down in English what they thought the Latin meant. They were given a Latin poem or one of Cicero's orations and made to translate it word for word into English. They had to hunt around, experiment, erase, and try again; look up words and check up constructions. They were worrying about Latin, not about English. They went through a primitive pattern-practice for so many years that later, when all they could remember was some Latin tag, they were so used to an unself-conscious manipulation of English that they went on with it. When Latin went out of the schools and English took its place, English suffered. The fear of doing wrong that had attended the Latin was transferred to English; English writers couldn't take English for granted any more. Then they had to be bright; they had to study hard to master it.

We don't want to go back to those days; we have too much that is important to learn in school and college. We have to find a new way to become at ease with English, not through ignorance of it but through knowledge. If we have any faith in knowledge, we believe that the person who has worked hard for it is better than he would have been without it, more effective and more capable. And what is there better to know—for people who have to live in the world and make their living there—than the workings of the language system by which we all communicate with one another? Since writing is not something you know like physics but something you do like swimming, you can work from knowledge and through knowledge to the skills you seek. You come finally to take English for granted and let it work for you while your mind focuses on what you are saying. You can choose words, build them into sentences, build the sentences into paragraphs, and the paragraphs into articles and stories, because you have proceeded step by step and practiced each step until you have mastered it.

We never write unself-consciously, for writing is not merely putting down on paper the way we speak. Writing brings two systems together into one, as two rivers come together at a fork and continue downstream as one. We start with the massive background of our native speech, modified as we grow older and come into contact with other ways of speaking. Here experience is valuable; in many ways the public-school graduate, who has moved from the company and language of the uneducated to the company and language of the educated, has a wider range than the children of the children of culture who know only cultivated speech. Such a range can let us move freely in any company.

Speech is one current approaching the confluence of influences. The other is the tradition of English writing, a noble tradition that began with *Beowulf,* the Anglo-Saxon epic, and King Alfred's prose, when readers were few and writers were fewer. This tradition continues unbroken to the present day, a tradition of craftsmanship and care. Speech is local, personal, and individual, largely contemporary; history is buried in it, but where only the expert can see it. The writing tradition is ancient, general, and universal; all the present English-speaking nations treasure the same central body of inherited masterpieces; yet writing, too, is contemporary. Here the child of culture has an advantage, for our culture is this tradition. Each of us must bring these two streams into one and develop a style of his own.

Earlier we displayed the patterns and word-classes of English and provided exercises by which you could play with substitutions. The effect of these is to give you the control of the English sentence from within that the eighteenth-century writer achieved by means of Latin. In Chapter 26 we developed this pattern practice, so that you could apply it to units as long as the paragraph and push it into efforts at staying within the limitations of verse. We recommend that you work in frequent short bits, daily if possible, and mainly for yourself, not for other readers. If you are beginning late to care about your writing, progress will be slow as you develop a sense of the sentence as an instrument of your expression. As Ben Jonson says, "If it come in a year or two, it is well." You are laying the groundwork for a lifetime.

Writers offering advice to young people tell them to "Imitate." We may discount this advice, because most professional writers who give it are addressing youngsters who want to be professionals and who have a fair idea of what they want to write: creative literature, poetry or fiction. The person who does not "want to be a writer," who merely hopes to make himself a firm and honorable place in his profession or business, will have to develop some skill in expressing his thoughts. Is this good advice for him? If so, how does he choose models to imitate? He should imitate, because by imitation he learns how other men have brought complicated matter into order and transferred that order to paper. He should choose three kinds of models: 1) the recognized experts in the field he hopes to work in; 2) articles, papers, speeches, and essays on any subject that attract him as adequate and forceful handling of their material; and 3) creative work, because it is so highly organized that it serves well as models for organization of other matters.

We may look again to the eighteenth century and to one of its most distinguished writers, Benjamin Franklin. Franklin tells in his *Autobiography* how he went about developing his style. He was first and last a practical man—printer, postmaster, and finally statesman—and he aimed at a plain manner of communicating his thoughts. "Prose writing," he says, "has been of great use to me in the course of my life, and was a principal means of my advancement." When he was about fifteen he argued with a friend who was more fluent and could put down his arguments. The discussion passed into letters, and Franklin "determined at improvement."

About this time I met with an odd volume of the *Spectator*. I . . . read it over and over, and was much delighted with it. I thought the writing excellent, and wished, if possible, to imitate it. With this view I took some of the papers, and making short hints of the sentiment in each sentence, laid them by a few days, and then, without looking at the book, tried to complete the papers again, by expressing each hinted sentiment at length, and as fully as it had been expressed before, in any suitable words that should come to hand. Then I compared my *Spectator* with the original, discovered some of my faults, and corrected them. But I found I wanted [lacked] a stock of words, or a readiness in recollecting and using them, which I thought I should have acquired before that time if I had gone on making verses; since the continual occasion for words of the same import, but of different length, to suit the measure, or of different sound for the rhyme, would have laid me under a constant necessity of searching for variety, and also have tended to fix that variety in my mind, and make me master of it. Therefore I took some of the tales and turned them into verse; and, after a time, when I had pretty well forgotten the prose, turned them back again. I also sometimes jumbled my collections of hints into confusion, and after some weeks endeavoured to reduce them into the best order, before I began to form the full sentences and complete the paper. This was to teach me method in the arrangement of thoughts. By comparing my work afterwards with the original, I discovered many faults and amended them; but I sometimes had the pleasure of fancying that, in certain particulars of small import, I had been lucky enough to improve the method or the language, and this encouraged me to think I might possibly in time come to be a tolerable English writer, of which I was extremely ambitious.

Here is pattern-practice like the translations from Latin which provided an outside organization against which to exercise the language. We may assume that the verse was pretty bad; we are lucky it has not come down to us. Franklin worked within the language; he had to proceed by trial and error, having neither an adequate analysis of English nor the opposition of Latin to throw light on English.

Building a Chain of Sentences

A THEME, an essay, an article, or a book is just one word after another, one sentence after another. Unlike the stretch of the utterances of conversation which seldom run to any great length (because the other speaker is ever ready to cut in), the stretch of written sentences can run to many pages and be composed over a month, a year, or half a lifetime. It has to be cut into manageable segments: parts, chapters, sections, and paragraphs. Yet the end must always be seen in the beginning; sentences, paragraphs, sections, chapters, and parts feed into each other; and the last sentence, the last paragraph, the last section and chapter wraps up the whole. A written composition of any length has a "box" design which is very satisfying to the reader; the beginning tells him where he is going, and the ending tells him where he has been.

Organizing your writing to come out this way is not a matter of starting with big jobs and working down to small, unless you have a natural aptitude for organization. You begin with the sentence and the paragraph; when you have these under control, you push on to the larger units. The sentence is a short string of linked words, and the paragraph is a short string of linked sentences. All parts of the sentence and all parts of the paragraph are not of equal importance. Since you want to end with the strongest impression, the last words of the sentence and the last sentence or two of the paragraph count the most. Next in importance is the beginning, for you want to start with something that will lead the reader in. If we give a "weighted value" to each of these parts, we mark the end with the number 1—to signify first importance—and the beginning with the number 2. What comes between we mark 3. That gives us the recurring sequence 2 3 1, which may be applied to both sentence and paragraph. When we have learned to handle these units according to this sequence, we can push on to the whole theme, article, or book. We need not apply these values rigidly, but have them in the back of the mind as we write.

In a box paragraph the first sentence is a "lead," as in the paragraph above where it tells us that the paragraph is to be about organization. The paragraph pinpoints the particular organization we are interested in, and then the second-to-last sentence sums up and recurs in different words to the idea of the first sentence, tying up the whole. The last sentence "releases" the paragraph by touching on a qualification of the idea. We schematize such a paragraph quite simply by using numbers and arrows:

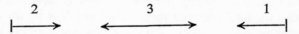

Having in mind the end of a paragraph when you begin it does not mean that you have to proceed according to a rigid plan. You write the first sentence or two to lead into your subject; then you develop your idea. The matter of your paragraph varies; it is simply a manageable bit of what you have to say, enough to take up several sentences. When you begin, you do not always know whether you will run to one, two, or more paragraphs; as you go along, you sense that you want to "take a tuck" in your discourse and start again. You glance back at your lead sentence, looking for something you can pick up and turn to a neat ending. You restate the same idea in about the same words, restate it in slightly different words, summarize what you have said and promise to go on, or just echo some phrase from the beginning. Writing is improvising, and you have plan enough in mind if you plan to do what comes naturally at the proper time. (Note the play on **plan,** with the rephrasing of the idea of not proceeding "according to a rigid plan.")

You have to take a flexible attitude toward paragraphs, because you need to have in mind what your reader can take as a single unit. For some newspapers you simply give up the whole idea of the paragraph and indent every second or third sentence—the second if your first is fairly long, the third if the others are short. These "paragraphs" are not really divisions of your subject; they are a trick to lighten the page so that it is not a mass of solid print. For most readers, paragraphs that run to half a double-spaced typed page are long enough. For sophisticated readers who read a great deal for pleasure and profit, you can run one paragraph to two-thirds or even a full page without leaving them winded. It is well to have one or two new beginnings on each page for the same reason that you write short paragraphs for the newspaper: they make a lighter, prettier page. Going over your manuscript before you retype it, you may want to look for a chink in a long paragraph where it can be cut to give you the overall effect you want. You keep your subject and your likely readers in mind.

The paragraph is a string of linked sentences. The first sentence should clearly point to the next; each of the following sentences should look both ways, reminding and promising at once. The final sentence should bring the paragraph to a stop, suiting its rhythm to the final, fading juncture, so that it feels like an end. Sometimes the final sentence should also set things up for the next paragraph, but that is a tricky thing to accomplish and can be omitted. Here is where your pattern-practice and substitution within the sentence pay off, for if you can write adequate and graceful sentences, you can easily link them. The English sentence, like a railroad freight car, has built-in couplers; it is no trick to connect one to another. One sign of inept writing is a succession of blunt statements unrelated to each other; the succession must be a chain.

We link one sentence to another in various ways. One way is to repeat a word—a key word like **way** in this sentence. Thus a series of sentences (**N V . . . N V . . . N V . . .**) may be linked by having a single form serve as **N** in each. Another way is

to state an order of succession, as **one** and **another** do here, keeping the same form as **N** but varying its modifiers. A third way is to
keep not only the same form but the same form with the same
referent: **Business must earn . . . Business must serve . . . Business must survive . . .** It is well to keep the headword of the
noun-group as close as possible to the verb-marker or the verb-
headword; its post-modifiers in the noun-cluster should be fairly
short. After the verb, noun-clusters can run to almost any length
without confusion. A fourth way is to keep the same form with the
same referent, pinning it down closely by means of a determiner
such as **the, that, these, those** or **its, his, their,** etc. And a fifth way
is to keep the same referent as **N** in a series of sentences, varying
the form by the use of pronouns: **it, he, they,** etc. The reader is
helped by such signals to keep the thread of the discussion in mind;
he is not left to flounder in the middle of the paragraph; your
sentences pass him from hand to hand.

Several other devices give the paragraph unity. One works something like the theme music played for each character in *Peter and
the Wolf;* it is so simple that some people avoid it. It is to use the
same words, sometimes exactly, sometimes slightly varied, to refer
to your subject. In these lines the paragraph has been our subject,
and we have called it "paragraph" wherever we have mentioned it,
with no fancy variations. If President Dwight D. Eisenhower had
been our subject, we would have named him in full, then permitted
variations within these words: **President Eisenhower, the President,
Mr. Eisenhower, Dwight Eisenhower.** We would not go beyond
them to **the former General, our great leader, or the Man in the
White House.** Such embroidery weakens the writing. Whenever we
use the **N** in the **N V** pattern to refer to President Eisenhower in
this paragraph, we would stay within the full title.

A second device is parallelism, writing several sentences to the
same basic pattern and allowing ourselves only enough variation
to avoid monotony. A third device is to delay the central **N V** pattern in some of the sentences, letting an introductory expression
come first, and putting the link into that expression (or not, as we
choose). Such a word as **but, yet, still, nevertheless,** or **however** indicates the addition of an idea, addition with some kind of contrast or opposition, or a qualification of the preceding idea. **V-ing**
beginnings are good: **Concerning this matter, the President notified
Congress that . . .** Adverb (word, phrase, or clause) beginnings

are good: **When so many people protested, the President . . . Afterwards, Mr. Eisenhower . . . At the first report of these actions, . . .** A fourth device is variation, but this one is tricky: it demands that you hold the theme and develop the idea without letting your concern for structure show. It takes a good deal of thought and practice.

The box paragraph is one in which the end is foreshadowed in the beginning, and the beginning is reflected in the end. It works well with any kind of writing: description, narration, cause and effect, or a simple line of statements. It can forewarn and reflect in words alone, in ideas and words, or in ideas alone. Its value is that it offers a satisfying completeness at the end of each unit. By giving the reader one nicely organized and neatly tied-up package after another, it holds his attention. The box paragraph flatters the reader by seeming to admit him to the order of your thinking; it does not really admit him to any more than you want to tell him at the moment, but it seems to. It builds his confidence in your control over your material and the language by presenting him with recurrences that obviously have not fallen by chance. It puts a rhythm into your writing with very little trouble and without any limitation whatever on what you say. You have only to construct a linked series of such paragraphs to produce a paper of any length you choose.

The Fabric of Prose Composition

"WORDS fail me!" people complain, sure that they know too few words for what they have to say. This or that is too beautiful, too complicated, or too something or other to be captured in words. We have cautioned against being overwhelmed by this feeling and setting out on a panicky effort to build a vocabulary. The chances are that you have a perfectly sufficient vocabulary for any reasonable purpose of expression. If you have grown to maturity within our society, you know enough words and enough meanings for them to communicate adequately. You may know more words than the entire language has offered to its greatest writers, such as Shakespeare or Chaucer—more words than were drawn upon for the King James Bible of 1611. If you do not command these words and have them available for your writing, your difficulty lies more in failure to call on them than in ignorance of them; your real trouble is lack of practice and of insight.

Word-counts are always deceiving, since the recesses of the mind are closed to the calculating machine. Still, one count may suggest the truth about words. For the two hundred English words repeated most often in print, the *Oxford English Dictionary* records some 14,500 discriminated meanings. An apparent deficiency in vocabulary may be merely an inability to build sentences which pinpoint those meanings. People have been known to starve in the midst of abundance because they could not tell good nourishing food when they saw it, and possibly writers languish from malnutrition because they hunt for a special word where a common word can serve if it is given a chance. Good style is not a matter of pulling big words down from the sky and using them to frighten your readers into the dictionary habit; it is a matter of making the most use of the commonest repeated elements. We speak of the texture of cloth, which differs from fabric to fabric; but as cotton weavers have shown ever since chemistry faced them with rayon and nylon, differences in texture depend as much on the weave as on the thread. It is the same in writing English. Words are important; more important are the sentences we weave them in.

The common words are good precisely because you and other people know them. They are common because they are useful; they are useful because they trigger responses in the reader. An unfamiliar word, as we know from experience, is simply a hole in the sentence until you find out what it means. A word may be familiar because it is old or because it is new; new words and new meanings for old words spread very quickly in our age of mass communications. Any television addict knows what a picture tube is and can distinguish audio from video troubles in his set. **Picture** and **tube** are old words in new senses; **audio** and **video** are new words, at least to the general reading public. All are quite familiar, but they differ: **picture** and **tube** each have many possible meanings as we use them in sentences; **audio** and **video** have very few. We can substitute **sound** and **sight** for **audio** and **video,** gaining a good deal not because they are more precise in meaning but because they are less. In use they suggest more because of all the other meanings we do not intend but cannot quite suppress when we apply them to television. They stir up echoes in our memories; these echoes are valuable to the writer.

The question occurs: familiar to whom? Americans talk about "the average person" and then go on to assume, each one, that he represents the average. An individual circulates in society and is simultaneously a member of several different speech-communities. He shares with each a vocabulary of familiar words that he cannot carry into the others: in the family, names that embody family traditions of long standing; in his age group, a private coinage often including disrespectful terms for outsiders such as teachers; in his trade or profession, its technical terminology; in his reading, the Latin-Greek-foreign vocabulary of the literate; and in his sports, clubs, and church, the language of devotion and ritual. No person is average, but each of us must make the discovery for himself that he is not average. He winnows his total vocabulary for terms that he can freely use anywhere. Familiar words are the words that most people know, the words of common use.

Any given idea provokes in the mind alternate sets of words to express it; if one set does not suit the occasion, you have to pick, choose, or combine them to achieve the most adequate display of your meaning. The texture of prose is a warp of words woven into a weft of structures, best achieved by holding some consistency in the associations stirred by the words you use and the patterns you use them in. We may distinguish four areas of vocabulary from which you may pick freely as you write; each gives a special quality to your style. They are 1) the words of common experience, 2) the words of comparison and imagery, 3) the words of literary reference, and 4) the vocabulary of allusion.

THE VOCABULARY OF COMMON EXPERIENCE

YOU can find the words of common experience in your dictionary by looking for entries that run to some length. The etymology may be quite long in such an entry, but that length is not of first importance, since most of it may be devoted to the word's prehistory before it came into English. A word's life in English is indicated in its spread and range by its numbered definitions. The words of common experience have from ten to fifty separate definitions; often they are entered also in a string of phrases in which they cannot be separately defined. Usually these words also are listed under two, three, or even four word-classes: a noun like *hand* has verb, adjective, and adverb listings which indicate class shifts of long standing. Words of common experience are names for the parts of the body, **head, hand, foot, eye,** and other names such as **house, home, store, road, way;** verbs like **look, see, smell, give, get, sell, buy, walk, run, go, come, talk, sing, think;** adjectives like **cold, hot, warm, fast, slow, dark, light, smooth, rough;** adverbs like **hard, fast, quickly;** and of course all the structure-words. Using only the word **hand,** we have expressions like **at hand, on hand, in hand, handy, left-handed, heavy-handed, even-handed, handily, hand** (someone something), **unhand, handle, mishandle,** and so on. These are the bread-and-butter words of our language; they are the first words we learn in a foreign language; without going outside them we can express a good deal of what we have to say.

To show the power that lies in such words, let us look at one of the great short poems in English which has in it only one "uncommon" word, **diurnal.** The poem shows something of the shock the living feel at death, not as it strikes one's self but as it cuts close:

> A slumber did my spirit seal;
> I had no human fears:
> She seemed a thing that could not feel
> The touch of earthly years.
>
> No motion has she now, no force;
> She neither hears nor sees;
> Rolled round in earth's diurnal course
> With rocks, and stones, and trees.
>
> WILLIAM WORDSWORTH

THE VOCABULARY OF COMPARISON AND IMAGERY

FROM the vocabulary of common experience we move easily into the vocabulary of comparison and imagery—a means of presenting the unfamiliar in terms of the familiar—which acts constantly to expand the expressive range of common words. We tend to relate what is new to what we know; what we know best is the central core of experience through which all men and women pass as they are born, grow up, marry, have children, age, and die. Thus any coming into being is a birth, like the birth of a nation, the birth of the blues, the birth of television. Thus water runs, time marches, incomes grow, troubles beget troubles, nations wither, and hopes

die. If we look in a dictionary at any word which has many meanings, we find that some are frozen metaphors (a metaphor is an
implied comparison, and **frozen** here is a metaphor) which some
one person began centuries ago and other people continued. Staying close to the names for parts of our own bodies, we find that
potatoes have eyes; cabbages, heads; and corn, ears. A reporter
has a nose for news, rivers have mouths, mountains have feet, and
tables have legs. A man is fingered for a crime; he knuckles under;
there is a body of opinion. Cars have knee-action, pipes have el-
bows, laws have teeth. What is true about these words is true about
any word which comes into common use; it is soon extended into
new areas of meaning. We could learn much about the use of words
by sitting down with a dictionary and looking up the common
words, the words everybody knows, and testing to see how many
uncommon thoughts can be expressed in them.

In a world where the little area of what is known is a candle in
the surrounding dark, each person holds his vocabulary and its
word-classes as a shield against the unknown, against what has not
been named. If he can apply a word he knows by some extension
to the new and nameless, he has achieved a kind of victory over
it by drawing it within the order of his thinking. Thus the settlers
in Colonial America gave familiar names to the plants and animals
they found: the robin, the polecat (skunk), the mountain lion, and
the buffalo. When the airplane first came into the American Army,
it was treated as a kind of cavalry; flying officers wore spurs on
their boots for no purpose, they said, but to keep their feet from
sliding off their desks. The first armored regiments were also put in
the cavalry; obviously armor was a new way to ride to war. The
menace of armored vehicles was suppressed in the simple name
tank. The internal mysteries of the atom were made familiar by
talk of distance, orbits, and constellations; and the infernal power
of thermonuclear devices was averted by calling them bombs. This
classifying in familiar terms holds the real nature of the newly discovered unknown on the edge of consciousness until we become
used to it and can face it squarely.

The value to the writer of comparison and imagery is immense,
in that it extends the reach of his vocabulary without burdening
it with new terms and sending him on a career of word-making or
word-finding. He is like the traveler in France who can pull American dollars out of his pocket and spend at will until he can get to

a bank and exchange his money. He is able at once to exploit the words he knows and keep his reader comfortable among the words the reader knows, even though the matter being discussed will lead into new worlds of thought and experience.

A further reach of comparison and imagery lies in the extended use of technical vocabularies, a use which depends on a generally spread knowledge or half-knowledge of the special terms. Thus we can take a term from boxing and apply it to a girl, **She's a knock-out;** we can say that we have been **saved by the bell** or **saved by a long count.** We **lead with our chins** in business and social affairs; we **give them the old one-two.** We can use the language of baseball: **Mendes-France struck out at London;** of football: **The Allied forces tried an end run at Anzio** or **President Eisenhower went into a huddle with a team of finance experts.** We can use the language of horse racing: **In the postwar race for the auto market, the independents seem to have been left at the post.** We can use the language of mining: **Nothing he tried ever panned out;** of chemistry: **The Rejection of EDC acted like a catalyst in the pot of European diplomacy;** of gambling, of animal husbandry, of farming, of engineering.

All this extension of our present vocabulary is not a mere matter of language. The comparison is not only a comparison of words; the writer must make his comparisons by observations in the world; he must see that certains things are like certain other things that he knows. The city boy who said, "The hens are cackling like a bunch of old women," seems to be reversing a comparison, but he may have been working from the unknown to the known. The writer is fenced by his native language; he can make only the comparisons it admits. A Frenchman cannot speak in French of the foot of a mountain or of the outdoors; and he calls a potato an earth-apple as we cannot, because the word **apple** does not have the same reach in English as in French. Within these limits, beginning with the previous classifications of his language which sort experience, the writer can sort new experience and look for similarities to what he has words for. He must watch out for comparisons which are just a matter of words, like "The mother grabbed her child in one fell swoop," since **fell** means 'terrible,' and the comparison was originally to the deadly dive of a hunting falcon. Where he sees a valid likeness, he illuminates his writing and pleases the reader by putting that likeness into words.

The language of comparison and imagery can be trivial or profound, but as a whole it is within the grand tradition of English
writing. Our great phrasemakers have been men of insight who
have seen likenesses. The likenesses sometimes take form in a single striking phrase, sometimes in an extended comparison, and
sometimes in an elaborate book-long allegory like *Gulliver's
Travels* or Orwell's *Animal Farm,* where the hog, the dog, and
the horse represent human beings acting like hogs, dogs, and
horses and producing tyranny. Like any other adventure in language, these comparisons take daring: the beginning writer will
turn off some that will make him feel silly. If he persists with intelligence and with the faith that this way of writing is an effective
way—though not always effective for him—he will sharpen his
perception of the world around him and his use of English at once.

THE VOCABULARY OF LITERARY REFERENCE

MANY students who enter college confess freely that they do not
enjoy reading and that they do as little as possible. They often imply that they intend to continue reading as little as they can get by
with—an attitude that leaves the faculty with its scholarly degrees
and the librarians with their stores of books wondering just what
the students think they are coming to college for. It also leaves the
teachers of writing wondering how you go about teaching non-
readers to write, and if you do, who in the world they will write
for. Since reading is a much simpler task than writing, you can set
out to produce non-writing readers and produce them; but a non-
reading writer is a rare bird with a dim future as an unread writer.
When a reader is more learned, more knowing, and more generally
sophisticated than a writer, he doesn't read him. He looks around
for another writer who can in some way enlarge his world; he drops
the writing which can only contract it. If you want to write and be
read, you have to read.

Anyone who writes—unless he aims at a juvenile audience—has
to assume that his readers know their business: they are skilled,
competent, experienced readers. Just as he assumes that an expression from baseball or politics will be more familiar than the special
thing he is saying (so that it will be safe to say, for instance, that a
certain advance in chemistry is only a minor-league triumph in research), so he assumes that a reference to ancient or modern litera-

ture, history, or one of the sciences will speak directly to his reader. Making that assumption (he must make it, or he will be working under wraps), he can give his writing a quality that the literate reader finds attractive: the effect of a meeting of minds on a civilized level. He cannot do it unless he himself is well-read.

If he is careful, he can also make his meaning clear to the not-so-well-read. When Secretary Dulles said to a New York audience that in dealing with the Chinese Communists the United States government would be slow to anger, anyone could understand him. Even so, the CBS Television News proudly photographed a verse in the King James Bible and presented it on the screen. Dulles was also echoing the language of the Bible for the special understanding of those who know the Bible. And CBS proudly submitted itself to the nation as one of the knowing. The special import of Dulles' Biblical echo is a little hard to pin down; we may take it as a hint to the world that this nation among Christian nations proposes to act not on expediency but on principle based on the word of God. Further hints of various kinds can also be spun out, but with less and less chance of being in Dulles' mind when he spoke.

Reflections of literature of this kind may be either direct or indirect. A writer may say, "Before he entered the church, he listened for a while to the siren song of business," in which the words **siren song** recall to readers a bit of the *Odyssey*. In place of "It is mine, and I like it," he may echo Touchstone in *As You Like It:* "An ill-favour'd thing, sir, but mine own." President Franklin D. Roosevelt echoed Mercutio in *Romeo and Juliet* in a comment on a labor-management dispute, "A plague on both your houses!" One may say, "Everything he did turned out well" or echo the Bible, "Whatever he touched prospered in his hands." Characters from literature may serve as types of people: Miranda for sweet innocence; Hotspur for rash, headlong courage; Dogberry for the dumb cop; Mrs. Malaprop for women like Mrs. Ace on the radio who get words mixed up; Portia for a woman lawyer; and Mentor for an athletic coach. Some writers—and some college professors—have such vast recall for their reading that their thoughts naturally take form in the words of Hazlitt, DeQuincey, or Montaigne. Quite often the phrasing is so natural and so subtle that the innocent reader never guesses that the composition is not free and original.

The effect of such literary reference or echo is an interesting texture in the writing. At its best it is a straight, clear statement that anyone can understand, well-read or not: it fits "horizontally" into the line of meaning of the writing. It also has a "vertical" dimension, a depth of significance that develops out of its roots in older, well-known literature, where it fits into a different line of meaning. Calling the United Nations Assembly the "parliament of man"— which it is, truly enough—recalls to the reader the prophetic, hopeful lines of Tennyson's "Locksley Hall," which are only hinted at in the phrase. Writers picking titles for their works have mined the standard authors for phrases like "The Green Pastures," "Deliverance from Evil," "The Arrow and the Song," "Let Mr. Chips Fall Where He May," "A Little Less Than Gods," "The Hand of Cain," and so on. Crudely done, literary echoing can run into the trite and kill the effect intended.

Ordinary people who have no great knowledge of literature to draw on know in its place a great number of proverbs and pithy sayings that serve to make a point. "There's more than one way to skin a cat," "Every dog has his day," "A bird in the hand, you know," "When thieves fall out," "Business is business," "Handsome is as handsome does," and so on. For a writer who has a point to make that one of these sayings will serve, either directly quoted or indirectly echoed, this proverb lore is always at hand.

THE VOCABULARY OF ALLUSION

THERE is also allusion to the popular interests of the day, to events, persons, popular songs, incidents—to the whole history of our own times, wherever it seems to bear on what the writer has to say. Passing events seem to make little impression as we go through them, except when they happen directly to us; otherwise what we hear over the radio, read in the papers, or see on television seems as remote as Caesar's conquest of Gaul: "Storms Batter British Coast," "Siamese Twins Separated, One Dies," "Vast Turbines in Cavern Provide Canadian Power," "Former Veep Now Junior Senator from Kentucky," "Army Cuts Draft Calls," "British Marilyn Monroe Visits U.S., Decries Sex," "Vishinsky Dead, U.N. Pays Last Respects." Eddie Fisher sings "Count Your Blessings" at the President's request. "Let Me Go, Lover" fills the airways in place of "Teach Me Tonight" (Oh, to be a teacher!); Milton Berle loses his sponsor to Jackie Gleason; and NBC, which starts the day at 7:30 a. m. with Dave Garroway and "Today," ends it at 1:00 a. m.

with Steve Allen and "Tonight." All this happens on the fringes of
our activities as we take our bodies through the things we have to
do between bed and bed again.

Allusion to the passing scene is a means of pinning your work
down in time and drawing on experience which you share with your
contemporaries. The very background nature of much that comes
to us by press, radio, and television, at the movies, the arenas, the
theaters, and the concert halls gives it a peculiar emotional impact;
we recall what we were doing in the past in terms of the songs we
were singing and the headlines we were reading. It is not unusual
for a writer dealing with some event of a few years ago—like the
flight of the first jet aircraft in 1942 at Muroc, California—to go to
the library and read through the newspapers, news magazines, and
other periodicals of the day for "atmosphere." Then, with his sense
of the circumstances refreshed, he can enrich his treatment of the
event by putting it into its setting. What did the papers say the day
the Liberty Bell cracked? Did they take the cracking as a symbol,
and if so, of what kind? The mention of a popular song can recall
to the reader the room he stood in when he heard it, the people
who were with him, the job he had then, and even the clothes he
wore. Our lives are webs in which these things are threads.

The Texture of Personal Style

THE beginning writer is inclined to see writing rather narrowly and
walk too narrow a line. He knows that between his graduation from
high school and his graduation from college much has happened
to him besides the knowledge he has gained. He is a larger person
with a considerably enriched life. All this has taken place over a
specific stretch of time, not just any time; his college life is part of
his whole complicated activities of the period. How can he work
his maturity and development into his writing so that the writing
shows something more than merely increased skill in making sentences?

The writer must, of course, stick to his subject, whatever it is.
Where a precise technical vocabulary is essential, he uses it; he uses
it the more freely the more certain he is that his probable readers
know the field. When his probable readers know less about the subject, he winnows the technical vocabulary, looking for what can be

translated into everyday English. He is left with certain terms of specialized meaning that he has to use. He follows his first use of each term with a definition which will hold for his paper, as we defined *phoneme* and *morpheme* in this book. He spreads these terms as thinly as he needs to, embedding them in the vocabulary of common experience. Using comparison and imagery to draw the reader into partnership, he relates what he is saying to the reader's knowledge of the way things go in the world. He achieves a civilized tone by reference to the literature which the educated man can be expected to know wherever such reference illuminates. He draws on the homely wisdom of ordinary people in proverbs and similar expressions; and he links his writing with reality by allusion to the passing scene, giving the matter he is writing about a place in the general cultural setting.

By this process he builds the texture of his style. The process is not easy, and it demands a good deal of self-exploration. "Who am I," he asks, "really? A young adult in the second half of the twentieth century, localized in time and space, child of my parents, member of my family; having had my schooling in specific schools; having traveled where I have been and seen what I have seen; having learned my favorite sports, songs, dances; having read just what I have read and studied what I have studied; having made my friends and my enemies—being the person that I am, what do I have to say and how best can I say it? How can I bring myself to bear as a whole person on what I have to talk and write about, so that it is me speaking—me, an individual, unique and never to be repeated, at this particular point and spot of time? I am not what I was yesterday, nor what I will be tomorrow; I may be wiser later, but I take myself as I am now, and I now express what I think now about the matters I think about."

We remarked early in this chapter that a dullard cannot take the road to a command of written English and remain a dullard. He has to take an easier road.

One Thing after Another in Proper Order

OUR civilization has what has been called a "rage for order," but it involves a large number of disordered people who are unaware of the systems they belong to or the classifications of the things they handle every day. Many of these are young people who come here and go there as they are expected to, but they preserve a sense of free individual choice because they are young and innocent and moved by internal directives that society has not yet brought under control. The community provides "play space" for them because they are young; it is only as they grow into adulthood that they realize how small the space actually is and how carefully fenced, how briefly they have been permitted to stay in it, and how thoroughly they have been excluded as grownups. When they turn eighteen and register for military service, get a job, marry, and have children; or even when they walk down a sidewalk between other people's lawns, drive a car or ride a bus, they soon learn that what was once "cute" when they did it is no longer treated with indulgence. Their movements are limited to paths which have been laid out for them, often for hundreds of years, and they walk those paths or walk into trouble.

Order is imposed upon us by the community because of the masses of people involved, the incredible number of things, and the pile-up of knowledge which characterize modern society. These things cannot be handled individually; they must be sorted into classes, subclasses, and subsubclasses for convenience and efficiency. We cannot go back; the people, the things, and the items of knowledge increase day by day. Larger and larger masses of land are occupied, and cultures which once could live in indifference to each other wash to a line of meeting, face to face. Farmlands become villages, villages become suburbs, suburbs become precincts and boroughs of cities simply for the sake of order as older patterns break down and become inefficient.

Before 1859, geology, biology, and physiology were separate studies, but they were brought together by Darwin in that year in his *Origin of Species*. Physics, chemistry, and astronomy have been linked by mathematics into one overall view of the universe; and the social sciences—anthropology, economics, geography, government, history, and sociology—are being forced into theories acceptable to all the various disciplines. Psychology spins a web between zoology and the social sciences. Scientists of all sorts, philosophers, theologians, and artists are finding that they have to face each other's concepts of man and his place in the universe. The pile-up of knowledge has forced them to it and they cannot go back.

We have no choice; either we master the order of things or it masters us. The repairman taking a sewing machine apart has to do it in the order established by the maker of the machine; the maker had to build it in submission to his materials. A person buying or selling property has to perform certain acts in a specified sequence, or he takes or gives a defective title; a student entering college has to go to a certain office and start from there. A graduate looking for a job finds himself limited to a certain kind and range of jobs; he is either too little or too well qualified for others. There is a place, it seems, for everyone and everything, and each must be in its place.

The universal demand for order is an obligation laid upon a writer by the people he writes for; as reader he demands it in what he reads. We cannot do as Emerson only a hundred years ago is said to have done. When a breeze from a window scattered his notes all over the stage, the people in the front rows leaped to gather them up. Emerson took them as they were handed to him, stacked them in a disordered pile on the pulpit, and then, picking the first one off the top, he began to speak. He handed out separate nuggets of wisdom, and his audience was willing to accept them. We have to refine and shape our thoughts or no one will take them, no matter how valuable they are. We give out the pennies, nickels, dimes, and quarters, each related to the others; just possibly we have gone off the gold standard of wisdom, too. If we can't count it, we don't want it.

The universal demand for order is also a discipline for the writer, for in our society we demand that the order expressed in language have some relation to the inherent order of the matter discussed. We are looking for truth; we ask for statements of fact. Among the Chinese, truth in this sense is not important; truth in their sense is a consistency within language, not a statement of the way things are as much as a model of the way things should be. Their demand is that the writer express the order he desires; our demand is that the writer find the order he expresses. To find it, he faces away from language toward life in all its complexity; he looks outward not inward for order, toward people and things and knowledge. He orders his writing to express what he has perceived.

We thus have two systems of order at work in each body of writing; they must be adjusted to each other. One is the "box" order of presentation which we mentioned: the choice of a "lead" which will draw the reader in, the discussion of the matter itself, and at the end a strong statement or restatement of the point the writer most wants to pound home. The other system of order is the relationship which the writer finds in his subject by studying it and which he must present as honestly as he can. Is this order not the same for everybody, for any writer? No, here is where the writer impresses his own mark. Being who he is and what he is, he approaches his subject with special insight and special knowledge; experience has prepared him to see it in a unique way. If you know astronomy and the sea, you read Melville with different eyes from those of the person who knows neither, but has some knowledge of law and anthropology. If you have tinkered with cars as a hot-rodder, you approach aircraft as mechanisms; if you are an artist, you are caught by the sheer stark beauty of the line of flight. Then you fit your special perceptions to the needs of your readers.

Any recipe in a magazine shows in a raw way the interaction of these two systems of order. First there is a picture of the dish in full color, and a mouth-watering description of its taste. Then there is a list of the ingredients in their exact quantities: "2 cups flour, 1 cup milk," and so on. This list is followed by the order of combining: "Sift the flour into a bowl, add the milk slowly, stirring constantly," and so on. Finally, there is the promise that if you combine these ingredients in these exact amounts and in this exact order, you, too, can serve this dish and become renowned in your dining room.

The recipe demands no breakdown of the list into classes: wet and dry ingredients, powders and solids, or basics and flavorings, though it might. The problem of such classification is one that always faces the writer; it is one of levels of relationship, of parts within wholes, of classes within classes. Any matter we look at can be taken apart in different ways, depending upon our interest. The process is one of "abstraction." We do well when we think of abstracting to remember that all language is abstract. No word is a full and complete representation of any specific thing. **Chair** refers to this chair, that chair, or any chair; we only know which chair when the word is used in a sentence that tells us as a whole which one. And **chair** refers to a general broad outline, shape, and use; the scratches, marks, or design of any particular chair are ignored.

The smallest unit of language that can point to any specific chair is the utterance (in writing, the sentence). **Chair** refers to a class of things. Chairs are furniture, but so are tables, desks, pictures, and rugs. **Furniture** is a class of manufactured objects; **manufactured objects** are a class of objects in general, some manufactured, some natural. And so on. We class by levels, depending on our interest.

Abstraction is a natural process which we constantly perform with the eye. Let us say we are looking at a single blade of grass in a forest. Withdrawing a little, we see the grasses; they are of various kinds. Withdrawing more, we see grasses and flowers, then grasses, flowers, and bushes, each of many kinds. Withdrawing more, we see grasses, flowers, bushes, and trees; among the trees, elms, maples, locusts, pines, firs, and oaks. Withdrawing further, we see the forest as a whole—the watered forest of the temperate zones. This is one kind of forest, and there are others: the rain forests of the coasts, the evergreen forests of the North, the jungles of the equator. The closer we are, the more specific detail we see; the more removed we are, the more we see the overall groupings.

When we apply knowledge to what we see, we come out to a different result. It is a shock to open a book of botany and discover that plants are classified quite differently on the basis of their internal structures. The grasses belong to the same family as towering bamboos; the juniper and the red cedar are members of the pine family; the pink flowering redbud is a legume; the box elder is a maple; ashes are olives, except for the mountain ash which is grouped with the hawthornes in the rose family; the thorny locust is a brother to the pea. The classifications of the casual eye give way to the exact ordering of the student of plant structures. Yet, for many purposes, a tree is still a tree, and the waving grass is grass.

The recipe also offers a sequence of actions in what we call chronological order—the order of time—one thing is done after another. This common order of narrative provides its problems. When we describe the actions of one thing or one person, we can begin at the beginning and go on through to the end. When we introduce a second person or thing, we have to decide whether to handle their actions together in a single sentence or follow one for a way and go back and pick up the other. Introducing a third, fourth, and fifth, we have to figure out some method of grouping the lines of action and carrying them along to the same end. Novelists face this problem in varying degrees; probably the great Russian novel, *War and Peace* by Tolstoy, tangles itself most daringly of all in this problem. This novel treats many specific men and women moving at will in complicated societies grappling in the Napoleonic War. The classic manipulation of many threads occurs in the great battle scenes. Any ex-G.I. who pressed his face into the dirt and lost contact with the men on either side should appreciate the sweep and control of this complex interweaving of individual actions related in time and space.

Description which deals with objects in space offers comparable problems. Should you start with an overview of the whole and work down to details, or take the details one by one and finish with the big picture? Your decision is often determined by the "lead" you choose; if it is a detail, you go from detail to detail; if it is a general treatment of the whole, you move then to the details. There are advantages either way. Your eye is like a movie or television camera, starting away back or away high and zooming in on the object (such as a building), coming down to a façade, to a door, then through the door to the object of your interest inside. Or it can pick out significant details one by one to set the tone and withdraw until the whole object is framed in a long view. Keats was almost a perfect scenarist in "The Eve of St. Agnes":

> St. Agnes' eve—Ah, bitter chill it was!
> The owl, for all his feathers, was a-cold;
> The hare limp'd trembling through the frozen grass,
> And silent was the flock in woolly fold:
> Numb were the Beadsman's fingers, while he told
> His rosary, and while his frosted breath,
> Like pious incense from a censer old,
> Seem'd taking flight for heaven, without a death,
> Past the sweet Virgin's picture, while his prayer he saith.

The details tell us it was a cold night.

The beginning writer walks too narrow a line. If he is given something to write about, he goes up with his eyes fixed on it and beats his head against it. He needs rather to back away from it and see it in its setting; he should look around and see if he knows anything like it. Comparison is not merely a matter of phrase and sentence; it can be the means of giving backbone to the writing. The very fact that individual items—persons, places, things, or ideas—are complex can be turned to our advantage instead of being permitted to work against us. Nothing else can be exactly like any one thing; when we put similar things beside it, we see what is common to all and what is peculiar to each. Arranging these similarities and differences can give us alternate sets of order to use between the introduction and conclusion of a paper.

A simple example will illustrate. Somewhere in a blank space we put a dot:

There is not much we can say about this dot. It is black and round; it stands in a certain relation to each of the four sides and each of the four corners. All relations change, however, when we introduce a second dot:

This dot, too, is black and round; it has its own relations with each side and corner. It has something else: it has a relation to the first dot, a relation that cannot exist without it. The two form an axis; we can draw a line between them.

We get a further change by introducing a third dot:

This third dot is also black and round, and has its own relations to the sides and corners. With each of the other dots it forms an axis, which lets us draw two more lines; this time the lines enclose space. If we imagine each dot to be an item of some sort—a person, place, thing, or idea—we can relate them as individuals and as a group to the whole setting, and we can use each one to set off the others.

From the dots we can proceed to principle: It is hard to write about any one thing alone and apart from other things, because it is hard to get hold of it. It offers a smooth round surface difficult to penetrate; its relations do not help much when they are to things different from itself. Two things are somewhat easier to handle, because they relate immediately to each other and set up a tension of similarities and differences; each sets off the other's relations to things different from both. Three things are much easier to handle than either one or two things. Each sets up a tension with each of the others and gives us enough relations so that we can deal with the three as a group. With things different from themselves, the items relate separately and all together.

One might object that items do not fall like this in nature, even dots, by isolated ones and twos and threes, but at random and in large numbers.

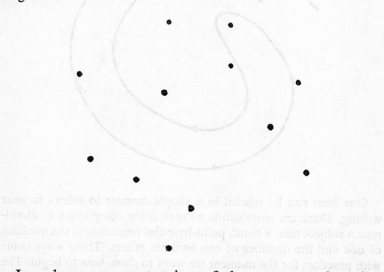

In such cases we must make or find arrangements that relate them: by triangles, or by some other linking; but we should not separate them and try to take them one by one:

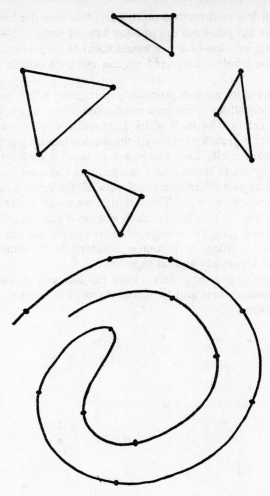

One item can be related in a simple manner to others in your writing. There are more subtle ways of using comparison to illuminate a subject than a blunt, point-by-point treatment of the qualities of one and the qualities of one or more others. These ways come with practice; for the moment we want to show how to begin. The simplest procedure is to treat item A (the subject) thoroughly, then move to B and to C. If item A has three aspects we want to touch on, we get a pattern like this:

A. (the subject)
   1.⎫
   2. ⎬aspects of A.
   3.⎭
B. (a similar item)
   1.⎫
   2. ⎬aspects of B.
   3.⎭
C. (another similar item)
   1.⎫
   2. ⎬aspects of C.
   3.⎭

An alternate way of approaching your subject A in this pattern is to sneak up on it by way of B and C. You lay down the general characteristics of the class, briefing your reader, in effect, on what to expect of a thing like A. Thus you have laid the ground for a thorough treatment of A in the light of characteristics which you and your reader understand. In the process of digging around for the characteristics of the type and looking for good examples to use as B and C, you learn a good deal about A which you cannot learn from it directly. The pattern of the whole paper would be as follows:

  I. Your lead: Some striking and interesting aspect of
     A or the type it belongs to
 II. Your discussion:
    B. A typical example of the type.
      1.⎫
      2. ⎬The qualities of B.
      3.⎭
    C. A second example.
      1.⎫
      2. ⎬The qualities of C.
      3.⎭
    A. Your subject: the one you are really talking
      about.
      1.⎫
      2. ⎬The qualities of A.
      3.⎭

III. Your conclusion: The nature of A in its relations
to the type, and its meaning to the reader.

Suppose your subject were something like a popular tract on the
Seven Sins from a medieval manuscript (A). You read around in
medieval religious literature in order to find out how your tract
(A) fits into it. You find it in certain ways quite unusual, in other
ways typical. You pick two other tracts (B) and (C), which are
good examples of the type. Then you lay out your paper according
to the pattern:

I. Your lead: The medieval approach to sin and how
it differs from ours. Popular tracts on the sins and
the treatment by classification.

II. Your discussion:
B. A typical tract quite popular in the Middle Ages.
1.⎫
2.⎬ Its characteristics.
3.⎭
C. A second tract, much the same, but slightly different.
1.⎫
2.⎬ Its characteristics.
3.⎭
A. Tract A, the one you are presenting.
1.⎫
2.⎬ Its characteristics.
3.⎭

III. Your conclusion: Your tract (A) is a special case,
showing the breakdown of the medieval attitude
and the beginning of modern ideas on sin.

This approach, simple as it is, can be quite sophisticated in its
handling and in its treatment of details; it gives your information
to readers in manageable segments. It also lets you build to a cli-
max, always effective in writing, by treating less important matter
first. It is easy to handle in the writing and, perhaps more important, it guides you in your reading. You know from the start
what to look for.

A somewhat more subtle and more difficult order to control is
the analysis of A, B, and C into their qualities, and the presentation of A, B, and C by characteristics. Letting A, B, and C stand

for the subject and two similar objects, and letting 1, 2, 3 stand for characteristics, we get the following pattern:

I. Your lead: Some striking or interesting aspect of A or the type it belongs to.
II. Your discussion:
    1. A characteristic of the type, as it appears in
    B. A typical instance.
    C. Another instance.
    A. Your subject.
    2. A second characteristic, as it appears in
    B.
    C.
    A.
    3. A third characteristic, as it appears in
    B.
    C.
    A.
III. Your conclusion: Taking A as a whole in the light of these comparisons, its nature is . . . and its meaning to the reader is . . .

This approach is not only more subtle but more involved, for you have to take all the information with which you might begin a paper according to the other patterns and make a further breakdown of it before you begin to write. It, too, offers manageable segments of the information to the reader. Suppose, for instance, your subject (A) is a sports car which you have found interesting enough to write about. The treatment works out about as follows:

I. Your lead: Car A is a very individual product of an imaginative designer, with startling speed and handling characteristics.
II. Your discussion:
    1. The motor, as it is seen in
    Car B.
    Car C.
    Car A.
    2. The body, as it is seen in
    Car B.
    Car C.
    Car A.

   3. The wheel-and-axle system, as it is seen in
       Car B.
       Car C.
       Car A.
 III. Your conclusion: Taking car A as a whole, we have
     a machine capable of such and such top speed,
     with remarkable streamlining, carrying capacity
     and comfort, and with unusual cornering ability,
     considering its size and cost.

Obviously the order of writing is not a matter of language alone. It is built by observations carried on outside language in the world of people and things. It is built by facing your subject on its own terms, in its relations to other items like it, and in its relations to other items different from it but affecting it. We can go astray in our writing through ignorance of the language system and how it works; we can go astray through ignorance of ourselves and other people; and we can go astray through ignorance of the world in which we all live and carry on our daily activities. We can go right in our writing and be read, if we make sure that we know about language, men, and society and put that knowledge into what we write, whether it is a letter, a report, a set of instructions, a poem, a story, or any creative composition whatever.

Last Words

WE PROMISED in our "First Words" a new vision of language and a new orientation of thought. The vision is admittedly partial; no man and no era has ever had the last word on any subject. This vision is partial like the morning sun half-revealed on the horizon. There is some light now; there will be more light later as we build up information about important areas where we are ignorant. Yet the outlines are now clear, and they are substantially as we have traced them in this book.

A human being is born into a language which has its origins in unrecorded prehistory. Like the physical world he walks about in, his linguistic world has its center in him and goes where he goes. It has immediacy to his senses and the effect of having been provided by nature. It is there as the land of his birth is there, as the plants and animals are there, and the birds that test the atmosphere. He may move from mountain to plain, from desert to seacoast, and feel some preference for one or the other, but they are physical facts, brute and absolute, and he knows that his attitude is irrelevant. The mountains do not walk at his wish, nor the seas dry up. No more than this does language accommodate itself to the will of any man. Himself at the center, it stretches away from him by minute gradations of change to the incomprehensible, unless some barrier intervenes, with the incomprehensible on the other side, nearby. Like a continent or an island, language is brute, absolute; our attitudes towards it are irrelevant. The only sane attitude for modern man is one of cool acceptance of the fact that he hears what he hears and reads what he reads.

Any other attitude toward language is irrelevant, a burden to the spirit, and a throwback to those haunted minds which saw demons in volcanoes, imps in kindling wood, angry gods in earthquakes. The buses run to Paracutin these days; tourists, clicking shutters and chewing gum, watch the volcano being born in a cornfield. There are still some mysteries about the crust of this globe and the tensions within it which burst out in tremors and flowing lava, but we know enough to approach them with curiosity, unemotional and unalarmed. The only sane attitude to take toward language is comparable: acceptance of its myriad ways, unemotional and unalarmed.

No human society shapes its attitude toward language on the knowledge of scholars; individuals do but groups do not. In this respect the most sophisticated gathering of cultivated Americans at the cocktail hour does not differ from drum-beating savages on the African veldt. Nor does it differ from a chain gang at lunch along a Florida road. There is the same visceral fear and rejection of the outsider, the same mythology, and the same misplaced ethical sense that the stranger with different ways is a good man inexplicably gone wrong, to be pitied or censured by those who know better. As the Greeks called themselves "children of light" and all other men barbarians, so the Eskimos call themselves Innuit, "the real men," and find other names for other men; so the barbered heads bob together in Boston, St. Louis, Dallas, or San Francisco, whispering, "He's really not one of us; he makes such odd mistakes in grammar." Down on the corner the gang hunches close and the word goes around, "He don't belong; he talks funny." A hundred years of Darwin leaves us with eight million anti-evolutionists within our national borders and millions more still undecided; a hundred years of linguistic study leaves this continent with a hundred million literates of all grades wrapped in the dark shades of primitive attitudes toward language.

A new vision of language brings a new orientation of mind and a new freedom from such mythology. If a given way of speech is a community's way, then the outsider in one community is, in a sense, a delegate from another. The language of each community is its inherited way of meeting felt or unfelt needs, its means of communication, its commonly accepted system of signals. There is no demon within it, but a fine principle of utility: when the community develops other needs, it will develop other language. Each individual within each community partakes of its language as far as he needs to; and when his needs outrun the needs of the community, he breaks out into a wider world of language. All languages—all words, all forms, all patterns—go back in the same honorable line to the same honorable origins; perhaps over the threshold of prehistory, they go back to the same ancestral knot of speakers, just as the same bedrock underlies the earthy overmantle of the globe in all its myriad forms.

Any man may have his prejudices as to the speech he likes to hear, as he has his prejudices about food and drink. To see language clear does not mean an abdication of taste and choice. There are those who like the mountains and those who like the sea. To see language clear means to shake oneself free from word magic, the sense of a mystical communion between words and things. It means freedom from egocentrism, the feeling that our own speech is the center and standard of the visible universe; our own speech is merely the center of our own little world of language which falls away into differences on all sides. To see language clear means to see it as a form of human interaction, an inert signaling system whose only life is in the messages that pass over it, a code about which moral, logical, and religious judgments are irrelevant and social judgments interesting but futile. To see language clear means to control it with a sure sense of its capacities and its resistances, so that we always put more in than we expect to come out at the other end. To see language clear means to make distinctions within language, between language and thought, between codes and messages, between men and the garbs they wear in society. To see language clear means to set the mind free: men of free minds are free men.

A NOTE ON THE TYPE

IN WHICH THIS BOOK IS SET

The text of this book was set on the Linotype in a face called Times Roman, designed by Stanley Morison for The Times (London), and first introduced by that newspaper in 1932.

Among typographers and designers of the twentieth century, Stanley Morison has been a strong forming influence, as typographical adviser to the English Monotype Corporation, as a director of two distinguished English publishing houses, and as a writer of sensibility, erudition, and keen practical sense.

In 1930 Morison wrote: "Type design moves at the pace of the most conservative reader. The good type-designer therefore realizes that, for a new fount to be successful, it has to be so good that only very few recognize its novelty. If readers do not notice the consummate reticence and rare discipline of a new type, it is probably a good letter." It is now generally recognized that in the creation of Times Roman Morison successfully met the qualifications of this theoretical doctrine.

Composed, printed, and bound by Kingsport Press, Inc., Kingsport, Tennessee. Paper manufactured by P. H. Glatfelter Company, Spring Grove, Pennsylvania.

A NOTE ON THE TYPE
IN WHICH THIS BOOK IS SET

The text of this book was set on the Linotype in a face called *Times Roman,* designed by Stanley Morison for *The Times* (London), and first introduced by that newspaper in 1932.

Among typographers and designers of the twentieth century, Stanley Morison has been a strong forming influence, as typographical adviser to the English Monotype Corporation, as a director of two distinguished English publishing houses, and as a writer of sensibility, erudition, and keen practical sense.

In 1930 Morison wrote: "Type design moves at the pace of the most conservative reader. The good type-designer therefore realises that, for a new fount to be successful, it has to be so good that only very few recognise its novelty. If readers do not notice the consummate reticence and rare discipline of a new type, it is probably a good letter." It is now generally recognized that in the creation of *Times Roman* Morison successfully met the qualifications of this theoretical doctrine.

Composed, printed, and bound by Kingsport Press, Inc., Kingsport, Tennessee. Paper manufactured by P. H. Glatfelter Company, Spring Grove, Pennsylvania.

THE FOUR GREAT WORD-CLASSES

NOUN N	VERB V	ADJECTIVE A	ADVERB A͜
CHANGES IN WORD-FORMS			

N	I, me; you; he, him; she, her; it.	V		
N-'s	my, mine; your, yours; her, hers; its.	V-s to-V V-ed	A-er	A͜-er
N-s	we, us; you; they, them.	V-ing	A-est	A͜-est
N-s'	our, ours; your, yours; their, theirs.	V-ed/en		

THE WORKING UNITS

WORD	WORD-GROUP	PREPOSITIONAL PHRASE	CLAUSE

THE BASIC STATEMENT-PATTERNS

ONE: **N V N**	TWO: **N V N N**	THREE A: **N V** B: **N V A͜** C: **N V A**

SELECTION

a as **D** selects a word beginning with a consonant.
an as **D** selects a word beginning with a vowel.

N in **N V** selects **V-s**.
N-s in **N V** selects **V**.

N selects singular pronoun.
N-s selects plural pronoun.

I selects **am, was.**
he, she, it select **is, was.**
you, we, they select **are, were.**
If N, though N, etc.,
  may select **were.**

REPETITION WITHIN THE PATTERNS

COMPOUNDING	APPOSITION

END PUNCTUATION

PERIOD	SEMICOLON	DASH	QUESTION MARK	EXCLAMATIC MARK

FORMAL PUNCTUATION

PERIOD	COMMA	COLON	SEMICOLON	DASH	PARENTHES